Smugglers and Saints of the Sahara

Smugglers and Saints of the Sahara describes life on and around the contemporary border between Algeria and Mali, exploring current developments in a broad historical and socioeconomic context. Basing her findings on long-term fieldwork with trading families, truckers, smugglers, and scholars, Judith Scheele investigates the history of contemporary patterns of mobility from the late nineteenth century to the present. Through a careful analysis of family ties and local economic records, this book shows how long-standing mobility and interdependence have shaped not only local economies but also notions of social hierarchy, morality, and political legitimacy, creating patterns that endure today and that need to be taken into account in any empirically grounded study of the region.

Judith Scheele is post-doctoral research Fellow at All Souls College, Oxford University. She is a social anthropologist who has conducted extensive fieldwork in Algeria, Mali, and, more recently, Chad. She is the author of *Village Matters: Knowledge, Politics and Community in Kabylia, Algeria* (2009).

African Studies

The African Studies series, founded in 1968, is a prestigious series of monographs, general surveys, and textbooks on Africa covering history, political science, anthropology, economics, and ecological and environmental issues. The series seeks to publish work by senior scholars as well as the best new research.

A list of books in this series will be found at the end of this volume.

Smugglers and Saints of the Sahara

Regional Connectivity in the Twentieth Century

JUDITH SCHEELE
University of Oxford

CAMBRIDGE
UNIVERSITY PRESS

CAMBRIDGE
UNIVERSITY PRESS

32 Avenue of the Americas, New York NY 10013-2473, USA

Cambridge University Press is part of the University of Cambridge.

It furthers the University's mission by disseminating knowledge in the pursuit of education, learning and research at the highest international levels of excellence.

www.cambridge.org
Information on this title: www.cambridge.org/9781107533813

First published 2012
First paperback edition 2015

A catalogue record for this publication is available from the British Library

Library of Congress Cataloguing in Publication data
Scheele, Judith, 1978–
Smugglers and saints of the Sahara : regional connectivity in the twentieth century / Judith Scheele.
p. cm. – (African studies series ; 120)
Includes bibliographical references and index.
ISBN 978-1-107-02212-6
1. Algeria – Commerce – Mali. 2. Mali – Commerce – Algeria. 3. Algeria – Relations – Mali. 4. Mali – Relations – Algeria. 5. Borderlands – Algeria. 6. Borderlands – Mali. I. Title.
HF3883.Z7M427 2012
382.0965′06623–dc23 2011049205

ISBN 978-1-107-02212-6 Hardback
ISBN 978-1-107-53381-3 Paperback

Contents

Maps and Photos

MAPS

PHOTOS

Acknowledgements

This book is a debt incurred – most importantly with my hosts, friends, and informants in Algeria and Mali: the Bakraoui family in Tamantit, especially Saïda, al-Bakri, Fatima and all her sisters and brothers, who hosted me in Tamantit and put me in touch with their cousins, in particular al-Hadj Mohammed, who in turn granted me access to the family library. I am also indebted to their cousins in Adrar: Moustapha, ʻAtiqa, her mother, and Rachid, who helped me at first find my feet in the south; and Rachid's mother, who put me up in Algiers. Also in Adrar, I am grateful to the Kalloum family, in particular Yousef, Zoulika, and Meriem, for their indefatigable hospitality and advice; and their cousin Mekki, for access to the family archives and family history. I am grateful to Mounir Akacem and Brahim, for their friendship and patience, and Mounir's family in Tamanrasset and Algiers. I also thank the Cherfaoui family for their never-failing hospitality, in particular Najat, Nasera, and Asma; their neighbours, Miriam, Messaouda, and her cousin Hanna; and their families, as well as Dahman and Fatiha, for Kabyle reminiscences in the *grand sud*. I am indebted to Professors Chouchane, Houtiya, and Bendara for their advice and access to relevant documents; and the shaykh Bilkabir in Mtarfa for granting me full access to his richly furnished and well-organised manuscript library and for assistance in producing digital copies. I thank Shaykh Maʻzūz in Talmin and Shaykh Tayyeb in Kusan for granting access to their archives, and Mehdi Titafi, then director of the Adrar national manuscript centre, for establishing first contacts. I owe more than I can say to Zineb and the Ferjani family for their hospitality in Aoulef and Adrar and for facilitating access to Shaykh Bāy's vast library; and to ʻAbd al-Qādir Layl, PDG and ʻAbd al-Karīm Dahadj for their life stories, so generously supplied. I am equally indebted to Zineb's uncle Karim Moulay for his generosity, delicious dinners, and valuable insights and her aunt Zahra and niece Lalla Aicha in Bamako for their hospitality and warm welcome. In Tamanrasset, I extend thanks to my hosts, the Bajouda family: Mehdi and Fatma, his fine sense of humour and her unforgettable cheerfulness. I am much indebted to Al-Hadj Abdelkarim for his profound knowledge and contacts in Tamanrasset, Tit, Gao, and on the road in between. I thank Abdallah, Khadija, and Hammou Zafzaf for their hospitality in Tit and Dadda Halawa for her help in Tamanrasset and her hospitality in Timbuktu and Algiers, her colleague Deija for her time, and her niece Mama for her warm welcome. I am grateful to Ighles and his team for treating me like royalty on the long road to Gao, and his family, especially his sister, for their help and hospitality. I owe a debt of gratitude to Mina and Abdullahi in Gao for their unquestioning hospitality and to the Awlād Dahi, especially Matou and Moustapha, for their hospitality in Bani w-Iskut and in Gao and its surroundings, and for their help in and with al-Khalīl. I am much obliged to the Arab traders in the Souk Washington in Gao, who readily submitted to my questions; and especially to Amar, and to Hamza and his family, for their help and hospitality. I further have to thank Cheibou and Fatouma for long evenings spent chatting in Gao and Cheibou's father for his hospitality in Bamako; the Ahl Arawān more generally, for their hospitality in Bamako, Timbuktu, and Arawān. Omar Kabyle, stranded in Gao, for his friendship, unfailing support, and kindness. I am grateful to the staff at the CEDRAB for their patience and knowledge; Al-Mukhtar for his hospitality in al-Khalīl; and my hosts in Kidal and Aboubakrine ag Ghissa for his help with administrative hurdles in Kidal; and Tayyeb and Fatiha for their kindness and friendly reception in Aïn Séfra.

I would further like to thank Bob Parks and Karim Ouaras at the CEMA in Oran for looking after me administratively and for providing the occasional break on the coast, as well as an ever-lively forum for intellectual debate, and the ISH in Bamako for providing a research permit for Mali. Funding for this research was provided by the British Academy (small research grant no. SG-47632), and by two post-doctoral fellowships held at Magdalen College and All Souls College, University of Oxford, respectively, which provided ideal settings for preliminary research and writing. Most especially, I would like to thank Paul Dresch for detailed comments on draft versions of this book: the overall intellectual debt that I owe him is impossible to put in words, as is his and his wife Melinda's never-failing support and friendship. Morgan Clarke,

Simon Quinn, Julien Brachet, Armelle Choplin, and Peregrine Horden have read all or parts of this book at various stages, and their comments and insights have proven priceless, as have those provided by two anonymous reviewers for Cambridge. Charles Grémont and Abderrahmane Moussaoui generously hosted me in Aix and Marseille and shared their intimate knowledge of northern Mali and southern Algeria with me; Charles further made me aware of the manuscript treasures kept at the Institut de France in Paris. An early version of this book was presented as the Evans-Pritchard lectures 2009 at All Souls College, and the result benefited greatly from questions and comments made during these lectures, in particular by Wendy James. Some of its ideas were tried out in the workshop "Navigating Northwest Africa: Towards an Analysis of Saharan Connectivity?" (coorganised with James McDougall), held at Magdalen College in September 2008: I would like to thank James and all the participants at this workshop for their contribution and debate, especially Ann McDougall to whose scholarship this book owes a great deal. These ideas were further tried out on unsuspecting students who took a post-graduate option course here in Oxford on the Sahara in early 2011, co-taught with James McDougall: again, their contributions are much valued. Lastly, many thanks go to Julien Brachet for drawing (and patiently re-drawing) the maps included in this volume.

Introduction

> The Saharan oases constitute for most observers an opaque and paradoxical universe, whose inhabitants appear as sometimes tightly shut off from the world and fixed on their "ancestral" practice, sometimes as part of complex relationships with other populations that might be very far from them, both geographically and culturally. The intensity of relations would even seem proportional to their physical isolation … This leaves us with the question as to how these outside relations can be articulated with local terms of technical and social organisation, without finally undermining their specificity and autonomy. (Guillermou 1993: 121)[1]

It is very cold in al-Khalīl, and there is not much to eat. Even water has to be brought by large tankers that cross the border from Algeria to Mali and carry it over the fifteen kilometres that separate the town – if this is what it is – from its Algerian twin, Bordj Badji Mokhtar. The nearest cities on the Malian side, Gao, Timbuktu, and Kidal, are all more than a day's drive away, on unforgiving mud-tracks that carefully circumvent all human settlement, and where teenage drivers practice at night with no headlights.[2] The Sahara is far from pretty here, no rolling dunes or palm gardens, just a vast flat plain with no protection against the constant wind and sandstorms, the beating sun, and the emptiness of a distant horizon. Men spend their days huddled near their trucks or shops, their faces covered with indigo veils, wearing thick leather jackets and Algerian army boots over their long shirts and baggy trousers,

[1] All translations from French and Arabic are my own, unless stated otherwise. Names have been changed where necessary.

[2] For the location of all places mentioned in the introduction, see Map I.1.

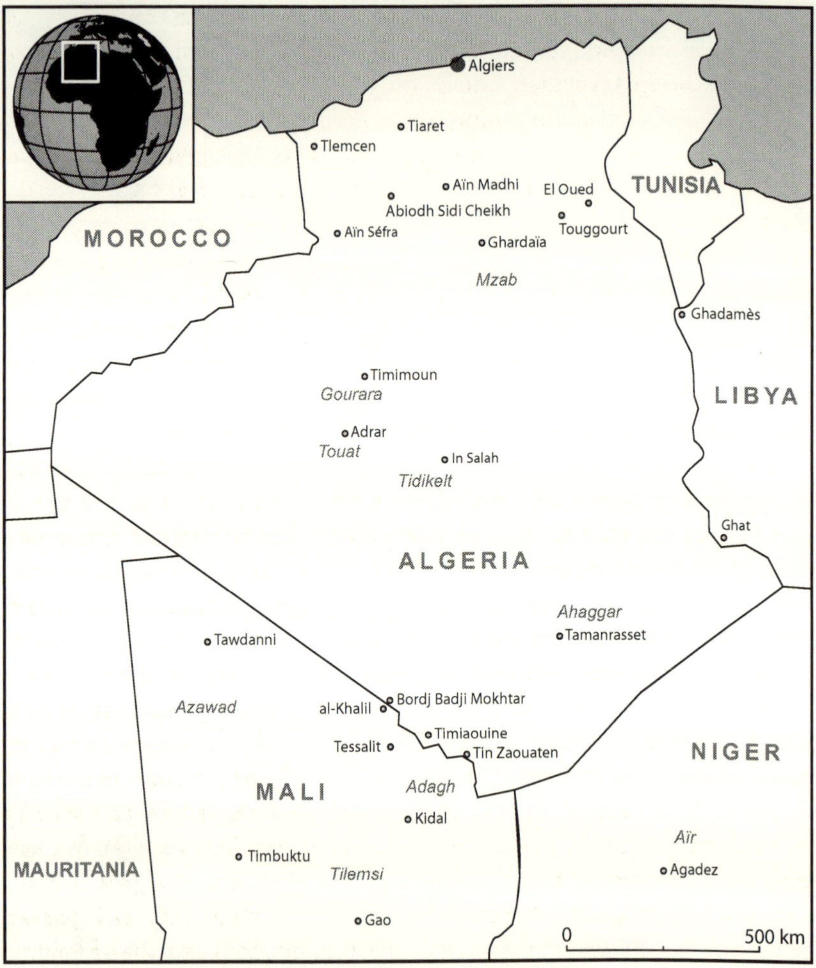

MAP 1.1. Algeria and northern Mali.

playing cards, boasting, shivering, smoking and drinking tea: life is fast in al-Khalīl, but the days are long, and are best described, in Spanish-inflected Algerian Arabic, as utter *miseria*. The few women in al-Khalīl are of little virtue, and are always hungry, with the exception of local Tuareg women married to Khalīlīs whose husbands have bought them generators so that they can watch Jackie Chan videos. There are few children, all smoking incessantly. As the evening draws in, people gradually get up, stretch, adjust their veils, and begin to load cars and trucks, fill tanks, and check their satellite phones. Customers arrive from the other side of the border: a bad-tempered Algerian soldier, haggling over a car, kneading his cap between his sinewy hands and twitching fearfully on his spindly legs at every sound of steps behind him; several well-nourished and rosy-cheeked Algerian traders crossing over from Bordj with "good business" and a pronounced interest in such improbable items as the latest Mauritanian fashion in Moroccan upholstery for the wife back home; a small and skinny Mauritanian, bent with age and moral doubt, waiting for the appointed time to carry some camels across the border, and meanwhile trying to find food and to keep control over his teenage apprentice; the pony-tailed drug-smuggling neighbour from Chad haggling over a secondhand satellite phone and inviting people for dinner; a group of rather nervous youth from Gao, waving their AK47s while looking for a spare tire; the inevitable West African migrants, grey with fatigue and visibly bearing traces of repeated stints in Algerian prisons.

Although al-Khalīl is marked on no map, every child in the area knows it: it is *'āṣima ta'l-frūd*, the capital of illegal trade in the northern Malian desert, and it is booming. Its oldest permanent house was built in 1993; at that time, it served as a store for arms for the separatist rebellion of the early 1990s.[3] Fifteen years later, al-Khalīl has developed into almost a town, with shops, restaurants, hostels and call-centres. Its scattered habitations – several hundreds of them, with at times a score of inhabitants each – stretch far into the surrounding plain; at its outskirts, *coināt* or "corners" of future buildings stake out claims to further construction sites as far as the eye can see. All construction material is imported from nearby Algeria, and manual labour is usually provided by sub-Saharan migrants. There are two mosques; a primary school is under construction; there is a health centre and the remains of a gendarmerie. Houses, however, are rare: most people live in what they call *gawārij* (sing. *garāj*), from the French *garage*: large courtyards capable of holding several trucks, enclosed by high concrete walls and protected by solid iron gates, with two or three rooms in a corner serving as a shop, storage place, kitchen and shelter for the night. True Khalīlīs are always on the move, and al-Khalīl is never the same two days in a row. People travel through, stay in a *garāj*, and leave the next day: in the unlikely event of a raid by Malian security forces, little would be found there but a ghost town. All traders who come to al-Khalīl are necessarily connected to one

3 Since national independence in 1960, northern Mali has been shaken by a series of rebellions and droughts, mainly turning on questions of regional and local sovereignty, and the role of and access to the state; on the 1990s, see Maiga (1997) and Ag Youssouf and Poulton (1998); for a more nuanced appraisal of the sociopolitical context, see Grémont et al. (2004).

garāj, where they sleep and eat for free, and can pass the night undisturbed, protected by the owner's arsenal of guns, fierce reputation, and sturdy doors. In exchange, they conduct all their trade in the *garāj* and rarely change allegiance.

Al-Khalīl exists because of its close connection to Bordj Badji Mokhtar: it is primarily a transhipment point for smuggled goods of all kinds. Flour, pasta, and petrol come down from Algeria on small jeeps, on antique trucks, or even on the backs of camels and donkeys. Livestock and cigarettes come up from Mali, the former on the hoof or on the back of trucks, the latter on relatively new Toyotas. Veils, perfumes, jewellery, incense, and furniture arrive from southern Morocco and Mauritania, places at the forefront of feminine fashion with harbours wide open to Chinese imports; these commodities are often traded by women, who travel themselves, in jeeps, or who send their drivers. Narcotics arrive from Mauritania via the Western Sahara, or from the Gulf of Guinea, and travel around the southern tip of Algeria through Niger and Chad to Egypt, and thence to Israel and Europe. Arms come up from long-standing crisis zones, such as Chad, or are unloaded in the large ports of the Gulf of Guinea and are sold throughout the area. Four-by-fours of dubious provenance are supplied with Mauritanian paperwork to avoid the costly customs clearance that they would otherwise be subject to throughout West Africa. Passengers travel up and down, perching on the top of heavy loads, tending livestock, or paying dearly for secret passage: temporary labour migrants from Mali, women with new babies on their laps visiting relatives on either side of the border, sub-Saharans on their way north, freshly turned back by the Algerian security forces or temporarily resident in al-Khalīl. Although al-Khalīl owes its existence to the vicinity of the Algerian border, it has by now in itself become a point of attraction, and sometimes drivers make considerable detours to take advantage of the relative security, efficient infrastructure, and various services it offers to those who have friends or family there: car repairs, spare parts, currency exchange, paperwork, credit facilities, and information.

Rather than as a town, al-Khalīl is thus perhaps best understood as a truck-stop – as a node in various overlapping networks that derive their power and standing from the outside and that have little to do with each other. Every *garāj* stands for a set of trade networks that it can draw on in times of need. These networks in turn bind local residents more closely to friends and relatives scattered throughout the Sahara on either side of the border than to their next-door neighbours. "If something goes wrong," people say, "you need to have friends – friends and guns – but you can hire guns, you cannot hire friends." On closer inspection, the various institutions that might turn al-Khalīl into a town turn out to be optical illusions. The health centre, constructed by the Red Cross in a brief spurt of interest in the border region fifteen years ago, is still waiting for the doctor, a "Bambara" (the local shorthand for southern Malian) who "got lost" on his way. The primary school is far from finished, and there is no teacher – and very few children, in any case, and these are more interested in learning about trucks than alphabets. The gendarmerie post is similarly empty, and here everybody knows what happened: "the government built this post, a nice building, you can see, and then they sent soldiers with guns, *suwādīn* ('blacks,' that is to say people from southern Mali) who were already shaking with fear when they arrived. They lasted two days: on the second night, we stole all their guns, and we never saw them again." The two mosques were constructed with private funds, but even they can hardly be taken to represent "Khalīlī society." At least one of them, people say, was built by a notorious drug dealer, to show off his wealth and perhaps even to buy his place in paradise, but nobody ever goes to pray there – quite simply, because nobody ever prays in al-Khalīl: for al-Khalīl is a place of corruption, and their prayer would wither on the tongue.

Al-Khalīl is a place of corruption, and this, from a local point of view, is the true reason why it cannot be a town. People forget truthfulness and religion as soon as they breathe its air; they act like animals when they get there: it therefore remains beyond the bounds of "civilisation" and part of the *bādiya* (steppe, wilderness). This is why "proper" women should never live there; conversely, because there are no women and hence no families, it is impossible for men to lead a "good life" here. Crouching over their tea and numbing their empty stomachs with cigarettes, young men might like to boast of their freedom, which implies the absence of mothers, wives, and table manners as much as, or even more than fast cars, heroic deeds, and familiarity with the vastness of the desert. Most Khalīlīs are young men, and the atmosphere in the *gawārij* oscillates strangely between a school trip and a cowboy film, with frequent casualties. However, they know that in actual fact women, and the "civilisation" women represent, are indispensable to al-Khalīl, inasmuch as women are pivotal to the various social networks that allow it to survive. Every Khalīlī dreams about leading a "real life," which means getting married and investing in a house elsewhere, ideally several hundred kilometres further north in southern Algeria, where the amenities of "civilisation" – a fridge, satellite TV, running water – are most easily come by. Successful traders are those who own houses in large Algerian towns, Adrar or Tamanrasset, staffed by one or several wives, in addition to livestock and real estate in northern Mali and perhaps even Bamako, the Malian capital in the south of the country. Conversely, it is only the "immoral" business of al-Khalīl that allows the traders' wives and families to live a "modest" life back in the civilisation of Malian or Algerian towns, a life of scholarship, prayer and female leisure and seclusion. Both in the economic and the social sense, and on the level of aspirations, al-Khalīl therefore remains a half-world that, by the revenue it generates, helps to make and maintain place elsewhere, while remaining tributary to the various outside places and routes it represents.[4]

This is equally true where relations to regional states are concerned. The vicinity of the Algerian state is crucial to the functioning of al-Khalīl: it creates and maintains the international border without which smuggling would be meaningless; it has long subsidised Algerian production of staples, leading to considerable price differentials – and hence profits – either side of the border; it provides the necessary infrastructure, water, food, and well-maintained tracks; last but not least, by all accounts, state officials are deeply involved in all aspects of transborder business. Nonetheless, the residents of al-Khalīl take great delight in insisting on their statelessness and total independence. But even here, images of the state remain central to all assertions of autonomy: *kull garāj dawla wāḥida* (every garage is a state in itself), as people like to boast. Algerian soldiers are the stereotypical "other" and are described as "worse than dogs"; and people laughingly claim to belong to the "popular and democratic republic of al-Khalīl," echoing the official title of Algeria. Past stints in prison are frequently invoked, and life in al-Khalīl is described as their antithesis, as the only way in which men can be men. But again, manliness *à la Khalīl* requires guns, friends, and fast four-wheel-drive Toyotas, and thus considerable means. These are best acquired through properly illegal traffic, which in turn, it is commonly alleged, is not merely organised by state officials, but also run just like a state. People say that the "mafias" that organise such traffic have "ministries," "delegates," and "security services," all managed with the strictest discipline, and that recruitment is made on an exclusively individual basis that pays no heed to prior family

[4] The term "half-world" is taken from Chapman's (1978) analysis of the "Gaelic vision" in Scottish culture, which he describes as a necessary part of a larger opposition that serves to define both "Scottish" and "English" traits, and which hence cannot be understood on its own.

or other social ties and obligations. Despite the constant boasting of their exploits, bravery, and courage, most drivers I spoke to were painfully aware of their dependence on the *patrons* – very few among them own their own cars – and of the fact that they are risking their lives to make other people rich. Al-Khalīl, then, might look like a bastion of autonomy, but it remains in fact a necessary part of something larger, to which it is always tributary: it makes no sense on its own, but it needs to be understood with reference to the various networks, outside connections and power relations that make it what it is.

Harsh, cold, unstable, and bearing all the trappings of "modernity," al-Khalīl hardly brings to mind images of immutable Saharan oases sheltered by shady palm gardens supplied by camel caravans, images of, say, the fabled trading towns of Timbuktu in northern Mali or Ghadamès in contemporary Libya. Khalīlīs themselves, however, like to stress continuity over change: al-Khalīl is, according to them, but the "child" of the more historical trading posts in northern Mali, such as Kidal or Gao. Al-Khalīl is "the same as" the Sahelian quarters that grace all southern Algerian cities: it is just another visible manifestation of what has always been going on in the area. Much of this is rhetorical, of course, but al-Khalīl's intrinsic and very visible outside dependency, as well as its brutal cosmopolitanism, fake autonomy, immorality, and adaptability to change might indeed provide clues for understanding the area more generally. As a place in the making, al-Khalīl forces us to question preconceived notions of Saharan settlement, exchange and regional unity, and to develop a new conceptual framework that can grasp it not as an exception but as an indicator of lasting features of Saharan life: this is what this book attempts to do.

THE OTHER FACE OF THE MEDITERRANEAN

Al-Khalīl is not alone in its economic vitality: if we believe in statistics, the Sahara is perhaps the fastest changing, most dynamic, and wealthiest region of the African continent. Urbanisation has been rapid over the last decades, as has demographic growth, caused by in-migration rather than high birth rates, and the Sahara contains some of the world's largest known resources in oil and natural gas.[5] As a result perhaps, governments

[5] Figures on urbanisation are mainly available for Algeria (see Côte 2005), where 80 percent of all Saharans now reside in cities or towns, and Libya (Pliez 2003, J. Bisson 2003). 95 percent of all exports from Algeria and Libya are crude oil or gas, accounting for 30 percent and 60 percent of GDP, respectively. Libya ranks ninth in worldwide proven oil

in the Maghreb especially have made considerable efforts to integrate their Saharan territories into the nation-state, an effort that in many cases has paid off. Southern Algeria, for instance, sports modern cities with urban facilities, relatively efficient transport networks, numerous universities, almost nationwide Internet and telephone coverage, strictly imposed national security, and rates of schooling comparable to many European countries (Côte 2005). Libya, for its part, has revivified Saharan agriculture through heavy investment in mechanised irrigation and deep wells, as a showcase of the victory of man over sand (Pliez 2003, J. Bisson 2003). This means that urban structures have changed. Although a strong case can be made for the structural outside dependency of Saharan cities (Pliez 2003, Bensaâd 2005a), the past variety of external sources of investment is now marginalised by the economic and political power of Maghrebi states, whose oil-fuelled financial resources have dwarfed any revenue that might be made from agriculture, causing people to abandon outlying oases in favour of administrative centres and their immediate hinterlands. In Niger and Mali, meanwhile, ecological and political changes have led to new patterns of residence and economic exploitation (A. Marty 1993), and even here, state revenues and development aid have become central to local power struggles and livelihoods, alongside booming cross-border trade (Nijenhuis 2003, Giuffrida 2005a). If images of a uniquely Arabic- and Tamasheq-speaking Sahara of taciturn camel herders have little or no historic underpinning, they certainly falter when confronted with the observable multilingualism of contemporary Saharan cities and oases – that house Chinese workers, Middle Eastern teachers, Malay migrants, Pakistani preachers, European tourists, Mauritanian traders, Malian tailors, Cameroonian builders, Nigerian fraudsters, and Ghanaian barbers, alongside national in-migrants from the north (Boesen and Marfaing 2007).

Although these developments and the growing importance of transnational connections are increasingly visible in scholarship on the Sahara, conceptual frameworks that would allow us to integrate them into Saharan history and society more generally have been slow to develop. On the one hand, there are in-depth studies on Saharan localities, mainly produced by geographers, anthropologists, and historians, and mostly published in French, many of which speak of urbanisation, "modernisation,"

reserves, and Algeria sixteenth – tenth in natural gas reserves. Prospecting for oil is underway in northern Mali, while Niger and Mauritania have just started exploiting their own, in the former case to supplement a more longstanding extraction of uranium.

agriculture, and the state. Southern Morocco is especially favoured here (Bencherifa and Popp 1990, Alaoui and Carrière 1991, Bellakhdar et al. 1992), as are Tunisia (Attia 1965, A.-F. Baduel and P. Baduel 1980, Bédoucha 1987, Morvan 1993, V. Bisson 2005) and, to a lesser degree, Mauritania (Leservoisier 1994). Others provide excellent studies of the ecology and sociopolitical history of pastoral groups, in particular in Mauritania (Ould Cheikh 1985, Bonte 2008) and the countries of the Sahel (E. Bernus 1981, Casajus 1987, Bourgeot 1995, Grégoire 1999, Grémont 2010). The scant literature on the Algerian Sahara reproduces similar divisions between more or less sedentarised nomads (Ben Hounet 2009), analyses of urbanisation in the northern Algerian Sahara (Côte 2005), and anthropological works that focus on "traditional" oasis towns in the Touat (Moussaoui 2002) and the Gourara (Bellil 1999–2000). But most of these studies pay relatively little attention to comparative questions or even regional connections, which they relegate to the footnotes, or, at best, treat as tangential and subsidiary to the "real" matter at hand. Even a book (J. Bisson 2003) that purports to review the Sahara as a whole and provides a broad bibliography and far-ranging series of case studies makes little effort to elaborate a regional or even truly comparative framework.

Transregional mobility, on the other hand, is at the heart of the perhaps most popular – and certainly the best-funded – topic of contemporary Saharan research: trans-Saharan migration.[6] Here, mobility is key, to the point where the more sedentary inhabitants of the Sahara, as well as local socioeconomic particularities, become almost invisible. This is problematic on two accounts. Although, in fact, most researchers point to the statistical insignificance of truly trans-Saharan movements and the importance of regional logics and developments (Brachet 2009, Choplin 2009, Marfaing 2010), it adds to the visibility of trans-Saharan migration, thereby helping to create it as a "problem" whose

[6] The recent literature on trans-Saharan migration is too large to be summed up in a footnote, but see, for instance, Bensaâd (2002, 2005b, 2009), the relevant chapters in Marfaing and Wippel (2004), Pliez (2004, 2006), Bredeloup and Pliez (2005), Ba and Choplin (2005), Brachet (2005, 2009), Streiff-Fénart and Poutignat (2006, 2008) and Choplin (2008, 2009); for a complete bibliography, see de Haas (2007). Most scholars working in the area are well aware of the political implications of their studies and themselves stress the importance of Saharan logics and concerns and the detrimental impact of EU migration policy; nonetheless, the fact remains that although the study of trans-Saharan migration prospers, little to no work has been conducted on migration systems internal to the Sahara, and even less effort has been made to link such questions to larger issues of mobility and regional interdependence.

more subtle underpinnings are rarely heeded by the international media, nor by students drafting research proposals. More importantly, perhaps, these studies lack in historical depth, and thereby implicitly postulate a break between contemporary realities and the past, between mobile and sedentary Saharans, immigrants and locals, towns and villages (but see Brachet 2009). Migration and mobility hence appear as exceptional solutions to a crisis, rather than as longstanding requirements. If connections are drawn with the past, these tend to be either rejected out of hand – and for good reasons, such as refuting direct parallels between contemporary migration and the historic slave trade. Or else, they are hinted at rather than demonstrated (see, e.g., Pliez 2003). In much the same way, local specificities are often flattened out, and one gets little sense of how regional migration relates to contemporary Saharan societies more generally.[7]

History seems to be much better equipped to deal with longstanding and far-reaching connections: after all, the study of trans-Saharan trade has long been central to historical research on the area (McDougall 2005).[8] And indeed, trans-Saharan trade, in particular as seen through local archives, has been the subject of a series of excellent recent studies that invariably hint at the close interaction between trade and agriculture, mobility and sedentary societies, thereby potentially providing a long-term perspective on more contemporary developments. Paul Pascon (1984), after a careful study of the accounts of a leading religious family in southern Morocco, shows the close interdependence between regional and international trade, from the 1840s onwards. Ghislaine Lydon (2009a) traces the commercial and kin connections established by the Moroccan Tekna in the nineteenth century throughout Mauritania and beyond. Pierre Bonte (1998a, 2000) describes local trade in grain, dates, and cattle as the mainstay of Mauritanian commercial fortunes in the nineteenth and twentieth centuries. Ulrich Haarmann (1998) shows the regional involvement of Ghadamsī merchants from southern Libya, and their combined trading in trans-Saharan and Saharan goods, from the eighteenth century onwards. Dennis Cordell (1977) indicates the investment in regional trade and agriculture by the Sanūsiyya Sufi order, in Libya and beyond, whereas Stephen Baier and Paul Lovejoy (1975) describe a regional "desert-side economy" in Niger, based on the exchange of local

[7] Boesen and Marfaing (2007) is an exception here.

[8] For classic examples of studies of trans-Saharan trade, see Newbury (1966), Bovill (1968), Miège (1981) and, more recently, Austen (1990, 2010). On the importance of trade for early modern European fantasies of the Sahara, see Mollat de Jourdin (1984).

produce and staples.[9] But little effort has been made to combine these case studies into an overall coherent framework, and to point out their wider implications.

It is thus mainly in studies of the "Orientalist" kind, mostly situated in a distant past and undertaken from a purely scripturalist vantage point, that the connectedness of Saharan localities and societies appears most clearly. In his account of the *Arab Conquest of the Western Sahara* (1986) and other works (1975, 1990), T. H. Norris describes a world of migration, where locality is secondary to mobility. John Hunwick (1985) and Mohamed Nouhi (2009) analyse the interplay between universal Islamic scholarship and local society, while Charles Stewart (1973), Timothy Cleaveland (2002), and Bruce Hall (2011) show the close connection between scholarship and social hierarchy. Rainer Osswald (1986, 1993) underlines the importance of Islamic law and legal sources for historical study, as does Chouki El Hamel (2002a) – and talking about Islamic law automatically involves some degree of striving towards universal and external models, a search for "extensive types," as Jacques Berque (1953: 150) put it for the Maghreb. Connections between scholarship and commerce run through these accounts (see, for instance, Batran 2001 and Bonte 2001), as do stories of settlement and "civilising missions" in the wilderness of desert wastes (Cleaveland 1998). But most of these works focus on Mauritania, and there remains a real gap in the literature where the Central Sahara is concerned. More importantly, the Sahara thus described remains strangely disembodied, with little concern for the welfare of sheep, goast, camels, palm-trees, and irrigation systems. Mostly this is due to the nature of the sources: they are exclusively of a religious kind and deal with times bygone. Where historical records are patchy at best and writing tends to be bound up with religion, more practical information seldom survives. But some of it also seems to stem from a lack of interest, as though the more material aspects of Saharan life are rightly beyond the scope of the historian's gaze – and rare indeed are historians who are aware of the rich anthropological literature on the area.[10]

As a result, and to put it rather bluntly, there is a tendency to represent the Sahara as divided into two incompatible halves: one regional, dynamic, open, cosmopolitan, fluctuating, controlled from the outside,

[9] Although most of these examples speak of a world in which European commerce and imperial pretensions were already a reality, similar patterns can already be detected earlier: in seventeenth-century southern Morocco (Gutelius 2002) and Mauritania and Senegal (Webb 1995a).

[10] Lydon (2005, 2009a) is an exception here.

and strangely disembodied; the other local, remote, static, bounded and constantly under threat by any kind of change or outside involvement. This dichotomy is projected onto time and space alike: cities are seen as fundamentally distinct from agricultural oases, and contemporary developments, as distinct from past evolutions. This is certainly partly true. The Sahara is changing fast, and local residents feel overwhelmed or literally over-run by outsiders. Nonetheless, we need to be wary of easy assumptions of historical boundedness and self-sufficiency, and study continuity as well as change carefully, and from the bottom up: neither might be located where they meet the eye. A conscientious reading of historical sources shows that in the Sahara survival inherently depended on exchange and that settlement was fragile and unstable (Pascon 1984, Gast 1989). "Oases," wrote Denis Retaillé in 1986, "only exist within networks of relations." This means that the relationship between the local and the regional is crucial, and an object of study in its own right. But this is easier said than done. Conceptual frameworks that are sophisticated enough to analyse the complex interplay between the local and the regional without losing ethnographic depth and texture are few and far between, not merely in the Sahara.[11] Much hinges here on the way in which both the "local" and the "regional" are defined: "regional" or even "global" studies can hardly be achieved by a mere adding on of more research conducted at individual sites, or, alternatively, by an exclusive focus on normative categories of homogenisation (Fardon 1995). Rather, we need to rethink our implicit assumption of the – historical and conceptual – priority of place over movement.

Historians, and especially economic historians, have made some headway in this, with anthropologists in their wake. Wallerstein's (1974–89, see also Braudel 1967–79) world system theory might by now seem rather crude and unilateral to most, but it clearly states the impossibility of understanding the local without reference to its position within larger logics of production and exploitation.[12] Approaches to regions marked by a high degree of interdependency and longstanding patterns

[11] This remains so despite the large number of calls, by now already somewhat old-fashioned, for anthropological studies of "globalisation" (most famously, Appadurai 1996).

[12] For an attempt to apply Wallerstein's theories to the historic Sahel, see Kea (2004). Similarly, Scott's (2009) opposition between "civilised" valley states and "Barbarian" hill people, partly derived from older descriptions of the Maghreb (see Montagne 1930a, and Gellner 1969) has the merit of showing the close conceptual as well as economic interdependence that cross and maintain geographic as well as "cultural" and political boundaries: being a "Barbarian" without a civilised neighbour is pointless, and the reverse is of course equally true.

of exchange also provide useful models: paradoxically perhaps, seas and oceans are especially prominent here, such as the Atlantic (Linebaugh and Rediker 2000, Klein and Mackenthun 2004), the Indian Ocean, and the Mediterranean. Studies of the Indian Ocean especially have stressed the importance of local conceptions of regional connections (Ho 2006); the crucial role of small-scale peddling, regional ecological imperatives, and technical innovations in the shaping of transregional connections (Parkin and Barnes 2002); power relations that were not based on territorial control, but that were delocalised as social networks radiating out from commercial hubs and city-states acting as safe storage spaces (Chaudhuri 1985, 1990, Pearson 2003); the close relations between notions of local religious and intellectual legitimacy and regional status (Freitag and Clarence-Smith 1997, Markovits 2000); and the development of a particular kind of "cosmopolitanism" in trading cities (Simpson and Kresse 2007) – all points that are also prominent in the Sahara.

Meanwhile, in the Mediterranean, Horden and Purcell's (2000) *The Corrupting Sea* attempts to reformulate Braudel's (1966 [1949]) classic essay on the "unity of the Mediterranean" by developing a new model of regional unity altogether.[13] In the Mediterranean, they argue, climatic and geographical conditions are such that small areas tend to specialise or become ecological niches, and that seasonal instability must be taken as given. Life hence depends on exchange, or, in their words, "connectivity." It makes no sense to think of places in isolation; rather, the local is made and maintained by regional interaction. In turn, regions are never given but are developed through sustained communication and can at times include places situated at considerable distance, while excluding areas close by. Hence, although both the creation of local ecological niches and the existence of regions are vital for survival, the form these take can never be taken for granted. Meanwhile, the presumed importance of long-distance trade over regional exchange mostly proves an optical illusion: within such economic regions, people need to exchange staples in order to survive; but this low-level daily exchange, unspectacular as it is, often escapes the notice of historians and their source material, while nonetheless providing the infrastructure for much trans-regional commerce. The distinction between the local and the regional is thus one of scale rather than of kind, as the one is already and necessarily contained in the other: "places" appear as nodes of particular density in overlapping networks of connectivity.

[13] See also Purcell (2003). For critical discussions of the *Corrupting Sea*, see Harris (2005) and Malkin, Constantakopoulou, and Panagopoulou (2009).

Horden and Purcell's argument promises to provide a useful framework of analysis for the Sahara. Geographically, the Sahara is most frequently defined by the absence of regular rainfall and vegetation.[14] Notwithstanding the conceptual shortcomings of such a definition, it indicates the prevalence of ecological and climatic conditions that lead to extreme regional specialisation and hence interdependence, in a wider context of overarching insecurity. Storage, exchange, and the spreading of risk are vital, and this can only be achieved when relying on widespread networks of support; here as in the Mediterranean, connectivity is a necessary precondition for human survival. Moreover, research based on local archives shows that oases are never given by "nature," but necessarily depend on the delicate interplay between favourable environmental conditions and human investment and planning: with their complex and costly irrigation system, high demand for labour, and long-term investment in arboriculture, oases necessarily depend on initial outside investment and mostly also on continued maintenance, and are thus by definition part of larger wholes (Pascon 1984, Pliez 2003). As a result, dense and continuous exchange – within regions defined by direct ecological complementarity – was a prior condition for all kinds of Saharan settlement. Trans-Saharan trade necessarily relied on such regional infrastructures, but did not determine them. Therefore, wider patterns of connectivity cannot be taken as given, but need to be studied from the bottom up. On the southern fringes of the Sahara, studies taking into account questions of human ecology have been more sustained, indicating that the boundaries of the relevant regions of intense exchange often straddle the borders of the Sahara proper, are eminently political, and change over time.[15] Moreover, where Horden and Purcell, by the nature of their sources, had to privilege the material, an analysis of the "regions" that matter in the contemporary Central Sahara can, in addition to trade statistics and direct observation, draw on the moral and conceptual models that structure these regions from within. These models show the overwhelming importance of social and spiritual considerations in the imagination and hence the making of place and region: human

[14] The Sahara is currently defined as either the area between the limits of productive date-palms to the north and *hād* (*Cornucala monacantha*) to the south, or as lying between the limit of 100 mm of annual rainfall to the north and of 150 mm to the south (Capot-Rey 1953). All these limits remain inherently flexible because of variations in rainfall and patterns of cultivation. Moreover, they only rarely correspond to local practical and conceptual boundaries.

[15] See, for instance, Baier and Lovejoy (1975), S. Bernus (1981) and Bourgeot (1995), and, perhaps less subtly, Webb (1995b).

ecology and the management of scarce resources might be all important, but such resources include people and social prestige as much as water rights – or price differentials caused by national borders.[16] Both "place" and "region" are thus never monolithic or stable, or even presocial, but remain inherently dependent on human volition and commitment.[17]

AL-KHALĪL AND SAHARAN CONNECTIVITY

Although the harsh reality of life in al-Khalīl appears at first sight far removed from such theoretical reflections, on closer inspection, they can help to explain its incongruities, while in turn indicating more longstanding features of regional Saharan ecologies. Thus, for instance, al-Khalīl's rapid growth seems to carry the promise of equally rapid decline. The history of the Sahara reads like a long account of the rise and fall of particular trading centres; early travel accounts never quite match in their appreciation of respective markets.[18] French archival records are littered with ruins and misery: at times, we can guess that shifts in trade routes took place within living memory, sometimes more than once, pointing to their inherent flexibility and dependency on sociopolitical as well as geographical factors.[19] The advancing French colonial army caused trade routes to be diverted, and oases to decline irreversibly, to a degree perhaps hitherto unknown; but the ease and speed with which such transitions took place

[16] Much – but not all – of this outside reference in the moral making of place is expressed with reference to Islam; and, by their very nature, world religions presuppose reference to a distant centre and a transcendental moral model. This tension between localising and universalising tendencies has been observed throughout the Islamic world: see E. Peters (1976), Lambek (1990), Bowen (1992), Henkel (2005), and Ho (2006).

[17] This is, of course, an anthropological trope, and one that ultimately relates back to Evans-Pritchard (1940).

[18] See, for example, Mauny (1961). The various early Arabic accounts compiled and translated in Levtzion and Hopkins (1981) abound in descriptions of abandoned towns. Thus, for instance, al-Idrīsī, writing in the twelfth century: "Eight stages north of the location of the Saghwa tribe is a ruined town called Nabranta. In the past it was one of the famous cities, but according to what is related, sand overwhelmed its dwellings until these fell into ruins, and covered its waters until these dried up. Its population diminished and at the present time only their remnants live there, clinging on to the remaining ruined homes out of affection for their native place ... South of it [Santariyya] is a town called Shabrū, now in ruins, but which was in the past most populous. Its buildings have crumbled, the waters dried up, the animals fled and its landmarks have become unrecognizable. Other than a sterile remnant of palm-groves, only decaying ruins and blurred traces remain" (Levtzion and Hopkins 1981: 120 and 125).

[19] These reports are accessible in the French Centre d'archives d'outre-mer (CAOM) in Aix-en-Provence, see in particular boxes 22H26, 22H45, 22H68, 24H45 and 24H53; and compare to Carette (1844). For a more detailed discussion of these materials, see Chapter 1.

point towards a more longstanding inherent flexibility. The reasons for the fragility of al-Khalīl, meanwhile, are obvious: all its vital necessities, including water, are imported from Algeria, and were they to stop, were trade-routes to shift, al-Khalīl would disappear as quickly as it developed, adding to the many ruins that dot the Sahara, while another similar trading post would probably mushroom up elsewhere. And al-Khalīl is no exception here: similar staging posts litter the national borders between what is now "North" and "West" Africa, from Mauritania to Chad.[20]

Al-Khalīl's physical appearance similarly reflects its inherent dependency on the outside. It is tempting to describe its *gawārij* as modern-day *fanādiq* (pl. of *funduq*, inn, caravanserai), fulfilling similar functions: storage, lodging, trade, organisation of transport, communication, protection, and, at times, the possibility of keeping strangers under lock and key.[21] Each *garāj* stands for a particular network of traders, which in turn refers to a certain region, linking places of origin and investment to suppliers, truck routes, markets and transhipment points on either side of the border. As a result, al-Khalīl is spatially fragmented, and has little existence as a town in itself: there are no communal institutions or meeting places; people not only receive their food but also derive their social and legal identity from networks that connect them to the outside; inasmuch as al-Khalīl makes no sense on its own, Khalīlīs are necessarily from somewhere else, and have created their own cosmopolitan hierarchies. Conversely, while al-Khalīl depends on outside input, money and prestige earned there makes places elsewhere, being invested in houses, livestock, land, shops, marital alliances, the maintenance and extension of kinship ties, and education "back home": al-Khalīl might be the "child" of older trading centres in the area, such as Kidal, Timbuktu, or Gao, but it has also helped to build large parts of its "mothers." In terms of bulk, most trade in al-Khalīl is in staples destined for local markets: biscuits, pasta, flour, and semolina exported from Algeria. This echoes a longstanding historical emphasis on exchange of cereals and pastoral produce for dates that was long essential for local survival and created overlapping regions of economic interdependence.[22] Most trade in al-Khalīl is

[20] Hence, for instance, the example of Arlit and Dirkou in northern Niger, near the border with Algeria and Libya, respectively (Brachet 2009). This is also true further south, see, for example, Roitman (1998) on "garrison-entrepôts" in Chad.

[21] For a detailed account of the history of *fanādiq* and similar institutions in the Mediterranean, see Constable (2003).

[22] Some of these regions are already reflected in archaeological sources, see, for example, Mattingly (2003) and Nixon (2009). For trade statistics, see CAOM 23H111, 23H31 and 23H102; and Chapter 1.

organised by networks whose reach is limited to one, at best two, intermediate trading posts, while transregional trade – such as the international cocaine trade – inevitably involves collaboration between different trade networks. The reach of these regional networks mostly overlaps with areas of longstanding economic interdependence. Al-Khalīl is thus a half-world that necessarily makes reference to several overlapping larger wholes. This is equally reflected in its connections with the regional states that are crucial for its existence, but in relation to which it posits itself as an opposite, as a moral negation of centralised and external rule.

Most importantly, perhaps, al-Khalīl shows that the making of place is a moral as much as an economic problem. Although al-Khalīl might for all intents and purposes look like a town, it lacks in morality and is therefore locally understood to be part of the *bādiya*, the steppe or wilderness. As such, it remains beyond the bounds of civilisation and is described as potentially dangerous to "proper" family life and sociabilities. This is perhaps why, in their interminable boasts, Khalīlīs endlessly endorse "traditional" morality, as though they were trying to integrate al-Khalīl within known frameworks of excellence and moral propriety: al-Khalīl is described as a place where men can be men, although everybody knows that the moral autonomy and social responsibility this implies are often illusory. In the Mediterranean, Horden and Purcell (2000: 108) talk of nodes of density within overlapping networks of relations in preference to cities: perhaps as important here is the "moral density" of such nodes, whether expressed in terms of tribal excellence or Islamic observance. This opposition between the *bādiya*, the steppe or the wilderness, and the *qariya*, the village or settlement, reoccurs in most local sources and tends to frame oral history and contemporary moral judgement beyond al-Khalīl, not as irreducible and exclusive opposites but as poles on a sliding scale.[23] Most settlements in the Sahara are said to have been founded by saints, following divine guidance. A *qariya*, seat of civilisation, is always an achievement and relates to larger projects of civilisation, generally bound up in Islamic standards of justice and order. As such, it can as easily be swallowed up by moral shortcomings and internal strife as by shifting sands and greedy raiders. Inversely, by giving universal names to things and transactions, the Islamic revelation lends a promise

[23] Although it might be tempting to see here an endorsement of oppositions familiar from earlier literature – that between nomads and settlers (see especially Gautier 1927) – this is a moral, not a geographical or ecological distinction: well-ordered nomadic camps are part of the *qariya*, and "immoral" settlement belongs to the *bādiya*. For a discussion of similar notions among Tamasheq speakers, see Casajus (1987).

of permanence to the inherent fragility of Saharan life and settlement: if necessary funds and people come from the outside, so do notions of legitimacy, knowledge, and status, at least conceptually. Intellectual and moral connectivity, and related problems of containment, are hence as crucial to the making of Saharan human ecologies as irrigation practices and regional patterns of exchange.

ANTHROPOLOGY AND HISTORY

Al-Khalīl, as an extreme example of Saharan connectivity, thus appears as an ideal place whence to introduce this book that attempts to approach parts of the Central Sahara as a dynamic set of overlapping regions, studied from the bottom up and by following the movement of goods, people and ideas as and when they occur, for a period that stretches from the late nineteenth century to the 2000s. "Place" here is not seen as an inevitable starting point that needs to be overcome in order to produce a regional study, but rather as an ecological riddle in itself, whose making requires considerable and permanent effort, both in terms of economic investment and moral endeavour. Such an intellectual project is of course ambitious and stretches beyond the limits of traditional anthropological fieldwork or even historical research; ideally, it would be the result of a longstanding collective endeavour in an area that – like the Mediterranean – abounds in archival resources and secondary literature. Such collaboration is lacking in the Sahara, and this book should hence be taken as a first step in a possible direction that Saharan research might take, rather than as an attempt to cover the impossible. Even so, its underlying ambition requires some methodological flexibility. Simply put, the material presented in this book is derived from sixteen months of ethnographic fieldwork, undertaken from 2006 to 2009, staying with families in Tamantit near Adrar, Tamanrasset, and Gao, with occasional trips to Timbuktu, Bamako, Aïn Séfra, Aoulef, Aïn Madhi, and al-Khalīl (see Map I.1). Further material is derived from local manuscript archives, which are generally held in private collections and are laborious to access at times; none of these archives had, in any case, ever attracted the attention of Western – or even Algerian or Malian – scholars, so directories, summaries, and secondary accounts are lacking.[24] Some additional information is gleaned

[24] This is gradually changing, with growing government and public interest in the Algerian national manuscript heritage; see, for example, Bouterfa (2005) and Abdelhamid (2006); see also Scheele (2010a).

from the French colonial archives, held in Aix-en-Provence, in Bamako, and in local town halls in the northern Mali. Although most of these are easily accessible, many have not yet been fully classified, as, in Aix at least, priority is generally given to documents from the Algerian north; meanwhile, access to French colonial archival documents held in rural Mali requires much negotiation, luck, and patience, as they are neither catalogued nor open to the public.[25]

Beyond this apparent ethnographic simplicity, however, problems soon become apparent. "Multi-sited fieldwork" has by now become virtually obligatory for anthropologists.[26] Yet in areas where most of the sites that matter are situated beyond the linguistic and infrastructural facility of the West, its difficulty should not be underestimated. Anthropological fieldwork is of its very nature limited by the bounds of sociability and patience: as I had learned in earlier research (Scheele 2009a), it is difficult enough to get to know even the smallest village after two years of residence; to repeat the attempt several times over within one single project is painful, and potentially frustrating and leads to nagging doubts of superficiality and incompetence. This is perhaps even worse in the Sahara, where everyday multilingualism, especially on the southern edge, is humbling; where travel is arduous, and at times dangerous; and where, more generally, it is unacceptable to wander around on your own and to go where you please without prior consultation. Saharan mobility is often surprisingly static, as people get stuck behind national borders and as trucks are trapped in the sand; the "sites" of mobility are often difficult to pin down, and, like the hedgehog in the fable, or indeed the fabulous riches of trans-Saharan trade, always seem to be one step ahead of the curious ethnographer. As a result, the obvious multisitedness of my research hides a much narrower scope: most of it was conducted in Arabic, with brief forays into French and bad Songhay, and relied on family networks that might well span thousands of kilometres, but that nonetheless strive to maintain their internal coherence: physical location, in many cases, was only of secondary importance. Similarly, it only describes a small fraction of the contemporary Sahara, suspended as it were from a handful of

[25] For a vivid description of the municipal archives in Kidal, see Lecocq (2002: 29, published as Lecocq 2010). For a thorough exploration of the Saharan archives held in Aix-en-Provence, see Brower (2009).

[26] The term was first coined by Marcus (1995). For contemporary developments, see Rabinow and Marcus (2008). In actual fact, ethnographers only rarely conducted fieldwork on one single place or even village, but rather collated information from different sites and sources, but the Malinowskian myth of "single-sited" fieldwork has long stood as an unquestioned albeit impracticable norm.

fragile settlements on an uncertain line that connects the Algerian Touat to Gao in northern Mali. In a sense, then, what follows is but another village monograph, but the village in question is stretched out over a third of the African continent, as though it had been sketched on a balloon and then blown up. As a result, much of my fieldwork – and perhaps some of the most valuable parts – was conducted in the "in-between" spaces or "non-places" that allow and maintain this "stretched out" community: on the back of trans-Saharan trucks, for instance, squatting on smuggled loads of biscuits; in a *garāj* in al-Khalīl; in the makeshift dwelling of Sahelians in the cities of southern Algeria; or by the side of desert tracks, waiting for transport or watching urgent repairs. Although, more often than not, the company by the roadside would continue the gossip where we had left it off "back home," and although familiar faces would appear in the most unlikely times and locations, this means that I never achieved the kind of profound local knowledge that a more reduced geographical scope might have made possible. Moreover, after such excursions into the *bādiya*, returns to the shade of palm-trees in Tamantit, the quiet oasis in southern Algeria where my fieldwork began, appeared at times incongruous and restrictive, especially when I had picked up habits that were shocking to my erstwhile hosts, but this incongruence – much as my own reliance on regional networks – perhaps best reflects the flavour of contemporary Saharan life, torn between attempts at local moral containment and the maintenance of necessary connectivity.

Local archives similarly turn out to be a potentially poisoned chalice. Happy as I was as I stumbled across "real evidence," which everybody agreed locally – and probably also in my home university – would allow one to do "proper research," the sheer abundance of "papers" of unknown worth and interest and the almost total absence of any prior framework of analysis turned out to be an additional source of headaches and doubts. Reading manuscripts requires special training, and despite much talk of interdisciplinarity, dabbling amateurs are easily resented by specialists, perhaps rightly so. Yet specialists in Saharan vernacular manuscripts are few and far between: when I presented documents photographed in the Sahara to Orientalist colleagues, they generally laughed, wishing me good luck; a publication sent to an Islamic studies journal sparked quite as many concerns about the "oddity" of the source texts as about my own interpretation. Beyond technical difficulties, the need to take into account universal systems of knowledge and legitimacy in all aspects of local studies puts fieldworking anthropologists in much the same position as historic Saharan *shaykh*s resident in remote oases: painfully aware of the relevant intellectual debates, whose centres nonetheless always remain just out of reach, emphasising, once more, one's own marginality and uncertainty. Further, important as the written word is to anthropological knowledge, it is also dangerously seductive, seeming to provide "real" evidence where in fact it only makes a partial statement, expresses an impossible aspiration, or provides detailed minutiae without any obvious relevance. Questions of authorship, readership, and context thus remain crucial and are often difficult to answer from the rudimentary material itself, in a context where oral memories are increasingly scarce: especially in Algeria, people have very consciously moved away from the "superstitions" of old and are loath to be reminded of them. In this sense, colonial archives are easier to deal with, as their bias is more familiar, although even there, dangers of the deceptive precision of statistics and the objectivity of the written word loom large and need to be kept in mind.

The limited heuristic validity of written sources is further aggravated by their patchy nature. This is particularly true of local archives. There are few centralised record-keeping institutions in the area, and the legitimacy of those that exist is limited and people prefer to keep their own documents. Archives are thus shaped by their contemporary owners' interests and care, and willingness to share.[27] Moreover, they tend to give an impression of stability that is often illusory. Standard legal handbooks, such as the *Nawāzil al-ghuniya*, a collection of legal opinions (*nawāzil*, sing. *nāzila*) compiled in the Algerian Touat in the late eighteenth and early nineteenth centuries, were copied until recently, and are today described locally as representative of "the past" more generally – and indeed notes were added to it as time went on. Contracts drafted in the early 1800s are often indistinguishable from their counterparts penned more than a century later, unless they bear a date, and they are inevitably filed together, by subject rather than date. In much the same way, oral history is often difficult to date and gives a false sense of permanence, while genealogies seek to establish equivalence rather than comment on historical developments. Locally, then, the emphasis is on continuity rather than change – and indeed, this promise (or illusion) of permanence and stability seems to have been one of the reasons why writing was quite so popular in an area otherwise struck by instability and insecurity. Nonetheless, the vast majority of documents and memories available today refer to the late

[27] The main manuscript sources drawn on in this book will be described more fully when they are first mentioned, and a brief summary of each is given in the bibliography.

nineteenth and twentieth century, and there is no doubt that the period treated in this book is one of tremendous change, change that could justly be described as fundamental and irreversible. The French colonial army arrived in Timbuktu in 1893, and in the Algerian Touat in 1899, having done all they could to upset regional trading and political systems ever since their conquest of Algiers in 1830. With the introduction of truck-transport in the 1940s, the considerable impact of World War II, decolonisation, and the oil boom, local societies were literally turned upside down. The documents used and the events described in this book are thus the result of unique historical circumstance. If this book stresses nonetheless continuity as well as change, and sometimes draws parallels between precolonial and colonial sources, or, with due caution, extrapolates from colonial times to what might possibly have gone on before, this is not to postulate Saharan historical stability. Rather, it is in order to nuance the dominant rhetoric of fundamental rupture, and, more prosaically, because this is all that my sources allow me to do: otherwise, we would have to shy away from larger questions altogether.

OUTLINE OF BOOK

This book, then, is the result of compromise, of a certain methodological heterodoxy and of a good deal of improvisation. This is reflected in its plan, which tentatively turns things upside down in order to invert the commonplace conceptual relationship between movement and place. Chapter 1 shows the historical underpinning of the regional connectivity that is still apparent in al-Khalīl but that can be traced, with the help of local and colonial archives, to earlier times. It suggests that we should shift our focus from studies of trans-Saharan trade, on the one hand, and isolated Saharan communities, on the other, towards an approach that encompasses them both, showing their intimate interdependence. Chapter 2 illustrates these points further, relying on history as told by four of the most influential Algerian trading families with ties in northern Mali and Niger. It shows both the importance of regional trade and the various circumstances under which it might expand into larger ventures. Nonetheless, the social and moral, and mostly also the economic focus of such families remained regional, with a strong emphasis put on the making of place and a constant striving for containment in the face of actual vulnerability and vital engagement with the outside. Chapter 3 continues stories of trade and regional exchange into the present. It illustrates how moral rather than legal categories continue to determine local classifications of regional trade: it is meaningless, therefore, to treat international drug or even people smuggling independently of regional trade more generally. Locally, debates inevitably hinge on the tension between vital outside connections and moral containment, and various illegal transborder activities are primarily judged according to their social impact, expressed in religious terms: the *frūd al-ḥarām* (illicit trade) stands to the *frūd al-ḥalāl* (licit trade) as state-like "mafias" compare to family-based transregional networks.

Chapter 4 looks at similar patterns not in terms of livelihoods, but inasmuch as they inform notions of ideal order. Throughout the region, local identity and hierarchies are debated and explained in terms of real or putative outside connections and potential mobility. The most common expression of these outside connections are genealogies that, despite their appearance of equality, potentially encompass everybody in a universal and inherently hierarchical scheme of Islamic history. Today, such universalising projects are much resented and counteracted by the growing influence of nationalist thought and categories; yet in the interstices of the modern nation-state, they continue to function, causing much embarrassment to the "cousins" thus united. Chapter 5 describes how this moral connectivity was played out in the realm of the political and the legal. Although the Central Sahara was routinely described as "lawless" both in French colonial and older Arabic external sources, local archives show a strong concern with the *sharīʿa*. Yet, beyond classical notions of bounded communities, local political representation seems to have focused on irrigation systems managed by co-owners: property rather than residence seems to have been key. Ownership, however, remained essentially decentralised: within the overall framework of connectivity, there is no reason to assume that particular political emphasis was placed on locally bounded communities. Rather, what mattered once more were notions of civilisation, achieved by turning the local, through reference to the Islamic revelation, into part of a universal whole. This social and moral connectivity continues to inform life in contemporary Saharan settlements, as illustrated in Chapter 6. Using the "ghetto," independent social and spatial arrangements set up by West African migrants, as a trope rather than as a sign of the migrants' failure to integrate, it shows that Saharan cities more generally are described, by their residents, as conglomerations of socially and economically autonomous districts, distinguished by their inhabitants' real or putative place of origin, and who are seen as more closely connected to their often geographically distant "cousins" than to their next-door neighbours. Similar notions of spatial and social segregation can be discerned in smaller Saharan settlements and throughout the historical record. Publicly, and rather like al-Khalīl, cities are portrayed as nonentities: as nodes in overlapping regional networks, housing an essentially mobile population, with a clear emphasis on distinction rather than integration, despite frequent interactions and interdependencies on the ground.

1

Founding Saints and Moneylenders

Regional Ecologies and Oasis Settlement

Timbuctoo …
And much I mus'd on legends quaint and old
Which whilome won the hearts of all on Earth
Toward their brightness, ev'n as flame draws air;
But had their being in the hearts of Man
As air is th'life of flame: and thou wert then
A center'd glory-circled Memory
Divinest Atlantis, whom the waves
Have buried deep, and thou of later name
Imperial Eldorado roof'd with gold:
Shadows to which, despite all shocks of Change,
All on-set of capricious Accident,
Men clung with yearning hope which would not die.
(Tennyson 1829: 5–6)

The mere mention of trans-Saharan trade evokes images of tremendous riches lost in the hazards of arid lands, of camels loaded with gold, cloth, ivory and ostrich feathers, of coffles of half-starved slaves dragging themselves across the desert on bleeding feet, brutally driven by powerful merchants. These images, however little accurate they might be, can be traced a long way back through European literature, even – or rather especially – to times when direct knowledge of the West and North African interior was scarce.[1] Although disproved by most firsthand accounts, accessible to the European public from the mid-nineteenth century

[1] For an overview and analysis about how this image developed and remained surprisingly constant over time, see Mollat de Jourdin (1984), Fall (1982), and Benjaminsen and Berge (2004).

onwards, these images were so resilient that less dramatic descriptions of trans-Saharan trade were discredited, rather than letting them question the myth as such.[2] This can partly be explained by the nineteenth-century thirst for evasion and romanticism, Tennyson's "yearning hopes which would not die"; but this image also became necessary to justify French imperial progress in the Sahara, and to invalidate international sniggering at the "Gallic cock scratching the sand" with tangible proof of Saharan Eldorados. Compared to this myth, trade on the ground was often found wanting: the streets of Timbuktu were covered with dust rather than paved in gold, and the French conquering army was first and foremost impressed by the misery of Saharan settlements rather than by their hidden wealth. Nonetheless, rather than renounce the legend, each time when the French occupied yet another "central trading post" and found it disappointing, trade was seen to be just one more step ahead. Caravans, it was claimed, had "just been diverted" to neighbouring oases, and local economic "stagnation" was blamed on the "apathy" of those who had remained behind, or on the "premature" (and rather half-hearted) abolition of slavery.[3] Notwithstanding, throughout the colonial period, most attempts to capture trans-Saharan exchange from the north proved vain, and most romantically imagined oases turned out to be a disappointment.[4]

2 The best example here is the long debate about the veracity of René Caillié's (1830) account of Timbuktu. Caillié was the first European to have visited the city in 1828 and to have come back to tell the tale, which however corresponded little to European imaginations of a vast city paved in gold. Debates over the authenticity of his account were caught up in national rivalries and moral prejudice (Heffernan 2001); yet a significant part seems to have been played by the general reluctance to give up a more positive image of Timbuktu and with it the unlimited exotic potential of trans-Saharan trade.

3 Reports on the "decline" of trans-Saharan trade are too numerous to be mentioned here in full. For a few examples, see "Lettre du Colonel Cauchemez, commandant militaire des Oasis sahariennes au général commandant la subdivision de Laghouat," 24/11/1900, CAOM 22H33; "Rapport de tournée du Capitaine Dinaux, chef de l'annexe d'In Salah. Ahnet, Adrar nigritien, Ahaggar, Aïr septentrional. 3 mai au 29 octobre 1905," CAOM 22H68; "Lettre du lieutenant colonel Pont commandant supérieur du cercle de Biskra au général commandant la subdivision de Batna," 30/05/1891, CAOM 10H30; "Lettre du consul général de France à Tripoli au ministre des affaires étrangères," 16/07/1989, CAOM 10H32; and R. Hardy, "Une terre qui meurt: le Touat," 30/04/1933, CAOM 10H86. See also Holsinger (1980: 65).

4 For accounts of such attempts, see the various documents on state-organised or -sponsored trade missions kept in CAOM 24H53. This of course does not mean that there never had been any trans-Saharan trade, but rather that it was flexible, and that, by the early twentieth century, much of it had been turned away by railways in Senegal, Ivory Coast, and especially Nigeria: see Johnson (1976), Baier (1977), Bonte (2000), and McDougall (2002). Similarly, the railhead at Aïn Séfra (1887) and then Colomb-Béchar

Although the Saharan "Atlantis" thus stubbornly remained out of reach, romantic images of trans-Saharan trade persisted. Even now, there is a tendency to portray trans-Saharan trade as distinct from and independent of Saharan trade, while the latter is often seen as relatively unimportant and of little sophistication.[5] This presupposes a clear separation between trade, settlement, and "traditional" agriculture; and indeed, as seen in the introduction, most research implicitly postulates a break between the two, investigating either one or the other. In line with the overall argument sketched out earlier, this chapter attempts to overcome this separation, by treating both trade and settlement as central, but never autonomous elements of Saharan regional ecologies. As highly specialised monocultures relying on complex irrigation systems and arboriculture, hence on heavy initial investment and considerable planning, few oases were self-sufficient. This means that they need to be understood in relation to broader political, economic, and social logics of which they were a necessary part. Vital interdependence, however, meant dates and cereals rather than ostrich feathers and gold: these goods were produced and exchanged within the Sahara, as they had little value beyond it, and the patterns of exchange that they gave rise too are best described as intra- rather than as trans-Saharan.

Archival evidence shows that the majority of these vital supplies were drawn from neighbouring and ecologically complementary areas, with which individual oases were linked through numerous social and political ties, and established patterns of travel or even seasonal migration. As a result, the Sahara was covered in overlapping areas of pastoral migration and intense exchange. These areas were determined by sociopolitical allegiances as much as by climate and pasture; their limits were thus flexible and varied from year to year. Nonetheless, in their general pattern, they were of astonishing longevity, and we can take them to roughly indicate ecological "regions," held together by economic complementarity, the regular movement of people, the ability to extend protection and engage in reliable transactions, investment in property, marriage, and other social ties. Oases, meanwhile, tended to be situated at the points where these regions overlap: we can hence think of them as places of safe storage and investment, but also as transhipment points and nodes

(1906) in western Algeria acted as a powerful magnet for regional and
in the northwestern Algerian Sahara and southeastern Morocco: see I

[5] See for examples most of the classics on this subject: Emerit (1954), M
(1968), Hopkins (1973), and Miège (1981), but also more recent wo
(1990, 2010).

in larger socioeconomic patterns of connectivity. As even specialists of trans-Saharan trade concede in their footnotes, much trans-Saharan trade had to rely on this preexisting regional infrastructure,[6] hence its adaptability and flexibility, and perhaps also the recurrent image of decline: while regional patterns of exchange show at times astonishing historical stability, the ways in which they could be combined for long-distance trade varied with circumstance. The inherent outside dependency of most Saharan settlement, coupled with a structural necessity for regional exchange, informs the conceptual framework of this book; this chapter illustrates its economic background, drawing on local Arabic and French colonial archives and oral history.

OASIS AGRICULTURE

From a purely local point of view, the existence of oases is puzzling. As Paul Pascon (1984: 9) noted after careful study of local account books of a powerful and wealthy *zāwiya* and trading post of Ilīgh in southern Morocco[7]:

> The considerable investments that are necessary to start the irrigation of the smallest plot of land, the cost of the development and the maintenance of intensive arboriculture in an extremely dry environment cannot be justified solely by their financial return nor even by general economy. Furthermore, we noticed very often that, for various reasons (political, military, demographic, and so on), oases decline long before they have finished paying back the initial capital outlay. We might thus be surprised by the optimism and the volontarism of the founders of oases, or in other words by their naivety, if we only consider the economic benefit that they might hope for. Maybe there are other than financial rewards, other benefits, or maybe other obligations of a system within which the agricultural sector is only a necessary, albeit loss-making, part.

What is true of the relatively well-watered Sūs al-Aqsa is perhaps even more applicable in southern Algeria, in particular in the greater Touat (Map 1.1), which has virtually no natural water supply beyond

[6] See, for example, Baier (1980: 142), Austen (1990), Webb (1995b), and McDougall (1985, 2005).

[7] A *zāwiya* (pl. *zawāyā*) is a religious stronghold, school, and pilgrimage site, funded through endowments and donations. It is mostly constructed around the tomb of a founding saint and managed by his descendants or followers. In many but not all cases, *zawāyā* are affiliated to Sufi orders. In the Sahara, much emphasis is put on their functions as hostels, safe storehouses, and regular or seasonal markets (see below, and Chapter 5). Larger *zawāyā*, such as Ilīgh, further acted as financial institution, extending loans to traders, leasing land to sharecroppers, and organising and funding caravans.

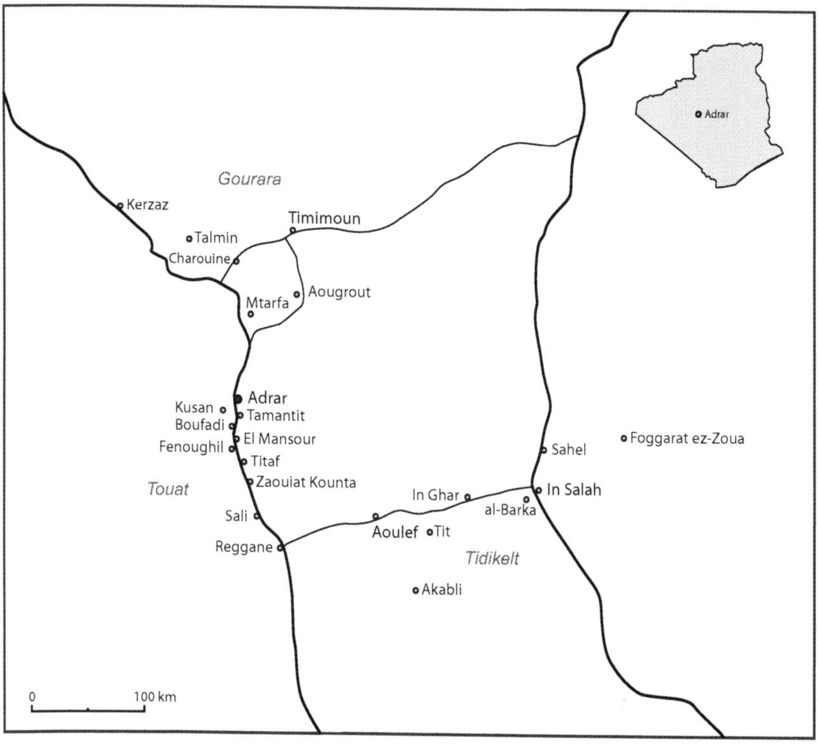

MAP 1.1. Gourara, Touat, and Tidikelt.

underground reservoirs common to most of the Sahara, and whose sparse pastures do not allow any reliance on animal traction to work simple wells.[8] Water is drawn from water tables using undergrounds canals (*fagāgīr*, sing. *faggāra*, see Photo 1.1) that tap higher lying water reservoirs, often located at a great distance, and that, on a carefully calculated slope, bring it to the place of settlement.[9] This is only possible in

8 Images of oases clustered around natural springs are hence of no heuristic value here, although there are some particular cases, especially in the southern Sahara, where settlement feeds on naturally occurring water: Agadez in northern Niger would be an example here. But even in the northern Sahara, where, within the southern scope of the run-off of the Atlas mountains, oases constructed around natural springs are common, such springs still require an elaborate system of irrigation canals and water management that are often ascribed to past outside influence or intervention. For an excellent description of one such system, see Bédoucha (1987).

9 *Fagāgīr* are more commonly known in the literature as *qanāt* or *khaṭṭāra*. On *fagāgīr* in the Touat, see Cornet (1952), Lo (1953–4), Capot-Rey and Damade (1962), Grandguillaume (1975, 1978), and Vallet (1973). For similar systems elsewhere, see Beaumont et al.

PHOTO 1.1. *Faggāra* and water divider.

low-lying lands and valleys, where indeed most historic oases are situated; nonetheless, locations of oases are never just "naturally" given, but owe their existence quite as much to strategic choice and technical skill as to the natural environment. Conversely, this means that any kind of settlement requires heavy initial capital outlay, a large and necessarily imported labour force, and constant maintenance works.

Although it is impossible to know just how much initial investment was needed, the sheer size of local irrigation systems can at least give us an impression of scale: in the 1950s, in the region of Adrar alone, Capot-Rey and Damade (1962) measured 2,000 km of *fagāgīr* – ten times more than the Parisian metro in the same year – for an overall population of barely 40,000 people. It is easier to estimate running maintenance costs: because *fagāgīr* are dug in relatively soft soil, they start silting up from the moment they are put in use. Further, they continually diminish the water table thus tapped and, in order to ensure steady supply, need to be extended on a regular basis. In the eighteenth century, debates about who should pay for the maintenance were a common concern in legal disputes brought before the *qāḍi* and recorded in collections of legal cases

(1989). For theories of the first introduction of *fagāgīr* to the Touat, see Wilson (2006); for contemporary attempts to revive them, see Khadraoui (2007).

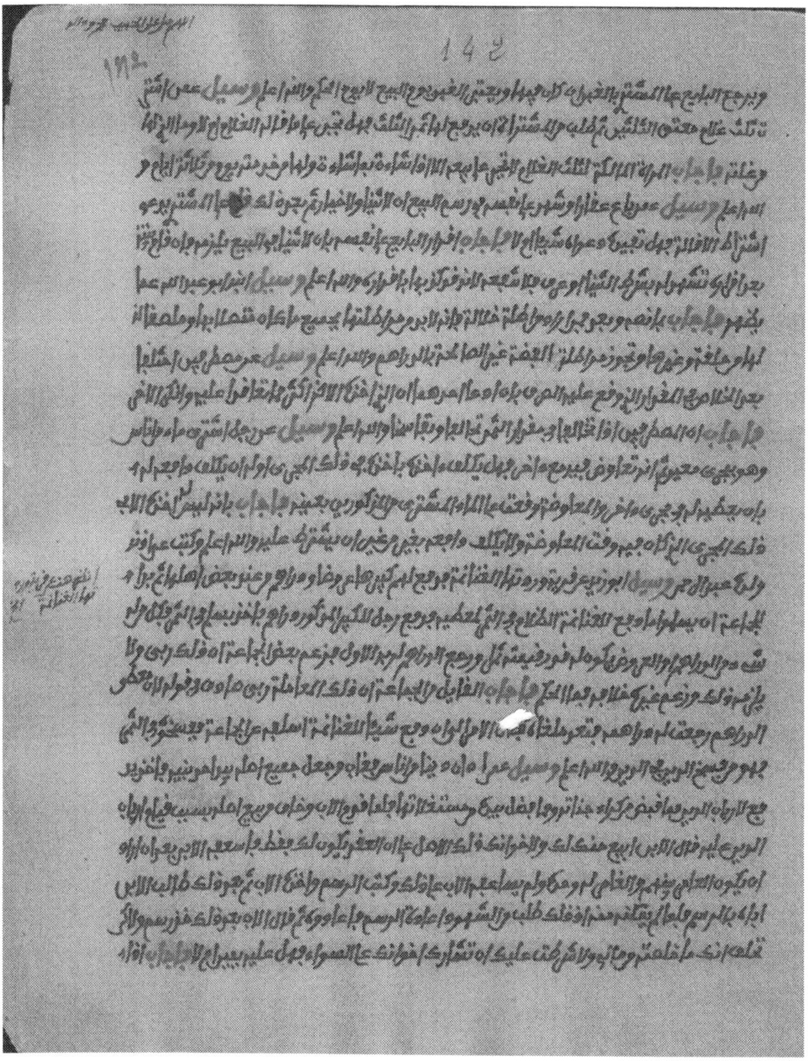

PHOTO 1.2. Nawāzil al-Ghuniya.

and precedents (*nawāzil*, see Photo 1.2).[10] In the early twentieth century, local water registers (Photo 1.3) routinely mention large obligatory

[10] See, for example, Grandguillaume (1975), citing the *Nawāzil al-ghuniya* (henceforth NG), a collection of legal cases (*nawāzil*) brought before the *qāḍi* Abū ʿAbd Allāh Sīdi al-Ḥājj Muḥammad b. ʿAbd al-Raḥmān al-Balbālī (born 1155 AH/1742 AD, died 1244 AH/1828 AD) and his son Sīdi Muḥammad ʿAbd al-ʿAzīz (born in 1199 AH/1776 AD). It was widely used as a reference work throughout the greater Touat, to the point that, when the French

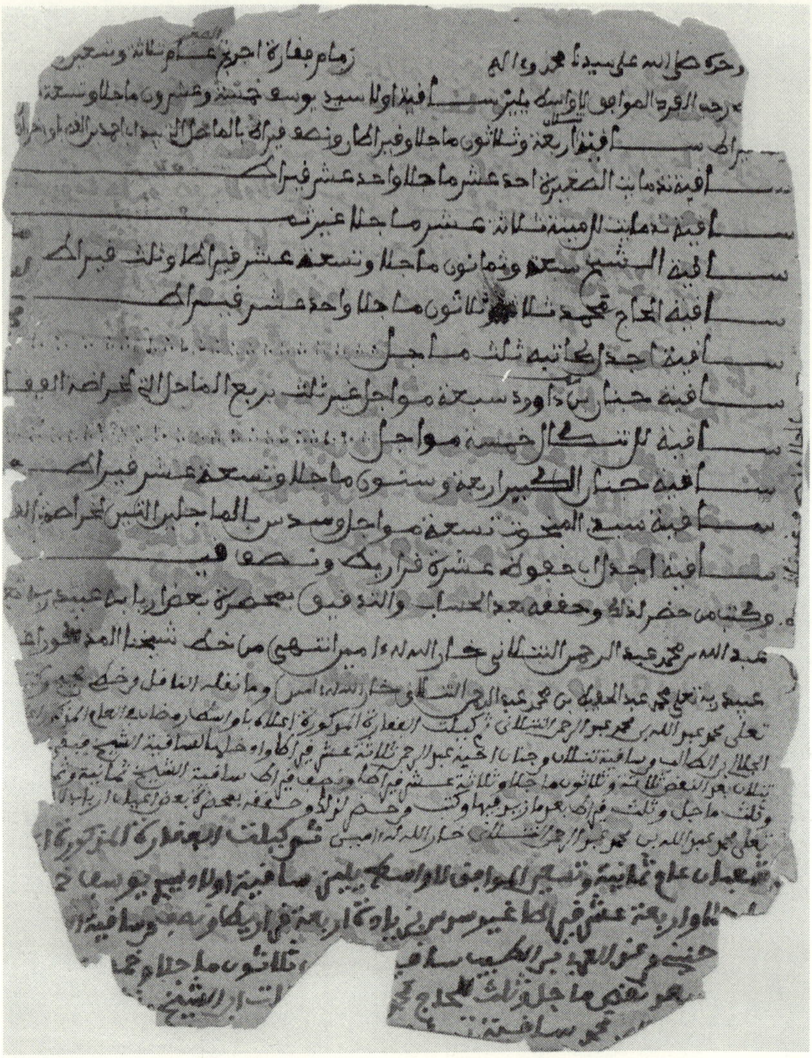

PHOTO 1.3. Irrigation register.

contributions or collective endeavours of fundraising "for the emptying" (*li-kabūyihi*) or the extension (*nafakh*, literally "swelling") of *fagāgīr*

colonial army arrived in the early twentieth century, they took it to constitute local "customary law." The copy referred to here is the one held in the library of Shaykh Bilkabīr in Mtarfa (courtesy of the *shaykh*). Other *nawāzil* collections that were commonly used in the area include the *Nawāzil al-Zijlāwī*, the *Nawāzil al-Janṭūrī*, the *Nawāzil Ibn Salamūn*, the *Nawāzil Shaykh Bāy*, and the more widely known *Nawāzil al-Qaṣrī*.

and subsidiary irrigation canals (*sawāqin*, sing. *sāqiya*).[11] In 1962, the *qṣar* (pl. *qṣūr*, fortified settlement) of Tit in the Tidikelt spent just under half a million francs (the equivalent of 7,500 euros in today's money) on the yearly maintenance of their main *faggāra*, collected from owners and users who were to be counted in hundreds rather than thousands. In addition to this, smaller sums were expended for the desilting of subsidiary canals and on drainage; altogether, the maintenance of irrigation works was the one most important expense registered by the assembly, dwarfing all other items of spending. The only way in which they could meet these costs was by appealing to outside investors and entrepreneurs, whom they remunerated in water shares and land.[12]

Even more than capital, the establishment of oases needed people, most of whom were necessarily brought in from the outside. Digging *fagāgīr* was a dangerous business, and desilting older and unstable underground water canals perhaps even more so, leading to frequent casualties, as did the harsh living conditions in the oases. Labour was mainly drawn from the south, and brought to the Sahara by force: the Touat not only traded in slaves to be used elsewhere (Ennaji 1994, Cordell 1999) but consumed a large number of them, if only to ensure its own survival.[13] Again, too little is known about the development of the Touati oases to be able to calculate the labour needed or to estimate the necessary infrastructure and capital to bring and keep them there, but it is certain that a concerted and far-reaching effort was necessary, especially if we bear in mind that the Touat could not feed any pack-animals, or indeed sustain a large population before the *fagāgīr* were established. Throughout the nineteenth century, it was commonplace for French military administrators, civil servants, and businessmen to petition not merely for the maintenance of slavery but for active state involvement in the slave trade, in order to keep

11 Water registers are the most common form of local documentation. They mainly concern one particular *faggāra*, recording the current division of water shares between its owners. I am drawing here on the registers of the *fagāgīr* Adjalloune and Rawḍat al-Ḥājj in Timmi in the Touat (*Zamām al-Faggāra*, ZF), established in the 1940s and 1950s, courtesy of Shaykh Belaïd. These registers will be discussed in more detail in Chapter 5.

12 This is based on the notebook of the assembly of Tit (*Sijill al-Jamāʿa*, SJ) that records municipal expenditure, income and decisions from 1962 to 1977, courtesy of ʿAbd Allāh b. ʿAbd al-Karīm. This document will be discussed in more detail in Chapter 5.

13 The first census established by the French administration records 10 per cent slaves, 43 per cent *ḥarāṭīn* or descendants of slaves, and 47 per cent "whites" in the Touat. In certain settlements, especially those with extensive irrigation and gardens, the proportion of "blacks" almost reached 70 per cent ("Recensement," 1911, CAOM 23H91). These figures have to be treated with caution, however, and cannot be relied upon: for a further discussion of their limitations, see Chapter 4.

alive both the southern oases and trans-Saharan trade.[14] After the turn of the twentieth century, such projects became politically untenable, but the threat of labour shortage and theories of a particular "aptitude" of black Africans for manual labour in the Sahara led to repeated attempts to settle "voluntary" sub-Saharan French soldiers in the oases.[15] Although these attempts were a spectacular failure, they show that the shortage of labour was considered a serious problem and understood to be intrinsically connected to the interruption of transregional relations. Today, although the contemporary Touat clearly does not lack people or indeed immigrants, at least half of all *fagāgīr* have ceased to function, as nobody is willing to undertake the arduous "slave labour" necessary for their maintenance – apart from, in some rare cases, "illegal" sub-Saharan migrants (Pellicani and Spiga 2007).[16]

Setting up an oasis and maintaining it, then, was a technical, logistic, and social achievement. Yet on the face of it, it hardly looks worth the effort. Although date palm oases look impressive and can, at times and in favourable conditions, produce a considerable surplus of starch in the forms of dates, in environments that were as unforgiving as the Central

[14] J. Vallier, "Rapport à la chambre de commerce," 13/07/1876; "Lettre du Président de la Chambre de commerce d'Alger au préfet du département d'Alger," 28/10/1879; Margueritte, "Rapport sur la question de commerce avec l'Afrique centrale," 10/03/1860, all kept in CAOM 22H26; and "Lettre de Laperrine, commandant militaire supérieur des Oasis Sahariennes, au Gouverneur Général de l'Algérie," 22/01/1907, CAOM 12H50; see also Martin (1908: 230–4). Despite lip service paid to abolition, French policy on the ground was rather flexible and used the prohibition of slavery mainly to punish "hostile notables" (Cordell 1999, Brower 2009, 2010). Many high-ranking members of the French colonial army, administration and commerce spoke out in favour of the maintenance of slavery, describing it as a "civilisational duty," see, for example, Baude (1841: 314–18), Bodichon (1847), Chancel (1858, 1859), and various documents kept in CAOM 22H26; further, "liberated" slaves were often entrusted to French allies, where they were clearly understood to be a reward rather than a responsibility: see for instance "Lettre du général Poizat commandant la Division d'Alger au Gouverneur Général de l'Algérie," 29/06/1889; and "Lettre du général Détrie commandant la division d'Oran au Gouverneur Général de l'Algérie," 2/11/1890, both kept in CAOM 12H50.

[15] In this way, they would be closer at hand to defend France against an increasingly populous Germany; meanwhile, they could cultivate the soil, revive local agriculture, and "regenerate the local black race." See, for example, "Note sur la question noire en Algérie"; and "Lettre du Gouverneur Général de l'Algérie au général commandant le 19e corps d'Armée," 23/04/1913, both CAOM 3H13.

[16] This is not to suggest that there is any kind of continuity between the slave trade and contemporary migration, as has been claimed by some researchers and especially journalists. Yet we should keep in mind that the influx of Sahelians and nationals of other sub-Saharan country, greedily absorbed by the local labour market, has been crucial for the current economic boom. For a fuller discussion of this, see Chapter 6.

Sahara, they could hardly be relied on to sustain life independently.[17] In a good year, Martin (1908: 306–8) calculated, the oases of the Touat yielded enough to allow their inhabitants to live off one kilogram of dates and 300 grams of cereals a day, but the latter figure already included imports, and throughout the greater Touat, "stout people were a real exception" (ibid. 352). Indeed, he added, the oases are constantly declining demographically (ibid. 361), and French reports of the time invariably noted the small number of children in the oases, concluding that the population of the Touat could not reproduce itself independently.[18] In 1909, a few years after the French colonial conquest, the French colonial administrator of the Touat described the "material situation of the indigenous population" as "none too rosy (*peu brillante*)": most people lived on "one single meal a day" consisting of "a few dates."[19] Even if exceptionally good harvests occurred at times and allowed for large profits, any crisis – always to be expected in the fragile Saharan environment – would lead to starvation, if no other resources were available to fall back on: and indeed, in 1906, confronted with the French imposition of taxes, many oasis dwellers saw their only chance of survival in abandoning their settlement altogether and tried instead to survive by "hunting game in the desert" (Martin 1908: 383). In 1907, and again in 1933, due to transport restrictions and camel requisitions further north, customary pastoral migrations from the Tell were interrupted, making the usual exchange of dates for grain impossible; in 1907, this caused utter misery and starvation; in 1933, local inhabitants had to survive on a diet of 3 kilograms of cereals and 20 kilograms of dates per month. Although such a diet provides roughly enough calories to survive for a time, it is lacking in vital nutrients and will eventually lead to starvation; and most local labourers tried to get away from the oases if they could somehow dodge

[17] For examples of more productive oases, see Wilkinson (1977) on Oman, and Bédoucha (1987) on Tunisia.

[18] "Recensements des populations du Touat," 1911 to 1950, CAOM 23H91, and "Recensement du Touat," 1933, CAOM 10H86. This is a common problem in societies based on slave labour: see Meillassoux (1986).

[19] "Rapport annuel, annexe du Touat," 1909, CAOM 23H91. The structural insufficiency of local agriculture is echoed in much earlier accounts. In the fourteenth century, Ibn Baṭṭūṭa had described Būdā, then the largest oasis of the Touat, as follows: "Then we arrived at Būdā, which is one of the biggest villages of Tuwāt. Its land consists of salt and salt pans ... There is no cultivation there nor butter nor oil. Oil is only imported to it from the land of the Maghrib. The food of its people is dates and locusts" (Levtzion and Hopkins 1981: 304).

French administrative restrictions.[20] Similarly, in the Tidikelt, local agricultural production, even where it could be exchanged for imports, was never quite enough to feed the local population; at times of crop failure, the deficit would have spelled disaster had there not been other sources of income.[21]

The French colonial army was to learn this lesson as soon as they attempted to establish permanent military bases in the area in the early 1900s. Even the maintenance of the most rudimentary military infrastructure, staffed by half-starved northern camel-nomads, turned out to be absurdly expensive. Between 1909 and 1929, In Salah, the main oasis of the Tidikelt, produced an annual trade deficit that amounted on average to more than 900,000 francs (equivalent to more than 500,000 euros in today's money), while taxes, including market taxes, never rose above 30,000 francs plus forced labour. In bad years, the annual deficit could rise to 1.5 million francs; virtually all reports complain about the chronic "*disette de numéraires*," while some mention camel-loads of gold being shipped south to make up the difference.[22] Of course, we cannot conclude from the French colonial situation what went on before: the presence of a French garrison considerably increased the overall population, and much of the deficit can be explained by army supplies and salaries paid out to soldiers and used to buy costly imports.[23] Further, the French presence inevitably upset regional patterns of exchange, thereby largely creating the misery they were complaining about. But the exceptional nature of the French colonial period allows us glimpses of an earlier system: in "normal" times, when the French were not there to settle the bill, other kinds of outside resources and means of storing surplus, diversifying income, and spreading risk must have been available.

20 "Rapport annuel, annexe du Touat," 1907, CAOM 23H91; and R. Hardy, "Une terre qui meurt: le Touat," 30/04/1933, CAOM 10H86. Such a diet would provide just 2,000 kcal per head. Adults performing heavy agricultural labour would need almost twice as much, or be, over time, severely undernourished (according to figures taken from M. Davis 2001: 39).

21 Throughout the following, figures are taken from the "Rapports annuels, annexe du Tidikelt," 1909–29, CAOM 23H102.

22 "Rapports annuels, annexe du Tidikelt," 1907, 1910, 1913, 1928, 1951 and 1952, CAOM 23H102. In 1945, the administrator of the Touat noted that "even in the best years, the economy of this country necessarily shows a deficit," "Rapport annuel, annexe du Touat," 1945, CAOM 23H91.

23 In 1906, the French army confiscated half of all cereal supplies, reducing daily rations to 150 grams per head (Martin 1908: 308). At that time, there were 600 soldiers stationed in the Touat and Gourara, and 300 in the Tidikelt.

MONEY AND DEBTS

The relative monetisation of oasis economies similarly points towards their porosity and integration into larger financial networks. Marouf (2005: 67) mentions early coinage stamped in the Gourara and, perhaps more importantly, shows how monetary values were notionally central to local measurements, even to those that at first appear most archaic: water measurements, such as the ubiquitous *ḥabba*, he suggests (following Martin 1908: 23), are derived from the size of grains of barley (hence from a measure that is not indigenous to the Saharan oases), which in turn – at least nominally – governs the gold and silver weight of standard coins.[24] This is probably not true historically, but as both Martin and Marouf were relying on local explanations, it shows the emphasis placed locally on monetary values and their universal validity. Meanwhile, Chentouf (1984: 83) claims that there never had been local coinage but mentions a remarkably large variety of different currencies used in the greater Touat. His list can be further expanded, drawing on the French colonial archives: the Spanish "*dourou*" (piece of eight, from *pieza d'oro*), the French *dourou* (gold piece of five francs), the *riyāl* (silver coin), the *rabī'a* ("quarter," which Beaussier 1958 has as a piece of silver worth 50 centimes) and the *waqiyya* ("ounce," worth 30 centimes by the late 1950s). A 1900 report on trade with the Ahaggar further mentions the *mizouna* (0.055 francs), the *tlétti* (0.2 francs), the *settoujour* (0.4 francs), the *tlétaouokt* ("three times," 0.75 francs), a silver *riyāl* worth 2.5 francs, the Maria Theresa dollar called *mithqāl* and the piece of five francs called "*cinco*," whose values are "surprisingly stable."[25] In the 1940s, *quḍāh*'s registers refer to *dūru*, franc, *salad*, and sometimes *riyāl* – by then, however, these all seem to correspond to multiples of French francs, the *dūru* representing the five francs gold coin, and the *riyāl* corresponding to a silver piece worth one franc.

Money seems to have been used widely in the late eighteenth century already. In one case recorded in the *Nawāzil al-ghuniya*, the *qāḍi* reminds a seller that he has no further claims on a buyer after the sale is concluded,

[24] This is a standard account for weights found throughout the Middle East, often with no factual backing, and probably has little grounding in reality. Marouf gives no conclusive evidence for this assertion, and at least one of the "coins" he mentions, the *mithqāl* ("weight"), is more likely to have been a weight of gold dust (perhaps based on Roman or more probably Middle Eastern precedent) rather than a stamped coin (see also Johnson 1968, Garrard 1982, Webb 1982).

[25] "Note sur le mouvement commercial qui s'est produit entre In Salah et le pays Touareg pendant l'été et l'automne 1900," CAOM 22H50.

unless the coin (*sikka*) used on the day of purchase is deficient. In the latter case, he is to be reimbursed, "in gold or in goods."[26] Other questions address the kind of weight that ought to be used to measure money, and how jewellery is to be converted into silver.[27] Yet others mention money-changers quarrelling over the rate at which they had exchanged coins.[28] Sales contracts established in the second half of the nineteenth century, fifty years after the *Ghuniya*, give a similar impression. In 1846, ʿAbd al-Raḥmān b. al-Ṭālib Yūsuf bought from his brother Muḥammad uncultivated land, paying four *mithqāl* and a half; the year after, Shaykh Maʿzūz paid four *mithqāl* and 18 *mizunāt* for various plots of land, trees, and water shares.[29] Both transactions took place in Talmin, a minor *qṣar* situated between the Touat and the Gourara, and known neither as a centre of learning nor of trans-Saharan trade. By the first decades of the twentieth century, after the French colonial conquest and when documentation becomes more plentiful, all goods were routinely evaluated in money, with the help of "customary experts" who had, it seems, long been in the habit of using money as a standard of account. Hence, an inheritance document from the *qṣar* of Kūsān in the Timmi dating from the 1910s or 1920s translates everything, water, land, houses, and even two outdoor toilets, into *mithqāl*.[30] Similarly, an inheritance document drafted in 1944, concerning the legacy of Abū Ibrīk b. Abū Aīʿīsh, includes:

> half of the square that is part of the house that is the inheritance of Sīdi al-ʿAzīz worth 10 francs. And the water: … five *ḥabba* and 13 *qīrāṭ* and ten *qīrāṭ* of the big *qīrāṭ* worth 976 *dūru* and ten *salad*. And with it 13 *ḥabba* minus a sixth from Abnakūr worth 513 *dūru* and three *ḥabba* from the *faggāra* of the *qṣar* Bitulk worth six *dūru* and three big *ḥabba* from the *faggāra* Sīdi ʿAlī in the *ghāba* [pasture] worth nine *dūru*. And three quarters of the price of the female donkey of ʿAshūr b. Nājim worth 244 *dūru* minus one franc and 5 *salad*. And three quarters in the donkey of Hansanī b. al-Ḥājj Aḥmad worth 75 *dūru* and the small donkey worth 50 *dūru*.[31]

These monetary evaluations, as well as referring to an external standard of value, make it possible to own shares of property, such as half a square

[26] NG: 139.
[27] NG: 142.
[28] NG: 142.
[29] According to documents kept in the private archives of the Maʿzūz family (*Wathāʾiq Talmin*, WT), n° 4 and 6, consulted with the courtesy of ʿAbd al-Qādir Maʿzūz.
[30] According to documents kept in the private archives of the Balbālī family in Kusan (*Wathāʾiq Kūsān*, WK), courtesy of Shaykh Tayyeb.
[31] *Sijill al-qāḍi*, SQ: 25.

in somebody else's house, or three-quarters of a donkey, that have no immediate practical use-value unless they are understood as investments or representations of rights that might be held by absentee landlords or traders as much as by local families.

This, however, does not mean that we are dealing here with a modern cash economy. Monetary value itself fluctuated wildly and always remained socially determined (see Chapter 5). Moreover, all sources agree that cash was scarce.[32] Even the unit of account, the gold *mithqāl* was "fictional ... a currency that does not exist or rather does not exist anymore"[33]; and it often happened, as inheritances were divided locally, that several heirs could not be paid off, as no money was available to do so. Money was often merely used as an accounting standard, and perhaps also to better meet Islamic requirements of fixed and immutable value (see Chapter 5). Yet this emphasis on monetary value despite the lack of ready cash might also point to the existence of deeply rooted networks of debt and credit. As one French army officer noted shortly after the conquest:

> In fact there is happening in the oases what is happening elsewhere. The poor, always improvident, consume quickly at the time of harvest everything they have. Thus the price of cereals and dates goes up fast to reach each year the double and triple of the normal rates. Forced by misery, the small landholders or *khammās*, *ḥarāṭīn* or negroes, buy on credit what they need for their subsistence to be reimbursed at the next harvest. In reality these are six-months credits that are granted by large landholders with an interest of 200 to 300%. This makes the poor totally dependent on the rich.[34]

Fifty years later, another report states that "in the Sahara, the regulation of private trade is inseparable from all social progress," due to the "total control of traders over all transactions" and the "scandalous usury" they practice when selling goods on credit, to the detriment of small farmers and workers.[35] An earlier detailed study of local retail notes that all small shopkeepers in the oases acted in fact as agents for larger traders, to whom they were constantly indebted.[36]

32 See, for instance, the "Rapports annuels, annexe du Tidikelt," 1928, 1951, 1952, CAOM 23H102; or the "Rapports annuels, annexe du Touat," 1907, 1910, 1912, 1922, CAOM 23H91. See also Martin (1908: 383).

33 "Note sur le mouvement commercial qui s'est produit entre In Salah et le pays Touareg pendant l'été et l'automne 1900," CAOM 22H50. For a similar observation, see "Rapport annuel, annexe du Touat," 1922, CAOM 23H91.

34 "Rapport annuel, annexe du Tidikelt," 1909, CAOM 23H102.

35 "Rapport du CHEAM sur le Sahara," 1958, CAOM AffPol 2178/6.

36 Fraguier, "Le commerce du Touat," 1948, dissertation submitted to the Centre des hautes études d'administration musulmane (CHEAM, later known as the Centre des hautes

Although this situation was certainly aggravated by French taxes and the development of truck trade by the 1950s, it was not altogether new. Oral histories as recounted today by trading families and that mainly recount events dating from the late nineteenth and the early twentieth centuries invariably mention moneylenders and mortgages, while family archives of successful traders contain notes of debts owed them by small-scale farmers or traders, and petitions by local religious dignitaries for small loans of money or goods. The following note, drafted probably in the 1930s, is typical here:

> Praise be to the one God and the prayer of God on our lord Muḥammad and his family. To the blessed our darling and our lord ʻŪmar b. Mūlāy al-Jilālī a thousand greetings to you and the mercy of God from the writer. And after this welcome our son and make possible for him a pound of sugar and 100 g of tea. Be patient and do not be sharp about us, God willing one day we will give you the borrowed money, we will come to you and settle our debt. And this is written by al-Maḥfūẓ b. Bayyiḍ, God be pleased with him. And add to this a pound of sugar and 100 g of tea with one pound of sugar and 50 g of tea.[37]

Other documents record the regular payment of monthly instalments of much larger debts owed to ʻŪmar, amounting to several thousands francs. In the 1920s and 1930s, ʻŪmar himself borrowed large sums of money from Oran (see below, and Chapter 2).

While ʻŪmar's documents refer to the French colonial period, problems relating to loans, repayments, and pledges already recur much earlier and are common throughout the eighteenth-century *Ghuniya*. Thus, the father who, harassed by creditors, disappeared, making all his mobile and landed property over to his son on the understanding that the latter would either return it to him once the immediate danger had passed, or else share it with his siblings.[38] Or the debtor who saw all his property, garden and water, confiscated by his creditors, with the exception of a certain quantity of salt that he bought in Timbuktu with borrowed

études sur l'Afrique et l'Asie modernes), available at the Centre historique des archives nationales (CHAN) at Fontainbleau.

[37] From the collection of documents held by Mekki Kalloum in Adrar. ʻŪmar al-Jilālī was his grand-uncle, a Zuwī and a prosperous trader in Timimoun (see Chapter 2). The sources tell us little about debt collection, and as Ghislaine Lydon (2009a: 336) notes for Mauritania, and Paul Pascon (1980: 707–8) for Morocco, in the unstable environment of the Sahara where control over people is the key to wealth, granting credit and the potential obligations that derive from it are often the best way of saving money.

[38] The son refused to do so, and the case was brought before the *qāḍi*. NG: 142–3.

money, and whose exact value was now disputed.[39] Other questions address the modalities of payment, giving us a glimpse of their potential complexity: can debts be paid in the form of other goods, such as slave girls, even if they are of lesser value? Can one debt be set off against another, or changed into shares in future transactions, such as forward buying (*salam*) of wheat or slaves? Can a debt be sold to somebody else against a fixed fee, leaving the buyer to come to an agreement with the debtor? Who is liable for money given to an envoy to pay one's debt abroad, if the envoy embezzles it and denies ever having received it? What happens if a pledge given for a debt – a carpet or guns, for instance – is damaged or lost?[40]

Moreover, the large number of cases concerning mortgages (*ruhūn*, sing. *rahn*) on land, water, and harvests indicate that debts were deeply rooted in all aspects of local production. Debts, pledges and mortgages were common even between family members: hence ʿAbd al-Qādir b. ʿAbd Allāh, who, owing a certain sum of money to his sister Maryam, offered a piece of land as a pledge and then "travelled abroad." Impatient, Maryam succeeded in selling the land with the help of the *qāḍi*, without consulting her brother or waiting for his return.[41] Similar arrangements were current between husband and wife.[42] Sometimes, mortgages explicitly linked landholdings to trade: as in the case of a house with a garden given as a guarantee to a third party who advanced money for goods to be delivered at a later date. Until then, the creditor reserved himself the usufruct of house and garden. Yet such an arrangement, said the *qāḍi*, is illegal, unless the pledge (*rahn*) was transformed into a sale with right of restitution (*iqāla*).[43] More generally, the *iqāla*, one of the most common subjects discussed in the *Ghuniya*, often seems to have hidden a loan against interest (*ribā*), thereby avoiding prohibition by the *sharīʿa*.[44] It was common practice to sell a garden for a limited time, against an

39 Should it correspond to the price of salt in Timbuktu, or should the salt itself be delivered to the Touat? NG: 206. For a similar case, see NG: 146.

40 NG: 138, 212, 213, 206, 216–17.

41 NG: 216. Lydon (2009a: 233) similarly notes the frequent use of written contracts between family members.

42 See, for instance, NG: 219–20.

43 NG: 218.

44 Lydon (2009a: 304–6) describes the *iqāla* as a sale with right of restitution. Although in the *Ghuniya*, some such use is made of the term (such as the case concerning the sale of a "very fat" camel that suddenly died a few days later, NG: 147–8), most cases of *iqāla* clearly refer to hidden interest payments.

immediate cash payment, to then continue working it, while paying the usufruct – in other words, a set proportion of the harvest – to the buyer, until the initial sum could be reimbursed. Once the delay had run out, the buyer could take full possession of the garden. This explains the frequent disputes over the exact nature of the usufruct that had to be paid: did it include all agricultural produce, or just dates, or just garden vegetables and not dates?[45] It also explains the large number of sellers attempting to recuperate their property a few days after the *iqāla* had run out, as well as the many squabbles over who had to pay for necessary repairs on properties while they were held as *iqāla*.[46] And finally, it helps us understand the *qāḍī*'s insistence that the *iqāla* was a sale, not a loan, and that it was illicit to use it, "as many people do," to hide interest payments.[47]

PROPERTY RELATIONS AND REGIONAL PATTERNS OF INVESTMENT

Debts, then, were a common feature of oasis economies, in agriculture as much as in trade, indicating that even the most basic "subsistence" activities were closely bound up in larger regional or even transregional commercial relations.[48] But, if money and debts made outside investments feasible, who provided the money in the first place? Some investors and landlords seem to have operated on a regional or even local basis, establishing overlapping rights of property throughout neighbouring oases. Local registers of individual *fagāgīr* mention frequent buying and selling of water shares, alongside leases and mortgages. Although the provenance of buyers and sellers is never explicitly mentioned, certain names recur throughout the region, indicating dispersed holdings. One Abū Flīja, for instance (whom we shall meet again), owned water shares throughout the Timmi and Tamantit.[49] *Quḍāh*'s registers are more explicit here. In 1347 AH (1929 CE), Sīdi Muḥammad b. Sīdi Muḥammad al-Ḥusayn set up a *ḥubus* (pl. *aḥbās*, endowment) for his children, including water from six

[45] NG: 139.
[46] NG: 139–40, 141.
[47] NG: 139.
[48] As Horden and Purcell (2000: 272) note for the Mediterranean, notions of "subsistence agriculture" are largely meaningless – "subsistence is suicidal" – in environments where stability is exceptional and crises have to be expected: any long-term project of settlement and agriculture has to be based on a reliable surplus in order to face future hardship, or else include other sources of income that are independent of local conditions.
[49] I am drawing here on the ZF, and the registers of the *qāḍi* of Timmi (*Sijill al-qāḍi*, SQ), from the 1930s through to the 1950s, courtesy of Mohamed Bakraoui.

different *fagāgīr*; three years later, he added water from the same *fagāgīr* plus an additional one, before reconfirming the *ḥubus* with further modifications in 1362 (1944) before the French-appointed *qāḍi*.[50] What was true of water was equally true of land, trees, and storage space. Most legacies were spread through various oases, and were dealt with in a series of documents, all drawing on different sets of local experts. Hence, in April 1944, the inheritance of Sīdi Muḥammad al-Sharīf was the subject of five independent documents, concerning property held in different places; al-Mahdī b. al-Ḥājj al-Ṣadīq al-Tiṭāfī, deceased in July of the same year, owned gardens and water-rights in his home *qṣar* of Tiṭāf but also, and to much greater value, in Tāmasat, Sīdi Yūsuf, Būyaḥia, 'Antha, Muḥammad, Tamāsakh and Ighīl.[51] More generally, in inheritance cases brought before the *qāḍi*, ownership that was limited to one *qṣar* was exceptional.[52]

In addition to this, land, houses, and storage space were frequently owned by people from beyond the neighbouring *qṣūr* (pl. of *qṣar*), including nomadic pastoralists, religious scholars and foundations (*zawāyā*, sing. *zāwiya*), and regional merchants. Revenues from gardens and landholdings and reliance on oasis storage capacity were central to regional nomadic economies.[53] Indeed, the term "*qṣar*" or "fortress" that is locally exclusively used to refer to Saharan settlement instead of the classical Arabic term "*wāḥa*" (oasis) indicates a local emphasis on safe storage and defence rather than on settlement and agriculture for its own sake (see also Capot-Rey 1956). Hence, Tuareg Ahaggar regularly travelled to Aoulef in the Tidikelt to exchange pastoral produce and cereals for dates, and owned storehouses there.[54] The Awlād al-Mukhṭār, who, in the late nineteenth century, were among the wealthiest residents of the neighbouring In Salah, used to be pastoralists who had invested gains made in regional trade in "beautiful gardens" throughout the Tidikelt. They now engaged in "prosperous date and grain trade" by proxy, by supplying capital to

50 SQ: 20–1.

51 SQ: 16–20, 34.

52 Much of this might simply have been but the result of strict observance of the Islamic law of inheritance, that grants shares to both sons and daughters, whether they have married locally or not; and when dealing with a *qāḍi*'s register, such observance is of course to be expected. Nonetheless, such strict observance in an agricultural and nominally locally bounded society in itself warrants explanation (see Chapter 5).

53 This is the case more widely for most pastoral economies, for comparative examples see Bonte (1981) and Marx (2006).

54 Chardenet, "Aoulef," n.d. (early 1900s), CAOM 22H50. See also Nicolaisen (1997 [1963]) and Gast (1968).

caravaneers, many of whom were probably their cousins, or by employing them as wage-labourers.[55] Pastoral nomads from the Algerian northwest, who had long supplied the Gourara in cereals invested in real estate in their habitual ports of call, as well as in their summer pastures in the Tell (Bugéja 1930), while their poorer cousins were employed as seasonal harvesters, of wheat and dates.[56] The Arbāʿ, nomadic pastoralists in the central northern Algerian desert, owned storage space, houses, and gardens in the *qṣar* of Aïn Madhi, that were indispensable for their household economy (Geoffroy 1887). In Aïn Madhi, according to the same author, "settlement was only developed with regards to the seasonal needs of the nomads"; inhabitants of *qṣūr* either made a living by renting out storage, or by guarding houses and stores that were directly owned by nomads.[57]

Aïn Madhi was also the seat of one the two rival Tijani *zawāyā* that drew gifts and donations from throughout the central Sahara and beyond, owned palm gardens scattered through the region and entrusted large numbers of livestock to nomadic dependents.[58] *Zawāyā* were religious strongholds, mostly constructed around the tomb of a saint, and at times connected to a Sufi order. They acted as centres of scholarship and religious and legal training throughout the Sahara, but they were also instrumental in the organisation of trade and agriculture, relying on their far-reaching regional connections and drawing on funds granted them as donations or endowments (*aḥbās*).[59] They thereby bound various

[55] Simon, "Notices sur le Tidikelt," 20/06/1900, CAOM 22H50.

[56] Bonète (1962), and see "Lettre du général commandant la division d'Alger au Gouverneur Général de l'Algérie," 21/10/1877, CAOM 24H117.

[57] Again, this is reflected in the historical record. Hence, Ibn Khaldūn: "Among the division of these B. Wamānū … are the clans of B. Yāladdas, though some assert that they belong to the Maghrāwa. Their homelands are strung out to the south of the farthest and the middle Maghribs behind the above-mentioned erg which encompasses their settlement. In their homelands they have built *qṣūr* and strongholds and have made gardens of palms and grapes and other fruits. One of their homelands lies three stages to the south of Sijilmāsa and is called Tuwāt. It consists of some 200 *qṣūr* strung out from west to east, of which the most easterly is called Tamanṭīṭ, nowadays a flourishing place and a point of departure for merchants who pass to and fro between the Maghrib and the land of Mālī and the Sūdān" (Levtzion and Hopkins 1981: 339).

[58] See Arnaud (1861); the various reports on the *zāwiya* kept in CAOM 16H44–5 and 51–3; and G. Hirtz, "Étude sur Laghouat, les Larbaâ, les Mekhalif, la zaouïa d'Aïn Mâdhî," 1950, CAOM 8X192. For the history of the Tijaniyya, see Abun-Nasr (1965); for its contemporary position in West Africa, see Triaud and Robinson (2000).

[59] For descriptions of individual *zawāyā* that underline their economic importance, see Hammoudi (1980), Pascon (1980), Triaud (1983), Elboudrari (1985), Gutelius (2002). Gellner (1969) has famously described *zawāyā* and their living representatives as necessary arbiters in an acephalous system. Subsequent research, in particular in Morocco, has shown that this was only one possible way in which a *zāwiya* might gain regional

sedentary and nomadic populations together in complex networks of overlapping ownership, protection, and donations, providing initial funding for agricultural and commercial projects, and redistributing surplus. Hence, the Awlād Sīdi Shaykh, the dominant tribal and religious federation in the area, invested in houses and storage places in the Gourara and Touat[60]; several *zawāyā* had long been set up in their name throughout the greater Touat, owning large gardens as *aḥbās* and worked by slaves or *ḥarāṭīn* given to the *zāwiya*. These *zawāyā* acted as markets and travel lodges, and sent their revenues back to the mother *zāwiya* in Abiodh Sidi Cheikh, in the Algerian northwest (Map 1.2).[61] Descendants of the Awlād Sīdi Shaykh, settled in these *zawāyā* and locally referred to as Zuwā (sing. Zuwī) or Ahl 'Azzī, in turn were granted land and endowments in the Ahaggar, in the extreme south of contemporary Algeria, where they had long acted as religious scholars, teachers, and regional traders.[62] Here, drawing on *ḥarāṭīn* labour from In Salah and income derived from husbandry and commerce, they established new agricultural settlements that were structurally similar to those of the Tidikelt albeit adapted to local hydrological conditions.[63] In some cases, regional trade routes shifted in order to pass through such new agricultural settlements, especially if the founder was still resident there and was sought after for his protection, both spiritual and political: this was the case with the village of Tit near Tamanrasset, set up by a descendant of Mawlāy Hayba's, *shaykh* of one of the most influential *zawāyā* in the Tidikelt.[64] While the Ahaggar's oldest villages were established no later than the second half of the nineteenth

dominance: *zawāyā* could also act as intermediaries with the central state, or attempt to establish small regional "states" on their own (see, for instance, Hammoudi 1974, Mezzine 1987). In all cases, it seems, successful *zawāyā* tended to project their power and protection over property and saw the vivification of land as part of their mission.

60 On the Awlād Sīdi Shaykh, see Leclerc (1858), Boubakeur (1999), and Bahous (2001).

61 Simon, "Notices sur le Tidikelt," 20/06/1900, CAOM 22H50.

62 Voinot, "Reconnaissance du bassin supérieur de l'Igharghar et visite du Sud du Ahaggar et de l'Ahnet," winter 1905–6, CAOM 22H72; "Rapport annuel, annexe du Tidikelt," 1919, CAOM 23H102; and Simon, "Notices sur les districts du Tidikelt," 21/05/1900, CAOM 22H50.

63 For a more thorough description of these recent settlements and of the agricultural and commercial activities of the resident Zuwā, see de Barrère, "Contribution à l'étude de l'évolution sociale du centre de cultures d'Idélès," unpublished typescript held at the library of the Maison Méditerranéenne des Sciences de l'Homme (MMSH) in Aix-en-Provence (no date, probably 1960s).

64 "Rapport de tournée du Capitaine Dinaux, chef de l'annexe d'In Salah. Ahnet, Adrar nigritien, Ahaggar, Aïr septentrional," 3/05 to 29/10/1905, CAOM 22H68. On the *zāwiya* Mawlāy Hayba, see "Notes sur les personnages influents du Touat, Gourara, Tidikelt," 1893, CAOM 22H36.

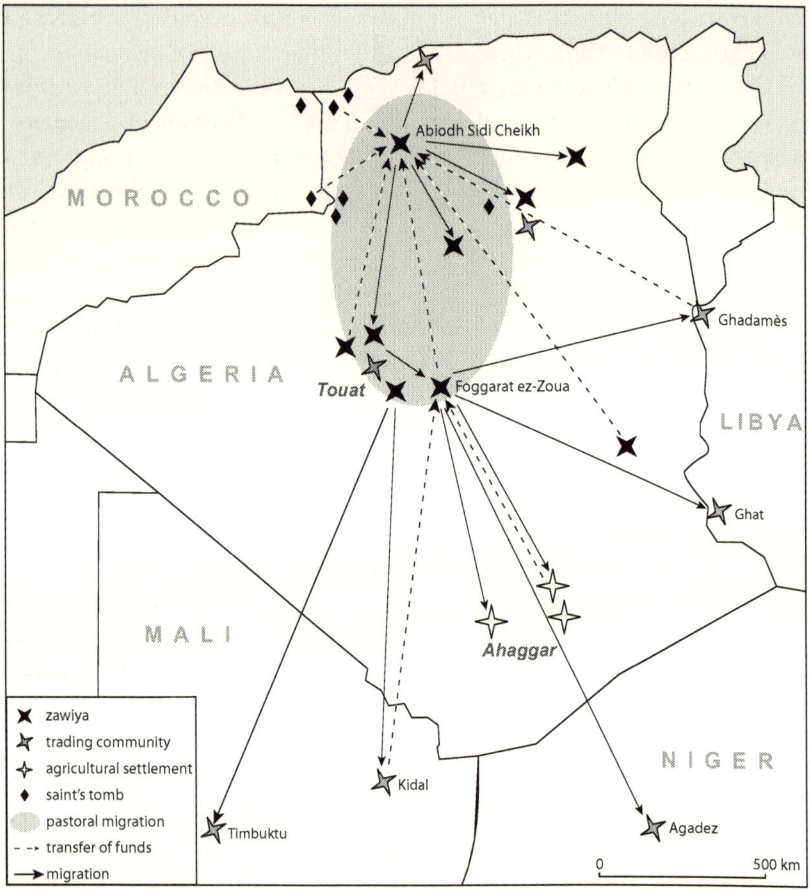

MAP 1.2. The Awlād Sīdi Shaykh.

century, settlement elsewhere seems to go back further: in 1903, a French officer on tour in the Aïr in what is today northern Niger encountered several *ḥarāṭīn* from the Tidikelt at Agadez, who were keen to "return" to the Ahaggar.[65]

Further south, the Kunta, a religious federation that emerged in the Malian Azawād in the late seventeenth century (Whitcomb 1975,

[65] "Lettre du capitaine Métois, chef de l'annexe d'In Salah au commandant militaire des oasis," 19/07/1903, CAOM 28H2. In one archival document, the *mrabṭīn* (descendants of regional saints) from Tit are themselves described as descendants from a branch of the Ahl 'Azzī established in the *zāwiya* of Maabed near Ghadamès. See "Renseignements sur les populations du Gourara, Touat, Tidikelt. Zaouias, ordres religieux, soffs," CAOM 22H55, and Chapter 2.

Batran 2001), established *zawāyā* throughout the Azawād, but also in the Mauritanian Hodh, the Tilemsi in contemporary Mali and in the Algerian Touat.[66] There they taught Islamic sciences and initiated adepts to the Qādiriyya. Their "students" (*talāmīdh*) were often in a position indistinguishable from clients and could be put to work herding, trading, and tending gardens (P. Marty 1920). Well provided with manpower and funds, the Kunta came to dominate the salt trade in the Western Sahara (McDougall 1986), and regional trade more generally (Géneviѐre 1950). In the late nineteenth century, the Kunta *zāwiya* of Akabli in the Tidikelt, for instance, received gifts and endowments from throughout the Azawād, and invested them in agriculture and scholarship locally, as well as in regional trade. By then, the annual caravan from the Touat to Timbuktu was organised in and by the *zāwiya*, relying on allied tribes.[67] Further south, the Kunta Shaykh Bāy's *zāwiya* and garden in Téléya near Kidal flourished, as his *ḥarāṭīn* and students cultivated wheat, tobacco, and vegetables alongside dates and looked after a large number of cows, donkeys, horses, and camels used for transport and trade with the salt-mines of Tawdanni north of Timbuktu. The *zāwiya* had been founded by Bāy's father in the second half of the nineteenth century, with money derived from regional trade and pious donations.[68] Incidentally, Shaykh Bāy himself was married to a woman from the Awlād Sīdi Shaykh (P. Marty 1920: 119).

The Kunta and Awlād Sīdi Shaykh were not alone in transforming their spiritual power into the tangible *baraka* of crops and flocks. Other palm gardens in Tessalit and Kidal were planted by "*mrabṭīn*" (religious scholars) either from the Tidikelt or from the Kunta, relying on *ḥarāṭīn* labour whose descendants are still defined as a category apart.[69] The *zāwiya* of Kerzaz, seat of an independent Sufi order, owned 65,810 palm trees, in addition to several thousand goats and sheep kept by their clients

[66] On the Kunta, see Leriche (1946), Whitcomb (1975), Bibed (1997), Batran (2001), and Hūtiya (2007). Their genealogical claims and current status will be discussed in more detail in Chapters 3 and 4.

[67] Chardenet, "Akabli," n.d. (early 1900s), CAOM 22H50.

[68] On Shaykh Bāy and Téléya, see P. Marty (1920: 119–37) and de Gironcourt (1920: 147–9). See also Shaykh Bāy, "*Ta'rīkh Kanāta*," Manuscript n° 2407/90, held in the de Gironcourt collection (CG) at the Institut de France in Paris; and Arnaud, "Monographie de Baye," 1918, ANM Fonds anciens 1D305; and see Chapter 4 for a discussion of some of his writings.

[69] On the palm gardens in Tessalit, see the relevant documents kept in the Archives du cercle de Kidal (ACK) in Kidal; on the longevity of social distinctions, see Clauzel (1962: 145).

on northern pastures. It further received donations from the inhabitants of the Touat, but also from contemporary Moroccan tribes and from Tlemcen in the Algerian northwest; in 1950, its leading *shaykh*, born in Tahoua in contemporary Niger, was on tour in West Africa collecting donations.[70] In southern Morocco, the *zāwiya* of Tamgrout described by Abdullah Hammoudi (1980) and David Gutelius (2002) owned 10 per cent of all irrigated land in the Dra'a valley, as well as 35,000 palm trees throughout the area; meanwhile, the *zāwiya* of Ilīgh mentioned earlier invested heavily in irrigation in its immediate vicinity and beyond (Pascon 1980). More generally, *zawāyā* seem to have been conceived of as agricultural and pastoral investments with regional links as well as spiritual centres: when the *qāḍi* of Timmi in the Touat appointed a new *shaykh* for the *zāwiya* of nearby Fenoughil, he explicitly "entrusted its command with its earnings and expenses (*jalaban wa daf'an*)," and the appointment was not only endorsed by the "leading personalities" but also by "the owners of the funds" (*wulāh al-umūr w-arbāb al-ṣurūr*).[71]

Lastly, land, water, and palm trees were often more or less directly controlled by regional, or transregional merchants. Hence, the Bani Mzab, the region's most successful traders, systematically invested their profits in palm gardens and water-rights throughout the south: in the 1860s, people from Melika alone owned 4,500 palm trees in Metlili and Ouargla, posing endless problems of taxation to the incoming French administration.[72] They also invested in the greater Touat (Chaintron 1957) and in the Ahaggar: in 1962, Capot-Rey and Damade noted the large share of water-rights in the Touat owned by traders or retired soldiers who were originally from Metlili or the Mzab, 800 km further north, and who had invested their earnings in water shares, thereby considerably raising their market value. In some oases, they "were heading the field" in water ownership (1962: 106). Meanwhile, in the Ahaggar, French colonial officers worried that the "Tuareg patrimony" in its entirety was about to fall into the hands of Mzabi merchants.[73] As seen earlier, both the Zuwā and the Kunta were

[70] Albert, "La zaouia de Kerzaz," CAOM 22H70; and "Commissariat de la politique en AOF, Affaires politiques musulmanes, Rapport trimestriel, 1er trimestre 1950," CAOM 28H1.

[71] SQ: 23. This echoes the French archival record: "The *zawāyā* are private enterprises that own endowments and whose only aim is to relieve the poor and to host distinguished guests" ("Rapport annuel, cercle du Touat," 1939, CAOM 23H91). They hence appear structurally similar to *qṣūr* more generally: see Chapter 5.

[72] "Lettre du général commandant la division d'Alger, au sous-gouverneur de l'Algérie," 21/01/1862, CAOM 22H13.

[73] "Monographie du Territoire militaire des oasis sahariennes," 1951/1952, CAOM 10H86.

religious scholars, but also successful regional traders and entrepreneurs. Formerly nomadic Sha'anba, who had long been employed by the Bani Mzab as transporters, caravaneers and agents, bought land, water, and palm gardens locally, or in the Touat and Gourara near their summer pastures and markets.[74] As, with commitment to the French cause, the Sha'anba grew rich and were among the first to invest in trans-Saharan truck trade, this trend continued. In the 1950s, the perhaps most successful Sha'anbī merchant was described as follows:

> Whatever the exact amount of his fortune, we can say that al-Ḥājj Aḥmad is one of the richest men in the Sahara: he owns a villa, several rented houses, stores, gardens, water-rights, cars, trucks and coaches. I do not think that he owns any stocks or shares or that he keeps gold or banknotes in his safe; however, he often buys some real estate: houses, gardens, palm-trees with which he will later on endow one of his children.[75]

Traders also invested in local agriculture in more roundabout ways: they are often cited, both in oral memories and in the French colonial sources, as the ultimate owners of debts. Hence, in 1893, a Zuwī resident in the Gourara suggested to the French military command that, rather than attempting to conquer the Sahara oases by force, they buy up the debts that his fellow Zuwā, acting as commercial agents and presumably local moneylenders throughout the region, had with Mzabi merchants. In this way, the French could easily become the legal owners of all the land they might wish to take by conquest. Although the French colonial command was tempted, they thought that such an approach was "too expensive," but the underlying message of economic interdependence is clear.[76] In 1889, the French intercepted a caravan of slaves, owned and guided by Zuwā, who were taking the slaves to the Mzab as a repayment of goods that had been advanced to them on credit.[77] In 1897, a Zuwī from Foggarat ez-Zoua in the Tidikelt complained to his brother Aḥmad in Ouargla, who was acting on behalf of Mzabi merchants, about difficulties encountered when collecting money from his debtors, all local people; in 1903, the French arrested a Sha'anbī caravaneer who was carrying

74 Ibid.; and Campens, "Les Chaamba du Gourara," dissertation submitted to the CHEAM in 1962. See also J. Bisson (2003: 210).

75 A. Reynaud, "Les commerçants transsahariens," Mémoire du CHEAM, n° 3018 (1957), CAOM 20X6. For further discussion of al-Ḥājj Aḥmad and his family, see Chapter 2.

76 "Lettre du général Marmet commandant la subdivision de Médéa au général commandant la division d'Alger," 25/06/1893, CAOM 22H38.

77 "Lettre du général Poizat commandant la division d'Alger au Gouverneur Général de l'Algérie," 13/09/1889, CAOM 12H50.

money sent by the *qā'id* (Moroccan-appointed headman) of Timimoun in the Gourara to pay his debts to a Mzabi settled in El Goléa, half-way between the Mzab and the Gourara.[78] Although "Mzabi merchants" at times seems to be used, alongside "Jewish banker," as a shorthand for all powerful investors and moneylenders in the region, there is no doubt that Mzabis indeed handled considerable funds, not least because they had access, through Jewish intermediaries based in Tripoli or Mogador, to credit facilities with European banking houses.[79] Yet even though at least some of the money spent and lent in the Sahara oases can thus ultimately be traced to sources from beyond the Sahara, moneylenders as remembered in oral history are always Zuwī or Sha'anbī, and personal trade relations and direct investments on the ground remained firmly anchored in regional logics.

WHEAT AND DATES: REGIONAL PATTERNS OF EXCHANGE

A similar pattern emerges from a closer analysis of trade on the ground. Although financial networks were extensive and often reached beyond the Sahara, the majority of goods traded were destined for regional exchange between complementary producers: cereals against dates, mediated at times by pastoral produce such as dried meat, wool, leather, cheese, and salt. Such exchange involved few outside professionals, and mostly took place within one "region" of habitual pastoral migration or frequent exchange that could be covered in one journey and while remaining under the same political protection. These regions could stretch to up to 1,000 kilometres, but they only ever connected one major settlement area with another: predesert northwestern Algeria with the Gourara, for instance, or the Ahaggar with the Tidikelt. The majority of trade goods only moved

[78] "Lieutenant Mathieu, chef d'annexe d'El Goléa au Commandant supérieur du cercle de Ghardaïa," 22/09/1903, CAOM 22H62; and "Lettre du général Collet Meygret commandant la division d'Alger au Gouverneur Général de l'Algérie," 16/06/1897, CAOM 22H55.

[79] Some of these intermediaries in turn owned shares in Manchester cotton mills. See "Le Ministre de la Guerre au Gouverneur Général de l'Algérie," 28/04/1851, CAOM 22H13; and "Rapport annuel, annexe du Tidikelt," 1911, CAOM 23H102: "Muslim caravaneers have in Tripoli associates who are often close relatives, and who are in charge of selling and buying. These transactions are negotiated with people from Tripolitania, generally Jews, who import English cotton made in Manchester on their order by factories in which they often hold shares: this is the case with the houses Grebib, Nahun, Hafsan for example. One member of each of these families lives in England." See also Amat (1888) and Holsinger (1979, 1980). On commerce and credit arrangements via the Moroccan port of Essaouira (Mogador), see Schroeter (1988).

within these regions. Take, for instance, In Salah, the main market of the Tidikelt: in 1906, the French administration registered the arrival of a total of 3,000 pack-camels. Just under two-thirds came from the Ahaggar carrying thirty quintal of butter, three quintal of dried cheese, eleven of dried meat, seventy of cereals; 154 *mahāra* (riding camels), 74 donkeys, 7,456 sheep; 23 camel saddles, and 130 pieces of Sudanese cloth: all local produce, apart from the last two items, which probably came from the Aïr in what is today northern Niger. In exchange, they took away 3,000 loads of dates, and certainly some unrecorded trade goods or money to make up the sums. A thousand camels from Ouargla to the northeast brought cloths and manufactured goods; sixty camels from Ghadamès, in contemporary Libya, carried tea and cotton cloths, imported probably via Tripoli. Compared to this, direct trans-Saharan ventures were negligible: only one caravan, composed of sixty camels, travelled further south than the Ahaggar, to Timbuktu and the Aïr in what is today northern Mali and Niger, respectively.[80]

Hence, in terms of bulk at least, the majority of goods traded in In Salah in this year were produced regionally, and destined for local consumption or resale. More importantly, all camels were from neighbouring areas, inasmuch as there were no major settlements between them and the Tidikelt, and as they were situated within the same area of habitual pastoral migration. The Ahaggar, long bound to the Tidikelt through pastoral exchange, migration and numerous social ties, were responsible for the largest share of trade. And 1906 was by no means exceptional: from 1909 to 1929, regionally produced goods on average accounted for at least 30 per cent of the value of all the goods traded in In Salah, a proportion that at times could rise as high as 70 per cent.[81] Transport on camel-back remained in the hands of regional pastoralists and caravaneers throughout, with the major share – between 60 and 90 per cent – falling to the Ahaggar.[82] There is no doubt that this emphasis on regional trade was caused partly by the interruption of trans-Saharan exchange by the French colonial conquest and by the diversion of West African trade goods to the coast. Yet regional supplies were always necessary to ensure the survival of oases, whatever additional economic activity they might pursue – and the overall value of trans-Saharan trade through Tripoli,

[80] "Rapport annuel, annexe du Tidikelt," 1906, CAOM 23H102.

[81] "Rapports annuels, annexe du Tidikelt," 1906–29, CAOM 23H102.

[82] This was although the Ahaggar developed from the 1900s onwards a flourishing salt against millet trade with Bilma. See Keenan (1977) and the annual reports on trade on Tamanrasset and Bilma, CAOM 23H102 and 28H1.

even in its heydays in the late nineteenth century, was but three times the deficit registered for In Salah two decades later.[83] Moreover, some reasons for the preponderance of regional trade were clearly social: even local investment in trucks from the 1930s onwards long followed regional patterns (see Clauzel 1960, and Chapter 2). Grain imports from north-western Algeria to the Tidikelt, carried by pastoral nomads, remained stable until the late 1930s, long after most trans-Saharan transport had been taken over by trucks, thereby suggesting that trade relied on pastoral mobility and logics of regional solidarities and mutual obligations as much as on abstract calculations of profit.

And indeed, regional trade was central to pastoral economies. A yearly budget established in 1887 for a nomadic family from the federation of the Arbāʿ on the northern edge of the Algerian Sahara – who, incidentally, had invested in a garden, house, and storage space in the *qṣar* of Aïn Madhi – shows that about a third of the family's annual income derived directly or indirectly from trade. The family spent the late summer near Tiaret in the Tell, where they exchanged dates, butter, cheese, meat, blankets and sometimes their own labour force against grains and imported manufactured goods, sugar, and tea. They then returned to Aïn Madhi, harvested their fields, and travelled on to the south, to exchange cereals, imported goods and their own pastoral produce against dates. In the meantime, they placed their surplus of wool with the inhabitants of Aïn Madhi and neighbouring *qṣūr* to be spun and woven into blankets or clothes (Geoffroy 1887, see also Bonète 1962). The Arbāʿ were but one federation among many: further West, the various tribal groups related in one way or another to the Awlād Sīdi Shaykh functioned in similar ways; in the centre and east, the Awlād Nāʾil, Sīdi ʿAṭba, and Shaʿanba did the same; while to the south, the Taïtoq and Ahaggar followed a reverse pattern of migration and exchange.[84] Elderly Tuareg from the area of Kidal and Tessalit in northern Mali still remember the departure of frequent caravans loaded with cheese, butter, skins, and dried meat towards the Touat, where they had regular correspondents and where some of their children were sent to acquire a basic education in the regional *zawāyā*;

[83] According to figures taken from Baier (1980: 237, 246). Paul Lovejoy (1984), comparing estimates for regional salt trade and trans-Saharan trade in pre-colonial Niger, came up with similar proportions.

[84] For an overview of pastoral migrations and French attempts to regulate them, see the vast amount of paperwork kept in CAOM 24H117. For a more general discussion, see Carette and Warner (1846), Bernard and Lacroix (1906), Capot-Rey (1942), and Boukhobza (1982); for individual case studies, see Cauneille (1968), Keenan (1977), and Romey (1983).

indeed, these journeys were seen as an indispensable passage to manhood, and various types of commercial associations were known to allow young men without means to take part in them. Marital alliances within these regions of vital exchange were frequent, and early labour migration to Algeria followed similar patterns and often relied on longstanding social ties.[85]

These regions further overlapped with areas of political and spiritual influence, and the ability to extend protection and guarantee transactions. Hence, as previously seen, the Kunta *zāwiya* of Akabli on the edge of the Tidikelt was able to organise caravans to Timbuktu, twenty days' travelling to the southwest because of their privileged relations with and spiritual allegiance from Arabic-speaking tribes from the Azawād that allowed them to extend their protection to all traders travelling as far as Timbuktu or Gao, but not further.[86] Zuwā and Ahl 'Azzī excelled as traders and caravaneers because they had long acted as teachers and scribes throughout the Ahaggar, had married locally and invested in real estate throughout the region and could therefore travel freely in the area.[87] Conversely, "legitimate" raiding was restricted to places and people beyond the limits of one such area of frequent interchange, beyond which not only neighbourly feeling but also religious descent and prestige lost much of their sway. In the early 1900s, a *ghazū* (raiding party) from the area of Béchar in what is now Western Algeria had to spend sixty days on the road before they found people who were distant enough to be raided; once beyond their immediate neighbours, they had little qualms about plundering villages inhabited by scholars, although, thirty days earlier, they had showered their neighbouring *shurafā'* (descendants of the prophet) with presents.[88] But regional traders and pastoralists could also act as proxies to help recuperate stolen goods: when, in summer 1901, a large caravan owned by a Tripoli merchant was raided by

[85] Hence, Intallah, the current "customary chief" of Kidal, spent parts of his childhood studying the Qur'ān in the Touat (and speaks excellent classical and Algerian Arabic). On caravans from the Adagh to the Touat, see Mohammed Mahmoud, "Rapport de tournée," 25/01/1963, ACK. On early labour migration, see "Lieutenant Butaye au capitaine commandant le CMTH, Oued Tahara," 17/12/1953; "P. Chalmont au commandant du cercle of Gao," 11/12/1958; and the "Déclaration" by Ekawel ag Ewana, 13/07/1961, all kept in the ACK.

[86] Chardenet, "Akabli," n.d. (early 1900s), CAOM 22H50.

[87] Simon, "Notices sur les districts du Tidikelt," 21/05/1900, CAOM 22H50; see also Dinaux, "Rapport de tournée" and Voinot, "Reconnaissance."

[88] Albert, "Une razzia au Sahel (novembre 1902 à février 1903)," CAOM 22H70. For different categories of raids among Tamasheq-speakers in Niger, see Claudot-Hawad (1996).

Tuareg from the Ahaggar near Ghat, negotiations were opened by people from Ghadamès, relying on their close ties to Ghat and on local religious scholars. By October of the same year, a part of the raided goods and three thousand camels had been returned via Ghat, while negotiations continued.[89]

REGIONAL EXCHANGE AND TRANS-SAHARAN GOODS AND TRADERS

If it is relatively easy to identify regional bulk trade, it is difficult to single out trans-Saharan ventures. Apart from a few exceptions, such as ostrich feathers, many goods could have been destined for either, and, as they changed hands frequently on the way, we can only guess at initial intentions and destinations. On the one hand, the fact that certain goods eventually crossed the Sahara does not necessarily indicate the presence of trans-Saharan traders. Lists of goods traded regionally almost always included some transregional items. In 1900, the Ahaggar exported carpets and woollen cloth from the Gourara (produced with wool obtained from the northern nomads), and sold, alongside pastoral produce, leather-ware from the Aïr, lances from Zinder in contemporary Niger, and cloths from Mali and Niger. Although such transregional goods only amounted to a small fraction of their loads, they allowed for profits of up to 150 per cent.[90] The Arbāʿ carried cereals and dates, but also found room for "perfume, knick-knacks, jewellery, coffee, tobacco, cloths, ostrich feathers, incense and musk" (Geoffroy 1887). Pastoralists from northwestern Algeria peddled transregional goods to outlying *qṣūr*, and played an important role in the slave trade, as part of their seasonal migrations; the same was true for Shaʿanba and Zuwā further east.[91] Slaves intercepted by the French recount having travelled on tortuous ways and in small groups, passing from the hands of one regional trader or pastoralist to the other.[92] Hence, all of fourteen slave children and teenagers whose caravan was caught in

[89] "Lettre de M. Pichon, résident général de France à Tunis, à M. Delcassé, Ministre des Affaires étrangers," 30/12/1901, CAOM 22H45.

[90] "Note sur le mouvement commercial qui s'est produit entre In Salah et le pays Touareg pendant l'été et l'automne 1900," CAOM 22H50.

[91] "Lettre du Préfet du département d'Alger au Gouverneur Général de l'Algérie," 5/10/1906, CAOM 12H50; "Lettre du général Poizat commandant la Division d'Alger au Gouverneur Général de l'Algérie," 13/09/1889, CAOM 12H50; and "Lettre du général Swiney commandant la division d'Alger au Gouverneur Général de l'Algérie," 13/07/1892, CAOM 22H13.

[92] "Rapport au sujet des nègres et négresses qui ont fait l'objet des transactions au Mzab et à Ouargla, par le commandant supérieur de Ghardaïa," 30/11/1905, CAOM 12H50.

1880 on its way from Figuig in southern Morocco to Bou Semghoum in western Algeria had been captured by Arabic-speaking tribes from the Azawād in northern Mali, and had then been conveyed to the greater Touat where they were sold to Figuig merchants, who in turn sold them on to their current owners once they had reached Figuig.[93]

Conversely, the presence of trans-Saharan traders – or traders from beyond neighbouring oases or pastoral regions – does not necessarily indicate that they were primarily concerned with trans-Saharan goods, as emerges very clearly from Ghadamsī commercial correspondence kept in Timbuktu.[94] The bulk of the letters conserved in Timbuktu date from the nineteenth and early twentieth century. Traders from the Libyan city of Ghadamès had long counted among the wealthiest long distance traders resident in Timbuktu.[95] Despite their reputation as trans-Saharan merchants, and wide-ranging trade and credit networks, their letters are only marginally concerned with trans-Saharan or imported goods, mainly various kinds of cloth. References to these goods are generally interspersed with accounts of regional commerce, and one letter might concern salt as well as incense and *kuḥl* (black colouring used primarily as makeup). Indeed, such goods were often produced locally and sold regionally, and only became trans-Saharan if the prices they fetched in the Touat were too low. Ghadamsī traders frequently instructed their Timbuktu agents to dabble in the regional trade in agricultural staples, if economic circumstances were favourable. Not surprisingly, then, most letters were sent from the Touat or at most Ghadamès, with frequent reference made to regional markets such as Djenné just south of Timbuktu, Arawān to the north of it, and the salt mines in Tawdanni, and to regional pastoralists providing transport, such as the Kunta, Barābīsh and Tajakānat. Where the Ghadamsī traders engaged in transregional trade, that is to say trade beyond one of the economic regions defined on the preceding section, they mostly relied on existing regional caravans for transportation, and acted through agents resident in the Touat.

Due to this close involvement in regional exchange and production, even those trans-Saharan traders who travelled across the Sahara rarely

[93] "Lettre du général commandant la division d'Oran, au Gouverneur Général de l'Algérie," 29/03/1880, CAOM 12H50.

[94] The letters consulted are kept in the Centre de documentation et de recherches Ahmed Baba (CEDRAB) in Timbuktu; see especially MSS 2708–36, 2757–77, and 6092–4.

[95] Hence, when the Moroccan army conquered Timbuktu in 1591, officers were lodged in the Ghadamsī quarter of town, the only one that corresponded to their standards of comfort and "civilisation."

crossed it in a straight line. Rather, they tended to move from one pastoral region to the next in a rather erratic way, exchanging their goods on the way and paying more attention to regional economic logics and circumstances than trans-Saharan designs, in a fashion reminiscent of Braudel's (1966 [1946]) *cabotage*. Hence, the Awlād Zinān from the Tidikelt, who according to French sources, "for a long time ... maintained in the Sahara the reputation of adventurous merchants":

> Their caravans travelled to the Adagh carrying woollen clothes and cotton cloth that they exchanged for gold dust and ostrich hides. They then carried on to Timbuktu with loads of salt taken on at Tawdanni. In Timbuktu they bought the shiny cotton cloth that is so sought after by the natives of the Tidikelt, returned via Ghat and Ghadamès where they exchanged the gold and the ostrich feathers from the Adagh for cotton cloth from Tripoli, for tea and sugar ... Then they returned to the Tidikelt where they sold their new trade goods.[96]

Haarmann (1998: 28) notes that for similar reasons of infrastructure and regional ecology, goods from Bornu bound for Timbuktu often transited via Ghadamès and the Touat, thereby crossing the Sahara twice. Similarly, in the late nineteenth century, all trade from El Oued necessarily passed through Ghadamès; the supply of transregional goods such as slaves was fuelled by regional needs in basic staples and complicated debt relations with merchants in Ghadamès and Tripoli, mediated via local Suwafa traders, peddlers, and pastoralists.[97]

This interdependence of regional and transregional trade was furthered by practical constraints. On the one hand, professional traders only rarely owned pack animals (Austen 1990, see also McDougall 2005). Successful camel breeding requires full-time pastoral nomadism: as a general rule, good pastures were at a certain distance from oases settlements and trading hubs. The Tidikelt, the "greenest" of the three regions that constitute the greater Touat, had barely enough pasture to feed one thousand camels, not even a third of what was needed to supply it in necessary staples; and this number quite simply could not be increased, despite efforts made by the French administration to do so.[98] This also the large value – 244 *dūru* or 1,220 francs, more than that

[96] Chardenet, "Aoulef," n.d. (presumably 1900s), CAOM 22H50.

[97] "Lettre du lieutenant colonel Pont commandant supérieur du cercle de Biskra au général commandant la subdivision de Batna," 30/05/1891, CAOM 10H30.

[98] "Pastures are too distant and too poor. It is possible to keep grown camels, to artificially feed sheep destined for slaughter, but husbandry will never succeed unless people revert to pastoral migration or keep their animals with the Touareg": "Rapport annuel, annexe du Tidikelt," 1906 (a similar observation was made again in 1911), CAOM 23H102.

of an average house – given to "three quarters of a female donkey" in the inheritance record cited previously. Moreover, the donkey mentioned here is exceptional: oases inheritance documents rarely make reference to livestock, and quantities of livestock listed by Martin (1908: 223–5) for the southern oases are remarkably small. As a result, traders from the Tidikelt generally stayed put and entrusted their goods to Ahaggar caravaneers for transport south because the latter could, within their own pastoral region, assure not just the haulage but also the protection of their goods.[99] Similarly, the Bani Mzab preferred to invest their profits in water and real estate, and relied for transport on their pastoral neighbours, in particular Sha'anba and Zuwā.[100] The Sha'anba especially were excellent caravaneers, as potential raiders were more often than not their own cousins or at least in-laws.[101]

On the other hand, even if traders had owned camels, these would have been of limited use for trans-Saharan trade. Due to variations in pasture and the nature of the terrain, camels were bred as regional specialists, and southern camels would rarely venture further north than the Touat, nor would owners of northern camels like to see their animals attempt to reach the stony Ahaggar. Initial French attempts to supply Saharan garrisons in one uninterrupted journey proved to be a logistic disaster. In 1900, for a supply caravan to the Touat, 3,200 camels and 1,062 camel conductors had been requisitioned in Aflou near the Mediterranean coast, but one thousand more had become necessary by the time the caravan had reached the half-way point at Aïn Séfra, as almost half of the camels had died on the way – or refused to continue, as "numerous dead camels form the preceding convoys were lying on the road ... smelling very bad." Things only improved as the French army command decided to delegate transport to pastoral nomads, or to imitate preexisting regional patterns of exchange.[102] Therefore, even in cases where trans-Saharan

99 Simon, "Notices sur les districts du Tidikelt," 21/05/1900, CAOM 22H50.

100 Margueritte, "Rapport sur l'organisation à donner aux sept ksour de la confédération du Mzab," 14/02/1865, CAOM 22H13.

101 Didier, "Projet d'organisation du Gourara et du Touat," 5/05/1896, CAOM 22H56; "Renseignements sur la région d'Idelès," 1893, CAOM 22H38; "Rapport du chef de bataillon Meynier, commandant les oasis, au Gouverneur Général de l'Algérie," 28/05/1914, CAOM 28H2; and Cauneille (1968). On raiding, see "Lieutenant Mathieu, chef d'annexe d'El Goléa au commandant supérieur du cercle de Ghardaïa," 22/09/1903, CAOM 22H62; and "Le général commandant la division d'Alger au Gouverneur Général de l'Algérie," 4/08/1860, CAOM 22H13.

102 Barthel, "In Salah et l'archipel touatien," 15/04/1902, CAOM 10H22; and "Rapport du Lieutenant Chourreu, chef du 6e convoi de ravitaillement d'Igli, sur les conditions dans

merchants ordered trans-Saharan goods, direct trans-Saharan shipping remained impossible until the introduction of trucks in the 1930s, and trans-Saharan necessarily had to collaborate with regional intermediaries. This regional underpinning of trans-Saharan trade on all levels goes some way towards explaining its great flexibility, with regards to both the routes chosen and the quantities transported: regional trade by necessity survived the collapse of larger patterns of exchange, and these various regional economic systems could easily be strung together in a new way if the opportunity arose. This might explain the various suggestions made by influential local traders to the French army command, proposing to set up new routes and totally redirect trade, if only enough capital was forthcoming[103]; and the fact that trans-Saharan trade never was quite where the French army commanders expected it to be, but rather, like the hedgehog in the fable, had always already moved one step ahead.

CONCLUSION

In the greater Touat, oasis economies cannot be understood if they are treated apart from regional logics of exchange and investment, be they economic, social, political, or spiritual. Local archives show that, throughout the greater Touat, property was rarely localised, and bound traders, farmers, scholars, *shaykh*s, and nomadic pastoralists into ties of mutual obligations, hence spreading risk among ecologically diverse and geographically dispersed sources of income, which could absorb exceptionally high gains through redistribution, as well as mitigating moments of crisis. Consequently, oasis economies were pervaded by monetary and debt relations, even in the absence or lack of available cash. Although some of these debt relations ultimately can be traced to places well beyond the Sahara, they were generally mediated by regional traders, for whom trade was but a subsidiary activity to investment in land or husbandry. These were the same traders who, often doubling up as nomadic pastoralists, provided most basic staples to oases, thereby maintaining regional patterns of exchange and vital interdependence. These regions

lesquelles le convoi a été effectué," 29/12/1900, CAOM 22H33. The impact of such camel hecatombs on the local economy was without doubt devastating.

103 See, for example, the suggestion by al-Hadj Aoumallâh from Ghat, proposing to re-route "the Sudan trade" via El Oued on what was then French territory, if only the French could supply him with an initial capital of 300,000 francs: "Lettre du général Fontebride commandant la subdivision de Batna au général commandant la division de Constantine," 19/04/1895, CAOM 10H31.

way, these narratives echo parts of the argument made in the preceding chapter: irrigation (and people) are a blessing brought in from the outside; local settlement is hence never autonomous, but by definition part of a larger moral system. But these legends also reflect aspects of historic reality. As seen in Chapter 1, and as will further be illustrated in this chapter through an analysis of the fortunes of four Algerian trading families, living potential saints and religious families and federations have long played an active part in the establishment of settlement in the Central Sahara, to the point where the successful making of place is often read as a central attribute of sainthood: gardens are visible manifestations and hence post facto proofs of *baraka* and therefore of saintly origins. It is perhaps not surprising, then, that even today, successful local trading families of religious descent use the image of the settling saint to pattern their own family history and hence to legitimise both past endeavours and their current social position. There thereby provide an insiders' view of the patterns described in Chapter 1: family history tends to begin with regional trade in staples, aimed at investment in livestock and real estate, in other words, at the making of place. Trans-Saharan trade only became relevant when circumstances were exceptionally favourable. In the four cases presented here, this was mostly due to the economic, political, and technical changes caused first by the colonial conquest and then by the gradual incorporation of the Algerian and Malian Sahara into a volatile international economy. The Second World War black market thus laid the foundation of contemporary fortunes, reinvested either in regional economies or in contemporary smuggling. Similarly, the diverging economic policies of independent Algeria and Mali were eagerly seized, primarily by those who were already well established in regional trade.

Yet, seen from the inside out, traders tend to stress continuity over change, while emphasising the fickleness of wealth acquired in trans-Saharan trade, as opposed to agriculture and regional exchange. If successful traders are today described in terms otherwise reserved to sainthood, their "civilising mission" also exposed them to many risks. After all, the *bilād al-sūdān*, the stereotypical "land of the blacks," is, from the southern Algerian perspective, home to all kinds of transgressions, and, perhaps, more importantly, clearly beyond the control of regional kin networks. Moreover, traders could only succeed if they established close ties with their host societies. Women and marital alliances were crucial for this, but too close a commitment to the host society could easily result in a lack of containment – physical, financial, and moral – and stories of husbands and sons "lost" or "bewitched" on their travels are legion. Trans-Saharan trade hence tends to be opposed, in contemporary accounts at least, to much less prestigious, but also much less dangerous regional commerce, arguing for a long-term normative emphasis on regional rather than transregional connections – an emphasis that, as seen in the preceding chapter, was clearly reflected in patterns of investment and alliance.

AL-MAKKĪ AL-MARKĀNTĪ, OR HOW TO LIVE UP TO A LEGEND

The first historic trans-Saharan trader of some renown that I came across in the Touat was al-Makkī b. al-Jilālī, nicknamed "al-Markāntī," a descendant of the Awlād Sīdi Shaykh (see Chapter 1) long settled in the Touat.[4] Al-Markāntī's story was first told me by his grandnephew and namesake, Mekki Kalloum. Mekki runs several businesses, one of which is the largest and best-equipped *ḥammām* in Adrar, situated in his own villa near the city centre, of luxurious Ottoman style, and in constant expansion. The house is bustling with activity, with sons and nephews, all employed in one of Mekki's various businesses, rushing in and out accompanied by a profusion of in-laws and grandchildren. Mekki has a degree in sociology; while I was there, he was interviewed on national television about the long-term effects of French nuclear experiments in nearby Reggane; he is as fluent in French as in Arabic, or perhaps a little more so. He owes much of his current wealth and influence to the fact that he had been involved with the ALN (*Armée de Libération Nationale*, the Algerian nationalist fighters) during the war of independence, when he established contacts with the great and mighty; after independence, he was instrumental in setting up the Algerian police in the area, before he decided to move back into business. Although most of his activities are by now centred on Adrar, there was a time when he, just like his illustrious uncle before him, had dabbled in trans-Saharan trade, buying secondhand cars and spare parts and tires in France, driving them across the Sahara, and selling them in Mali, Niger, or Burkina Faso. In the 1980s especially, this was a highly profitable way of obtaining convertible currency.[5] This changed with the devaluation of the franc CFA, the currency common to most French-speaking West African countries, in the mid-1990s and the growing insecurity in Mali and Niger,

[4] "Al-Markāntī," a term derived from Italian, is Algerian Arabic for "wealthy trader" or "coloniser."

[5] Conversion of the Algerian Dinar into international currency used to be heavily restricted, while the franc CFA used throughout most of French-speaking West Africa was linked to the French franc in a fixed exchange rate.

and Mekki had to give up on this lucrative sideline.[6] He still owns land in Gao in northern Mali, however, and says that he would certainly return there if circumstances were once more favourable. After his departure, his son spent several years in the Malian capital Bamako staying with friends and "doing business." He has recently come back, bringing with him several Malian "friends" who are now working in subordinate positions in the *ḥammām*. More generally, the Kalloum family is known throughout Adrar for its wealth, high level of education, and commercial success; like Mekki, they have been successful in converting their ancestral prestige into contemporary education and political influence, without neglecting family connections with the Awlād Sīdi Shaykh.

According to Mekki, his granduncle al-Markāntī was born in Abiodh Sidi Cheikh in the second half of the nineteenth century. With the French conquest, some members of his family decided to settle on a more permanent basis in Timimoun, where they had long had their summer pastures and owned some gardens, and where many Zuwā had settled before them. Once established there, al-Markāntī's brother Aḥmad was the first to venture into trans-Saharan trade. He went to the Adagh in what is today northern Mali, taking all the family fortune with him. Despite his initial success, he was held up and robbed of all his goods on the way to Bamako. He managed to take refuge in the city and sent letters to his family back home imploring for help. His brother al-Makkī was chosen to set out on his rescue, but had no money to finance his journey. He thus took the weighty decision to collect all the family gold, including his mother's and sisters' jewellery, and travelled up to Oran on the Mediterranean coast to negotiate with a Jewish moneylender. He received 3,000 francs, converted them into goods, and set out for Bamako where he rescued his brother. The two of them then went up to northern Mali together and set up shop in Kidal, with so much success that al-Makkī decided to stay, while Aḥmad returned to Algeria. In Kidal, al-Makkī built the first proper house in mud bricks and introduced tea to the whole of the Sudan.[7] He

[6] The value of the franc CFA, linked to the French franc and then the Euro, was reduced by 50 per cent on January 11, 1994. Even today, this is often seen as the official end of any hope for sustained prosperity in West Africa, as it stands as a symbol for the structural adjustment that generally followed it. For more background, see Conte (1994), Mbok (1994), and Dupraz (1994).

[7] The introduction of tea to the Sudan is a "civilisational achievement" claimed by North African traders throughout the Sahara: see for instance Lydon (2009a: 24). In al-Markāntī's case, although tea was indeed introduced by North African traders to northern Mali, this probably happened earlier, in the last decade of the nineteenth century (see the numerous manuscript *qaṣā'id* about tea conserved in the CEDRAB; for comparable information on the Moroccan Sahara, see Leriche 1953).

grew immensely rich, invested in land and livestock in the area, and set up the first gardens of Kidal, thus, at least in oral memory, truly behaving as a *sharīf* (descendant of the prophet) should.[8] He brought various members of his extended family over to Kidal to help him. After his death, however, the nephew who had been left in charge of the family business in Kidal squandered it all, succumbing to the temptations of Sudanese life. Both the family fortune and their house crumbled, bearing silent witness to the fickleness of earthly wealth and of young relatives weakened by too familiar an acquaintance with the *bilād al-sūdān*.

This legendary account of al-Markāntī's fortunes sets the pattern for local trading family histories more generally: all speak of independent enterprise, initial failure, exposure to great risks, a period of incredible success, the construction of houses and various civilising endeavours. But they are also all said to have failed in the next generation, usually due to the corrupting influence of the Sudan. In this case, however, the story is somewhat nuanced by the family archives, a motley collection of letters, bills, receipts, and petitions, both in French and in Arabic.[9] These documents show the importance of regional trade and investment in agriculture as well as the family's involvement in dense networks of local and transregional credit. Trans-Saharan trade appears rather as a supplementary business that only became possible when the French colonial government improved transport infrastructure in the early 1940s, while profits continued to be invested locally, in livestock, houses and gardens.[10] According to these documents, al-Makkī moved to Timimoun in 1906, after the arrival of the French army for whom he probably hoped to act as a supplier. He bought a house in the *fīllaj* (village), that is, the French-constructed part of the city, worth the stately sum of 850 francs. He nonetheless retained his main residence in Abiodh Sidi Cheikh, where a payment was made to him a year later. First traces of trans-Saharan activities only appear in the 1940s: a telegram sent by "Ben Djilali" in Kidal to Khada b. Mekki in Timimoun, promising a rapid shipping of goods; and again in 1947, a

[8] Historically speaking, this is rather unlikely: the gardens that can still be seen in Kidal were probably set up earlier, in the late nineteenth century, and by traders from the Tidikelt, as most people who worked them initially were *ḥarāṭīn* from In Salah and neighbouring *qṣūr* (Clauzel 1962).

[9] These family archives are kept by Mekki Kalloum in his house in Adrar; I am very grateful to him and his family for granting me access to them.

[10] In the improvement of trans-Saharan roads under the Vichy government, see Guitart (1989) and the numerous reports kept in the Malian National Archives (ANM) in Bamako, Fonds Recents 1Q217, "Relations commerciales avce l'Afrique du nord," and 1Q128, "Relations commerciales avec l'Algérie, 1940–1942."

dispatch note for a bag of 104 kilograms of goods, sent with the French transport company CGTS. Throughout his life, al-Makkī's main focus of investment remained Abiodh Sidi Cheikh, and he seems to have trusted in husbandry rather than trade. In 1960, his son Muḥammad gave full power of attorney to his elder brother Larbi, for several hundred sheep and camels kept near Abiodh Sidi Cheikh under the care of a salaried shepherd; that herd seems to be the bulk of al-Makkī's legacy. At that time, both of al-Makkī's sons had their main residence near Abiodh Sidi Cheikh.

Meanwhile, a third brother, 'Ūmar, ran the house and business in Timimoun. He had some limited interaction with the French administration: in 1927, he received a "gratification" for the good behaviour of a *spahi* (soldier in the French colonial army), indicating that he might have acted as a middleman for the French army, the perhaps most important purveyor of ready cash at that time (see Chapter 1). Mostly, however, his involvement was in local and regional trade, in particular with nomadic pastoralists from the northwest and near the contemporary Moroccan border to whom he was linked through myriad debt relations. Notes of small amounts of money advanced to small traders and private debtors abound (an example is quoted in Chapter 1), but at times the sums advanced were more considerable. Hence, in 1932, he lent a thousand francs to a local trader for two months, to be refunded "at the arrival of the caravan," presumably the one that linked the Gourara to the grain-producing areas of northwestern Algeria. Inversely, 'Ūmar seems to have received at least some of his capital from further north: in 1925, he borrowed 13,000 francs from Oran, to be repaid in instalments. Other documents indicate his close relation with local *zawāyā* linked to the Awlād Sīdi Shaykh, especially with the *zāwiya* of Amsāhil, to which he granted regular gifts and loans that never seem to have been repaid, and to whom he paid an annual *zakāt* of 30 kilograms of wheat. This indicates that he also invested in local agriculture: in 1936, he received a petition to grant the usufruct of one of his landed properties in the Gourara to one Sa'īd b. 'Alī Laḥmaha, in exchange for his part of the harvest. In 1941, the harvest for one of his properties amounted to a just over a ton of wheat and 175 kilograms of barley, slightly more than a tenth of which he paid to his *khammās* (sharecropper). A receipt dated 1948 concerning 85 francs paid for the fertilisation of palm trees confirms that 'Ūmar also owned extensive palm gardens in the Touat and Gourara.

The image of the settling saint with a civilising mission in the Sudan hence needs to be nuanced. However, the close connection between the brothers' trading activities, agriculture, and the making of place is beyond doubt, although the place thus "made" in any durable way belongs to the more familiar areas that had long been situated within the family's summer pastures and sphere of influence: Abiodh Sidi Cheikh, Timimoun and later on also Adrar, where al-Markāntī's legacy remains tangible. In Adrar, the compound of the Kalloum family, situated right next to the city centre, is known to all, and is generally taken as the visible sign of the family's wealth and success. By now, it has grown into a village of its own, and although the family owns houses throughout the Algerian west, including Abiodh Sidi Cheikh, this is where they meet for all important family events and religious holidays. The "village" is still surrounded by venerable palm gardens, although all the Kalloum brothers occupy white-collar jobs in town; and connections with Abiodh Sidi Cheikh and Timimoun remain intense, as witnessed by the continuous flow of visitors and repeated marital alliances with people from both places, mostly drawn from the Awlād Sīdi Shaykh. Moreover, the conceptual relationship between al-Markāntī and the Sudan described in the legend is by no means a thing of the past. Mekki fondly recalls his years of trading with the Sudan: in Burkina Faso and Mali, he says, with a little money worth nothing at all in Algeria, you are a great lord; as a white man and as an Arab, people respect you; and with money and some magnanimity you can do anything. Yet he also saw himself as continuing a valued family tradition of trading and "civilising" West Africa, through the magic of trade and money, but also and especially through language and religion.

And indeed, in his accounts of his own trading ventures in the Sudan, he and his granduncle al-Markāntī become almost undistinguishable. Thus, the story of Mekki's first contact with Malian custom officials:

> It was the first time I had been down there, and I was sitting in the cab of one of my trucks, the driver had gone to see the border officials. Things were difficult, and the *patron* himself came out to have a look at the truck, being quite rude, but then he saw me and his manner changed: he was very polite, asked me to come down, come to his house, meet his family, have lunch – first I didn't understand what was going on, but then he asked me and whether I knew al-Markāntī? Of course I did, I said, he was my grandfather's brother – and we do look much the same everybody says. We had lunch that day in the official's house, proper hospitality, you know, and ever afterwards everything was easy, we worked together for everybody's benefit ... He was a Guindo, a Dogon, and al-Markāntī had stayed with his family and Arabicised them, and then they became very important in Gao, this is why they all venerate him until today.[11]

[11] The Guindo are today an influential family in Gao. The current head of the family still remembers an Algerian merchant called al-Markāntī who had stayed with his family

Mekki revels in the recounting of legends: this is perhaps one of them. Nonetheless, it indicates the structural pattern and lasting meaning that he discerns in his granduncle's life-story: more than just a trader, he was a *sharīf* and descendant of one of the most influential religious tribal federations in North Africa. This remains the most important aspect of his personality and the key to his life and to his relation with the "south," much as it indicates Mekki's own potential calling. In this sense, then, al-Markāntī is the stuff of legends, not of history; and, despite the relatively abundant, carefully dated and apparently "modern" documentation that he left behind, he hardly seems to belong to the banal twentieth century.

ḤAMMŪ ZAFZAF AND THE KEL TOUAT

If al-Markāntī is the stuff of legends, Ḥammū Zafzaf is a reality to everybody in Kidal, by now the main town of northeastern Mali, and a mere day's truck journey away from the Algerian border. Local opinion was unanimous that, if I wanted to know anything about the history of Algerian traders in Kidal, he was the person to talk to, as he was the most senior of all "Algerians" in town. But as I arrived in Kidal, Zafzaf had just left in order to supervise his son's wedding in Tit, his home *qṣar* near Aoulef in the Tidikelt (whose founding legend was recounted at the beginning of this chapter). Having waited in vain for several weeks, I decided to look him up in Tit itself. In any case, I had long been puzzled by the large number of traders, especially in Kidal, who said that they had come from Tit, and by the equally large number of Tuareg who had travelled and sojourned there, although, according to all accounts, it was tiny, remote, old-fashioned and had almost given up its permanent struggle against the invading sands. And indeed, Tit, several kilometres off the main road linking In Salah to Aoulef, seems to belong to another age. Most houses are constructed of mud bricks, people continue to work the gardens as long as water is available, and the presence of the Algerian state is limited to a tentative patch of tarmacked road and a primary

in the 1940s when he was a child. In his account, however, the "civilising mission" is reversed: "One day my father came home with an Algerian he had met in Gao, who did not know the country but wanted to trade. My father was rich and influential, and offered to help him, and he could speak Arabic so they could communicate: thus al-Markāntī – he was not yet called that – stayed with us for several months, and my father taught him all he needed, and helped him sell his goods and buy new ones. He then came back almost each year to give us presents and so on, but then he just disappeared, we don't know where to."

school, whose director, 'Abd Allāh b. 'Abd al-Karīm, kindly agreed to act as my host.[12] As I explained the purpose of my visit, 'Abd Allāh quickly warmed to my undertaking: of course he knew Zafzaf, probably better than anybody else, as it had been 'Abd Allāh's own uncle, the former head of the *qṣar*, who had financed Zafzaf's and his father's first trade-ventures to the Sudan.[13] 'Abd Allāh's uncle had been the richest man in the *qṣar* and its largest landowner. He had wanted to invest in trade with the Sudan, but rather than travelling himself, an arduous undertaking that would not have corresponded to his wealth and status, he hand-picked sons of the resident sharifian families in Tit – locally described as descendants of the Awlād Sīdi Shaykh, just like al-Markāntī – and sent them on his behalf to the Adagh, the area that was to become Kidal in northern Mali. Zafzaf had been one of the many, and had become the most influential of them all. Although 'Abd Allāh had never been to the Sudan himself, his wife Khadīja had been born there, to a Sha'anbī father and a Tamasheq mother, and her maternal uncles were frequent visitors to their house in Tit. Khadīja was more than happy to take me to Zafzaf's house that very evening, and off we went – followed, at a respectable distance, by 'Abd Allāh.

When in Tit, Zafzaf lives in a very large mud-brick compound house in the old *qṣar*, in the quarter of the *shurafā'*. After a short conversation with his wife and several other female relatives, I was ushered into his presence in a large reception room of the other side of the house, the ground covered in colourful but rather worn hand-woven carpets, without the customary television set or gilded prints from Mecca. Wealth made abroad had clearly not led to conspicuous consumption, but rather, it seemed, to increased austerity. Zafzaf is a rather small man, tanned by the sun, with a pointy white beard, his eyes sparkling with energy and intelligence; he seemed not even vaguely astonished when I told him that having looked for him in vain in Kidal, I had come to Tit (800 kilometres and an arduous Saharan crossing further north) to meet him. After having protested his bad memory and general ignorance, he embarked with great delight on his account of the history of Algerian trade in Kidal – in Arabic, although I am convinced that he was also fluent in French, Tamasheq, Songhay and various other languages necessary for trade in

[12] Many people from Tit, including a larger part of 'Abd Allāh's own family, have by now settled in Tamanrasset, and contacts were thus easy to establish.

[13] His uncle had been the elder of the *qṣar*, and it was 'Abd Allāh who showed me the various administrative documents produced by the assembly of Tit that I have drawn on in Chapter 1 and that are described in more detail in Chapter 5.

the area. 'Abd Allāh respectfully crouched in a corner, his earlier assertions of the preeminence of his own family having all but vanished, although he occasionally attempted to direct the conversation "scientifically" as befitted his role of a school-director.

Zafzaf went for the first time to Kidal to follow his father, who had long travelled there on a regular basis to sell all kinds of goods imported from the Tell, especially cloth, and to buy livestock in exchange. Zafzaf's father was very successful, and with the arrival of the French colonial army, he decided to set up a shop in Kidal, initially in a *paillote* (grass hut), although he was soon forced by the French administration to construct in mud bricks.[14] He thus built one of the first houses in Kidal, alongside other traders from the Touat, all *shurafā'* from Tit, Reggane, or Sali. Zafzaf helped his father in the shop, and travelled many times on camel-back from Tit to Kidal and back. As his father grew older, he settled with him in Kidal on a more permanent basis, taking on all kinds of trade that came his way, initially with Algeria: livestock against manufactured goods and dates, and then increasingly also with southern Mali and nearby Niger. At that time, Kidal hardly existed: there was the French military post, the prison, some gardens, and then at quite a distance the Algerian village with the market, all constructed by Algerians. After a while, they were joined by Arab traders from Timbuktu and a few Mauritanians, who had been in the habit of trading with the Tuareg of the Adagh, but the "Kel Touat" (people of the Touat) always remained the majority, to the point where Malian Arab traders were generally subsumed in this category as well.[15] The Kel Touat tried to avoid French interference in their dealings as much as possible and were organised in a village committee with a village head, who regulated disputes and collected taxes for the French.[16] Zafzaf's father had been one of the earlier village heads, succeeded by traders from Reggane and Akabli; Zafzaf still remembered the names of all village heads drawn from the Kel Touat,

[14] This was due less to his "civilising mission" than to French regulations aiming to control the outbreak of fire; see the various relevant documents kept at the ACK.

[15] *Kel* is Tamasheq for "people," equivalent to the Arabic *ahl*. Sometimes, Algerian traders were quite simply referred to as *dioula*, the Mandé term used throughout West Africa to refer to Muslim traders. Hence, in Gao, the *quartier* of the *dioula* refers to the former Algerian quarter that is now predominantly inhabited by Arabic-speaking traders from Timbuktu (see Chapter 6). This very fluid terminology makes the use of archival sources sometimes problematic; most importantly, it indicates a predominant classification by profession rather than origin; for a further discussion of this, see Chapter 4.

[16] Similar Algerian trading colonies were set up in northern Niger at the same time: see Grégoire (2000).

and he and 'Abd Allāh took great delight in establishing and disputing it. Most names were familiar to 'Abd Allāh, although he had never been in Kidal himself, as they all belonged to a relatively small group of people known to his uncle, and who had at some point of their lives transited via Tit. From 1960 until 1982, Ḥammū Zafzaf himself was village head, until the position was abolished. This was when he set up the Association of Algerians in Kidal, and he has been its president ever since. Today, he has his main residence in Kidal, although he refuses to take on Malian nationality; he trades in "all kinds of things," mainly foodstuffs, with Niger and southern Mali, leaving, as he said with a knowing smile, the "more adventurous" (read: illegal) trade with the north to the young.

Some more background to Zafzaf's story can be gleaned from the French colonial archives kept in the Kidal prefecture. At the time when Zafzaf's father constructed his house in Kidal, Algerian traders had already settled for quite some time in Aguelhoc, on the road to the Touat. In Aguelhoc as well as in Kidal, the head of the village and French tax collector was Algerian at least until national independence.[17] Similar settlements were established throughout the area: in Tessalit, Menaka, and even in much smaller places such as Anefif and Tabankort. Most traders were from oases that had long been in touch with the Adagh, and they had, like Zafzaf's father, decided to set up shop rather than carry on peddling their wares (although many others continued to do so, even after the introduction of trucks). They concentrated on trade with the north, exchanging manufactured goods and dates with the local Tuareg for livestock, which was then sent on to the Touat. As the importance of trucks grew, Algerian traders, who had easier access to capital and could hence invest in heavy equipment, came to control most (official) trade with the Touat. Thus, of the thirty-four people who passed the border post between Algeria and French West Africa at Tessalit in November 1956, all but two were born in Algeria, and of the two "Sudanese," one seems to have been born in Aguelhoc to an Algerian father, while the other was from Timbuktu.[18] Locally, they acted as moneylenders and provided capital for trading ventures, as the frequent complaints about unpaid debts of large amounts of money – over 1,000,000 Algerian francs at times – let us surmise. One way of lending money was to provide credit for young Tuareg migrants

[17] P. Chalmont, "Rapport de tournée," 7/02–14/02/1959, ACK.

[18] Seven were born in Aoulef, six in Metlili, four in Adrar, two each in Ouargla and Sali, and one each in Timimoun (but his parents were from Metlili), Oran, Abiodh Sidi Cheikh, Aïn Séfra, Reggane, and Tunis ("Liste de personnes qui ont traversé le poste frontalier de Tessalit entre Adrar et Gao en novembre 1956," ACK).

seeking employment on building sites in Algeria. Thus, in 1953, an Arab trader in Kidal lent a she-camel to Mohammad Bakkay ag Rali, a young Tuareg of the Idnan in Kidal, against a first payment of 2,000 francs CFA. The latter used it to travel to Tamanrasset, worked on construction sites, sold the camel, and sent all his earnings – 16,000 Algerian francs – back to his creditor in Kidal. Unfortunately, the person who carried his money for him absconded to enrol in the French army to go to Indochina.[19] Conversely, at least some if not all of the profit made by the Kel Touat in the Adagh was invested in livestock, which was entrusted to local Tuareg, although, by the late 1950s, the Kel Touat had their own shepherd.[20] In 1953, when Sīdi Muḥammad, a trader from the Ahl 'Azzī, died in Kidal, his inheritance – or rather the part of his inheritance that was known to his brother in the Tidikelt – was exclusively made up of livestock, looked after by Tuareg Ifoghas.[21]

Ties between the Kel Touat and influential Tuareg families were thus close, and Algerian traders made most of their money by acting as intermediaries in regional trade and not by trans-Saharan ventures, while still partly relying on their Tuareg allies for transport. This is clearly expressed in a series of petitions that Ḥammū Zafzaf sent to the newly independent Malian government in 1962, protesting in the name of the "traders of Kidal" against the imposition of customs duties and the subsequent confiscation of trade goods. Here (probably somewhat dishonestly), he claimed that, because of their close involvement with the local Tuareg economy, traders often had to stay with the *badū* "for several months" buying "*dukkālī* [hand-woven rugs from the Gourara] and blankets and white cloth," and that they hence quite simply could not know about the "imposition of customs."[22] In a later petition, he exposed similar grievances and the negative effective of customs duties both on the "people of the village" (i.e., sedentary traders) and the "people of the desert":

As to the people of the desert (*ahl al-bādiya*): if one of them increases his herd and he patiently bears the hunger and the difficulty until the herd grows and he goes and he sells it in the Tuwāt, then he buys clothes and the like and then maybe he needs to buy some new equipment. Did he do this to be forced by one

[19] "Lieutenant Butaye au capitaine commandant le CMTH, Oued Tahara," 17/12/1953, ACK.

[20] "L'affaire de la chamelle de Sabba mint Abidine des Kel Touat," 14/11/1961, ACK.

[21] At the time of his death, he owned four she-camels, six cows, three camels, seven goats, and "a few animals kept with the Tuareg" ("Lettre de Thomas, chef de l'annexe du Tidikelt, au chef de la subdivision de Kidal," 23/04/1955, ACK).

[22] Ḥammū Zafzaf, "Risāla," 1962, ACK.

of the men of the government to pay damaging taxes, or did he do this to provide for his dependents? And the trader who buys from him: perhaps he buys from him with compassion, not for the love of profit but to set him free of need. As to the trader ... : he entrusts the *badawī* with some necessary goods. Then comes the man from the customs and by force collects duties (*khallām al-diwāna*) on what is not the *badawī*'s property, and on all his valuables although he is poor and deserves compassion and mercy. And this does not only happen to one but it happens to many, and this stops the trader from trading with the people of the desert.[23]

The thorny problem of customs and newly established national borders aside, this shows the close interaction between Algerian traders and local nomadic populations who imported goods from the Touat, their mutual interdependence, the predominance of regional trade, and the importance of credit extended to nomads.[24]

By all accounts, such close contact and mutual relations of trust were backed up by much further reaching social ties created with leading local families and especially with the Tuareg Ifoghas, whose claims to political authority in the area grew steadily under French occupation (Boilley 1999). The most important way of creating such ties was through marriage, most commonly by Algerian traders taking a second wife locally in addition to a first wife left in the Touat.[25] This was common practice among Algerian traders in northern Mali more generally: the first Algerian established in Gao in 1945, a *sharīf* from Sali near Adrar, took a second wife from among one of the leading Malian Kunta families, giving him "great standing among the Africans";[26] another Algerian trader married the daughter of the *amenokal* or federal head of the Kel Rela, a high-status Tuareg federation straddling the Tidikelt, the Ahaggar and the

[23] Unsigned petition, n.d. (presumably also 1962), ACK.

[24] The problem of customs and smuggling endured, sometimes leading to the confiscation of caravans and trucks by the Algerian and Malian authorities, and to subsequent tensions between both governments (see, e.g., "Lettre au commandant Ahmed Mahmoud," 6/02/1963, ACK). Lecocq (2002: 74) mentions restrictions on exports to the north among the causes of the 1960s rebellion. Trade, or rather, as it was now called, smuggling, continued nonetheless: in 1963, the regional Malian governor Mohammed Mahmoud mentioned dozens of caravans bound for the Touat, with several hundred sheep each ("Rapport de tournée," 25/01/1963, ACK).

[25] This was a longstanding practice in the area, as were the complications resulting from it. See, for instance, a case recorded in the *Ghuniya*, in which the daughter of a Touati trader born and resident in the Sudan had exchanged parts of her inheritance with another Touati trader against indigo veils. The trader was now attempting to claim the land from her half-brother resident in the Touat (NG: 143).

[26] Reynaud, "Les commerçants transsahariens," Mémoire du CHEAM, n° 3018 (1957), CAOM 20X6 32.

Adagh in northern Mali.[27] Ḥammū Zafzaf similarly took a second and third wife on arrival in Kidal, and in many cases, the commercial success of Algerian traders is perhaps best described as an organizational feat by their various in-laws, providing the necessary transport and protection. Beyond considerations of commercial necessity, from a male point of view at least, marriage also became central to notions of the incomparable "sweetness" of life in the Adagh: many Algerian nostalgic reminiscences crystallise around the supposedly easy access to beautiful women in the Sudan. This is especially true of husbands, who clearly enjoy and often embellish their youthful memories, but it equally applies to the children born to such marriages. Hence, Khadīja, 'Abd Allāh's wife, who was born and brought up in Kidal, still fondly remembers living alongside her maternal grandparents in tents. At that time, she said, all Algerian traders had kin through marriage that lived in the country, and traders' families would spend more time in the *bādiya* than in town. Meanwhile, the mud houses, so conspicuously built in Kidal and so central to family accounts of "civilisation," were mostly used for trade and storage. Although Khadīja's father was killed in Kidal, although she moved back to Tit with her family when she was in her teens, and although none of her own children speaks Tamasheq or would ever dream about travelling to the Sudan, the Adagh in northern Mali remains for her almost an earthly paradise, her mother's country, where food was delicious beyond all comparison, and the desert strangely and beautifully alive.

Memories of transborder marriages are not always rose-coloured, however. Among women in the Touat, stories of absent fathers and husbands still haunt conversations, even today, indicating deep-rooted fears of the potentially irreversible intimacy of Algerian traders and their nomadic customers. The Kidal archives are full of petitions sent by despairing wives and mothers looking for their husbands, or at least asking them to pay maintenance for their children.[28] Worse, the fear of losing a husband altogether was always present, and in some cases justified. The son of another prominent Algerian trader gives the following account:

My father was travelling along the road that then still went via Tabankort and then Bourem, and he stopped in a camp and it was there that a woman bewitched

[27] On the role of the *amenokal*, see Claudot-Hawad (1990).

[28] For one such case, see "Lettre de Thomas, chef de l'annexe du Tidikelt, au chef de la subdivision de Kidal," 6/02/1952, ACK: "My father has left In Salah six years ago, he lives in Kidal whence he sends us nothing but a small allowance every summer. He left us his military pension of 320 francs every three months. We are four people to dress and feed and this money is not enough."

him. Real potent witchcraft: you know what the women are like in Mali. From one day to the next he forgot everything about us, his wife and children, and just lived with them in tents, tending his flock and drinking milk: he spent seven years like that, tending his flocks and drinking milk. And then one day suddenly, he woke up in the morning and remembered us, and he ran away. He met a cousin in Gao who brought him back: I still remember the day when he came back as if it was yesterday, we were living in Adrar in the house you know, I was coming back from school, and everybody was saying "he has come back! He has come back!" You couldn't get through to the door, so many people were waiting outside to have a look – and there he was, as if nothing had happened ... And then he set off again, but without disappearing again; but my mother was always fretting, we had been very poor while he was away, no money, nothing. He died when I was still very young, on the road, he must have been forty or so, not more.

Conversely, Malian wives left by themselves for too long when their Algerian trading husband was away in the Touat (and who might have been married against their will by a father desirous to further relationships with wealthy strangers) might find others more willing to stand by them. Thus, the daughter of Aḥmad b. Nājim, an Arab trader probably from Timbuktu, who, married to an Algerian dioula (trader) from Aguelhoc at the age of eleven, ran away during a prolonged absence of both her husband and her father in 1955. Now aged sixteen, she chose to marry a local Tuareg, and succeeded in gaining support for her cause by local Tuareg notables and scholars.[29] Children might also go missing: traders who had married locally, and then divorced the mother of their children, often despaired of ever seeing them again and routinely appealed for help to the French military commander.[30] Similarly, children sent by Algerian traders to work with leading Tuareg families, to "learn the trade of a camel-herd," but certainly also to forge important social ties, sometimes quite simply disappeared.[31]

Hence, such close social alliances did not necessarily lead to "multicultural" harmony but were often in themselves a source of tensions. Nonetheless, through them, the Algerian traders in the Adagh constructed a close web based on the exchange of people as well as goods that was indispensable to their success, but that also irreversibly altered

29 "Lettre de Ahmed b. Nâjim, commerçant à Kidal," sent on the 3/11/1955 from Tessalit, and the "Déclaration de Zeid ag Attahar," taken down by Capitaine Germain, 20/11/1955, ACK.

30 "Lettre du chef du cercle de Tahoua au chef de la subdivision de Kidal," 2/01/1953, ACK.

31 "Lettre de Thomas, chef de l'annexe du Tidikelt, au chef de la subdivision de Kidal," 15/01/1952, ACK.

their own way of life, and especially that of their children. This web of social relations eventually resulted in the development of a multilingual and multireferential society that in turn had an unmistakable impact both on Kidal and the traders' hometowns. Tit is a striking example here: although terribly remote in terms of modern transport, access and facilities, most of its inhabitants speak several languages, have travelled extensively, and have some kind of connection with the Adagh. The number of Tuareg from the Adagh who live there is surprisingly large. Most have family ties with former traders, and came to live in Tit either at Algerian independence or during one of the successive crises that sent large numbers of Malian refugees to Algeria. Thus, for instance, Bohanna, a Tamasheq from Adagh, who had grown up in 'Abd Allāh's uncle's household in Tit. Back in the Adagh in 1960, he joined the Algerian nationalist army there, obtained Algerian nationality at independence, and continued to work for the Algerian army until the 1970s, when he chose to settle in Tit.[32] His sister still lives there, in the "Tuareg" quarter, and although none of her children has any relation to northern Mali, they all speak Tamasheq and dress "Tuareg" fashion – or rather, in a way that is defined as such throughout southern Algeria (see Chapter 4). More generally, Tit shows a striking diversity, despite its remoteness and small number of inhabitants. Daily conversation might refer to rainfall in the Adagh as much as to purely Algerian matters, while property relations overlap and are equally complex. Its spatial layout appears as a direct reflection of its cosmopolitan history (see also Chapter 6): although, in terms of the number of its inhabitants, it is barely a village, it has two mosques, one old, one new, and several distinctive quarters, one for the *shurafā'* near the graveyard and shrine, one for the "Arabs," one for the "Tuareg," and one for the *ḥarāṭīn*, plus a more modern town centre with a primary school and some concrete buildings. Despite this obvious spatial segregation, everybody knows each other as a matter of course and multilingualism is the norm, giving Tit an atmosphere of worldliness that few Algerian towns now share. Hence, while traders from Tit quite rightly claim that they have constructed at least one section of Kidal, their in-laws, partners and cousins have clearly had an equally large share in the making of Tit.

[32] During the Algerian war of independence, the ALN set up base camps in northern Mali, especially after Mali itself had become independent in 1960 (see below). The ALN recruited widely among young Tamasheq and Arabic speakers in the area, thereby inaugurating a pattern of military involvement that, according to some (e.g., Keenan 2006a), lasts until today.

THE RISE AND DECLINE OF THE ZIJLĀWĪ EMPIRE

If Ḥammū Zafzaf is known to any child in Kidal and Tit, the Zijlāwī have a similar reputation in Adrar, and even more so in their hometown Aoulef in the neighbouring Tidikelt. The first members of the Zijlāwī family that I was introduced to in Adrar were two sisters, Zayda and Mouna. Most women in Adrar know Zayda as she trades in dresses, incense, and jewellery from Mali and Niger. "Sudanese" fashion has recently become popular in Adrar, and sells dearly (see Chapter 6). Her younger sister runs a private language school in town and is known and admired for her independence and initiative, and corresponding choice of husband after a first divorce. Both sisters were born to a Malian mother and brought up in Niamey. They speak several African languages, as well as Arabic and French, fluently. Their house in Adrar is always besieged by large numbers of guests, mostly women, cheerfully gathered around plentiful West African dishes. They include Mauritanian and Western Saharan traders, Arab refugees from Mali of the better sort, innumerable cousins with international life stories, and numerous friends from Adrar who come to buy or order clothes and other "exotic" goods with Zayda, settle debts, or just fancy a break from the surrounding sternness. Zayda majestically oversees the daily commotion, seated on a sofa under her own large picture, knows everything about everybody, and holds the house and the larger family together. Without her extensive knowledge and networks, my research would hardly have been possible, and I soon found that the title of "Zayda's friend" opened doors in most places I went to. Having benefited from her as a guide to the world of Malian immigrants and traders in Adrar, copiously abused the hospitality of her uncle Mūlāy Sharīf in Gao, and heard about the tremendous riches accumulated by the Zijlāwī wherever I went, I finally asked her to introduce me to the heartland of the Zijlāwī empire: Aoulef, near In Salah.

Aoulef is a medium-sized town on the main road that leads from In Salah to Adrar. In comparison with Tit, it has a rather modern and Algerian feel to it: it has a *lycée*, several *collèges*, various regional administrations, shops, a market, and regular public transport. Yet besides the cluster of modern concrete buildings, the town centre is dominated by two large buildings: the local *zāwiya*, of recent construction, financed by the Zijlāwī and led by their son-in-law Shaykh Bāy,[33] and the even larger

[33] Shaykh Bāy, the head of the *zāwiya* of Aoulef, is not to be confused with the Kunta Shaykh Bāy mentioned in Chapter 1 and discussed further in Chapter 4. The Aoulef

qaṣba Zijlāwī, made up of a cluster of individual houses ranging from mud-brick hovels to large comfortable concrete villas. Indeed, my insistence that the bus driver let me down at the Zijlāwī's house was the cause of great hilarity: "*shūfi dār Zijlāwī*" (look, this is the Zijlāwī's house), he said pointing at the whole of Aoulef, then including with a vast sweep of his arm the whole world. I nevertheless managed to find Zayda's late father's first wife, Maryam, who was staying on her own in a large and comfortable house, waited on by a black servant. Surprised at my unexpected arrival she rapidly composed herself (she was clearly used to surprise visitors from all kinds of strange places and with dubious claims of "relatedness") and, on my request, told me the story – almost a fairy tale – of the Zijlāwīs' rise to wealth, and showed me her family photographs. These were arranged in several large albums: her daughters, cousins, and her only son (the other one had died on a trip to Niger); brothers, nieces and nephews; in Aoulef for the *ʿīd*; in Niamey in bathing suits sitting next to a large swimming pool; end-of-year photographs from expensive private schools in Niamey; four-by-fours and travels down through the desert. Her daughter in her own private clinic in Niamey; her daughters' wedding pictures, dressed up in the elaborate Timbuktu bridal outfit, with Songhay braids, Malian *boubou*s or all in white, and with husbands variously from Timbuktu, northern Niger or Algeria. Another photo was framed and hung up on the wall: the Zijlāwī family in Niamey, maybe twenty years ago. The photo was oversized, in order to accommodate more than a hundred Zijlāwī of all ages, colours, dresses, and African hairstyles that still showed traces of the 1970s, all assembled in a large and beautiful villa near a swimming pool, with the "*grand patron*," the current head of the family, Sī Ḥammādi, in the centre of the photograph, smiling and keeping a close eye on everybody around him.

Family history starts in the early twentieth century, when, just after the arrival of the French, the first Zijlāwī, Ṭālib Sālim, arrived in Aoulef from the Wād Sūf near the contemporary Tunisian border. He was a Trūdī, that is to say from a group well known for their trading abilities and with prior connections to the area.[34] On arrival, Ṭālib Sālim was given a house in

Shaykh Bāy traces his descent from al-Ḥājj ʿŪmar Fāll (Bāy Bilʿālim 2004) and came to Aoulef from the nearby Akabli on the invitation of the Zijlāwī. He is the author of the multivolume work on the Touat (Bāy Bilʿālim 2005), and more generally a prolific writer, keen to exploit to the full the new technological resources offered by modern publishing, computers, the Internet, and the generosity of the Zijlāwī family.

[34] In 1891, the French Resident in Tunis notes that most Algerian slave traders supplying the market in Tunis were Awlād Trūd ("Lettre du Résident Français à Tunis au Gouverneur Général de l'Algérie," 15/05/1891, CAOM 12H50).

Aoulef by the *jamāʿa* (assembly) of the *qṣar*. He had already been married in the Wād Sūf and brought with him his three sons – al-ʿArbī, ʿAmar, and al-Bashīr. In Aoulef, he took another three wives: one from a local family, the Būsbaʿa, and the other two from the Kunta *zāwiya* of Akabli that had long been central to trade with the Adagh, Gao, and Timbuktu (see Chapter 1). Thenceforth, the major trade routes to the Sudan were controlled by Ṭālib Sālim's in-laws, while the Būsbaʿa had, in their own way, much experience of Sudanese trade. Until the arrival of Ṭālib Sālim, they had been poor, owning some land and a few houses on the outskirts of Aoulef. This poverty forced them to work as peddlers of Algerian trade goods in the Adagh and Tilemsi, much as Ḥammū Zafzaf's father had done. Their initial capital was provided by a Shaʿanbī moneylender who had a shop in Aoulef and probably received his own capital from Mzabi merchants based in Ghardaïa. He lent money to the Būsbaʿa taking their land, gardens, and houses as security. Like al-Markāntī's first venture, family lore abounds in stories of insecurity and the constant threat of total loss, as, on every trip to the *bilād al-sūdān*, they risked the family's whole fortune: they must have been keen to ally themselves with an energetic and perhaps also wealthy trader from the Sūf, while Ṭālib Sālim was sure to profit from their experience and abundant manpower. As this first alliance was repeated in all subsequent generations, the two families are by now virtually undistinguishable.

Ṭālib Sālim never went to the *bilād al-sūdān*, but concentrated on regional trade with the northeast, while entrusting others with the necessary capital to venture further south. His seven sons, however, travelled extensively in the south: al-Bashīr died on a trip in Tahoua, in central Niger; al-ʿArbī was involved in trade in Guinea; other sons and grandsons started plying the route to Gao, continuing the Būsbaʿa tradition of peddling (see Map 2.1 for the family's trade network). With World War II, this southern trade took a new turn: the Vichy government, fearful of an allied sea blockade, started to invest heavily in trans-Saharan road infrastructure, and truck trade became a viable option. More importantly, the war led to heavy economic restrictions in Algeria (which was technically a part of France) but not in French West Africa, and black markets were booming throughout the country.[35] Moreover, French West

[35] References to close ties between trans-Saharan trade and black market supplies in Algeria abound; see the various documents kept in CAOM 9H26. The Bani Mzab were especially active here, and they vociferously complained that the French were routinely violating the sanctity of their mosques which they suspected of being used as storages spaces for illegally traded foodstuffs and Italian guns smuggled in from Libya (see, e.g., the "Lettre des délégués de la population commerçante ibadite au Gouverneur Général de l'Algérie," 10/06/1947, CAOM 9H41).

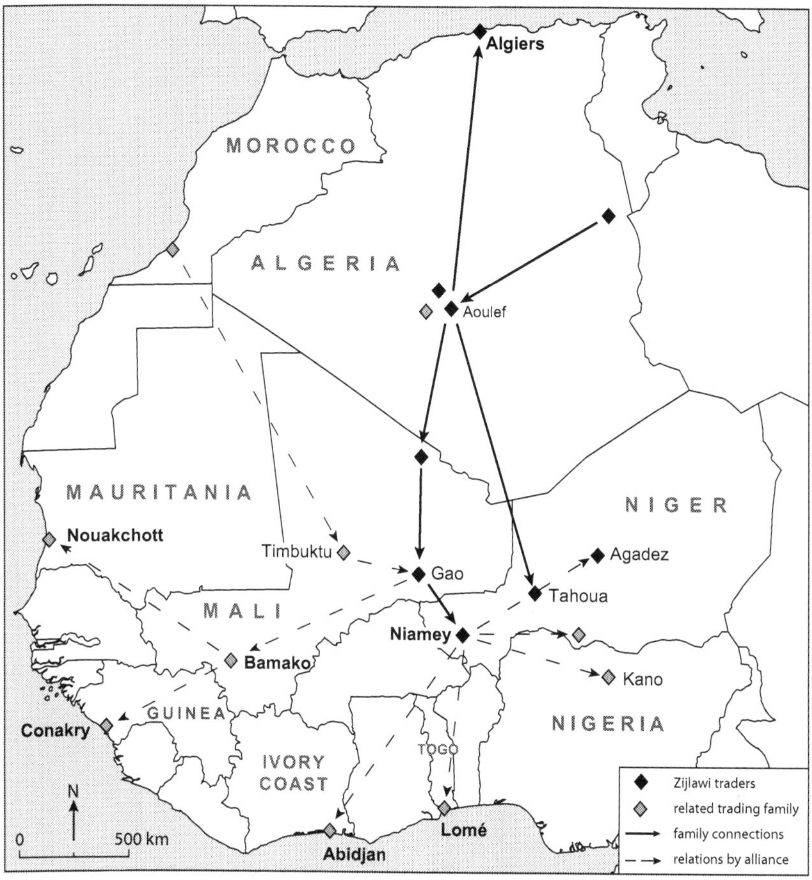

MAP 2.1. Zijlāwī trade and settlements.

Africa had long and uncontrollable borders with British colonies, Ghana and Nigeria, giving access to local produce such as palm oil, but also and primarily to cheap English imports, especially cotton cloth.[36] According to Daḥmān Būsba'a, who was in his late teens when the sudden bounty of multiple transborder smuggling dawned upon him:

We'd go down to the Adagh [in northern Mali], with our pockets full of money, and we'd find some *koro-boro* [Songhay, literally: town dweller] or *fulānī* [Haalpulaar] and buy his cows, put them all together and then pay somebody to drive them across the border to Niger, then Nigeria, where they would be changed for cloth that was loaded on trucks all the way to Gao. Sometimes, we'd

[36] J. Raynaud, "Rapport d'enquête administrative relative à un certain trafic de bovides, trafic de tissus," December 1948, CAOM AffPol/2188/7.

go ourselves all the way, and then: there was great misery in Algeria at that time, people were always hungry, but in Nigeria you would eat and eat, everything was *bāṭil*, free of charge … Or we'd give cash to people who bought their own cows and took them down, but if you didn't know them they would cheat you. From Gao to Aoulef, we went by camel. There was no need to hide: as long as we showed the nicest bits of cloth that we got to the [French] *commandant* so he could keep them for his wife, everybody was happy …[37] We made more money than you will ever see in your life, more than I will ever see again, it was as though you only had to stretch out your hand and people put gold into it!

Business was such that, in the late 1940s, Ṭālib Sālim's grandson, 'Abd al-Salām set up a permanent shop in Gao, together with his elder brother, to trade in more "legal" goods, mainly dates, manufactured produce, and livestock. There was no head of the village here as in Kidal, but trade was well regulated: Algerian traders delivered their dates and other goods to one central storage place, where prices were fixed. Local customers and retailers bought them through the storekeeper, who had often advanced their price to the original trader.[38] Moreover, traders claim that the whole market was owned and built by Algerians following the Algerian style – they had even brought with them stonemasons from Aoulef, or so the story goes.[39]

Nonetheless, here as in Kidal, commercial success hinged on the establishment of valuable connections with local societies; and here also, marital alliances were key. Yet although all marriages established some kind of connections, not all of these were considered publicly avowable; and even a brief comparison of the different life stories and attitudes of several Zijlāwī men shows that hardly ever two marriages were alike, depending, mainly, on the status of the wife chosen, her position within

37 Although I initially presumed that Daḥmān was referring to the administrator in the Tidikelt, documents I found later in the archives might indicate that he meant the administrator in Gao, Reben, who appears as pivotal in the organisation of cloth smuggling in the area during the 1940s, see J. Raynaud, "Rapport." People alleged that his dealings were so profitable that he routinely sent gold to France hidden in bars of soap.

38 This meant that traders from the Touat who did not know the country well would get fair prices and never had to hang around for too long; it also ensured lasting control over the market by those traders who had come first. A similar system has been reported from throughout the Sahara; see, for example, Pascon (1984) and Schroeter (1988).

39 After independence, an Algerian consulate opened in Gao, and the consul was often described as acting "like the village head in Kidal" – in other words, he was seen as a representative of the resident Algerian trading community (rather than the Algerian state) to the Malian government. Today, however, relations between traders and the consul are often tense: Algerian diplomats see Gao (probably quite rightly) as a punitive posting, "worse than Siberia," while traders mistrust officials recruited in northern Algeria, who "know nothing of the Sahara."

local society, and the recognition of this position by her future husband and his family.[40] 'Abd al-Salām represents perhaps an extreme case of an excess of "unsuitable" ties: when he settled in Gao, he was already married to a cousin in Aoulef. He then took another five successive wives in Mali: three Arab women, mainly from impoverished and low-status nomadic families living along the road that led from Gao to Adrar, and two Tuareg women who never bore him children. "This is just how things were done then," he says, "and marriage over there wasn't like marriage in Algeria: you turn up, you pay, and if you don't like her, you get a divorce. And Malian women are so beautiful." But despite this prevailing rhetoric of reversibility and "freedom," as soon as children were born to such unions, ties were forged that could never be cut. Hence, one of 'Abd al-Salām's ex-wives, Sharīfa, remembers her stint of married life rather more bitterly. Still of outstanding beauty, but of "lowly" descent, she was married to 'Abd al-Salām when she was fourteen, and divorced after she had borne him five children.[41] To be married to an Algerian trader in Gao was difficult, she says, as, used to the "free life" of the camp, she suddenly found herself locked into a house in Gao, not allowed to ever go out, cut off from her family, and looked down upon by her in-laws in the Touat. Now remarried with a much younger Malian husband, she has nonetheless chosen to settle in Adrar and visits Zayda daily, thereby clearly stating that she remains, for all intents and purposes, one of the Zijlāwī, and intimately bound up with the contemporary life and reputation of the family as a whole.

Nothing could have been more different than Zayda's father Muṣṭafā's second marriage. At an early age, Muṣṭafā followed his father to Gao, where they lived right in the heart of the marketplace, in a house that continues to be owned by the family – as, indeed, a large part of the market in Gao still is. They traded in livestock and dates, but also picked up any other "business" that came their way. Muṣṭafā's first wife, Maryam, my host in Aoulef, still remembers with a certain bitterness how her husband left by himself to settle in Gao, saying that the Sudan was not for women and children, only to then take a second wife in Gao. Nor did

[40] This point is valid beyond the Sahara, and has perhaps been made most convincingly by Ho (2001) for the Indian Ocean. The Saharan example shows, however, that the nature of marital alliances did not only change from one society to the next, but could vary from case to case, and according to status distinctions within the host and the sending society (for further examples of this, see Chapter 6).

[41] Local notions of nobility and hierarchy are complex, and will be discussed in more detail in Chapter 4.

the second wife know about the existence of the first, or, at least according to her daughter Zayda, she would have refused to marry him. After all, Lalla ʿĀ'isha was not like the Arab nomadic girls that ʿAbd al-Salām married for their beauty: rather, she was of a reputed sharifian family of Moroccan descent, whose father was perhaps the most influential trader in the region, whose uncle was *qāḍi* of nearby Goundam, and she had no need to throw herself away on an Algerian. Muṣṭafā had to gain more from the alliance than she did, as he well knew and as she constantly reminded him. And gain he did: much if not most of the Zijlāwī's success and ongoing popularity in the area stem from the good relations they established with their in-laws who still provide many political and social dignitaries in Bourem and Bamba on the Niger bend and are foremost among the people who can "do things" in Gao and its hinterland. Lalla ʿĀ'isha seems to have run the family much as Zayda does today, and Zayda clearly does not feel inferior in any way to her peers born to Algerian mothers, as other children of mixed marriages settled in the Touat often say they do. Hence, whereas ʿAbd al-Salām chose his wives despite their low status and relative lack of family connections, and is now an obscure shopkeeper in Aoulef slightly embarrassed by the reminiscences of past joys, Muṣṭafā, by his marriage and the numerous connections it led to, prospered beyond all expectations; and until today, much of the still blossoming "Zijlāwī empire" in West Africa relies on his initial investments and is run by his in-laws, defined in the broadest possible sense.

In 1960, with Malian independence and initially socialist economic policy, the Zijlāwī moved their business to Niamey.[42] They were not alone in doing so: a large percentage of the Gao trading communities chose to leave at the same time, including many Arabic-speaking traders of Malian origin. For Zayda's generation, Niamey rather than Gao is the site of most childhood memories, and indeed has come to stand for the *bilād al-sūdān* more generally; until today, this is where most of those members of their family who have chosen to stay in West Africa live. Among these "exiled" traders were Muṣṭafā's cousins Būsbaʿa – Daḥmān's brothers – and their wayward nephew, Daḥmān's son al-Mukhṭār. The Būsbaʿa were trading in all kinds of goods, imported from the West African coast as well as from the north; however, much of their business relied on imports from Algeria and was carried on trucks they owned themselves. At that time, large profits could be made in transborder trade, as, with independence

42 For a discussion of Malian economic policy after independence, see Châu (1992).

and subsequent economic reforms, most basic staples, such as powdered milk, flour, pasta, and semolina were heavily subsidised in Algeria, and the price differential between both sides of the border was considerable.[43] As a result, exports from Algeria to West Africa had become subject to heavy restrictions, but traders who could rely on efficient networks of support on either side of the border and on their own means of transport could relatively easily avoid these (for the ways this trade was conducted, see Chapter 3). In this way, the "Lahda" period – as the 1970s and early 1980s are generally referred to, Lahda being the trade name of Algerian state-produced powdered milk – laid the basis for many a fortune in the area. Yet the Būsba'a always supplemented their Lahda trade with legal commerce in dates and tobacco. Some of these were grown in their own gardens in the Tidikelt, where they had invested extensively in land and water; members of the family who had stayed in Aoulef provided the rest, bought directly from producers in the Tidikelt and the Touat, often against advance payment on a harvest before maturity: within greatly changed socioeconomic and political circumstances, they were thus perpetuating the kind of credit networks described in Chapter 1, and that had, once upon a time, financed their family's own initial trans-Saharan ventures.

While the Būsba'a brothers and their Zijlāwī cousins of the same generation represent a bygone age of wealth and prestige, their nephew al-Mukhṭār stands, until today, as a living example of the "corruption" of the Sudan. He is the son of Daḥmān's second wife, a Tamasheq speaker from Kidal, but he had been brought up in Aoulef by his stepmother, a fact that he still resents deeply. When he was just sixteen, his uncles called him to Niamey to assist him in their business. This is why, even today, everybody calls him "PDG" (*Président-Directeur Général*): in Niger, all official business had to be conducted in French, a language that remained foreign to his uncles, who were literate in Arabic and went about their daily business in Zerma and Hawsa, while al-Mukhṭār, who had been to school in Algeria during the war of independence, had some familiarity with it, and hence acted as the family's official representative. The unmistakable sparkle in al-Mukhṭār's eyes speaks volumes about what it meant for a teenage boy to move from the austerity of Aoulef and the surveillance of paternal kin suspicious of "Sudanese" children to the freedom of Niamey,

43 On economic policies in postindependence Algeria, see Benissad (1994) and Stora (1994). For an account of transborder trade in the 1980s and early 1990s from the point of view of northern Niger, see Grégoire (1998).

where everything seemed possible, where girls were plentiful, accessible, and beautiful and money could be spent by the fistful. And this, indeed, al-Mukhṭār set out to do: "it took my father decades of hard work to amass a fortune by the sweat of his brow; he worked, and I squandered it all, for nothing but the sake of it" – until, two years later, his worried uncles decided to remove him from office, and to put him on duty away from the temptations of Niamey, accompanying the company's trucks on their trips north and south. On these journeys, al-Mukhṭār became familiar with the hardships of desert travel, but also and especially with the delights of the Adagh, the Aïr, and Niamey, the large freight ports on the coast in Benin and Togo, and above all the cities of northern Nigeria, Kano, and Sokoto, where he still travels frequently "for religious reasons," as he puts it.[44] Al-Mukhṭār has now permanently settled in Aoulef, although he admits that he finds it difficult to fit in. To make time pass, he dabbles in politics: he was elected mayor of Aoulef several years ago, much to the displeasure of his family, as he won the elections with *ḥarāṭīn* support, and attacked the *shaykh* of the local *zāwiya* (his own brother-in-law) in his first speech. He had to resign two days later. Undaunted, he then stood for the presidential elections of 2004, one of the many candidates ignored by media and voters alike – "but we had such a laugh," as he says himself, with a big smile on his round face marked by years of the "sweet life."

Where stories of 'Abd al-Salām's seven wives are met with comprehensive smiles, al-Mukhṭār's tales are treated as slightly shameful jokes by men and are harshly judged by women. Nevertheless, they draw a picture, if clearly not of the realities, then at least of male images of life in the *bilād al-sūdān*. Thus the story of his "wife of a month":

> I was travelling with our trucks and another trader, a friend of mine. We stopped on the way between Kidal and Gao, somewhere around Tabankort. My friend said that he wanted to get married, so we pulled into a nearby camp and asked if they had any women to give us. The man came out and said he had two: a girl [i.e., a virgin] for 2,000 francs, and a woman [i.e., divorced or widowed] for 1,500. I said to my friend that this was no good, as he would certainly take the money for the girl and then set him up with the woman. The only way round this would be that I take the woman at the same time, so he is bound to give you the girl. That's what we did: they set up two tents for us, and we both got married that day. The next day we took our wives with us on the trucks, and went to Gao.

[44] Al-Mukhṭār is affiliated to the Qādiriyya that has important centres throughout northern Nigeria (see, e.g., Loimeier 1997). His office in Aoulef proudly displays photographs of a visit of a large group of Nigerian religious dignitaries to Aoulef, a visit that al-Mukhṭār had organised and hosted.

I stayed with mine for a month and then we divorced, but he took his back to Algeria and they are still married.

Despite the evident glee with which he tells this story – not a very repentant sinner – it has recently caused him some trouble, as a young man from Mali turned up in Aoulef, claiming to be his (only male) heir, fruit of the one-month marriage. Although al-Mukhṭār vehemently rejects his claims, muttering something about "genetic testing," his elders are putting pressure on him to do the "right thing" whatever the truth of the matter, rather than bring shame to the Zijlāwī name. More generally, the fear of "forgotten" children suddenly turning up in Aoulef is omnipresent, especially among women, who are loath to put up with unwelcome new heirs and divorced but nonetheless demanding former rivals. Meanwhile, al-Mukhṭār's "wildness" and stereotypical lack of containment is taken to be symbolic of the corruption of the Sudan more generally: his mother was from Mali, people point out, and even the most honourable Sudanese wives will produce "rotten" children that "eat" the family fortune within one generation: it is like witchcraft, *sihr*, women say, pointing to the veins in their forearms, "it runs in the blood." This observation applies to wealth as much as to children: nothing, it is implied, that has been earned in the Sudan can ever really prosper – unless it is converted into "proper" capital back home: gardens, water, houses, and Algerian wives and children.

At first sight, the contemporary fortune of the Zijlāwī seems to justify this gloomy prediction: the heyday of easy living in Niamey has clearly passed, and most Zijlāwī shops in the Sahel have closed down, their former owners now living retired in Algeria. Today, are seen as successful those members of the family who managed to convert their financial capital into landholdings or, even better, a good education and a position of influence within the Algerian administration. Most Zijlāwī who correspond to this ideal were born to Algerian mothers, and often regard their "Sudanese" half-siblings with some degree of resignation bordering on pity. Al-Mukhṭār's half-brothers, for instance, all completed school in postindependence Algeria, went to university, and became part of the first generation of civil servants employed in the south following the gradual political decentralisation in the 1970s and 1980s; for them, past trans-Saharan ties are but a vague memory, and al-Mukhṭār himself a living embarrassment. Indeed, on at least one occasion, Sī Ḥammādi, the current head of the family, sacked one of his nephews because the latter insisted on marrying a Malian wife: "the beginning of the end," according to Sī Ḥammādi, as such a marriage would necessarily produce "rotten" children, witness his own example and that of his wayward nephew, al-Mukhṭār. On a closer look, however, the Malian side of the family continues to be crucial to its success, as the "Zijlāwī empire" still prospers in the margins of Algerian territorial rule and respectability, employing a new generation of traders in lucrative enterprises throughout West and North Africa: many of these are related to the Zijlāwī by marriage rather than birth, speak Songhay instead of Arabic, and have little or no "natural" connection to their Algerian "homeland" that they nonetheless visit on a regular basis. And in times of crisis, even "Algerian" Zijlāwī might remember past connections. Hence al-Mukhṭār's youngest half-brother, Ṭayyib, who was instrumental in setting up a lucrative cigarette smuggling business in northern Niger, in the name of the current head of the family, Sī Ḥammādi, and whose career is described in Chapter 3.

Sī Ḥammādi himself is the living proof of the family's continuing good fortune: he is truly rich, not merely by Malian or Algerian standards. He owns several companies in various West African countries and acts as exclusive representative for many others. He has invested in sizeable real estate in Algiers and is busy constructing flats and office space in Dely Brahim, an industrial area at the entry of Algiers whose unfinished buildings often double up as more or less temporary homes for sub-Saharan migrants. He also owns a large colonial villa in Douira near Algiers, several flats in Switzerland, and one on the Champs Elysée in Paris. He is about to set up shop in Dubai, by now central to trade in electronic and all kinds of goods with North and West Africa (Marchal 2001). Most importantly, he actively keeps the family together: he manages his young relations and in-laws in Mauritania, Mali, and Niger, guaranteeing employment, economic opportunities, and financial security to those who are ready to work for it and agree to subject themselves to his will in all matters. Although his interference in his relatives' private life is often resented, his control is never rejected outright, as Sī Ḥammādi "never forgets anybody" and assures the well-being and protection of all family members, whether they are productive or not. This investment is especially visible in Aoulef, which from a dusty oasis has been turned into a showcase of the family's wealth and influence: a modern Algerian town with all facilities, utterly dominated by the Zijlāwī *qaṣba*, their large concrete villas that often remain empty, and extensive irrigated gardens producing nothing much, but where no Zijlāwī will ever go cold and hungry – a successful and conspicuous making of place, if ever there was one. Although many Algerian Zijlāwī, such as Zayda, by now live in Adrar, once a year, on the occasion of the *ʿīd al-kabīr*, Sī Ḥammādi insists that they all return "home," filling the villas, *qaṣba* and gardens with a motley and multilingual crowd of "proper" and "spoiled" children, divorced wives, in-laws, and hangers-on. More than anything else, this reunion defines who truly can claim to be a Zijlāwī, while marking the family's public investment in Aoulef and indicating their continued ability to expand, adapt, liaise, prosper and squander.

AKACEM: CAMELS, TRUCKS, AND RESPECTABILITY

In order to find a family of similar wealth to the Zijlāwī, we have to turn to the Akacem, the perhaps most influential Shaʿanbī family in the Algerian south. Yet although the Akacem's reputation is also based on their trans-Saharan ventures and commercial success, it is of a very different kind to that of the Zijlāwī. While al-Mukhṭār's standing for the presidential election is an obvious joke, the Akacem are on supposedly intimate terms with the "*pouvoir*," although their influence seems to have faded. They are at the heart of the respectable bourgeoisie in Adrar and Timimoun, and the current generation and sometimes even their fathers already have invested in education and influential administrative positions rather than trade. Thus, the first Akacem I met was a bank director rather than a trans-Saharan smuggler of high standing. Where al-Mukhṭār and Zayda speak fluent Songhay and Hawsa, Djamil is conversant in French culture and life; much as the Būsbaʿa and Zijlāwī, he seems to belong to a bygone place, but this place was not south of the Sahara, but central to Algeria: the multilingual, French cosmopolitan, and "sweet" Algeria of the privileged few of the rich decades after independence that was brutally lost in the late 1980s.[45] At the time when al-Mukhṭār, after a rudimentary and rather functional education, was travelling up and down the main trans-Saharan and West African trade routes, learning about ports and easy border passages, Djamil was following his father in his spiralling administrative career through Algeria, with stints in France. Other members of the family hold equally important positions in finance and

[45] Social and political tensions in Algeria had been mounting ever since the late 1970s. In 1988, they came to a head in open street riots (Benkheira 1990), followed by the public emergence of Islamist parties. The latter then went on to win the elections of 1991, which were cancelled by the army, leading to years of civil unrest (Martinez 1998). Although the issues at stake were complex, protesters clearly expressed resentment of the Francophile upper middle classes whom they described as having "sold out" to the former colonial power.

government; they live either in the central quarters of the Saharan towns, where they often were the first to build houses (see Chapter 6), or else they have obtained villas that were formerly owned by the French in Algiers' most exclusive and central quarters.

The Akacem are originally from Metlili near Ghardaïa and belong to the Bani Brahim, a sedentary section of the Sha'anba who long acted as transporters and agents for the Bani Mzab and repeatedly crop up as implacable moneylenders throughout oral memories and the archival sources.[46] As seen in Chapter 1, the Sha'anba had long been in the habit of trading with the Gourara and the Touat, alongside extensive commercial and kin connections with Ghadamès and the Ahaggar; they were also linked to the Awlād Sīdi Shaykh through ties of spiritual deference.[47] Among the region's dominant camel nomads, many Sha'anba quickly picked up on the opportunities offered by enrolment in the French army, although they equally distinguished themselves as versatile regional raiders throughout the French colonial period.[48] Aware of the supply needs of the French army, and the ready cash offered in exchange, they were usually the first to settle near the French forts on a more permanent basis.[49] In 1900, the first Akacem moved from Metlili to Timimoun, an area with which he had long traded independently. He set up a permanent shop in order to supply the French army and his fellow Sha'anba colonial soldiers, but he also continued to act as an intermediary between nomads from the Algerian northwest and oasis date-producers, often buying dates wholesale before harvest time. In 1921, at the age of fifteen, his nephew, Djamil's uncle al-Ḥājj Aḥmad was sent to Timimoun to help in the family shop. In 1934, now aged twenty-eight, al-Ḥājj Aḥmad established his own shop in Adrar, once

[46] See Chapter 1. On the Sha'anba more generally, see Cauneille (1968), who briefly mentions their success in trade; see Campens, "Chaamba," for their longstanding connections with the greater Touat. Much of the following paragraphs is based on Reynaud, "Commerçants," cross-checked with information given by al-Ḥājj Aḥmad's contemporary descendants and further archival reports.

[47] Campens, "Chaamba"; and Didier, "Projet d'organistion"; "Etat n° 1, cercle de Laghouat," 22/05/1879, CAOM 24H117; and "Renseignements sur la region d'Idelès," 1893, CAOM 22H38. On ties with the Awlād Sīdi Shaykh, see Leclerc (1858); "Note sur Mohammed ben Radja," 1893, CAOM 22H38; and the various documents on Bou Amama kept in CAOM 22H33.

[48] On Sha'anba recruitment for the French army, see Cauneille (1968), Grévoz (1994), and Laperrine, "Lettre au Gouverneur Général de l'Algérie," 27/10/1908, CAOM 1H44. For references on Sha'anba caravans and raiding, see Chapter 1.

[49] "Rapports annuels, annexe du Tidikelt," 1909 and 1910, CAOM 23H102.

more acting as a supplier to French troops. Simultaneously, he invested in regional date trade, buying supplies on the stalk in the Gourara or the Tidikelt and more generally advancing money to small-scale producers and peddlers: he was thereby acting like the stereotypical Sha'anbī moneylender encountered in Chapter 1. His clients and sometime debtors were primarily nomads from the Oranais, the Ahaggar, and southern Morocco. Although he started to use truck transport as soon as it became available, his capital was never quite sufficient to buy his own trucks, and he remained thus dependent on French transport companies, much as al-Markāntī had been before him.

This was to change with the Second World War, the "golden age" of trans-Saharan trafficking described earlier, when rationing in Algeria but not in French West Africa made trans-Saharan smuggling very profitable indeed. Al-Ḥājj Aḥmad and several other Sha'anba from Metlili, based in Adrar, Timimoun, Metlili, and In Salah, drawing on capital provided by a Jewish trader from Béchar, grouped together as the SOTRAT (*Société de transports automobiles du Touat*) and invested in trucks, mostly Italian army vehicles that had been taken by the French during the war and were now sold off cheaply. They imported cloth, soap, coffee, tea, sugar and peanuts; al-Ḥājj Aḥmad was in charge of buying goods and frequently travelled to Gao and Niamey, the capital of Niger. As seen in Chapter 1, he invested most of his profits in water, land, and houses in Adrar, Ghardaïa, and Timimoun and was soon counted among the richest and most prestigious landowners in the area. In 1948, however, custom officials started to crack down on illegal trade, and the SOTRAT was dissolved. A year later, al-Ḥājj Aḥmad bought his first two trucks, and started to export dates to the Sudan, alongside locally produced woollen cloth and tobacco and imported cloth and manufactured goods. He imported peanuts, coffee, and especially livestock. Despite the importance of the Sudan trade, he was careful to maintain his contacts with the northwest, in particular with influential *zawāyā* in the Tafilalet and Wād Nūn in what is now southern Morocco, whom he provided with generous funds. In 1952, he started organising annual pilgrimages by bus to Mecca, and often travelled with them, establishing contacts in "Tripoli, Benghazi, Alexandria, Cairo, Suez, Jeddah, Mecca, and Medina," to the great worry of the French administration.[50]

[50] "Rapports annuels, annexe du Tidikelt," 1949 and 1951, CAOM 23H102; and especially the "Monographie du territoire militaire des oasis sahariennes," 1951/1952, CAOM 10H86.

By the late 1950s, members of al-Ḥājj Aḥmad's extended family had built houses and set up shops in Gao and Niamey, whence they travelled to Timbuktu, Bamako, Maradi in southern Niger, Ouagadougou, and even Kano in northern Nigeria, and Lomé and Accra on the West African coast. In southern Algeria, al-Ḥājj Aḥmad was said to be able to make and unmake political careers; he had bought the monopoly for truck transport between El Goléa and Adrar from the French company SATT, while his brother, Djamil's father, had received an exclusive concession from the nascent CPA (*Compagnie des pétroles algériens*) to supply their research stations and digging sites and to provide transport. Al-Ḥājj Aḥmad was but one of a number of extremely successful businessmen who came to control southern Algerian and trans-Saharan trade at the time, the vast majority of whom were defined as Sha'anba.[51] Their at times brilliant careers were reenacted on a much more modest scale by an even larger number of their poorer cousins. Most of these were former soldiers who invested their military pensions in trade of livestock against manufactured goods and dates with the Ahaggar, the Adagh, and the Tilemsi, and then reinvested their profits in land and water rights throughout the greater Touat.[52] Khadīja's father, encountered earlier, was one of them.

Reynaud and other French administrators made a great deal of the "Arab sympathies" displayed by al-Ḥājj Aḥmad and his peers, fearing that they might all too easily be induced to support the "rebellion" (the Algerian war of independence that was then, at least in the Tell, in full course).[53] This is indeed one of the points best remembered by al-Ḥājj Aḥmad's contemporary descendants, who relish telling stories about the current Algerian president Abdelaziz Bouteflika's stay in their house in Gao and their support for other well-known dignitaries of independent Algeria. With Malian independence in 1960 and subsequent open support for the Algerian struggle for independence, northern Mali had become an important relay and recruiting ground for the Algerian *Armée de Libération Nationale* (ALN) – witness the sometime Algerian soldier Bohanna whose career was described previously. Near Tessalit,

[51] "Monographie du territoire militaire"; see also the "Rapport annuel, annexe du Tidikelt," 1949, CAOM 23H102.

[52] On small-scale Sha'anba involvement in the Sudan livestock trade, see the "Rapport annuel, annexe du Tidikelt," 1939, CAOM 23H102; on investment in land and water rights, see Capot-Rey and Damade (1962).

[53] "Monographie du territoire militaire." Literature on the Algerian war of independence is vast; for an overview, see Stora (1993) and Harbi and Stora (2004).

an ALN camp provided a safe hide-out for tired or wounded fighters who were recruiting among Kel Touat, who by then made up 80 per cent of the population of Tessalit, as well as among the local population; meanwhile, the independent Malian government continued to let a military airport near what was now the Algerian border to the French army.[54] ALN officers were based in Gao, whose elderly inhabitants still recall how "we used to go to see the Algerians when we were little, and they would make us stand to attention and sing *Qasamān* [the Algerian national anthem] and then give us sweets until out bellies ached."[55] As a result, trans-Saharan transport and supplies became crucial, both for the French army and the ALN: the Akacem, who by then held a virtual monopoly over such trade, were indispensable for both and knew it. They were not alone in this situation: other Touati traders similarly remember driving trucks "for Bouteflika" from Gao to Oran, to supply ALN forces with arms; as seen earlier, Mekki's intimacy with the *pouvoir* dates from these times.

As a result, the Akacem family managed to maintain their strong position in independent Algeria, although their trading ventures and transport infrastructure suffered from war-time changes and confiscations, the rapid devaluation of land, and economic reform in the 1970s. By then, however, the younger generation of the family were well established in administrative posts throughout the country: Djamil's father, for instance, occupied a series of high-ranking posts in the Algerian independent administration, and was for a time *walī* (prefect) of Aïn Séfra in the northwest, before he was pensioned off with an ambassador's salary. Meanwhile, the older generation, among them al-Ḥājj Aḥmad, had retired to their abundant gardens in Metlili. Although much of the family's wealth initially derived from trade with the Sudan, they have by now cut most relations

54 Both must have been aware of their immediate neighbours, but no incidents happened, although the freshly independent Malian government was clearly more worried about their uncontrollable allies than about their former colonial masters. See various reports kept in the Kidal archives, especially a "Lettre de Mohamed Mahmoud," dated 25/02/1962; for a brief discussion of this rather awkward situation, see Lecocq (2002: 104).

55 At that time, relations between the inhabitants of northern Mali and the ALN were cordial, although this soon changed as, with independence, disagreements about trade restrictions and confiscations became common (see, e.g., the very angry letter by the ALN commander of Bordj Badji Mokhtar, the Algerian border post, to the Malian commander Ahmed Mahmoud, dated 6/02/1963 and kept in the ACK, in which he accuses Malian custom officials of "acting like colonialists"). Lecocq (2002: 130) claims that the leaders of the first northern rebellion in the 1960s were counting on Algerian support for their cause – in vain, as it turned out.

with it, and, here as for al-Markāntī, no stories of disappearing husbands or unruly wives come to upset the well-defined bounds of respectability: rather than dependening on local connections or even longstanding spiritual ties and ambitions, the Akacem's success was largely based on their privileged access to transport, capital, and government officials. And, perhaps as a result, they remain at the heart of the regional bourgeoisie in southern Algeria and easily mingle with the Algiers upper classes. They occupy the town centres of Adrar and Tamanrasset, hold many important administrative posts there, continue to marry among themselves or with high-status families from the south or the Tell, set the social tone, and stand for utter respectability in all matters: their parties are as lavish as they are exclusive. Although many have invested in gardens in their "home" *qṣar* in Metlili, the places they have truly made by their commercial ventures are the major towns of the Algerian south – Timimoun, Adrar and Tamanrasset – large sections of which they own, and where most of their social relations are played out (see Chapter 6). Often the first settlers after the French army, they have maintained their influential position and their wealth due to their close relations with the state, which has at times put them in a position to subvert it most successfully. A few Sha'anba continue to be active in trans-Saharan trade, but mostly those who intermarried with people from northern Mali and Niger, and the horizons of "good" families such as the Akacem are by now unquestionably Algerian: they remember their forays into the Sudan with a smile, as a fleeting episode in a much more consistent and durable story of "colonisation" that was acted out in the Algerian south.

CONCLUSION

These stories of four trading families all paint very different pictures, bearing witness to the great diversity and changeability of trade and to the traders' necessary ability to adapt to evolving circumstances. Yet several points recur throughout, illustrating and further developing the argument outlined in Chapter 1. All traders began from a regional base and mostly traded in staples: either acting as brokers and middlemen between nomads from the northern gateways of the Sahara and Touata producers, as was the case with al-Markāntī, Ṭālib Sālim Zijlāwī and al-Ḥājj Aḥmad Akacem, or as peddlers of local produce and imported manufactured goods in northern Mali and Niger, as exemplified by Ḥammū Zafzaf and the early Būsba'a. Their ventures only became truly transregional when circumstances were favourable: al-Markāntī dabbled in trade with northern Mali after the French colonial administration had established a regular truck service; Ḥammū Zafzaf was encouraged by national borders and custom restrictions to draw supplies from further south; and the Zijlāwī and Akacem truly started to invest in trans-Saharan trade when, with World War II, profits on the black market were temptingly high. More generally, state involvement remained central to their success, through favourable economic policies and the complacency or active collaboration of state agents, from the Zijlāwī's early cloth smuggling to Mekki's contemporary efforts; the Akacem started their career as suppliers to the French army and then grew rich through smuggling and the Algerian war of independence. Moreover, all trading families invested most of their profits in land, water, houses, and agriculture. At his death, al-Markāntī mainly owned livestock, kept near his place of birth in Abiodh Sidi Cheikh, but other members of his family had acquired extensive gardens and houses in Adrar and Timimoun. The Zijlāwī have made Aoulef what it is today; the Akacem built the centres of Adrar, Timimoun, and Tamanrasset, and Ḥammū Zafzaf and his peers did the same in Kidal and Gao.

Whether situated in the traders' place of birth or in new rallying points set up along the way, such investments provide material backing for the conceptual pattern formed by "settling saints" throughout the region. Undertones of a "civilising mission" in the *bilād al-sūdān* are most apparent in al-Markāntī's story, but they equally inform accounts of the Sahel as given by Zafzaf and – indirectly through failure – in the Zijlāwī's family gossip. Yet such a moral "making of place," much as regional trade more generally, was only possible if traders became closely involved with local families and their ways of life. This involvement is most often represented in marital alliances: most traders discussed in this chapter, with the notable exception of the Akacem, took one or several local wives, usually in addition to earlier marriages back home. These relations were necessary for the organisation of trade, as traders relied on their in-laws for protection, information on routes and markets, and pack animals, guides, and conveyors. Yet it also had a strong impact on the traders' way of life, as southern Algerians were all too easily seduced away from their "civilising mission" by the "sweet life" of the *bādiya* and often built their costly and prestigious houses in the newly founded towns for show. Most importantly, such close entanglement with local societies led to never-ending problems of containment: people went missing, wives and husbands absconded, and children born to "mixed" marriages were never what they appeared to be. The wealth of the Sudan thus came as a poisoned chalice, bearing within it the seeds of decline – or this, at least, is how it is portrayed today. Nonetheless, the ties establish then continue to function today: transborder trade remains largely in the hand of the in-laws of Algerian traders discussed in this chapter. Similarly, as the next chapter will show, throughout the region, debates over morality and concepts of civilisation, rather than, say, economic viability or legal status, continue to underpin local classifications of trade.

3

Dates, Cocaine, and AK 47s

Moral Conundrums on the Algero-Malian Border

At first sight, the situation on the Algero-Malian border today seems very different from that described in Chapter 2: since Algerian independence in 1962, virtually all overland trade between Algeria and Mali has been declared illegal; further, since the 1980s and especially the 1990s, it is no longer in the hands of Algerians, but organised by people from northern Mali, mainly Arabic and Tamasheq speakers.[1] The selection of goods traded has expanded and now ranges from dates and livestock via flour, pasta, petrol, and cigarettes to guns and narcotics. Nonetheless, on closer inspection, parallels with the situation described so far soon become apparent. Although the majority of traders on the ground are by now nationals of Sahelian countries, the more successful among these have long been linked to the Algerian traders described in Chapter 2, as assistants or partners, but most frequently through marital alliances; others work as drivers for Algerian *patrons*. The same resemblance to the past is evident on a structural level: trade is still mainly concerned with high bulk and low value staples, such as pasta, semolina, powdered milk, and petrol. These are consumed within the region and are understood to be indispensible for local survival, particularly in northern Mali. Trade

[1] Research on borderlands in general and on transborder trade in particular has recently been popular in anthropology; see, for example, Amselle and Grégoire (1988), MacGaffey (1991), Roitman (1998, 2005), Botte (1999), Schendel and Abraham (2005), and Tagliacozzo (2005). They are mostly concerned with links between smuggling, state building, and globalisation: see in particular Bayart, Ellis, and Hibou (1999) and Bayart (2004); for a critical appraisal, see Bryceson (2000). See Grégoire (1998), Boubekri (2000), and Bordes and Labrousse (2004) for case studies of Saharan and related North African cases.

continues to be organised by regional networks and is mediated by family connections. It operates within areas marked and maintained by intense social interactions, many of which have grown out of the older regions of heightened connectivity described in Chapter 1, despite the fact that transport infrastructure has changed radically with the spread almost everywhere of truck transport and four-wheel-drive pick-ups.[2]

More recently, new kinds of trade have made their appearance, mostly dealing in cigarettes, arms, and narcotics. Such trade comprises unheard-of possibilities of social mobility, and has thereby put pressure on older ties of solidarity, dependency, and moral control. As much as smuggling is otherwise recognised to be a honourable occupation, these new kinds of businesses are strongly rejected as *ḥarām* (illicit) and as inherently destructive both to society and to the traders who engage in it. Drug smugglers, in particular, are portrayed as little better than beasts and as prone to all kinds of "fratricidal" violence, and *al-frūd al-ḥarām* (illicit smuggling) has in itself become an explanation for all kinds of moral shortcomings, including failed marriages. Most of these suspicions prove groundless, however, as even notorious drug smugglers prefer to invest their gains in recognised status symbols, such as marriage with "good families" and in licit enterprise, whether profitable or not. Moreover, everybody tacitly acknowledges that, with the economic situation being what it is, only *al-frūd al-ḥarām* can provide the funds necessary to lead a truly "moral" lifestyle and the houses, livestock, gardens, and religious education that are essential for it.

AL-KAMIYŪN: LIFE ON A DATE TRUCK

Moral classifications of transborder trade are perhaps best understood by looking at the kinds of vehicles used, the routes chosen, and the rhythm travelled at: inherently sociable and well-manned trans-Saharan trucks that ply routes known to all are opposed to fast and furtive four-wheel-drives that cross the desert by night with lone taciturn drivers. Travelling at a leisurely average speed of perhaps twenty miles per hour, trucks take

[2] This sectional organisation of smuggling not only illustrates, in keeping in line with Chapter 1, the crucial role played by regional infrastructures for international trade, but it also strengthens the argument that assumptions of a coherently organised and homogeneous "underworld economy" are largely illusory (Naylor 2002). In Bayart's (2004: 97) words: "The agents of 'transnational global crime' do not form a homogeneous sociological category either with respect to their internal organisation, their cultural repertoire, and their specialisation or with regards to their aims and their field of action. The latter mostly remain national or local, rather than truly global."

between five days and a week to get from Adrar or Tamanrasset in southern Algeria to Gao in northern Mali during the dry season, and up to three times as long during the rainy season in August. Truck drivers are known to all, their whereabouts never a secret, and even small children can identify the make of trucks and sometimes even individual vehicles from far off by the sound of their engine. They are the most economic means of transport between Algeria and Mali, and no truck would be complete without its twenty-odd travellers on the back, climbing on and off, and making themselves useful whenever manual labour is required. At the discretion of the driver, trucks carry family visitors, transborder peddlers, shepherds, and Malian labour migrants to Algeria. Women travel to visit members of their extended families on both sides of the border, sometimes with babies on their lap to be presented to their cousins, or to pick up birth certificates or other "papers" from the Algerian consulate in Gao.[3] They have their reserved seats in the cab and their own privileged position in the complicated hierarchy that governs truck society. Messages and letters are passed on, petrol bartered against food along the way, and goods dropped off in known depots in the *bādiya*; everybody has his or her own family to supply somewhere along the road, and twenty tons of dates and the truck's conveniently large tanks provide room not only for hitch-hikers, but also their often very heavy and large bags of illegal exports taken in guise of a salary by returning seasonal migrants.[4] Some trucks, especially those owned by Algerian businessmen, make for Gao in a relatively straight line; others, however, can be seen in the most improbable places in the Tilemsi, the *bādiya* between Gao and the Algerian border, acting as true *caboteurs*, peddling dates,

3 As a result of the many transborder marriages concluded by southern Algeria traders (as described in Chapter 2), and due to increasing transborder migration, residents of Algeria often have to travel south to pick up the necessary paperwork to get a passport, register a child, or get married. Others prefer applying for paperwork in the Gao consulate, which they see as easier to deal with than the more anonymous and less familiar offices of the Algerian bureaucracy north of the border. Conversely, many northern Malians prefer to get an Algerian rather than a Malian passport, as the former is seen to be more valuable in international terms; or else, they have two legal identities (often under two different names) that they use according to circumstances.

4 Very little has been published on Sahelian seasonal migration to Algeria, although there is no doubt that it has long been part of local household economies: see Chapter 1 for archival references on labour migration from Kidal to Tamanrasset. On structurally similar seasonal migration to Libya, see Spittler (1993), Pliez (2004), and Brachet (2009). Throughout the Sahel, such seasonal migration is often an essential part of the normal agricultural cycle (see, e.g., Cordell, Gregory, and Piché 1996, Hampshire and Randall 1999, and Rain 1999).

PHOTO 3.1. Trans-Saharan truck.

petrol, and exported Algerian goods against livestock among the local nomadic population.

With Algerian independence, exports from Algeria to Mali and Niger became illegal, with the exception of a short list of goods of supposedly local origin that could be "bartered" and that are, theoretically at least, exempt from taxation. Algerian second-rate dates "that you would not even feed to dogs" and Malian livestock figure most prominantly in this list, alongside more improbable items such as handwoven cloth and dried mangoes.[5] Traders need to be registered with the customs office in Adrar or Tamanrasset have sufficient capital and equipment, and, most importantly, an Algerian passport and official proof of several years of residency. This means that most officially declared trans-Saharan trucks are owned by Algerians but driven and looked after by people from northern Mali.[6] Hence, the truck I travelled with on my first trip overland to Mali

[5] For the full list, see the "Arrêté interministériel du 14/12/1994 fixant les modalités d'exercice du commerce de troc frontalier avec le Niger et le Mali," consulted at the customs in Adrar.

[6] Or else, Malian traders have to pass through a registered Algerian middleman. Further, they cannot export money, but only goods that they often find difficult to sell. Not surprisingly, then, according to official statistics (that Algerian custom officers themselves warned me would "only represent a tiny percentage of actual exchange"), trade with Mali and Niger is rapidly declining, as it has done ever since the devaluation of the franc

was owned by a Sha'anbī trader (see Chapter 1) from Tamanrasset, Nā'imī, whose family had been among the first to settle in the city, and who himself is married to a woman from a locally very influential Tuareg family. The driver, Ighles, was born and brought up in a nomadic camp in the vicinity of Timiaouine on the Algerian border, but he now lives with most of his brothers in a large house in Tamanrasset (see Chapter 6). Ighles's brothers all work in transport, and his eldest brother drives trucks between Adrar and Gao, also for an Algerian *patron*. Their sister Faṭma is married to an Algerian trader in al-Barka near In Salah, who met her on the road as he was peddling goods in the Tilemsi, as so many southern Algerian traders did (see Chapter 2), but she frequently travels to Mali to visit her mother. Like all truck drivers, Ighles works in a team of three, including a lubricator and a mechanic who are his maternal cousins and always travel with him. Another three men completed the initial equipage: two taciturn and excessively thin Tuareg resident in Tamanrasset with impracticable shoes, who were rather cagey about their reasons for travelling, and one young lad of eighteen, Didi, from Touggourt in eastern Algeria, on his first trip to the Sudan. We travelled in a convoy with a second truck, also owned by Nā'imī, and driven by Sīdi 'Alī, an Arab from In Salah, a skinny and melancholy man in his fifties, and one of the very few "real" Algerians who are today employed in the transborder trade as drivers. His crew was motley, including a Songhay from Gao with much trans-Saharan experience, and a couple of *ḥarāṭīn* from In Salah. Sīdi 'Alī was also conveying, free of charge, a Kunta *shaykh* who conspicuously led prayer throughout our journey.[7] Religious personalities often travel with trucks, and on a later trip, Ighles himself gave a lift to a Kunta *shaykh* from his mother's home area of Anefif, whom he treated with all possible respect, despite the latter's penchant for young girls and lewd jokes. Sīdi 'Alī told me much about his former travels, which had for many years taken him from Tamanrasset or In Salah to Kano and Sokoto in northern Nigeria, but whereas Ighles was at home as soon as he crossed the border into Mali, Sīdi 'Alī found himself in a foreign country, a world turned on its head, full of corrupt officials, tropical diseases, and sexual licence. As he was staying in Gao, in

CFA (see Chapter 2), and, by all accounts, traders who still run trucks to Gao do so either out of habit or social obligations or because they have "special reasons," that is to say, because they use legal trade to cover other, less legal and more profitable transborder activities.

7 On the regional influence of the Kunta, both as traders and scholars, see Chapter 1, and later in this chapter; and P. Marty (1920), Génevière (1950), and McDougall (1986).

a rather shabby *garāj* in the *quatrième quartier*, the Arab quarter of Gao and inevitable terminus of all transborder trade, waiting for his truck to be loaded, he was worried about malaria, and maybe a little less so about the various female visitors he received, who were all not quite young anymore, and who seemed to know him well. "Friends of Nāʿimī's," he said with a slightly embarrassed grin.

Sīdi ʿAlī was keen that I tell the world about the hardship of desert travel, and indeed, our days were long, and interrupted only by the five daily prayers. The truck moved slowly, but constantly, with little food and rest; this rhythm only changed in the event of a flat tire (of which we had about ten in six days) or more serious breakdowns, repaired with little or no matching tools and spare parts and much physical force and ingenuity (see Map 3.1). Other, more welcome interruptions were provided by encounters on the road: no truck could ever go past a stopped vehicle without asking whether they needed help, or offering the latest information on road security. All truck drivers know each other and the strength and weaknesses of their machines; they tend to stop in fixed spots at times when they know that they are likely to meet, and invariably share at least the three customary glasses of tea.[8] Drivers invite each other over for lunch and dinner, and some food is always offered to women travelling on other trucks. Moreover, Ighles invariably stops over at his mother's camp near Anefif, spends the night there with his cousins (while the other members of his team remain at a safe distance with the truck), and supplies her with basic staples, brought with him from Algeria: large bags of semolina, rice, powdered milk, and packets of biscuits. On every trip, he spends an afternoon at a Kunta shrine on the way, where he prays, makes offerings, and drinks tea with the resident Kunta family, leaving behind stores of basic foodstuffs. Similar norms of sociality and respect for family obligations govern the truck drivers' interactions with armed robbers and, to a lesser degree, custom officials. When we were held up by four armed men clamouring for their customary share of the load, they let us go past as soon as Ighles – who clearly had met them before – told them that he was travelling "with his family" (i.e., that he had a woman on board), and they apologised: even bandits attacking trucks are

[8] With the introduction of trucks and the establishment of an (albeit rudimentary) road network in the 1940s (see Chapter 2), Saharan routes have became more predictable and unified than they were in the past, although the overall knowledge of possible and impossible trajectories and of other people's whereabouts must have always been of similar concern to traders. Conversely, well-equipped four-by-fours can pass virtually everywhere, and their drivers trade on their ability to escape detection.

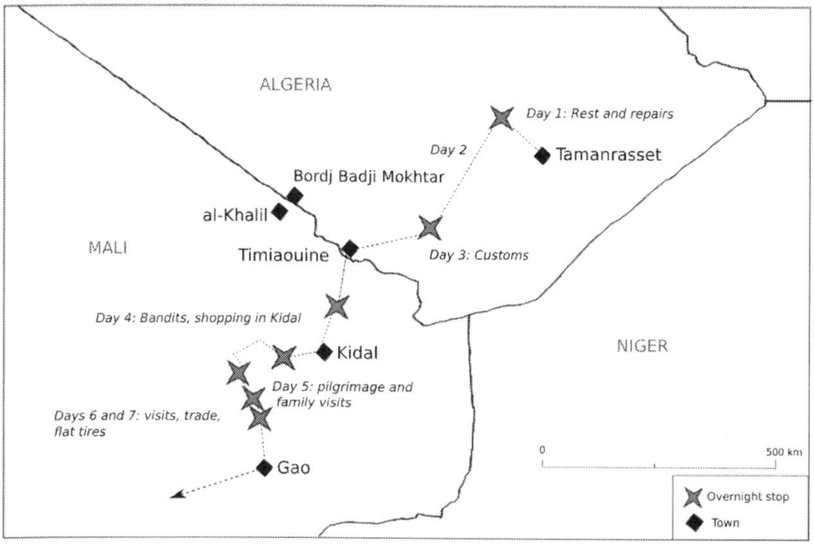

MAP 3.1. Truck trade between Tamanrasset and Gao.

thus bound by recognisable norms and social obligations.[9] Sīdi ʿAlī, more of a stranger in these lands, and who could not speak Tamasheq, was less lucky and got beaten up, before handing over the required petrol and provisions. Similarly, we passed the Malian border with no difficulties, after handing over the customary "presents."[10]

This inherent sociability of the truck trade means that it is difficult to qualify it as either "legal" or "illegal." The bulk of it, dates, indeed goes through customs, as does some of the livestock on the journey back north. But as the driving force behind this trade is the Algerian shortage of meat rather than Malian demand for dates, at least some of the money used to buy livestock is directly exported from Algeria or, rather, earned through less legal transactions on the way, especially the sale of petrol.[11] On each of his trips, Ighles carries enough staples to feed his extended

[9] This is reminiscent of the account of a *ghazū* given by Albert, "Une razzia au Sahel" (see Chapter 1). Similarly stringent social norms used to govern raiding throughout the area (see, e.g., Caratini 1989, Claudot-Hawad 1996) but are partly suspended for more illicit forms of transborder trade (see below).

[10] For the customary nature of these "presents" in the similar setting of northern Niger, see Brachet (2005).

[11] Even the legal "barter" of dates against sheep never takes place as a direct transaction: as in the past (described in Chapter 2), dates are sold in bulk to wholesalers in Gao, who distribute them throughout the country. Livestock is bought in small quantities from local producers, known or related to the drivers.

family and the Kunta sanctuary, and most members of his team do the same. Seasonal labour migrants on their way back to Mali often carry goods rather than money with them, staples again, but also building materials, bags of concrete or, as on one occasion, enough steel frames for the construction of a house. Women visiting their families on either side of the border never travel empty-handed but carry bags of veils, incense, gold, and perfume up into Algeria, bringing back more "modern" luxury items such as electronic goods, nappies, biscuits, sweets, and manufactured clothes. Most women in northern Mali have sisters or at least cousins resident in either Tamanrasset or Adrar, and transborder exchange is thus vivid, socially acceptable, and lucrative (see also Chapter 6). As a result, trucks tend to stop at known dropping-off points and hideouts in the *bādiya* before reaching Gao, to rearrange their loads and unload parts of it; some drop off most of the petrol in their tanks to unofficial "service stations" in the *bādiya*.[12] The reminder is unloaded in Gao itself, in one of the many *gawārij* in the *quatrième quartier*, before clearing customs on the other side of town. Hence, our first port of call was a *garāj* owned by a Timbuktien nicknamed Baba Gasoil. Its large courtyard was filled with large barrels of petrol, into which he siphoned whatever was left in our tanks, while two of his four wives took care of me and served large plates of boiled meat to the men. Baba Gasoil owns the largest petrol station in Gao and supplies most of the Malian military at special prices.[13] He acts as a host and local agent to many Algerian truckers, although such privileged relations need to be entertained carefully – while I was there, he fell out with Ighles, who straight away redirected his trade to a neighbouring

[12] This system of unmanned depots in the desert where goods could be stored quite safely until their owner picked them up again seems to go back a long time, see, for example, Laperrine's report of a raid to Tawdanni (Laperrine, "Tournée à Taodeni," 1906, CAOM 22H24) and cases of dispute over such goods recorded by McDougall (1985) and Lydon (2008). In contemporary Mali, such depots can be found around most towns, where large loads are left until they can be taken into town in smaller quantities. As everybody knows what belongs to whom, these depots are relatively safe, and although of course disputes are frequent, anonymous theft is quite difficult.

[13] The export of refined petrol from Algeria to neighbouring country is illegal, but, due to considerable price differences with its neighbours, it has become the mainstay of transborder economies: see Y. Chmirou, "Du pétrole bidon," *Marco Hebdo International*, May 2003, and "Trafic de carburant de l'Algérie vers le Maroc: les coupables en prison," *La Gazette du Maroc*, 10/11/2007, for the Algerian border with Morocco; K. Assia, "Le traffic de carburant en Algérie bat son plein," *Le Quotidien d'Oran*, 2006, for the south; and "Algérie: traffic de carburant vers la Tunisie," *Le soir d'Algérie*, 15/05/2010, for the eastern border with Tunisia.

garāj, as demand for Algerian goods – and especially Algerian petrol – is always high.

The trip from Tamanrasset to Gao might take anything between four and twenty days. Drivers and their assistants stay on either end for as long as it takes to reload the trucks and then set off again: this means that they spend more time on the road than "back home." Much of this, however, is not only due to their exploitation by ruthless businessmen but rather to their own taste: even where cities are within reach, they prefer to sleep out in the *bādiya*, which is "cleaner" and more peaceful, and, most importantly, theirs. Truck travel is a way of life, with its own hierarchy of driver, mechanic, lubricator, and mere hand, in which drivers are kings, a position earned less by appointment by a distant trader than through knowledge, hard work, and endurance. A driver's decision is difficult to argue with, and owners of trucks seem to have accepted that drivers travel at their own rhythm, or not at all. Truck trading is based on and creates its own social networks, which include families and local religious dignitaries as well as custom officials and traders on both ends and along the way; a hierarchy that might be at odds with Algerian official conceptions of value, but is, in northern Mali, understood to be central to local society. Ighles and his companions define themselves not as traders, and even less as employees, but rather, albeit with a slight ironic smile, as "nomads," *ruḥḥūl*. They pride themselves on their sense of direction and their gallantry, which sets them apart from Malian or "black" drivers, as much as on their mechanical skills and stamina. When Didi at one stop started to pray by himself at night, facing the wrong direction, everybody burst out laughing: they clearly did not produce many guides, then, in Touggourt or wherever he was from.[14] This intimate connection of truck trade with local categories of value and socially approved transborder connections explains why women should never go to al-Khalīl, but can safely travel on trans-Saharan trucks; and this is also why, from a local point of view at least, there is no doubt that the slow and meandering rhythm of truck travel, although trucks are quite as much involved in carrying smuggled goods as other means of transport, is morally sound.

[14] Touggourt is an important date-growing oasis in eastern Algeria near the Tunisian border. Equipped with mechanised irrigation since colonial times, it has become one of the centres of production for the famous Deglet Nour date variety, one of the rare Algerian agricultural products destined for export. As such, it is beyond the region of frequent interchange known to Ighles's equipage (i.e., the area between Gao, Tamanrasset, and Adrar) and follows social and economic logics that they are unfamiliar with.

AL-FRŪD AL-ḤALĀL: LICIT SMUGGLING

Ighles's subsidiary trade in pasta and semolina represents but a small proportion of staples brought across the border each day. Indeed, without this constant traffic, as all traders, *Chambre de Commerce* representatives, and customs officials readily admit, the people of northern Mali would probably starve.[15] This dependency is ancient, as shown in Chapters 1 and 2; it has been aggravated by successive food crises in Mali, with the growing difference of wealth between the two countries and the poor development of national infrastructure in Mali.[16] Neither Timbuktu nor Kidal are directly accessible by paved road; and travel by car – let alone by truck – from Kidal to the Malian capital Bamako takes at least three days. Bamako itself largely relies on expensive imports from further south. More importantly, transport in Mali is very dear, even by European standards, due to high fuel prices, high import taxes on vehicles, and considerable wear and tear on bad roads. In Algeria, on the other hand, petrol is cheap – *bāṭil*, free of charge, as people say – and the hard surface of the Tanezrouft, the uninhabited area of *reg* (hard stony surface) that lies across the border is easier to drive on than most Malian roads. Furthermore, from the former Algerian president Boumediene's economic reforms in the 1970s to the early 1990s when the World Bank imposed structural adjustment on the Algerian economy, basic food staples were subsidised in Algeria and thus were considerably cheaper than in Mali (see Chapter 2). Today, profit margins have dropped considerably, as, due to an explosion in prices in Algeria, price differentials on either side of the border have diminished.[17] Nonetheless, people continue to export basic foodstuffs illegally, because it has become a habit, because they have few other choices, and because many fail to include the wear and tear on their vehicles in their calculations of profit. Locally, people

[15] The following paragraphs are based on interviews conducted in Gao and Kidal, with the two presidents of the local *Chambres de Commerce*, but also with traders, drivers and their families, in winter 2007–8.

[16] For a brief history of food policy in Mali since independence, see Phelinas (1991, 1992).

[17] After structural reforms were implemented in the late 1980s, prices of basic foodstuffs in Algeria rose considerably, by up to a third in the worst years. In 1996, when some stability was reached, prices were on average five times higher than they had been in 1989. Forced by popular discontent, the Algerian government reverted to subsidising basic foodstuffs, such as bread and milk; in February 2010, the Algerian government announced that various basic products, including semolina, flour, couscous, and pasta, would be subsidised again, that prices would be kept low through regulation, and that subsidised produce would be prohibited from export.

have grown used to Algerian products, and, most importantly perhaps, they prefer to continue functioning within known social networks that for most inhabitants of northern Mali stretch north rather than south, generally go beyond the purely commercial, and that in turn need to be maintained by daily contact and traffic across the border – networks that have often directly grown out of the regional interdependence described in Chapters 1 and 2.

The traffic in staples is well organised, and flourishes in the grey zone between legal and illegal enterprise. Algerian traders or, more rarely, Malian refugees with Algerian nationality set up a trading company based in Adrar or Tamanrasset, with an outlet in Bordj Badji Mokhtar or Timiaouine on the Algero-Malian border (see Map I.1). They obtain permission to export large quantities of staples to either of these two border posts, on trucks. These trucks are unloaded as soon as they arrive. At nightfall, the goods are put onto smaller cars that come up from al-Khalīl or Kidal and shuttled across the border. Sometimes, even camels or donkeys are used, as they can easily evade controls by custom officials and allow people with little or no means to earn their (small) share of profits. These goods are either taken straight to Gao or Kidal or transshipped again in al-Khalīl onto Malian trucks that take the merchandise to Gao or Timbuktu. This last leg of the journey is either organised by full-time transporters who sell their goods wholesale to known traders or by traders themselves who order what they need from merchants in Bordj Badji Mokhtar or Timiaouine. Hence, one of the best-known traders in Timbuktu travels twice a month to Bordj for the pleasures of the road and in order to keep an eye on the quality of his goods. Hammed, an Algerian from Batna in the Algerian northeast who owns a well-stocked shop in Gao, usually buys goods from certain drivers he knows once they arrive in Gao. For important deals, his assistant, a Rgaybat from Tindouf in southwestern Algeria, travels up to al-Khalīl to negotiate with suppliers higher up the chain, while also benefitting from the occasion to invest in some trade of his own.[18] Larger traders own their own

[18] Tindouf has been an important commercial centre for trade throughout northern Mali, southern Morocco, and Mauritania since the mid-nineteenth century (Lenz 1884, see also Caratini 1989). Today, the town and the adjacent refugee camps – established with the onset of the war in 1975 and run by the independentist Polisario Front (for more detail on the Western Sahara conflict, see Hodges 1983, Lawless and Monahan 1997, and Zunes and Mundy 2010) – are allegedly involved in all kinds of illegal and illicit trade, partly fuelled through international aid, partly maintained by the legendary mobility and far-reaching commercial networks of its Rgaybat and Tajakanat inhabitants.

means of transport; hence, Abdessalam, the president of the *Chambre de Commerce* in Kidal, who owns the town's largest bakeries and petrol station, draws all of his supplies from Timiaouine, the nearest Algerian border post, and has them carried to Kidal on his own three trucks; if customs are "particular" one morning, or his trucks break down, there is no bread in Kidal, and the petrol station runs dry.[19]

Mostly, however, transport is run independently from retail, and as a result trucks and jeeps usually carry mixed loads. This was well reflected in a journey I undertook from al-Khalīl to Gao on the back of a four-wheel-drive Toyota, owned by an Arab from the Tilemsi resident in Gao whose brother ran a *garāj* in al-Khalīl. The owner drove the car himself, with the help of his teenage Tuareg apprentice, who crouched on the back with the merchandise. For this particular trip, he had rented the carrying capacity of his car to Lahcène, a trader from Algiers who was a rather unpopular figure throughout the area: he breathed guile and excessive fondness of drink, and, as he leered at my veil in a meaningful way, told me that he used to run a bar in Greece. Lahcène's own charge consisted in pasta, biscuits, and packets of juice, bought on his own account, and that, several days later, I saw him trying to sell to Hammed, the Algerian shopkeeper in Gao. He had sublet parts of the car's carrying capacity – and a seat in the cab – to a Malian Arab lady from Tamanrasset, who had her own load of goods, mainly pasta, to be sold in Gao. Lahcène had also sold eighteen passages to a very diverse crowd of migrants, including one woman, from Ghana, Guinea, Cameroon, Congo, and Nigeria on their way to Gao, and to three Malian Arabs and an elderly Tuareg from Libya, who was rather flustered by the lack of good manners displayed by everybody around him during the trip, when he was not worried about being squeezed to death by his hearty Nigerian neighbour.[20] On our arrival in

[19] Abdessalam has a long history of trading successes, risk taking, and failure and seems to be rather used to operating in the margins of legality. A Tamasheq speaker of a good Kidal family, his family lost everything in the famine of the 1970s; he then went to Burkina Faso and Nigeria to work as a trader, smuggling petrol across the border and growing very rich in a very short time – drugs are nothing compared to this, he says. He was busted by the customs and lost it all in a day (on petrol smuggling between Nigeria and Niger, see Grégoire 1986). He then started again in Gao, making money fast; the 1990s rebellion came along, and his house and new cars were burned to the ground. He now invests in "everything," just to make sure. He started the *Chambre de Commerce* in Kidal, lobbied for the opening of the first bank, and is among its major wholesale traders, but gossip has it that at least some of his capital is invested with his cousins who engage in rather less licit kinds of transborder trade.

[20] By all accounts, migrants travelling up and into Algeria used to draw on specialised transport, arranged in the "ghettoes" of Gao and Kidal. With the increasingly restrictive

PHOTO 3.2. Northern Malian traders.

Gao, we were immediately picked up by a customs official on a scooter, a close acquaintance of both Lahcène's and the drivers', who followed us to the *garāj* in the *quatrième quartier* that was to be the end of our journey. While I was helping the Arab lady to unload her various boxes of pasta, Lahcène negotiated with the officer and then immediately recovered most of the money paid from his West African passengers, with the help of the Songhay official threatening imprisonment.

Transborder trade in staples remains thus relatively "democratic": anybody with a four-by-four, some initial capital, and enough cousins along the road can become a carrier or else trade on his own account, and deals with Malian custom officials are commonplace and cheap. By all accounts, the same used to be true of cigarette and petrol smuggling. Cigarette smuggling took off in the early 1980s. Cigarettes, either Chinese counterfeit or real semiofficial imports, are unloaded in the major harbours on the Gulf of Guinea, whence they are carried north overland. They are redistributed

migration policy in Algeria, mainly caused by EU pressures, Gao has ceased to be a migration hub, and most migrants I met were either stuck in Gao or Kidal, having been expulsed from Algeria and waiting for things to clear up, or travelling south. For more detail on these ghettoes, see Chapter 6.

), cross the Maghrib and the Mediterranean, and are sold ...tern Europe. Most trade goes through Niger where it is ... Nigerien authorities provide escorts and receive 10 per ...all value of the merchandise, while entry in Libya and ...illegal.[21] Among the first to invest in cigarette smuggling were the Zijlāwī, with the intermediary of al-Mukhṭār's half-brother, Ṭayyib (see Chapter 2).[22] Sent by his uncle Sī Ḥammādi to set up a trade route through northern Niger, Ṭayyib quickly realised that he could only succeed if he managed to harness preexisting social networks:

> You need to find a tribe that is both weak but not too weak and strong but not too strong. If they are too strong, they will charge you lots of money and might just make off with all the merchandise, and there is nothing you can do about this. If they are too weak than you might get away cheaply, but they won't be able to help you when things go wrong, and usually that also means that they do not have enough men, guns and cars to do the job. I was lucky: I found an Arab tribe who were just right, with a young representative who was rather ambitious and intelligent and understood right away that I could make his fortune. I made sure that he had a good reputation, and then gave him a first load of cigarettes, on credit. That was risky: he could easily just have gone off with it and never be seen again. But he came back – I was so worried while I was waiting for him, in Agadez, wondering how I could ever face Sī Ḥammādi if he hadn't.[23]

The tribe provided men, guns, and cars; and Ṭayyib never inquired much into where they sold the goods. They had their own middlemen in Algeria and Libya who took cigarettes wholesale and sold them on the local market or to other transporters who carried them into Europe. Delighted by his early success, Sī Ḥammādi decided to branch out into production, and Ṭayyib thenceforth employed his talents designing cigarette packets and blending tobacco. A joint venture with a known American company failed, however, showing nevertheless that boundaries between "legal" and "illegal" ventures were fluid.[24]

[21] In 1995, these 10 per cent amounted to almost six billion F CFA (Grégoire 2000: 244). Brachet (2009: 124) estimates the overall trade to be worth 27 billion of F CFA in 2004.

[22] Between 1991 and 1996, much if this business was managed by the SOBIMEX, a Lebanese company based in London and operating mainly in Niger. The company was dissolved for tax fraud in 1996 (Grégoire 2000: 244).

[23] Interviewed in Adrar, March 2008.

[24] Nordstrom (2007: 22) claims that 50 per cent of all cigarettes traded worldwide are smuggled, and that, therefore, most large cigarette companies quite simply have to actively cater for it. For the rather difficult distinction between "legal" and "illegal" businesses, see MacGaffey (1991) and Roitman (2005).

PHOTO 3.2. Northern Malian traders.

Gao, we were immediately picked up by a customs official on a scooter, a close acquaintance of both Lahcène's and the drivers', who followed us to the *garāj* in the *quatrième quartier* that was to be the end of our journey. While I was helping the Arab lady to unload her various boxes of pasta, Lahcène negotiated with the officer and then immediately recovered most of the money paid from his West African passengers, with the help of the Songhay official threatening imprisonment.

Transborder trade in staples remains thus relatively "democratic": anybody with a four-by-four, some initial capital, and enough cousins along the road can become a carrier or else trade on his own account, and deals with Malian custom officials are commonplace and cheap. By all accounts, the same used to be true of cigarette and petrol smuggling. Cigarette smuggling took off in the early 1980s. Cigarettes, either Chinese counterfeit or real semiofficial imports, are unloaded in the major harbours on the Gulf of Guinea, whence they are carried north overland. They are redistributed

migration policy in Algeria, mainly caused by EU pressures, Gao has ceased to be a migration hub, and most migrants I met were either stuck in Gao or Kidal, having been expulsed from Algeria and waiting for things to clear up, or travelling south. For more detail on these ghettoes, see Chapter 6.

in Burkina Faso, cross the Maghrib and the Mediterranean, and are sold throughout Western Europe. Most trade goes through Niger where it is semilegal, as the Nigerien authorities provide escorts and receive 10 per cent of the overall value of the merchandise, while entry in Libya and Algeria remains illegal.[21] Among the first to invest in cigarette smuggling were the Zijlāwī, with the intermediary of al-Mukhṭār's half-brother, Ṭayyib (see Chapter 2).[22] Sent by his uncle Sī Ḥammādi to set up a trade route through northern Niger, Ṭayyib quickly realised that he could only succeed if he managed to harness preexisting social networks:

> You need to find a tribe that is both weak but not too weak and strong but not too strong. If they are too strong, they will charge you lots of money and might just make off with all the merchandise, and there is nothing you can do about this. If they are too weak than you might get away cheaply, but they won't be able to help you when things go wrong, and usually that also means that they do not have enough men, guns and cars to do the job. I was lucky: I found an Arab tribe who were just right, with a young representative who was rather ambitious and intelligent and understood right away that I could make his fortune. I made sure that he had a good reputation, and then gave him a first load of cigarettes, on credit. That was risky: he could easily just have gone off with it and never be seen again. But he came back – I was so worried while I was waiting for him, in Agadez, wondering how I could ever face Sī Ḥammādi if he hadn't.[23]

The tribe provided men, guns, and cars; and Ṭayyib never inquired much into where they sold the goods. They had their own middlemen in Algeria and Libya who took cigarettes wholesale and sold them on the local market or to other transporters who carried them into Europe. Delighted by his early success, Sī Ḥammādi decided to branch out into production, and Ṭayyib thenceforth employed his talents designing cigarette packets and blending tobacco. A joint venture with a known American company failed, however, showing nevertheless that boundaries between "legal" and "illegal" ventures were fluid.[24]

[21] In 1995, these 10 per cent amounted to almost six billion F CFA (Grégoire 2000: 244). Brachet (2009: 124) estimates the overall trade to be worth 27 billion of F CFA in 2004.

[22] Between 1991 and 1996, much if this business was managed by the SOBIMEX, a Lebanese company based in London and operating mainly in Niger. The company was dissolved for tax fraud in 1996 (Grégoire 2000: 244).

[23] Interviewed in Adrar, March 2008.

[24] Nordstrom (2007: 22) claims that 50 per cent of all cigarettes traded worldwide are smuggled, and that, therefore, most large cigarette companies quite simply have to actively cater for it. For the rather difficult distinction between "legal" and "illegal" businesses, see MacGaffey (1991) and Roitman (2005).

In northern Mali, the cigarette trade seems to have been even less centralised, but organised in a similar way: people say that anybody with some capital, a car, and a few friends could apply to known central dealers, who would take them on trust because of their family's social capital and supply them with merchandise and credit, without trying to exercise undue control over their whereabouts or internal organisation. Petrol smuggling out of Algeria used to be organised in much the same fashion. Today, however, it seems that both cigarette and petrol smuggling are gradually being taken over by larger organisations, supposedly based in Algeria and Libya; these organisations employ northern Malians as mere drivers, and on a strictly individual basis. Such drivers do not own their cars, neither are they involved in the negotiation of prices either end; they are paid a fixed fee per journey undertaken and have no share in profits or indeed control over the route taken. The reasons given for this development vary, but they generally turn on falling profit margins, especially in the cigarette trade, which means that smaller traders find it more difficult to make a living, and on growing pressure by state officials who confiscate or even burn loads and cars if they apprehend smugglers, a loss that is impossible to sustain for smaller traders.[25] Meanwhile, larger organisations are rumoured to have the necessary protections to avoid retaliation altogether. And indeed, most cigarettes and petrol smugglers I knew were working not with friends and on their own account, but as salaried drivers for Algerian patrons.

A good example here are Rashīd and his cousin Muḥammad: a member of the Awlād Sīdi, a high-status nomadic family of religious descent from near Bourem in northern Mali with longstanding ties to the Zijlāwī (see Chapter 2), Rashīd was brought up in Bani w-Iskut, the Sahelian quarter of Adrar, where his mother, sister, and wife – a girl brought over from the northern Malian *bādiya* – still live (see Chapter 6). His job is centred on al-Khalīl, from where he drives every second day to Abalessa, the first petrol station in Algeria on the road to Tamanrasset, fills his various tanks, waits for nightfall, and then races back again – roughly 1,600 kilometres there and back, on bad mud-roads, and half of it in the middle of the night without headlights. Now in his early thirties, Rashīd looks both too old and too young to be his age: his lifestyle is clearly not conducive to fresh looks, but his position of relative dependence and insecurity

[25] This is part of a more general crack-down by border officials in the area, partly sparked by European security concerns and worries about immigration, that have so far mainly benefitted larger and more properly "criminal" organisations on the ground. For a similar observation in northern Niger, see Brachet (2011).

has not given him the demeanour of a grown man either. His cousin Muḥammad, who is in his mid-twenties, shuttles smuggled cigarettes between al-Khalīl and Adrar. His *patron* lives in Bordj Badji Mokhtar, owns several four-by-fours, and employs roughly a dozen young drivers, all Arabs or Tuareg from northern Mali, and all unrelated. Muḥammad grew up in Bordj Badji Mokhtar and went to school there, but as he was never quite Algerian enough despite his Algerian passport, he could not find a job, nor could he work in Mali where his Arabic education is of no use. It is doubtful in any case that he really would have preferred a subordinate and badly paid job in either country to driving a fast Toyota through the desert at night. When he was just sixteen, he was caught smuggling, arrested, and spent several months in prison in Adrar. The journal he kept in prison, and which his sister Lalla dutifully preserved, written in careful and somewhat halting school Arabic with at times improbable spelling, speaks of anguish, loneliness, and utter helplessness. He was released after the family, with their distant Algerian relations' help, presented a fake birth certificate that claimed that he was fourteen and thus not legally responsible; he picked up his job as a cigarette smuggler the next day, and later became involved in drug runs. Last year, he was caught again and has not yet been released; rumour has it that he is routinely tortured by the Algerian security forces, keen to obtain the names of his colleagues and *patron*; his family have almost despaired of ever seeing him again.

THREATENING THE ORDER OF THINGS

Personal animosities and "accidents" with the Algerian security forces set aside, *al-frūd* (from the French *fraude*), as the smuggling of staples is locally referred to, is recognised to be a respectable way of earning a living. Indeed, the term *al-frūd* has come to designate Saharan trade more generally, with not the slightest hint of shame; and children happily and very proudly describe their fathers as "*aṣḥāb al-frūd*" or smugglers. In some cases, however, traders who have grown rich in the Lahda or cigarette trade are loudly condemned, less for what they do than for who they are, or rather, who they used to be. As seen in Chapter 2, Algerian traders often intermarried with nomadic Arab families from the Tilemsi of subordinate status. They employed their in-laws as peddlers and subsidiary traders, thereby allowing the latter to accumulate experience and at times considerable capital. Most Algerian traders left northern Mali in the mid-1990s, due to the reigning insecurity (see Chapter 4), but also because they had reached retirement age and could not convince a son to replace them. More often than not, they passed their businesses on to their former employees, some say, under constraint: by then, Algerians felt less than welcome in Gao and always feared expropriation. Local Arab traders had also branched out into cigarette smuggling, and, rumour has it, the regional arms trade that was expanding fast as a result of the collapse of the Soviet Union and of increased local demand due to the widespread violence and fear of the early 1990s – thereby, according to local gossip, abetting or even actively encouraging "fratricide" (see Chapter 4). Some had gained further experience in refugee camps in Algeria, in the 1970s, 1980s, and 1990s, where by all accounts the black market sale of international aid was rife.[26] Forcefully "encouraged" to leave Algeria in the late 1990s, they converted these new skills and their knowledge of southern Algerian trade routes into booming commercial activities. Today, all of these traders are collectively referred to as "Tangara Arabs," with reference to the main Arab village on the track between Kidal and Gao.[27]

In everyday conversations, the term "Tangara Arab" inevitably implies disdain, if only through reference to an identity that hinges on assumed ties with a minor and neglected settlement of no prestige: "They do not know who their own grandparents are," as Muḥammad's elder sister Lalla scoffed, "all they know is that they were the Kunta's slaves, they might have come from anywhere, and worse they do not even care."[28] Or, according to Mūlāy Sharīf, Zayda's uncle, "you shouldn't even call them 'Tangara Arabs' – do they really come from Tangara? Do they come from anywhere? How can it be then that they are so wealthy and Tangara is

[26] Following severe drought in the early 1970s, camps were set up by the Red Cross in Timiaouine and Bordj Badji Mokhtar, on the Algerian side of the Algero-Malian border. They were supplied by the Algerian Red Cross, and by all local accounts, corruption was widespread (for a more general appraisal of this, see Comité d'Information Sahel 1975).

[27] Tangara (officially al-Mostagham) is the largest Arab village between Gao and Anefif. Although many "Tangara Arabs" are actually from neighbouring villages or the *bādiya*, Tangara, as it has some shops that played an important part in the Lahda period, has come to stand for the area as such.

[28] According to local oral history, the Arabic-speaking population who are today resident in the Tilemsi between Gao and Kidal are descendants of Mauritanian tribesmen who followed the appeal of the Kunta for military help against the Iwellemeden, a then dominant and rapidly expanding federation under the leadership of Tamasheq speakers centred on Menaka. After their defeat, they decided to stay in the area but remained subordinate to the Kunta. This was probably part of the well-documented attempt by the Kunta Ahl Shaykh Sīdi al-Mukhṭār to extend their political influence to the east in the nineteenth century (see Shaykh Bāy, "Ta'rīkh Kanāta wa-'l-Sūq," MS n° 90 of the de Gironcourt Collection at the Institut de France in Paris; and P. Marty 1920, Urvoy 1936). On the Iwellemeden, see Richer (1924) and Grémont (2010).

but a heap of mud, no house constructed there, no school?" In popular explanations, this "rootlessness" quickly becomes ruthlessness and serves to explain their supposedly dishonourable success. Yet this explanation is perhaps best turned on its head: almost none of the activities really engaged in by most Tangara Arabs is seen as morally tainted per se, had they not allowed formerly "lowly" people to improve their status and now to "look down" on "people who are better than them." In the early 2000s, these tensions came to a head: until then, the Tangara Arabs had each year paid the *jiziya* ("tribute") to the head of the regional Kunta.[29] Now, with reference to their wealth and actual social standing in the area, they refused to do so; worse, they put forward their own candidate in the local elections, and, worse again, their candidate won.[30] In the aftermath of the elections, as Kunta continued to try and collect their "dues," violence broke out between Kunta and non-Kunta Arabs throughout the region, and several dozen people died before tempers cooled down; marriages broke up, sometimes violently; and many Kunta sought refuge among Tamasheq speakers in Kidal and its surroundings – remember Ighles's devotion to Kunta shrines and scholars.[31] Although by now, an uneasy peace has returned to the area, formerly high-status Arabs, and especially Kunta, strongly resent their former clients' success as destructive to proper social relations and ties; hence, perhaps, the commonly shared assumption that their fortunes must necessarily be based on "dirty," illicit, and fratricidal dealings.

The most notorious and publicly condemned "Tangara Arab" in Gao is Khuwī. Perhaps the richest inhabitant of Gao, he runs a large retail shop and owns an impressive number of petrol stations throughout Mali, as well as a booming transport business, both for goods and people, with regular overland services to Niamey, Bamako, and the Mauritanian capital Nouakchott. He has recently finished the construction of a vast villa in the *quatrième quartier* that takes up a whole housing block, is surrounded by

[29] Although throughout the Arabic-speaking world, the *jiziya* denotes the headtax paid by "protected people" (*dhimmi*s, Jews and Christians), in the Western Sahara, it is routinely translated as "tribute" paid by groups of lower status to their "protectors," with reference to an earlier history of conversion (see Hall 2011: 146).

[30] Mali experienced its "democratic transition" after the end of the military dictatorship in 1991. First parliamentary elections were held in 1997. For different perspectives on this process, see Tag (1994), Fay (1995a), Nijenhuis (2003), and Wing (2008).

[31] Nothing has so far been published on this "war of the Kunta" as it is referred to locally, apart from a small number of newspaper articles in the Malian national press. See for instance M. Cissé, "Gao: assassinat de quatre arabes Kounta: l'État tente de faire prévaloir la justice sur la vengeance," *L'Essor*, 8/01/2003; and C. Sylla, "Arabes et Kounta: le sang coule à nouveau," *Le Républicain*, 14/09/2004.

a high wall that restricts access to the selected few, and is rumoured to be the very epitome of wealth, luxury, and refinement in the midst of which Khuwī "sits on the ground on his own and eats rice with his fingers." Khuwī is from a poor nomadic family in the Tilemsi, who had nothing, he said, and he started off penniless, as a boy, selling cigarettes and sweets in the streets. Judging from his own account, he then went to Libya to work on building sites.[32] This is where he earned his first capital to set up his company, which specialises uniquely in trade with the south: he insisted that all rumours of his involvement in transborder trade with Algeria are totally unfounded, as even his supply of petrol comes in through the large ports, Lomé and Cotonou, although he has hired out some of his petrol tanks to the Algerian national oil company (Sonatrach) prospecting north of Timbuktu.[33] Popular versions of his rise to wealth confirm his modest origins in the Tilemsi, and especially dwell on his family's low status. His trip to Libya, however, is seen as his first involvement in unspeakably "dirty deals." Gossip has it that he collaborated with Algerians during the heydays of the Lahda period, making money on the side and then, in the troubled early 1990s, took over their businesses, allegedly by threatening his patrons with violence and eviction. His real fortune was made in arms dealing throughout the 1990s, smuggling cigarettes and "selling guns to blacks," as outraged Arabs would whisper behind closed doors. Today, he is taken to be responsible for the best part of petrol illegally exported from Algeria, and he is rumoured to be involved both in the drug trade and in people smuggling. These rumours are tenacious, although today Khuwī makes a great effort to legalise his business and to raise his educational, moral, and social standing. His piety is conspicuous; he has married a "very white woman" of noble origin; he invests in tea and date imports and employs several Kunta, one university-educated Malian and two others from Algeria, in his office to "square it all with the law" (and good "morals"), as the former proudly told me.[34]

[32] Migration from northern Mali and Niger to Libya has long been common in the area, and increased exponentially with the droughts of the 1970s and 1980s, and Ghaddafi's attempts to redefine Libya as an "African" power: see E. Bernus (1999), Grégoire (1999), and Pliez (2004).

[33] On Algerian oil prospecting in northern Mali, see C. Takiou, "Le Mali fait appel à l'Algérie pour trouver du pétrole," *Forum Algérie*, 24/11/2008; A. Koné, "Le ministre des mines en visite au bloc de Taodeni," *L'Indépendant*, 1/06/2009; and M. Benachour, "Nepad, grand gazoduc transafricain Nigal, contrats au Sahel ... Sonatrach part à la conquête de l'Afrique," *Algérie 360*, 26/12/2009.

[34] Not all traders of formerly lowly status try to use their newly gained wealth to better their local status; some clearly think that they have other fish to fry and other audiences to play to. Hence Muḥammad 'Abdī, originally a *ḥarṭānī* from the Touat, first came to

Yet the Tangara Arabs by no means hold the monopoly of envious whispers and moral criticism: the fratricidal violence of the 2000s is also widely acknowledged to have "corrupted" the Kunta themselves, upsetting internal as much as external hierarchies. As such, it serves as convenient shorthand to explain contemporary fortunes made in "illicit" trade, which tend to be traced back to moral shortcomings rooted in an excess of (the wrong kind of) violence. An example of this is Abidine, or rather, popular accounts of his startling career. Abidine is a Kunta Arab originally from the vicinity of Bourem near Gao, who now lives in Kidal in a large and very conspicuous villa, where he runs a shop selling rare treats – juice, chocolate, and cheese and ready-made clothes imported from Saudi Arabia – to a select and remarkably small group of customers. When I came to talk to him, Abidine smiled and said he knew all about me, from a friend (a drug smuggler from Niger whom I had met in al-Khalīl). He was at pains to show me just how outraged he was by my suggestions that he would know anything at all about drug smuggling or trade with Algeria. All he had, he said, was one truck that travelled overland to Lomé, to deal in clothes and sweets. Local stories about him, however, suggest that he had lived in the *bādiya* north of Bourem in rather squalid circumstances, engaged in small-scale trade and peddling for the account of some cousins of his, who had a shop in Gao. His good fortune only started in the 1990s, when, according to local gossip, he discovered his "passion" for killing and looting, and "in cold blood shot whole families, women and children, in order to fill his pockets or maybe only for the fun of it." He also made some money from arms dealing. With the "war of the Kunta" he moved to Kidal, again after having committed some notable massacres, "against his own former friends and brothers," that allegedly provided the necessary capital for his current business. Fleeing from revenge, he arrived in Kidal as the cocaine boom started and quickly invested in it, drawing on supplies coming in through Mauritania and – of course – Togo. Although such accounts have to be taken with a pinch of salt, they bear witness to the easy association between rapid social climbing, and accusations of

Gao working as a driver for his sharifian patron. He gradually took over the latter's business and now owns it fully; he is one of the wealthiest businessmen in Gao, and certainly the only one who can be seen in his shop, day after day, in shirtsleeves, sweaty, and very visibly hard at work. He has never tried to hide his low status, and he is excluded from the "better" Arab social circles: as people say, once a *ḥarṭānī*, always a *ḥarṭānī* – and he smiles with a resigned shrug. His ambition lies elsewhere: he has sent his two sons to business school in the United States, thus bypassing local social hierarchies altogether.

immorality, disrespect for proper social ties, or even, as in this case, an absence of all human feeling bordering on bestiality.[35]

MAFIA PROBLEMS

The Lahda trade has an ambiguous status in local perception: it is seen as an inherently honourable occupation that makes it possible to exploit the region's perhaps most important "natural" resource, the Algerian border, while strengthening family ties and relations. Yet where it leads to profound social changes and a questioning of regional hierarchies, some families at least consider it to be morally tainted, not for what it is, but for what it allows to happen. A similar sociocentric logic is at work in the moral judgment applied to other types of commerce that flourish in the border area: arms and drug trafficking and trade in stolen cars. Everybody locally agrees that the gun, car, and drug trade are firmly in the hands of large-scale centralised organisations locally referred to as "mafias." Guns come in from China through the ports of Lomé and Cotonou; cars are detaxed and provided with "official" Mauritanian paperwork in al-Khalīl; drugs come in directly from Colombia by boat, through the Mauritanian port of Nouadhibou or the ports of Cotonou and Lomé on the Gulf of Guinea, or by plane, mostly through Guinea Bissau. Those that arrive in Nouadhibou are picked up by drivers from the refugee camps of the Western Sahara, where they are repackaged and handed over to Khalīlīs, mostly Arabic- or Tamasheq-speaking young Malians, but also some Mauritanians, Nigeriens, and Chadians. They are transshipped in al-Khalīl, travel through Niger into northern Chad, where they change couriers once more before reaching the Sudan, Egypt, Israel, Eastern Europe, and eventually the big consumer markets in Western Europe. The large profits that can be obtained in the drug trade, and the low cost of transport and especially labour in the southern Sahara, locally serve to explain this formidable detour. More recently, people have started talking about whole planes, loaded with narcotics, chartered in Colombia, supposedly to fly to Eastern Europe. On their way, they stop over in the northern Malian desert – "you know what it is like up there, nothing but a huge landing strip" – unload their goods onto myriads of four-by-fours, commandeered from al-Khalīl by satellite phone, which

[35] A similar association between rapid economic success and illicit practices can be found throughout the ethnographic record: see for instance Ardener (1970), Taussig (1977), Geschiere (1997), and Ferme (2001).

then feed them into the normal circuit. Although I at first dismissed such stories as mere bragging, the recent "discovery" by the Malian army of a large plane wrecked near al-Khalīl belied my initial scepticism, showing that the "mafias" operating locally indeed have access to large capital and far-reaching organisational structures.[36]

And this is indeed the image that is conveyed locally. Although in local parlance, the word "mafia" can be used for quite a range of different organisations, "mafia" here implies a high degree of centralisation as well as close connections with relevant government officials.[37] Everybody can drive a car across the desert, and car trading is not illegal as such, but the "car-mafia" has ways and means of de-taxing cars in Mauritania, against a "small fee," and with all the necessary papers. Similarly, large-scale trade in guns needs official protection, and drugs cannot even be obtained unless buyers can present some generally recognisable security. "Mafias," then, are necessary where the stakes are high. This also means that they are organised. They are just like a state, people say: they have a president, his deputies, and various "ministries": the ministry of defence, which protects its interests and deals with all possible trouble; the ministry of foreign affairs, which goes out to prospect if there are new deals, and at times travels all the way to Colombia or China; and the ministry of justice, which controls and judges its members and makes sure they do not cheat. How much of this was made up by my informants on the spot, I do not know, probably rather a lot.[38] Yet it does illustrate one main

36 On 2/11/2009, the Malian military "discovered" a wrecked plane 200 kilometres north of Gao, which they said had come from Venezuela carrying up to 10 tons of drugs (AFP, 22/11/2009). Claims that this proved a link between the "international drug trade" and "Al-Qā'ida" seem to be unfounded, however (see also the conclusion).

37 Hence, small armed groups such as the one that stopped our truck between the Algerian border and Kidal, and that do not seem to have a central organisation at all, but are "open to all," are also referred to as mafia. Yet the word is never used for small and locally based smuggling networks. For classic studies of "real" mafias elsewhere, see Blok (1974), Gambetta (1993) and Varese (2001).

38 Conditions of research in al-Khalīl were, for obvious reasons, rather special: Muḥammad and his cousin Slīman, who drove me to al-Khalīl, thought my project was hilarious and, despite all my rather naïve attempts at discretion, went out of their way to tell everybody we met on the road that I was going to al-Khalīl to meet the *shifāt ta 'l-māfiya* (mafia bosses, from the French). The same scenario was repeated in al-Khalīl, where my host Lakhḍar relished bringing a large number of supposed "chiefs" to his *garāj*, telling me gleefully that I should interview them right there and in his presence. They were all charming and very talkative, some wanted to convert me to Islam, and all left me their mobile and satellite phone numbers, saying that I should meet their wives once I get to Adrar or Tamanrasset. As a result, the only guarantee of accuracy in what follows are the limits of the spontaneous inventiveness and creativity displayed by my informants.

point: mafias, in opposition to smaller smuggling groups or even tribal monopolies such as the one fostered by Ṭayyib Zijlāwī in Niger, are assumed to be organised according to a "modern" and very efficient division of labour, where what you see is always only a small part of a complex and, from a local point of view incomprehensible, whole. Their headquarters are invariably said to be based beyond northern Mali, some say in Algeria and Libya, others – more accurately perhaps – speak of Colombia: in any case, well beyond the reach of local or even regional social networks and the moral control and commitment they imply. Individuals employed by such organisations, albeit selected for their personal courage and bravery, thus have very little autonomy and power of decision, hence perhaps the clear parallels drawn between the mafia and the region's most powerful and violent states, Algeria and Libya, known to foster obedience rather than autonomy.[39]

Accordingly, recruitment to the mafias is made on an individual basis, irrespective of social origin. Mafias first inquire into the trustworthiness and seriousness of candidates and then entrust them with smaller runs, but they never just coopt existing networks or take people's recommendations for their cousins. Payment is made on an individual basis, in cars not cash: after three or more successful return trips, the driver owns the car, either to keep it and start his own business smuggling cigarettes or staples or to sell it on and continue with the mafia.[40] Drivers tend to start their jobs as apprentices when they are adolescents, hoping to move through the ranks as they grow older and eventually to become small-scale patrons themselves; in most cases, however, they fail, either by dropping out of the business altogether, or by dying or being maimed in accidents or shoot-outs with customs officials. This means that most drivers on the ground are very young, often barely in their twenties. Stories they tell at night around campfires in al-Khalīl where there are no older family members or women to inhibit or control them all speak of heroism, nomadic excellence, honour, and personal autonomy. They dwell on car chases, shoot-outs with the Algerian gendarmes, feats of extraordinarily fast

[39] Similar parallels between states and "mafias" are routinely drawn by social scientists and historian, pointing to the at times close relationship between organised crime and state building: see for instance Tilly (1985), Bayart, Ellis, and Hibou (1999), and Hibou (1999). This is not merely a contemporary phenomenon: see Barkey (1994) on similar developments in the Ottoman Empire.

[40] Economically, this makes sense: cars need to be brand new to be able to outrun Libyan and Algerian military vehicles, while even used jeeps are highly valued prestige objects locally, as they contain the promise of social advancement and future economic independence.

driving on treacherous desert tracks in star-less nights, on records held and broken for journeys often almost a thousand kilometres long, incredible navigational achievements, encounters with wild beasts, hunting stories, personal deals made despite the patron, duped police and soldiers, and covert references to available females in border posts. References to time spent in prison are less common, although the cruelty of Algerian prison officials does sometimes make for a good story; cousins and brothers die along the way, shot by the army or victims of equipment failure, but they play only a small part in tales of heroism. All stories are stereotyped, and they correspond to models of manliness, honour, and heroism that seem to owe as much to Hollywood films and local legends of heroic excellence as to the realities of the trade. They hence arrogate "traditional" models for social interaction, autonomy, honour, and manliness that local society otherwise denies to smugglers, both as young men and as dependent traders in marginal positions.[41] Yet smugglers know as well as everybody else in the area that, despite the rare individual success stories known to all, these claims to personal autonomy are largely illusory: they know that they are "the stupidest people in the world," as one put it in a thoughtful moment, who "just risk their lives to make other people rich." Much of the attraction of al-Khalīl is thus virtual and seems to lie in the stories themselves, stories that allow men to be great even if they are not rich, and to become rich if only they are great, and that more closely correspond to notions of generosity, honour, bravery, and Arab superiority than the realities of daily life in contemporary Mali ever could.[42]

This is perhaps one of the reasons why, for mothers, sisters, and older brothers back in Gao, drug smuggling is clearly beyond the pale, to the point where it becomes an almost magical explanatory trope for moral transgressions. First of all, they say, living in places like al-Khalīl and on the road makes it impossible to behave like a true Muslim, if only from a practical point of view: it is almost like living outside Muslim society altogether. In a very striking opposition to truck drivers, smugglers who drive fast jeeps never stop to pray, or even to eat; they shun other travellers,

[41] The notion of "honour" has been much criticised in anthropology as exoticising and essentialising, and as an anthropological cornerstone of an artificially created "Mediterranean" or "Middle East" (see, e.g., Herzfeld 1980, 1987). Nonetheless, there is no doubt that certain clusters of values pertaining to personhood and centred on notions of autonomy and protection run through the ethnography of both areas. For a classic piece on northern Algeria, see Bourdieu (1965); for a careful analysis in Yemen, see Dresch (1989).

[42] Gilsenan (1976) provides an excellent analysis of the aesthetics of lying among young men in northern Lebanon, who similarly use boasting to mask their real lack of power and autonomy and to nonetheless participate in local games of honour.

and there is no equivalent to the inherently sociable rhythm of travel – and the rosy stoutness that comes with it – that is cultivated by people such as Ighles. Although al-Khalīl would afford much time for prayer, and indeed has two mosques (see introduction), nobody ever seems to pray there. Even people who are known for their regular fulfilment of religious duties in Gao or Bani w-Iskut "forget" them as soon as they reach al-Khalīl. Nobody in al-Khalīl can lead a proper family life, as there are no families but only women of debatable virtue. These circumstantial arguments are backed up by a more substantial one: drugs (*mukhaddirāt*) are *ḥarām*, and any contact with them or with money earned through them is polluting. This means that any fortune derived from drugs can never be blessed (*mubārak*) but is barren (*māḥil*). Concretely, this results in sterility: drug smugglers grow thin with their wealth, and any investment made with drug money will necessarily fail. More importantly, considering the age and aspirations of most drivers, marriages contracted with drug money will be barren, or result in the early death of children or in their "rottenness" – just like the "mixed" marriages discussed in Chapter 2. Hence, no noble or self-respecting girl should ever get married to a drug trader, even if she is blinded by his wealth, as she would knowingly throw her virginity away, for "fake" bride-wealth, like a prostitute.[43]

If such marriages do take place, their supposedly horrendous consequences are recounted with great relish as ladies meet over tea, in particular by those who, though single, have never yet had the occasion to reject similar offers. In these stories, drug smugglers – like Abidine – appear as barely human: their wives soon find themselves abandoned, without maintenance, and unable to have recourse to their husband's family who had not been consulted on the marriage and for whom the husband had become "like a stranger." Worse, intoxicated by the wealth and violence of al-Khalīl, drug-smuggling husbands might not even recognise their own flesh and blood anymore and harm them if ever they return. Inversely, as seen previously, rapid accumulation of wealth by people of a formerly lesser status is directly blamed on the drug trade and is further associated with intracommunal violence, moral failure, and religious transgression, in short, with asocial behaviour. Yet despite the recurrent image of pollution, the crux of the matter seems to lie beyond Islamic classifications of licit and illicit substances. Car and gun smuggling, neither of which

[43] For comparable worries about the purity of money, the inherently destructive power of impure money and ways of cleansing it among the Nuer of southern Sudan, see Hutchinson (1996).

deals in illicit substances, are condemned in similar terms, and this harsh judgement can stretch to cigarette and petrol smuggling if organised by a "mafia." The real problem, then, seems to be the mafia in and of itself, which, like the state and the ubiquitous Algerian secret services, is seen as inherently destructive to "proper" social ties and to the right kind of region-bound and morally controllable connectivity, due to its emphasis on individual recruitment and enrichment, and due to its capacity to "turn people away from their families."[44] Drug trafficking introduces new sources of wealth to local society, sources of wealth that are out of proportion with anything else that might be available locally and that are clearly beyond the reach of local authority figures and their concomitant distributive networks. Much like the Sudan trade for the Algerian traders encountered in Chapter 2, mafias involve the wrong kind of connectivity that lays everybody involved open to uncontrollable sources of corruption that inevitably and irreversibly contaminate whole families, and make traders "forget" the most basic ties that bind them. Similarly, beyond notions of pollution, marriages with wealthy drug smugglers are problematic because they – like Algerian traders' marriages in the *bilād al-sūdān* – can be concluded without the consent and approval of the groom's family, hence undermining accepted practice and offering no recourse to the bride if things go wrong.

On the ground, none of these fears seems to be truly justified: although some drug smugglers indeed abandon their wives and small children, the vast majority do not; and rather than keeping the money they earned for themselves, they tend to use it to improve their social position by establishing prestigious marital alliances and investing in real estate and livestock, hoping eventually to be able to drop out of *al-frūd al-ḥarām* altogether.[45] Everybody can point to the large villas in Gao and the new quarters of Bamako, sites of lavish feasts and parties that gradually attract more longstanding Arab commercial elites, especially in Bamako, away from northern social pressures and logics. As smugglers are paid in cars, they often attempt to establish their own small-scale and family-based trade networks of the Lahda-kind or else set up their cousins or brothers

[44] Worries about the institutionalisation of extralegal associations and activities among Chicago street gangs are voiced in rather similar terms of moral disappointment: with the arrival of crack cocaine, gangs are seen to have turned from a "family" to a "corporation" breaching rather than maintaining "proper" social ties for the sake of individual profit rather than communal solidarity (Venkatesh and Levitt 2000).

[45] This striving for respectability and the social mobility it entails is common throughout the area and has probably long informed local social hierarchies; for a parallel example from Mauritania, see Cleaveland (1998) and Bonte (2000).

with transport and initial capital, hence furthering preexisting social ties rather than challenging them. Others, such as Abidine to some degree, Khuwī, or, it is rumoured, Abdessalam's cousins, invest the money made trafficking drugs in wholesale trade with Bamako or the major West African ports or, perhaps, in their cousin's Lahda business and petrol smuggling. Marriages with sharifian girls from known Timbuktu families who have recently been out of commercial luck are conspicuous, costly, and much talked about; they do, however, create family ties that cannot be denied, and are gradually normalised, with fewer and fewer qualms about the barrenness of drug money.[46] The two mosques in al-Khalīl were constructed by notorious drug dealers; in a less conspicuous way, drug smugglers often finance the religious studies and devotions of their brothers or parents and generously feed poor relatives. Some are very active in local missionary groups, especially the *Jamāʿat al-tablīgh*, leaving their capital and business in the hands of capable younger relatives.[47]

These attempts to resocialise illicit wealth provide the context for animated debates over whether drug smugglers should pray or not. One such debate was prompted by my astonishment and mirth as, while visiting with Sahelian friends in Adrar, I saw Lakhḍar, my host in al-Khalīl, who is, according to his friends, a notorious drug dealer, "born crook," and "compulsive liar," trundle off to the mosque in the company of al-Shaykh, a wealthy trader known for his religious commitment and active support of the *Tablīgh*.[48] I had never seen Lakhḍar pray in al-Khalīl, and initially put down his sudden religious fervour to his understandable

[46] Hence, the first "Tangara Arab" to have been elected to parliament, mentioned earlier, was married to a sharifian lady from Arawān near Timbuktu, whose family is at the heart of the "traditional" commercial and religious elite of the northwest; tellingly, however, they chose to settle in Bamako rather than in the north.

[47] The *Jamāʿat al-tablīgh* is an Islamic missionary group originally from Pakistan. Recently, it has been very popular throughout West Africa, and meetings are common both in Sahelian capitals and small settlements (see, e.g., Janson 2005, Lecocq and Schrijver 2007). For background to the movement, see Masud (2000).

[48] Lakhḍar's life story is one of a radical break with his past and home country: he left Mauritania to trade in Mali, and then, on his return, he was imprisoned – "just because he had done a bit of business," he said. After some time in prison during which he was regularly beaten and deprived of sleep, food, and human company, he was set free on condition that he work for "them" (i.e., the Mauritanian secret police). This consummated his break with Mauritanian society at large, and he then disappeared as fast as he could to al-Khalīl, swearing never again to set foot in his own country. This, of course, does not necessarily mean that he refused to work for the Mauritanian secret police, as many smugglers probably do. Indeed, on a later visit, the Mauritanian government had changed due to a coup d'état, and Lakhḍar had sold his *garāj* to try his luck in politics back home.

desire to accommodate al-Shaykh's opinions. My comments to that effect led to an animated discussion among the ladies present: some agreed with me that it might indeed be an outrage to God to pray whilst in the polluted state of a notorious drug dealer, and that Lakhḍar, by his truly immoral lifestyle, had forfeited all chances of salvation; others forcefully denied this. Drugs are not polluting as such, they said, but are criminal because they are destructive to other people, mostly, for that matter, Europeans. Drug smuggling is thus a crime against humanity, whereas not praying is a crime against God, and thus infinitely worse: "you open two different accounts, and beware you never mix human concerns with godly ones, or else think they are equal in value." Lakhḍar just sat by and smirked: economically successful, with two wives in Adrar and Tamanrasset and good connections to all those who matter, it is unthinkable that he would ever really be excluded from "good" society in northern Mali. Meanwhile, folk wisdom easily points to the relevant *suwar* in the Qur'ān that are renown for the protection of smugglers; amulets and other protections are readily provided to protect illegal and illicit ventures, at prices that acknowledge their special status. More generally, although locally, the *frūd al-ḥalāl* and the *frūd al-ḥarām* are construed to be mutually exclusive, in actual fact, most families engage in both, and limits between them are often fluid. Indeed, many a family's "moral life" of Islamic scholarship, female seclusion, and leisure depends ultimately on revenues generated by the drug trade.[49] Like the trans-Saharan trade of the early twentieth century described in Chapter 2, *al-frūd al-ḥarām* thus poses endless contradictions: it allows a life of apparent autonomy, independence, and morality, if only for the family back home, but it does so only by exposing traders to a life of risk, servility, and "corruption" that makes them inherently vulnerable to moral opprobrium.

CONCLUSION

Since national independences, Algerian restrictions prohibit virtually all exports to Mali and Niger. Nonetheless, much of northern Mali remains economically dependent on exports from Algeria, and regional trade in staples continues in patterns similar to those described in Chapters 1 and 2. This means that in the border area official distinctions between legal and illegal transborder trade are largely meaningless and are replaced by older oppositions between morally acceptable regional and inherently

[49] For a fuller discussion of the problems this causes, see Scheele (2009b).

dangerous transregional trade. This is directly reflected in the rhythm and social organisation of trade. Slow-moving trucks are seen as inherently sociable, whether they carry legal or illegal exports, as they are crucial for the maintenance of cross-border regional family ties and may transport women and whole families; their journeys are punctuated by social and religious duties, and they often act as travelling markets, suppliers of basic foodstuffs, and popular means of communication. Jeeps might carry staples smuggled out of Algeria and be driven by their owners or run by small family concerns: such business, technically illegal, is seen as totally acceptable, and indeed understood to be indispensable to day-to-day life in the border area. Cigarette and petrol smugglers, who are equipped with faster cars and generally stay aloof from roadside sociability, are rather more marginal to "good" society but, when they work in small networks following local norms of solidarity, are seen as relatively harmless. On the other hand, trading that is in the hand of the "mafias" – large-scale, transregional, centralised, state-like and impersonal organisations – is perceived to be morally tainted and inherently destructive to local society. Although such distinctions are often expressed in terms borrowed from Islam, opposing *al-frūd al-ḥalāl* to *al-frūd al-ḥarām*, and although some reference is generally made to the status of the substances traded – drugs are illicit and lead to pollution and barrenness – the logic that underpin such local moral judgment seems to be predominantly social. Trade becomes "immoral" when it ignores "proper" social ties, hierarchies, and regional control, or allows people to circumvent or even to publicly challenge them. Meanwhile, horror stories of the inherently asocial nature of notorious drug smugglers have become a convenient explanation for moral failures and "improper" violence more generally, of which the fratricidal "war of the Kunta" and the social reshuffling it led to is but the most widely cited example.

Such rigid distinctions have little reality on the ground. Most traders employed by the "mafia" do not use their wealth to question longstanding social ties and hierarchies, but rather attempt to better their position within them, by mounting careful marriage strategies, investing in legal enterprises, and spending time and resources on religious scholarship, both of the "traditional" and the more recently imported kind. As for the traders discussed in Chapter 2, the majority of their investments are carried out within the region, and in eminently "sound" ventures: houses, gardens, livestock, and trade in staples. Most networks cover all kinds of trade, and economic strategies are by necessity flexible, while the boundaries between the legal and the illegal, but also frequently between the licit and the illicit, remain fluid. Decisions as to who chooses what kind of trade depend less on "morality" than on age, with younger brothers of thoroughly respectable traders employing themselves as couriers for the mafia until they earn enough to set up their own small-scale and respectable trading network. As in Chapter 2, "immoral" and "moral" trade are thus inherently linked, one feeding into the other. This flexibility leads to never-ending moral conundrums back home: everybody agrees that drug smuggling is clearly beyond the pale, but everybody knows equally well that it is, in contemporary northern Mali, often the only way in which a truly "moral" lifestyle and concomitant high status can be maintained. This tension between a strongly felt need to extend social networks and fears about a resulting lack of control and moral containment echoes the preoccupations with "civilisation" voiced by the Algerian trading families encountered in Chapter 2. Further, it illustrates the eternal predicament of connectivity as described in Chapter 1: if place and civilisation are inherently dependent on outside connections, they become inevitably porous and vulnerable to outside meddling. Similar worries inform notions of local identity and social hierarchies, the subject of the next chapter, inasmuch as they remain intimately related to genealogical reckonings that, independent of one's will, establish quite as often the "wrong" as the "right" kind of connectivity.

4

Struggles over Encompassment

Hierarchy, Genealogies, and Their Contemporary Use

> As to the beginnings of the *sūdān* and the details of their circumstances in this land only God knows them, praise be upon Him. They are dead and with them died their stories (*akhbār*), and all that is left are the ruins [of their buildings] ... They were people who fate has obliterated, and not people who write and produce history (*yu'arrikh*) and remember their affairs (*yaḥẓaf akhbārihim*). They were like animals, all that was important to them was eating and drinking ... And this is all that is known about them and we [who] research into the ancient histories (*tawārīkh*) of the Arabs, as to these base people, there is no benefit for us in knowing about them.[1]

Reading through Saharan history and ethnography, one is struck by the recurrence of questions of social hierarchy and status distinctions, in endlessly varied terms, but that all seem to refer to a similar underlying logic of fundamental human similarity and internal moral distinction. Many attempts have been made to explain this underlying logic, first with reference to notions of race and past conquest, then with reference to property relations, and finally, most convincingly, by attempting to explain notions of degrees of nobility and its counterpart, servility, as given and

[1] Shaykh Bāy, "Note sur les anciens habitants de l'Adagh," ca. 1912, MS n° 95 of the de Gironcourt collection (CG), held at the Institut de France in Paris, as MSS 2407/1–223. His words strongly echo al-Idrīsī's much earlier (twelfth century) scathing remarks (that Shaykh Bāy might have been familiar with): "Of all the people they [the *sūdān*] are the most corrupt, addicted to many marriages, and most prolific in the production of sons and daughters. One can seldom find a woman among them who is not followed by four or five children. They are like brutes who do not care for anything in the world except eating and copulation. Apart from this they do not give a thought to anything" (in Levtzion and Hopkins 1981: 119).

abstract "indigenous categories."[2] All these explanations are valid and reflected in local rhetoric. However, they tend to favour the local over the regional and explain distinction in terms of the opposition between bounded categories or groups.[3] Yet beyond arguments from physical appearance, wealth, language, lifestyle, and nobility, on the local level, status distinctions are mostly expressed in noncomparative and universalising terms of descent: the most popular genre of historical writing are genealogies, or *tawārīkh*, "histories." These histories appear at first egalitarian – everybody supposedly has one – but establish hierarchical distinctions implicitly: descent is turned into genealogy by the historical consciousness of the people concerned, by their moral obligation to remember, that once more, as is clearly illustrated in the preceding quote, hinges on the distinction between savagery and civilisation. Further, regional genealogies invariably establish a certain degree of closeness to the central figures and places of the Islamic revelation that acts here not as a mere account of past events but rather as an active template for present and future social order. People hence derive their moral worth and concomitant contemporary status from their putative position in an overall scheme, encompassed by the one *ta'rīkh* that matters most: that of the Prophet Muḥammad, his descendants and spiritual ascendants, stretching back through all the prophets to Adam, and hence subsuming the history of the world in its totality (see Ho 2006). Rather than depending on an image of superposed ranks, genealogical models thus rely on notions of encompassment and range. Although there seems to be general agreement on the overall validity of such a scheme, and the possibility of a divinely ordained social order that could theoretically be known by all, individual positions within this scheme remain hotly disputed, and attempts to fix them once and for all – in writing, for instance – are necessarily controversial or even seen to be subversive.

[2] For case studies of status distinctions among Tamasheq speakers in Mali, Niger, and Algeria, see Clauzel (1962), Keenan (1977), Baier and Lovejoy (1977), E. Bernus (1990), Casajus (1990), Rasmussen (1992), Bourgeot (1995), Claudot-Hawad (2000), and Giuffrida (2005b). For similar distinctions among Hassaniya speakers in Mauritania, see Stewart (1973), Bonte (1989, 1994, 1998b), and Villasante-de Beauvais (1991, 1997, 2000). Similar hierarchies are common among speakers of black African languages throughout the Sahel; see, for instance, Olivier de Sardan (1984) and Conrad and Frank (1995).

[3] The most noticeable exceptions here are Cleaveland (2002), Hall (2005, 2011), and Bonte (2008), with their emphasis on genealogy and on the inherent flexibility of status, but see also Casajus (1990).

Genealogies, of course, do not explain status distinctions on the ground but rather provide an idiom in which they can be expressed, justified, and debated in a way that strikingly echoes the overall argument of this book. If Chapter 1 attempted to show that local ecologies are intrinsically dependent on regional connectivity, a genealogical vision of the world claims that local identity is equally so: an argument for human connectivity that implies a similar necessity of exchange and fears of potential corruption that might be caused by it, as became apparent in Chapters 2 and 3. This means that local identity, bound up with the outside, is inherently vulnerable and porous; meanwhile, local appreciations of the respective moral worth or credibility of putative outside connections might differ from one person to the next and over time. This porosity can lead to much embarrassment, especially at times when the bounds of "respectable" connections are redrawn. Hence, in the contemporary Sahara, with the growing impact of centralised states, nationalism, and the bounded and exclusive ethnic categories that accompany them, radically different notions of identity are put forward, putting pressure on earlier identities that relied on regional connectivity. Yet although southern Algerians might now look towards establishing prestigious links not with Islamic saints, but rather with northern state officials, older notions of human connectivity persist and become especially relevant as refugees and migrants from northern Mali settle in ever greater numbers in southern Algeria, often attempting to rely on older family ties and thereby causing much tension and mutual embarrassment.

STATUS, LABOUR, AND EXPLANATIONS OF HUMAN DIFFERENCE IN THE SAHARA

As the French colonial army advanced towards the Sahara, they were struck by the human diversity they encountered. An anonymous 1893 note on Ghat, for instance, describes the population of the city as a "mixture of all the people who, since its foundation, have met here for trade: white, black, half-cast, slaves, Arabs, Berbers, people from the south, people from the north, people from the east, people from the west."[4] This diversity, thought French army officers – themselves all too familiar with rank – was ordered according to a strict social hierarchy, established

[4] "Notice sur Ghat," 27/11/1893, CAOM 22H33.

along racial lines and following past conquest.[5] Hence, in 1902, Barthel described In Salah as follows:

The inhabitants belong to three races: the Berber race, the Arab race and the Black race. A. The Zenata from the Gourara and the Kebala from the Touat represent the Berber element; they are the old owners of the land reduced to client-hood by the victorious Arabs. They are generally settled and traders. B. The Arabs are partly nomads and partly settled (the great majority). Among them should be mentioned the *sharīf* plural *shurafāʾ* Muslims descending directly from the Prophet or making themselves out to be so and who have real authority. C. The negroes, slaves or liberated, are originally from the Sudan. They are employed as servants and provide the necessary manual labour for all agriculture. The *ḥarāṭīn* seem to be descendants of unions between white men (Berbers) and negro women; some authors however consider them to descend from the first local inhabitants that were subsequently dispossessed by the Berbers and then by the Arabs. They are agricultural labourers (*khammās*), schoolteachers, and day labourers, and are in consequence slightly more respected than blacks. Both groups are deprived of all political roles and are divided among the population in proportion to people's wealth.[6]

Other colonial reports claim that ways of life were equally a reflection, or even the result, of racial difference: according to Captain Pein in 1900, "the Touat is inhabited by a race that is totally different from the Arabs, that of the inhabitants of the *qṣūr* who only obey the nomads in as much as they are afraid of them and cannot live without them."[7]

French colonial notions of "race" at that time were rather confused: until the first decades of the twentieth century at least, they could designate occupational or linguistic groups as much as legal or political differences.[8] Moreover, there is no doubt that colonial rhetoric was heavily

[5] Explanations of social hierarchies in terms of racial differences and past conquests were familiar to French officers at the time, as, throughout the second half of the nineteenth century, opposition between indigenous "Gauls" and their "Frankish conquerors" were commonly used to explain French history and society (Thom 1990). Although French notions of race remained confused throughout (Hall 2011: 10, and see later), the science and vocabulary of human gradation in terms of race had further been developed to its extreme in the slave-owning societies of the Antilles, and, to a lesser degree, Mauritius (Cohen 1980, see, e.g., Vaughan 2005). For more general discussions of French racial theories as applied in Algeria, see Pouillon (1993) and Thomson (1993); for West Africa, see Conklin (1997).

[6] Lieutenant Barthel, "In Salah et l'archipel touatien," 15/04/1902, CAOM 10H22.

[7] Captain Pein, "Situation générale et projets d'occupation des oasis sahariennes," 28/12/1900, CAOM 22H33. For similar ideas, see Simon, "Notice sur le Tidikelt," 20/06/1900, CAOM 22H50.

[8] If in 1848, the French army officer Carette (1848: 13, 470) could still claim that the most important difference between Arabs and Berber Kabyle "races" was their language, their

influenced by local explanations of human difference, and by a shared need for labour. It was thus not so much the intellectual background than the practical purpose of French colonial officers that was at fault: as relational distinctions were turned into administrative categories within a modern bureaucratic state, they became decontextualised and over time developed a life of their own. Population censuses can stand as an example here: categories employed ranged from "Arabs, Berbers, *ḥarāṭīn*, negroes" in 1900 and "white, *ḥarāṭīn*, negroes" in 1901 to "*shurafā'*, *mrabṭīn*, Arabs, Zenata [Berbers], *ḥarāṭīn*" in 1933; in some years, population statistics were merely given by *qṣar*, by sex and age, by occupation, or as a mixture of several categories.[9] Where these shifting categories allow for comparison over time, figures indicate their incongruity: hence, censuses claim that between 1911 and 1933, throughout the Touat, the overall percentage of "whites" increased by 13 to 20 per cent, or even, in some places, by half, while that of "blacks" dropped by 40 per cent. At the same time, the overall population remained relatively stable, declining by 5 per cent on average.[10] Nonetheless, these figures are probably at least partly correct inasmuch as they capture changing social dynamics on the ground. French reports invariably note that the "labouring population" is disappearing as they speak.[11] This they blame on "racial

political organisation and their "rootedness in the soil," that is to say, sedentary agriculture, barely sixteen years later, his colleague Daumas drew more heavily on physical appearance and a rhetoric of the Kabyles' "Germanic origin," as manifested in their red hair and lighter skin (Daumas 1864: 186). Yet even then, ideas about race remained confused, and Ernest Renan (1873: 193) happily used the Berber example to develop his claim that nations were based on what we would today call culture (Renan 1882), whereas the most famous military ethnographers of the Kabyle, Hanoteau and Letourneux (1872: 1–2), ranked true "Berber-ness" with reference to political and legislative autonomy. On the development of the "Kabyle myth" and French racial thinking more generally, see Lucas and Vatin (1975) and Lorcin (1995).

9 Simon, "Notice sur les districts du Tidikelt," 21/05/1900, and "Recensement du Tidikelt," 12/09/1901, both CAOM 22H50; "Rapports annuels, annexe du Tidikelt. Recensement de 1906," CAOM 23H102; "Recensement des populations du Touat," 1911 to 1950, CAOM 23H91; "Recensement du Touat," 1933, CAOM 10H86.

10 Both the percentage of "blacks" and "whites," and the decline in the overall population varied widely form one *qṣar* to the next. Boufadi, for instance, lost a third of its population, both black and white, whereas blacks remained in a majority in Tamantit, whose overall population remained stable throughout. Cooper (1980: 164) cites similarly swift changes in colonial Zanzibar, where between 1924 and 1931, the number of "Arabs" increased by 70 per cent.

11 Until the early twentieth century, these worries had led to the (more or less) tacit endorsement of the slave trade (see Chapter 1); from the 1910s onwards, West African soldiers were to be settled, by force, in the Algerian oases. Yet such attempts failed spectacularly, as the imported *Tirailleurs Sénégalais* showed but little inclination to engage in

degeneration," and emigration to the Tell.[12] Yet most of it probably needs to be accounted for by initial category error, and categorical redefinition within changing power relations: at times, people were quite simply "dropping out" of their presumed category. In other words, if low status was indeed primarily linked to labour and coercion, it was a relational category, and no notion of bounded and homogenous entities, whether based on race, language or lifestyle, could possibly grasp it, while changes in the political environment would inevitably have an impact on it.

Alongside race, French colonial observers quickly noticed that social hierarchies dovetailed with unequal access to property, at least in the garden and water-owning societies of southern Algeria. The classic and widely quoted picture here was provided by Martin in 1908: in the greater Touat, the *shurafā'*, who made up 15 per cent of the population, owned more than a third of both water and palm trees; the *mrabṭīn*, 12 per cent of the population, owned just under a fifth of both; the "common people," just under a third of the population, owned a corresponding proportion of both water and palm trees; the *ḥarāṭīn*, 15 per cent of the population, owned 15 per cent of each; and the slaves, almost a tenth of the population, owned nothing at all. Local juridical documents, dating from the 1940s, confirm this picture: virtually all land that changed hands recorded by the local *qāḍi* was owned by and exchanged between *shurafā'* – although, of course, minor interaction among *ḥarāṭīn* might quite simply go unrecorded, if only to avoid the substantial fee that the

"slave labour," but rather flaunted their wealth and, according to the archival sources, bought local girls as slave-wives to take home with them: see "Note sur la question noire en Algérie," 1909; "Lettre du Gouverneur Général de l'Algérie au général commandant le 19e corps d'Armée," 23/04/1913; and "La main-d'œuvre noire au Sahara," 23/04/1914; Gautier, "Rapport sur la création des villages militaires pour troupes noires," 15/03/11919, all kept in CAOM 3H13. Hence, where the French officers had seen but racial homogeneity, their soldiers thought in terms of status and had striven to take their position in local society as high as they could – as owners rather than owned.

12 Every single annual report for the Touat mentions emigration as one of or even the main reason for its chronic economic difficulties. The French administration introduced passports and permits to make emigration more difficult, but Touata continued to migrate north anyway, illegally if need be. The larger cities on the coast, most famously Tunis, all had a "*shaykh* of the Touata" looking after new arrivals, and helping them to find employment, whether they had French permits or not ("Rapports annuels, annexe du Touat," 1906–51, CAOM 23H91; see also G. Marty 1948a, 1948b). The only way to slow down emigration, French officers thought, was by "limiting slave emancipation" and by encouraging former slaves to stay with their masters: "We need to use our authority to commit negroes to staying, as servants, in the families that employ them, while explaining to them that they are free nonetheless" ("Rapport annuel, annexe du Touat," 1908, CAOM 23H91).

qāḍi charged.[13] Twenty years later, Capot-Rey and Damade, describing the *faggāra* Ouarmol Kébir in the *qṣar* Ouled Hadj Mahmoun in Tamantit, note that of 360 *ḥabba* or units of water, 200 were owned by 35 *shurafā'*, 50 by 24 *mrabṭīn*, and 84 by 75 *ḥarāṭīn*; five were owned by nomadic Arabs, one by a "half-cast," and nine belonged to the quranic school and the mosque (Capot-Rey and Damade 1962: 106). A third of the water, or 120 *ḥabba*, were owned by two *shurafā'* alone; the authors remark further that the larger amount of water owned by *ḥarāṭīn* was "remarkable." If anything, then, unequal access to land and water had increased rather than decreased with French colonial rule. This situation remained strikingly stable after independence, notwithstanding the Algerian agrarian revolution, which was mainly concerned with the ownership of land rather than water. Hence, as Granier noted in 1980, agricultural property largely remained in the hands of 10 per cent of major sharifian landowners, while 40 per cent of the population had no access to land and water at all but increasingly refused to undertake agricultural labour thought to be demeaning due to its former association with slavery (1980: 662). Meanwhile, according to Guillermou (1993), local *shurafā'* maintained or even strengthened their high status by investing in modern agro-businesses and by becoming indispensable power brokers for the independent national government.[14]

From an economic point of view, this connection between land and water ownership and status is unsurprising: all survival in the area depends on the control of vital resources, especially water, which, as shown in Chapter 1, lends itself to investment and the accumulation of capital.[15] Moreover, as seen in Chapter 2, the ability to establish place and to control water, land, and agricultural production is central to local images of sainthood and religious status: there is no doubt that *baraka* is necessary to make the desert bloom, but it is also in turn proven by agricultural success. *Zawāyā* often owned large amounts of land as religious endowment (*aḥbās*), and

[13] This fee usually amounted to 5 per cent of the value of the goods transacted: see 'Abd al-Karīm b. 'Abd al-Ḥaqq al-Bakrī, *Sijill al-qāḍi*, and Chapter 5.

[14] For examples of one such family, see the Akacem, discussed in Chapter 2.

[15] In the literature on status distinction throughout the western and central Sahara, the recurrent link between certain forms of servility and irrigated horticulture is striking, see, for example, Clauzel (1962: 145) on *ḥarāṭīn* in the Adagh, and Bonte on the increase of slavery in Mauritanian as religious tribes turned to settled horticulture (Bonte 1989: 120, 1998a: 159). This does not mean that pastoral nomads did not rely on slaves for domestic labour and on freed slaves to tend their herds, but rather that different forms of servility were locally perceived to belong to different kinds of economic activities. For the close link between status "ethnic identity" and occupation in Mauritania, see Cleaveland (1998, 2002).

indeed needed them to fulfil their role properly: hospitality and generosity are among the most visible signs and obligations of high status throughout the region, as well as a way of binding people to centres of patronage; and among the many reasons for establishing oases, ideas of increased saintly prestige often seem to have played a part. Yet no direct and necessary equation can be established between landownership and prestige, and today, with the general decline of oasis agriculture, the importance of landownership has dwindled, retaining mainly symbolic value.[16] In line with our initial argument, the important factor here once more seems to be the control of outside resources, and most notably people, without whom water ownership is impossible, and landownership is meaningless; and indeed, despite great emphasis placed locally on property, property in land and water was always inherently fragile, due to the vagaries of the climate that could only be countered by an abundant labour force and access to other sources of income.[17] Hence, in contemporary Algeria, government salaries and some form of official recognition are indispensable both for successful agriculture and for the maintenance of full sharifian status more generally, not because Algerians tend to exaggerate their respect for the judgement of those who govern them – on the contrary – but because this is the only way in which *shurafāʾ* can be effective mediators between their adepts and worldly as well as spiritual powers, channel funds to the needy, and build up and maintain networks of support. What seems to be at stake here, then, is not landownership in itself but control over people and labour that is its indispensable precondition.[18]

This emphasis on control over people rather than control over land is backed up throughout the ethnographic and historical record on

[16] As labour is expensive, most land owned by sharifian families now lies barren, cutting a sad figure next to the well-tended tiny gardens owned by their *ḥarāṭīn* neighbours. Some landowners have taken to cultivating their gardens themselves, less, it seems, in the illusory hope of economic gain than as a way of maintaining their claim to the ownership of land (see also Bendjelid et al. 1999).

[17] Local legal documents frequently record cases of cultivated land reverting to waste (which, strictly speaking and according to Islamic law, cannot be owned), due to the absence of water or labour to maintain irrigation and palm groves, see for instance, SQ: 19, and NG: 145–6. See also Chapter 5.

[18] In the Sahel (and throughout sub-Saharan Africa more generally), scholars have long argued that what mattered was control over people, rather than land: see, for instance, Baier and Lovejoy (1975), Lovejoy (1983), Meillassoux (1986), and Rossi (2009), but see Guyer (1993). Arguments have even been made to see the very stratification of society as a response to uncertain economic and climatic conditions (see, e.g., Baier and Lovejoy 1975, 1977): in times of dearth, you can release your slaves to fend for themselves thereby easing the burden on scarce resources.

Mauritania and on Tamasheq speakers in the Sahel and central Sahara, where similar notions of status hold, although local vocabulary varies considerably. "Nobility" implies prestigious descent, but first and foremost the ability to protect and control other people and to receive gifts or taxes from them (Bonte 1989: 118); nobles, indeed, frequently do not "own" anything but can draw freely on everybody else's labour and resources.[19] This means that status categories are never fixed, but relational. According to Jean Clauzel (1962: 129), writing on Tamasheq speakers in the Malian Adagh: "It is often difficult to draw the line between the groups whose quality of *ilellan* [noble] is recognised and those whose is not, as everybody tries to convince themselves and especially to convince the others that the group to which he belongs is *elell*." Moreover, status categories and "ethnic groups" more generally are not thought about in terms of bounded groups but rather with reference to a model of excellence to which people correspond to varying degrees:

> Membership of the Tamasheq-speaking community is only ever acquired by degrees ... *Emajegh* ... the word that we translate as "Tuareg" and that indeed describes a Tuareg when compared to a non-Tuareg, also identifies the noble Tuareg when compared to a Tuareg of lowly birth, whether client, black-smith, slave or freedman. The Tuareg par excellence, the *emajegh* in the full meaning of the word, is noble. He is the one who embodies the qualities that define Tuareg identity: restraint, generosity, a certain refinement are often cited here, but the most distinguished is the ability to speak well. (Casajus 1990: 11)

These models of excellence were of two kinds (E. Bernus 1990: 44): secular, as described by Casajus, or religious, corresponding to the image of the settling saint developed throughout this book. This further increased flexibility on the ground: pastoral nomads of "warrior" descent could, by changing their lifestyle to more sedentary pursuits, redefine themselves as scholars (Cleaveland 1998, see also Bonte 1987: 68), although upwards – rather than sideways – mobility was clearly much more arduous, and costly. Moreover, although colour distinctions mattered and provided some of the vocabulary of status, and although there was a tendency, in the Maghreb in particular, to consider all "blacks" as potential slaves (El Hamel 2002b, see also Barbour and Jacobs 1985, Hunwick 1999a), even distinctions between "black" and "white" ultimately referred to unilateral descent rather than physical appearance (Hall 2011: 33): "Although

[19] A similar rhetoric of protection runs through the Arab world: see, for instance, Dresch (1989, 2009). See also Dresch (2006) for a summary of comparative examples from beyond tribal Arabia.

the ideas of race developed along the desert edge were color-coded (white, red, black), they were not based primarily on observable skin colour but instead on arguments about Arab and Islamic lineage." What mattered was the historic moment of conversion as an ever-repeated founding myth, defining certain groups as "bearers as Islam" and others as permanent "infidels" – an imagery that still informs contemporary Saharan visions of the *bilād al-sūdān*, as seen in Chapter 2.

A similar picture of variability and relationality emerges from a series of notes drafted in the early twentieth century, at the request of the French agronomist and explorer de Gironcourt, by the local Kunta scholar Shaykh Bāy, whose scant opinion on the *sūdān* was quoted at the beginning of this chapter.[20] In his notes, he divides people into *masākīn* (literally "poor"; people of low status) who are "servile and peaceful," some scholars, others herders, and "people of war," some protectors, others tyrants. Although this is a story of domination, Shaykh Bāy, himself a scholar, is clear that military power is not in itself a sign of nobility, and merely a precondition rather than a guarantee of political might. Conversely, failure to act in a honourable way inevitably leads to political downfall:

> The Kel Ahalwān are an evil tribe of tyrants ... They killed and looted and among them they were heroes known for victory. A single one of them was an army. They exaggerated their tyranny and they cut the roads of caravans coming from the Touat and elsewhere. They carried on like this until their political power disappeared and their strength lost all value. And the strongest and the weakest have dominated them since.[21]

Although Shaykh Bāy's notes thus seem to divide the world into the bounded groups, this division is immediately mitigated by his emphasis on fragility and flexibility.[22] Like the Kel Ahalwān, the Idnan were strong "until injustice entered among them"; the Taghat Mallat "used to be very rich in cows and sheep" until raiders took them all; and the Itakay

[20] CG, MSS n° 91–104. For my full translation of these notes and a discussion of their historical content, see Grémont (2010: 107–24 and 511–25); on Shaykh Bāy, see Chapter 1.

[21] CG, MS n° 101.

[22] This is not to say that the idea of bounded group identity was not at all available locally: Bruce Hall (2011: 77–80) carefully traces debate over the legal qualification of all military groups as *mustaghraq al-dhimma*, owners of illegal property who hence cannot legally claim possession of anything. The debate itself shows, however, that this is a rather tenuous argument, unsustainable in Islamic law and, more importantly perhaps, impracticable. Tribal groups certainly had notions of common responsibility, but these were rarely recognised in Islamic law, tended to be expressed in terms of genealogical "closeness," and remained negotiable (see, e.g., Bonte 2009).

Takāyan lost their dominance by foolishly attacking a Kunta scholar, leading to retaliation by the Iwellemeden.[23] Shaykh Bāy further takes great care to emphasise that most groups are linked to each other through ties of maternal kinship (*raḥm*), political alliances, or shared descent, and that they are ranked internally according to their degree of piety and conformity to Islamic ideals. Moreover, where de Gironcourt asked him for a neat grid of classification that, much like a population census and tax register, would leave nobody out of the picture, Shaykh Bāy primarily covers the few people in the region whom he considers as "having history" and hence as worthy of interest; as seen in the opening quote, questions about "vassals" and "blacks," put to him by de Gironcourt, he answers grudgingly, with little enthusiasm, or not at all. Hence, he describes the mostly low-status *imghad* as follows: "As to the *imghad*, there are too many of them to count them, and numbers cannot contain them ... Some have been here for three hundred years and some for two hundred years and some for a hundred years and some less ... They pay taxes to the Ilmidan."[24] History, then, or even accurate knowledge of one's identity, that is to say of one's exact position in the larger scheme of things, is in itself a privilege and clear indicator of high status.[25]

GENEALOGICAL GRIDS OF VALUE

Shaykh Bāy wrote his notes to cater for de Gironcourt's demands; but what he was really interested in, to judge from his own collection of manuscripts as well as from de Gironcourt's description of their encounter, were genealogies. "The sight of my manuscripts vividly aroused Bāy's curiosity," de Gironcourt notes, "he held out his hand and wanted to see the genealogies of *shurafā'* that were in my hands."[26] Shaykh Bāy was

[23] This is a period of Iwellemeden expansion (Richer 1924, Grémont 2010), and indeed most weakened tribes finish by asking for protection in exchange for taxation However, these stories of decline also indicate the flexibility of status categories and the ease with which people and, at times whole groups, passed from one to the other.

[24] CG, MS n° 102. Since the nineteenth century, the term *imghad* has usually been used in European sources as a one designating low status, comparable to the *laḥma* of the Awlād Ḥassān. Yet as both Claudot-Hawad (1985: 785) and Grémont (2010: 114) point out, the term *imghad* can in actual fact designate groups of different status in different places, including, in certain cases, "warriors" as opposed to "tributaries."

[25] This echoes, in a very different context, Sahlins (1983) famous observation that in certain social and historical systems, only kings and heroes have history.

[26] Otherwise, the *shaykh* was rather distant, according to de Gironcourt's (1920: 147) own description: "Wrapped in his frieze coat, whose hood stands up rigidly according to Moroccan fashion, Bāy shows nothing of his face, hidden under numerous folds of

not alone in his interest: even now, questions asked locally about human difference are usually answered in genealogical terms, and described as being closely connected to history; and the bulk of local historical writings follow genealogical patterns. Indeed, the Arabic term for history, *ta'rīkh*, throughout the region refers to what we would describe as genealogies: lists of names, journeys, and places that link local people to past ancestors, mostly known through their involvement in Islamic history. Hence, the history of the Arma, the leading Songhay-speaking families of the region, as recorded by Mūlāy Sharīf, a scholar based in Gao, in the early twentieth century, reads as follows:

And as to the father of the Arma, the people of Gao: they are two tribes, the sons of the *qā'id* Arkas and the sons of the *qā'id* Ḥamat. And the sons of the *qā'id* Arkas are four: Muḥammad and Kīj and Ghābil [sic]. And the sons of Muḥammad are four: Muḥammad al-Shaykh and Ḥamma and the *qā'id* Ghall and the *qā'id* Ghīl who is not the only one but the one who is known. And he had two children, Abū Bakr and his sister. And the children of Ḥamma are not here but they were two. Muḥammad al-Shaykh had five children.[27]

Arkas and Ḥamat link the families to the Moroccan army that conquered Timbuktu in 1591, while the repetition of the title *qā'id* indicates the uninterrupted line of rulers: until today, the traditional ruler of Gao descends from this line, and interest in Arma genealogy has by no means faded (see later discussion). On this particular manuscript, the genealogy of the Arma is followed by that of the local *shurafā'*, leading down to the author; the latter then passes seamlessly into an account of the kidnapping of a sharifian child from Mecca by a hostile army, and of the miracles performed by the child thereafter.

Shaykh Bāy's own genealogy, copied and presented to de Gironcourt in 1912, is presented in the same way:

In the name of God. As to the Kunta, their father is Sīdi Muḥammad al-Kuntī. And from him descend the Kunta who are in the Touat and those who are in Morocco and those who are here. And those who are here are the children of al-Wāfī and the descendants of al-Shaykh al-Kabīr who is the son of Aḥmad b. Abī Bakr b. Sīdi Muḥammad b. Ḥabīb Allāh b. al-Wāfī b. Sīdi

blue Guinea, but some dark skin and eyes with a young and sweet gaze, that he masks carefully after the first encounter by lifting his cloth as soon as he is seated, anxious to preserve this invisibility linked to prestige … After observing a long silence, some weak, almost plaintive sounds, come forth from his veils; his assembled companions bend forward, full of devotion: the saint is going to speak. He speaks in fact with a voice that is thin and frail, but clear, pleasing, almost charming."

[27] Mūlāy Sharīf, "Ta'rīkh al-Ramāt," CG, MS n° 87.

> 'Amar al-Shaykh b. Sīdi Aḥmad al-Bakkāy who is buried in Walata son of Sīdi Muḥammad al-Kuntī who is the father of all the Kunta. And he is the son of 'Alī b. Yaḥya b. Yaḥya also b. Ward b. Yahas b. Tamīm b. Sā'id b. Shākir b. 'Uqba b. Nāfi' al-Qurayshī the companion [of the Prophet] who conquered all of the Maghreb until he arrived in a place where animals die because of the sun. Then he returned to Ifriqiyya [present-day Tunisia] where he built [the city of] Qayrawan. He died near this city ... And the land of the Kunta used to be in Ifriqiyya. Then they moved to the area between the Touat and the Erg Chech and the Berber mountains. Until the beginning of the eleventh century when the Raggagda went south, and then in the middle of the century the Awlād Wāfī and the Awlād Sīdi al-Mukhṭār also.[28]

Here follows a detailed account, again in genealogical terms, of the passage of sainthood in the family, and the political influence held by them, sometimes in opposition, sometimes in subordination to the Iwellemeden, until the arrival of the French. The manuscript further contains a description of the establishment of Shaykh Bāy's *zāwiya* in Téléya and of his gardens in Tessalit (see Chapter 1).

These genealogies, by their nature, propose a different account of human difference than the sources quoted earlier. They do not identify groups, but individual people: no two persons can have exactly the same position on a genealogical grid, and those who are most the same – brothers – are also the most likely points of fission and conflict. Whereas colonial administrative explanations approach status differences from a locally bounded point of view, genealogies are universalising and derive status from past putative outside connections: they make local identity dependent on what happens or has happened elsewhere (although they need to be endorsed locally, and ultimately depend on *sam'a*, hearsay, see Powers 2002 and Touati 1992). They therefore do not explain places anymore than they explain groups: both need to be bounded off through an additional effort (although this effort might be commonly made, especially where low-status groups are concerned: see Hall 2011: 82). Further, genealogies never explicitly talk about status differences, but establish equivalence rather than distinction (Bonte 1987). Status is differentiated implicitly or through omission: genealogies only ever account for people who are already contained in their original premise; as in Shaykh

[28] Shaykh Bāy, "Ta'rīkh al-Kanāta," CG, MS n° 90. This account corresponds to general Kunta genealogical lore and early historical accounts, see, for example, Levtzion and Hopkins (1981: 12–13). For more information on the Malian Kunta, see P. Marty (1920) and Leriche (1946); for scholarship on the Kunta more generally, see Bibed (1997), Batran (2001), and Hūtiya (2007).

Bāy's notes, all the others fall through and become invisible.[29] Hierarchy is further introduced by reference to an overarching and universalising historical framework, based on the Islamic revelation, and to an implicit geography of value, with a moral gradient running from north to south. Not all ancestors and places of origins have the same moral worth, and those who are most closely connected to the Islamic revelation and its models of excellence, in particular the Prophet Muḥammad, are intrinsically morally superior. In turn, Islamic history is subsumed in Prophetic genealogy (Ho 2006), which therefore contains and implicitly ranks everybody else's descent: hence, *shurafā'* are "noble" because their genealogies are coterminous with history; they encompass the entire world, and, as a result, they have "cousins everywhere." Slaves, on the other hand, although by definition imported from the outside, are renamed on capture and deprived of their own genealogies, both ascending and descending: slave children are attached to their mother, or their mothers' master, not to their father, as if the intervening relation of property cut through the genealogical grid and modified it.[30] Hence, rather than in terms of localised rank, genealogies propose a reading of social hierarchies in terms of encompassment and range, within which putative past and potential future mobility and the ability to draw on geographically dispersed resources are key.

Moreover, genealogies, as universalising schemes, bear within them a promise of transcendent order: they are a model not of what the world is like, but for what it ought to be. History thereby becomes not so much an account of past events but a template for future action. As such, it is inherently controversial; and although most people in contemporary northern Mali at least would agree on the overarching validity of genealogical schemes, and in the possibility of knowing everybody's real and proper place in the world, attempts to fix such an order once and for

[29] The "Muzīl al-khafā fī nasab ba'aḍ al-shurafā'" (The Remover of secrecy about the genealogies of some *shurafā'*), written in 1837 in the Touat for a leading sharifian family resident in Tamantit, quotes a well-known Prophetic *ḥadīth* to the effect that no genealogy apart from that of the *ahl al-bayt* (literally the "people of the house," the Prophet's family) is worth recording: on the day of the last judgement, the Prophet will recognise no people apart from his own people, and no *nasab* apart from his own *nasab*. The text further notes that, in addition to written and witnessed genealogies, *shurafā'* can be recognised by the "signs of revelation" on the faces, their distinguished fragrance, and by the *baraka* apparent in them.

[30] See Meillassoux (1986). This, of course, does not mean that slaves have no kinship, or indeed family life and personal ties (see also Lovejoy 1983): what matters here are public representations and legal categories.

all in writing are deeply resented.[31] This is well illustrated by the example of Muḥammad Maḥmūd wuld Shaykh, sometime *qāḍi* of the Ahl Arawān, a group of Arabic-speaking sharifian scholars and traders from the Azawād settled Timbuktu. In 1933, at the height of French colonial rule in the area and relying both on French and Arabic source material, Muḥammad Maḥmūd wrote his only full-length manuscript, *Kitāb al-turjamān fī ta'rīkh al- ṣaḥara wa al-sūdān wa bilād Tinbuktu wa Shinjīṭ wa Arawān wa nubadh fī ta'rīkh al-zamān fī jamī'a al-buldān* (The book of the genealogist about the history of the Sahara and the country of Timbuktu and Shingiti and Arawān and small fragments of the history of all countries at all times). Despite this world-historical title, the *Kitāb al-turjamān* is mainly concerned with the history of Muḥammad Maḥmūd's own family, and especially his ancestor, Shaykh Aḥmad ag Adda, whose genealogy serves as a framework through which all other events are ordered and explained.[32] History begins with the *shaykh*'s arrival from al-Sūq, a legendary city north of Kidal, and his foundation of Arawān, north of Timbuktu, after he married the daughter of the head of the Kel Antassar, a Tamasheq-speaking group who trace their descent – and Muḥammad Maḥmūd elaborately backs them up in this – to the companions of the Prophet.[33] The following ten chapters (out of eighteen) deal with the *shaykh*'s genealogy, travels, deeds, and immediate descendants, with a rather brief reference to the 1591 Moroccan conquest of the area, mentioned mainly, it seems, because of an exchange of letters between the Sultan of Morocco and Shaykh ag Adda, concerning the lawfulness – or rather, lawlessness – of taxation of the salt mines of Taghaza.[34] Chapters eleven and twelve rapidly cover the years until the nineteenth century. Chapters thirteen and fourteen deal with the arrival of the first Europeans, the French conquest and their "ways of governing"; the remaining two chapters give an overview of the people of the

[31] This is in no way specific to the Sahara: similar observations have been made regarding attempts to reduce "tribal history" to one coherent narrative; see Dresch (1989) on Yemen and Shryock (1997) on Jordan.

[32] On Shaykh Aḥmad b. Adda, see P. Marty (1920: 239). Muḥammad Maḥmūd clearly had read Marty's works, and was much influenced by them.

[33] P. Marty (1920: 239) puts forward a rather different account of the foundation of Arawān. Al-Suq (Essuk) plays an important part in local imagination, as the legendary place of origin or obligatory passage of regional *shurafā'* (see, e.g., Badi 2002). Al-Sūq, today abandoned, is the site of several medieval graveyards with Arabic inscriptions (see Farias Moraes 2003) and has attracted some archaeological attention (see Cressier 1988 and Nixon 2009).

[34] KT: 8–11. On Taghaza, see McDougall (1980, 1990).

Azawād and Arawān and their respective genealogies and an account of traders and trade from the arrival of the Barābīsh in the early seventeenth century until today. This apparent imbalance in the division of chapters is partly counteracted by the length of these last two chapters that, between them, fill 38, or more than a third, of the 113 pages of the manuscript.

Chapter fifteen promises to

> mention the tribes who were living in the Azawād and its area and those who remain of them today, and to mention the Awlād Ḥassān and their link with Ḥassān and the tree of the genealogies of all of them, and to mention who was taken in by the people of Arawān who was not Barābīsh, and to mention the remaining [genealogical] trees of all Amāqil tribes, God willing, and to mention the Awlād Ḥassān who are in Adrar and Shinjīṭ and its area and other things such as the genealogy of Ḥassān and to include a reminder of the tribes of the *sūdān* and their origin.[35]

In its contemporary focus and all-encompassing ambition, this chapter diverges most clearly from the more familiar style of those that precede it, although it firmly espouses the genealogical principle established earlier. As promised, Muḥammad Maḥmūd recounts the standard genealogy of the Awlād Ḥassān and discusses at length the origin of the Tuareg.[36] He then proceeds to include all the "tribes of the blacks" (*qabā'il al-sūdān*) in this overall scheme. Following standard tropes of explanation, he states that all *sūdān* are descendants of Hām, the son of Noah, alongside the Berbers and the Copts. He then further divides them into tribes, ranking them by origin, and according to their ancestor's position in Islamic or Arab history.[37] Hence, the Wākarā and Sanagha and Wangara, families still known today as of great scholarly and social prestige, are descendants of three brothers, "vassals" (*milk*, or property) of a Yemeni king. Fleeing

[35] KT: 73.

[36] Muḥammad Maḥmūd relies here on standard genealogical lore, linking the Awlād Ḥassān all the way back to the legendary initial division of "all the Arabs" between 'Adnān and Qaḥṭān, and copiously referring to standard Islamic historical scholarship and genealogies, such as Ibn Khaldūn and an unnamed "leader of al-Azhār," legendary figures such as Ja'afar al-Ṭayyār, the Prophet Muḥammad's uncle, and local classics, in particular the *Ta'rīkh al-Fattāsh* and the *Wasīṭ* by Sīdi Muḥammad b. Sīdi al-Mukhṭār al-Kuntī (for a partial translation of the latter, see Leriche 1946). Similar overarching schemes were proposed by Arab genealogists and historians much earlier; see Levtzion and Hopkins (1981).

[37] Some of these "tribes" are recognisable as contemporary "ethnic" categories, such as the Bambara or Mossi. Others are now used as family names or *diamou*, encompassed within larger "ethnic groups," such as the Wangara (Oungara). Other terms seem utterly obscure. In other words, the terms used by Muḥammad Maḥmūd to refer to "tribes" (*qabā'il*) today refer to a whole variety of levels on which and ways in which people can be distinguished from each other.

oppression by the king's successor, they arrived in the *bilād al-sūdān*, where they settled. The two elder brothers married, the third had children by a slave girl; a fourth tribe, the Minka, is descendant of their slave. The eldest brother was accepted as a king by all people in the *bilād al-sūdān*; as to the Wangara, they are people of "scholarship, goodness and saintliness," counting among their ancestors a "great imam and martyr."[38] The Mūsh (Mossi), on the other hand, were descendants of "Banū Isrā'īl" before they converted to Islam; others, such as the Bingār, used to be *majūs*, but now, they are "strong in Islam."[39]

Other tribes were of less prestigious descent:

> As to the tribes Jinka and Saraka and Būbū and Tambir and Karnagā, the origin of these tribes is verily Noah [who] owned a female slave and of her 'Ās and Sūr and Kātū and Jār and Sabṭ [were born] and they were all girls ... indeed they became pregnant and every one of them gave birth to twins male and female. And Mās gave birth to Jink and Maybūtuwa and Sūr gave birth to Būbū and Sar and Kātū gave birth to Timbū and Hūb and Jār gave birth to Karanga and Sār and Sabṭ gave birth to Saraka and Nār. And when the children grew bigger, Noah peace be upon him permitted them to emigrate with their mothers and they settled in the region of the river and hunted fish to live and there came millet to them also. And they worked until they reached the age of marriage and Jink married Sarr and he was the father of the tribe Jink spelled with *jīn* and *nūn* and *kāf*. And Būbū married Maybūtuwa and he was the father of the tribe Būbū with *bā* and *wāw* and *bā* and *wāw*, and Karnagar [married] Sār and he was the father of the tribe Karnagar. And Tambū married Sabūr and he was the father of the tribe Tambūr; and Saraka married Sār and he was the father of the tribe Saraka with *sīn* and *rā* and *kāf*. And from that time they did not cease and they multiplied and they increased and they dispersed in the land until they reached the land of the *sūdān* and they increased in it.[40]

Or consider the Ham Tīn, Ham Wala, Sarbanar, Samshāk, and Kam: Muḥammad Maḥmūd describes them as descendants of five brothers – whose

[38] On the importance of the Wangara for the establishment, scholarship, and trade in both Timbuktu and Walata, see Saad (1983). The Wangara today claim common sharifian descent, although the term probably initially meant "Muslim trader": see Lovejoy (1978) and Lydon (2009a: 63–5).

[39] KT: 74. *Majūs*, literally "Mazdaist," is a general term to refer to any people with a learned religion that is neither Christian, Jewish, nor Islamic. The question of religion matters as it determines whether people could be legally enslaved or not: for a discussion of the longstanding debates over this issue and the easy slippage between "black skinned" and "heathen" that informs it, see El Hamel (2002b) and Hall (2011: 82).

[40] KT: 73–4. Muḥammad Maḥmūd here mostly seems to be repeating known genealogical lore that dovetails with existing economic specialisations and group identities that are said to derive from them (see Fay 1995b). Muḥammad Maḥmūd's innovation is thus mainly situated in his attempt to include all these accounts in one coherent framework.

father was a blacksmith in the service of the Christians and who had fled from the islands of the ocean to Gao at the time of the sultan Sharr Muḥammad Fāra. On his arrival in Gao, the father married one of the sulṭan's mother's slaves, and then became a famous bandit, "oppressor," and "road-cutter." He was defeated and killed by the sultan's forces, and his five sons were captured and settled in different places so that they could not unite again for mischief.

Implicitly, these stories – and Muḥammad Maḥmūd mentions many more of a similar kind – establish a clear moral hierarchy. All make reference to a past history of dependence and slavery, but while some establish "proper" descent, through the male line, coupled with a prestigious eastern place of origin, others dwell on descent from women and dubious places of origin, such as the "islands of the Ocean": presumably the Atlantic, associated with the Christians. Meanwhile, people without socially recognised genealogies – slaves and freedmen, or *ḥarāṭīn* – drop out of his explanatory grid altogether. "Proper" genealogies are further represented in the text through the inclusion of diagrams: Muḥammad Maḥmūd includes sixteen such diagrams, all of which are concerned with "Arabs"; eight of these refer to sharifian families; six to nonsharifian but religious families, such as the Kunta; and two describe the Awlād Aslīman and the 'Arīb, of political prominence in the region. Hence, genealogies vary in quantity as well as in quality; further, these genealogical distinctions are of more than merely antiquarian interest: the respective prestige or shortcomings of the genealogies recounted are directly reflected in the contemporary position and activities of the "tribes" defined in this way, ranging from respected religious scholars to heinous road-cutters. Through genealogy, Muḥammad Maḥmūd thereby maps all local differences onto a coherent framework of "universal" (i.e., Islamic history), within which any position carries a certain moral value, determined by its "closeness" to the central protagonists, in the spatial, genealogical, and temporal sense, or, conversely, by the "stain of original unbelief" (Hall 2011: 240) that their contemporary descendants are made to bear. Genealogy and historical unity thus equate with hierarchy; and such hierarchy is potentially all encompassing, whether people like to be included or not.[41]

[41] In most other historical writing in the area, such hierarchical ordering is avoided, leading to the long-term coexistence either of different versions or even of different kinds of history: for a Saharan example, see Echard and Bonte (1976), describing how Hawsa and Tamasheq histories as recounted by adjacent or even intermingled populations complete ignore each other; for an analysis of the coexistence of shaykhly and tribal history in

RACE, ETHNICITY, AND THE NATION-STATE

Mostly, it seems that they did not. Muḥammad Maḥmūd wuld Shaykh is even today a highly controversial figure; he was imprisoned almost immediately after Malian independence (Hall 2011: 314). Although the *Kitāb al-turjamān* is not the direct cause of this, it is generally seen to represent the "racist" political opinions that got him in such trouble. From a scholarly and sharifian family from Arawān near Timbuktu, Muḥammad Maḥmūd was, for a short time, *qāḍi* of the Ahl Arawān settled in Timbuktu, until he was forced to resign after quarrels with the local *'ulamā'* (Lecocq 2010: 54). He was among the region's staunchest supporters of the French project for the establishment of a separate Saharan territory (the Organisation commune des régions sahariennes, OCRS) that would remain under French guidance after the countries of French West Africa and later also Algeria had gained independence; to gain support for this project, he came to fame touring southern Algeria and northern Mali, and initiating petitions among notables in Ouargla, Tindouf, and Timbuktu.[42] His vision of Saharan relations and inherent connectedness, partly inspired by Paul Marty's work, was taken up by Marcel Cardaire, French colonial officer and fervent supporter of the OCRS, in order to argue for a coordinated policy of propaganda either side of the border, or ideally for the abolition of the border altogether.[43] The few Western scholars who mention him have been rather dismissive of Muḥammad Maḥmūd, stressing especially his "racism": he notoriously refused to pray behind a "black" imam (or this is how it is put today), and his house was among the first to be burned down during the "troubles" of the 1990s (Hall 2011: 300, see below). Yet Arab notables both in Timbuktu and in Bamako recount his "kindness," "extraordinary knowledge," and easy conversation: "he knew how to speak to everybody, and when he did, time swept past, it was like a glimpse of paradise." They also describe him as the last representative of a long line of Arab scholars in the area, a line that has now tragically come to an end: and the *Kitāb al-turjamān*, little read, is nonetheless seen as a central

Upper Yemen, see Dresch (1989). For various case studies from the Indian Ocean, see Simpson and Kresse (2007).

42 See the lengthy report kept in the French military archives in Vincennes (SHAT), box 1H4754/3; see also Lecocq (2002: 56–7) and the various documents kept in CAOM AffPol 2258/5. On the French project of an autonomous Saharan region under French guidance, see Boilley (1993).

43 "Rapport du chef de bataillon Cardaire sur les chaînes commerciales sahariennes," January 1957, CAOM AffPol 2261/7, see also Lecocq (2010: 52–8).

piece of evidence of the region's "true" history. As such, it is understood to be both precious and subversive: it came into my possession in a rather underhand way, as a photocopy of a manuscript, lent to me over the weekend by the assistant director of the Centre Ahmed Baba in Timbuktu, a relative of Muḥammad Maḥmūd's, who had it delivered "secretly" to the house where I was staying – which was also owned by an Arab.[44] Hence, although the *Kitāb al-turjamān* appears at first sight to be an obscure scholarly endeavour, accessible to the selected few, and of mainly antiquarian interest, as an attempt to fulfil the promise of permanence and completeness that is inherent in all genealogical endeavours, it is perceived to be inevitably dangerous, a potential source of conflict: an expression of deep-seated racism for some, and of "true knowledge" for others.

Beyond the contradictions inherent in his undertaking, Muḥammad Maḥmūd was even more at odds with the Malian nation-state. By its very nature, the latter stood for new and equally universalising claims to patterns of ordering and legitimacy that echoed those put forward, fifty years earlier, by the French colonial administration (Lecocq 2010: 98–101): first and foremost, those of nation-states, and their concomitant categories, ethnicity and race. Conceptually, these notions are opposed to genealogical visions of the world. Both claim to be universal (everybody "has" a race or a nationality, much as everybody has a position in a putative universal genealogical scheme, and those who do not – slaves and *sans papiers* – quite simply fall through the grids of recognition), but whereas notions of "race" and national identity claim that people within one group are not merely equal, but also the same, and that people beyond group boundaries are fundamentally different, a genealogical vision of the world – much as the "models of excellence" described earlier – postulates gradual continuity of positional difference where no two people are exactly the same, but there are no radical breaks, and people are all different in the same way.[45] Hence, genealogies, especially of the kind discussed previously, establish gradual but boundless hierarchies of differential access, whereas nationalisms – much like notions of

[44] There was no need for such secrecy: I could just as easily have consulted the manuscript in the CEDRAB, as Bruce Hall clearly has done (see Hall 2011: 305). For reflections on this need for – at times artificial – secrecy in knowledge production in the Arab world, see Dresch (2000).

[45] See also Dresch (2009). Such a model is perhaps most familiar to European readers from the biblical vision of the world; for a discussion of its gradual replacement by racial thinking in the very different context of India, see Trautmann (1997) and Ho (2004).

ethnic boundaries, racial difference, and bureaucratic efficiency – draw lines around defined groups and places. As a result, nationalism carries within it different notions of legitimacy (and often also of property), of the social as well as of the religious kind; and indeed, in many instances, it has at least nominally put forward a type of Islam that attempts to cut out mediation and intermediaries, that is to say, that aims to replace notions of differential proximity to God by mass access.[46] In practice, the distinction made here is of course overly schematic. As Bruce Hall (2011) has convincingly shown, notions of racial difference can coexist with genealogical visions of the world, as long as they remain subsumed within overarching status distinctions functioning in relational terms; and longstanding debates over the legal enslavement of "blacks" easily took a racial turn (El Hamel 2002b, see also Lecocq 2010: 95–7).[47] Similarly, the exclusive aspirations of nationalism often falter on the ground: one nationalism rarely ever resembles another, with state resources and wider regional connections playing a key role; more importantly, perhaps, conceptual replacements are rarely total, and state visions of the world might easily be subsumed within more longstanding ones, especially if they have such remarkable powers of encompassment as genealogical schemes. But the conceptual opposition between bounded groups and relational hierarchies remains good to think with.

In southern Algeria, the impact of Algerian nationalism, backed by oil revenue and legitimacy obtained in the war of independence, has been considerable. Much of this is due to the economic power of the state: if Chapter 1 made an argument for the inherent dependency of oases on outside investment in the past, today, this is even more true. Oasis agriculture has dwindled, as part of a general disinterest in agricultural production throughout the country, but perhaps first and foremost as a result of the chronic labour shortage that the French colonial administration feared already in the 1930s and that has increased exponentially due to the general rejection of agricultural labour as demeaning and notoriously low status. Meanwhile, regional Saharan trade has all

[46] This, of course, occurs with often-mitigated success: see Scheele (2007).

[47] Indeed, Hall's notion of race often seems undistinguishable from the genealogical logics described here: "The significance of the idea of 'race' in the Southern Sahara is really an outgrowth of the increasing importance attributed to ideas about lineage connecting people living in this remote region with noble figures from Arab-Islamic history … Whiteness is therefore not really about skin colour or physical characteristics of those who identified themselves as 'white'… rather, it lies in the accepted genealogical connection to important figures in the historical and religious pantheon of Arab Islam. Blackness by contrast, is defined by the lack of such connections" (2005: 345, 355).

but disappeared, or at least shifted to a few prominent trading posts, many of which are of recent construction, such as al-Khalīl, Bordj Badji Mokhtar, and the Sahelian quarters of Tamanrasset, Reggane, and Adrar (see Chapter 6). Access to water is now provided by technical infrastructure, such as drills and motorised pumps provided by the state (J. Bisson 2003, Bensaâd 2005a), and, more generally, all resources that matter and that enable a semblance of high status are controlled by the central administration. Whereas few (local) people now actively labour and low status has become a question of descent, snobbery and poverty, high status, and the concomitant ability to extend hospitality and patronage to dependents are necessarily connected with access to state resources and officials. Images of success, as transmitted in the national media and on international Arabic satellite television, correspond to northern notions of prestige and morality, within which ties with the south count for nothing, or even are stigmatised as a sign of "corruption": more generally, rather than as a potential source of wealth and status, the current image of the *bilād al-sūdān* has mostly been reduced to its most immoral aspects (see Chapters 2 and 6, and the following discussion). Algerian official Islam is state-centred, with salaried civil servants replacing locally known scholars of prestigious descent; although they might in actual fact be one and the same person, publicly avowable notions of religious legitimacy have thus changed, and claims to genealogically motivated preferential access to knowledge and grace are treated with suspicion, at least in public. As a result, high status is still about access, range, and connections, but these connections are now centred on the state and, where they cross national boundaries, are directed north and east rather than south. Hence, the moral north–south gradient, already discernable in the older genealogical literature, has been strengthened beyond recognition.

Although, on the ground, this means that locally influential families have generally attempted to obtain government positions, or at least to have their own status sanctioned by the state – a sanction that is easily granted, as egalitarian revolutionary fervour often fades when confronting the prospect of unrest in the south, where most of the country's natural resources are based – key positions in the local administration tend to be occupied by civil servants from the north. Teachers, shopkeepers, oil workers, restaurant owners, police, and army personnel are also predominantly of northern origin. These northerners are often unaware of subtle local status distinctions, or else less restrained by local codes of politeness; they are especially sceptical of the relative local disjunction between skin colour and status, in particular when the former tends to be expressed in colour terms, opposing "whites" (*bīḍān*) to *ḥarāṭīn* and "blacks" (*suwādīn*).[48] In the eye of the average northerner, low-status *ḥarāṭīn* and local *shurafā'* look much alike, equally black, and only barely Algerian; southern girls especially seem to suffer increasingly from a certain stigma attached to their skin colour and are exceedingly fond of quoting passages of the Qur'ān to the effect that such matters have no importance before God. Some such northern blunders are intended to be friendly but remain, nonetheless, unwelcome: Lalla, the cigarettes smuggler Muḥammad's (Chapter 3) elder sister, still remembers how, on a visit to Algeria and walking around the centre of Adrar wearing her *milḥafa*, the five metre all-body veil worn by Malian Arabs and Tuareg alike, she was accosted by a Kabyle (a Berber speaker from northern Algeria) who, taking her for a Tuareg "cousin" of his, launched into a long speech (in Arabic presumably) about Berber unity and their common fight against "corruption" and "exploitation" by the Arab majority. He simply refused to understand her insistence that she herself was of most noble and pure Arab ancestry and felt little inclined to associate with a "peasant" of unknown ancestry and European appearance.[49] Here, as for the French colonial censuses quoted earlier, clashing logics of hierarchy, belonging, and status – one genealogical, the other racial – lead to mutual incomprehension on the ground; however, whereas the French colonial administration failed to impose their point of view, the greater power and legitimacy of the contemporary Algerian state, the large number of northerners settled in the south, and especially the widespread striving to emulate northern Arab middle class values seem to promise a more successful replacement of local notions of identity.

As a result, in contemporary southern Algeria, the maintenance of sharifian status requires constant effort, both moral and material, as it implies abstinence from manual labour and permanent and unquestioning hospitality. The latter might sometimes be recompensed by offerings,

[48] This is the necessary result of status that is linked to unilateral descent. This does not mean that southerners are anymore "colour-blind" than northerners, but rather that questions of colour can be debated quite apart from considerations of status.

[49] In northern Algeria, claims to the official recognition of a separate "Berber identity," and concomitant interest in Berber culture and language have led many northern Berber speakers, especially Kabyles, to turn to the equally Berber-speaking Tuareg for the cultural and linguistic authenticity they think they themselves have lost due to Arab influence. Mostly, they are disappointed, as local Tuareg do not recognise them as "fellow Berbers," but rather as generic northerners of dubious morality and religion (see Chapter 6). For more details on the Berber movement and its rhetoric of "purity" (that is strikingly similar to that put forward by Algerian nationalism), see Direche-Slimani (1997) and Scheele (2009a); for an example of Berberist literature, see Chaker (1999).

but these are only drops in the ocean. Hence, the family I stayed with in Tamantit, who were from a poorer branch of the leading sharifian family in the area (descendants of the *qāḍi* of Timmi discussed in Chapter 5), are struggling to survive on small salaries earned by the parents and the two eldest children, while the income they derive from their remaining land-holdings, managed by the father's elder brother, is negligible. Although they scrape by in normal times, festive seasons such as Ramadan invariably bring with them their series of privations, mainly in order to be able to keep up appearances: new clothes need to be bought to celebrate the *'īd*, and hospitality is especially lavish on such occasions – and of course it would be unthinkable to neglect the daily offering of milk and dates to the mosque, even if this means that no such luxuries would be had at home that day. Lacking wealth, the women of the family are especially careful to cultivate full Islamic dress and piety, in addition to active involvement in local women's associations; an ethical striving that makes sense in their home *qṣar* but that remains unrecognisable to most inhabitants of nearby Adrar, where large parts of their lives are played out today and where their religious fervour is quite simply read as backwardness. If their more influential cousins have fared better, this is due to the privileged relations they managed to establish first with the colonial and then with the independent state: one brother has been appointed as regional head of religious affairs, another had a nominal position in the national oil company, a cousin is senator, and yet another branch of the family now occupies positions of responsibility in Algiers and beyond. In principle, there is nothing new about the difficulties encountered by poor *shurafā'* today: it seems likely that the Touat has always produced a surplus of *shurafā'*, many of whom most probably quietly "dropped out" when they saw themselves unable to support their high status. However, as seen in Chapters 1 and 2, for the more adventurous among them, travels to the *bilād al-sūdān* used to offer an eminently prestigious way out of poverty, or rather, an escape route away from the scrutiny of relatives and dependents. This route has now been blocked for most, as, from an indispensable way station, the Touat is gradually turned into a cul-de-sac.

In northern Mali, the state has been much less powerful, and, as seen in Chapter 3, former social hierarchies have evolved considerably but have barely lost their hold on the local imagination. People have challenged their own individual position in the system and continue to do so, but this is mainly due to their economic success rather than a general questioning of status distinctions: people do not try to abolish local hierarchies, but rather struggle to better their position within them. Status as derived from descent still counts, as debates over the true position of "Tangara Arabs," outlined in Chapter 3, show; nevertheless, here, as in southern Algeria, "noble" families struggle to obtain the means of their high status and often find their only hope of success in potentially illicit transborder trade, which in turn threatens their claim to hereditary religious excellence. Nonetheless, in domains where state recognition and funding are important, notions of identity have shifted, if only partly. The Malian government has long put forward an image of Mali in which northerners play little or no part; although Tamasheq speakers have gradually found their way into national curricula and television, if only as a folkloric marker of identity, Malian Arabic speakers remain excluded, to the point where Malian Arabs are routinely described as foreigners. This is especially visible in Timbuktu, where much funding has been channelled towards manuscript conservation, but where Malian Arabs are conspicuously absent from government- or NGO-sponsored activities, and where the language of research is classical Arabic, learned in Cairo or Tripoli by native Songhay or Bambara speakers.[50] More generally, with the growing availability of religious programmes on radio, television, audiotapes, and the Internet, sources of Islamic knowledge and scholarship have been diversified, and the privileged access to Islam claimed by many Arabic-speaking families – due to genealogical or linguistic proximity – is often doubted. Meanwhile, their Arabic is compared to Middle Eastern examples and found wanting.[51] Much like transborder ties in Algeria, the privileged connections Malian Arabs can claim to the north are now mainly treated with suspicion: they all too easily translate as involvement in transborder smuggling and "Islamic terrorism," in a context where foreign origin is increasingly read as a stigma rather than an asset. Here, then, the longstanding north–south moral gradient has been interrupted, if not reversed.

Yet the most powerful shift from genealogical to racial notions of distinctiveness was brought about by violence rather than government policy. In the early 1990s, after rebellions and a coup d'état by the army in Bamako had put an end to Moussa Traoré's military dictatorship, a second "Tuareg rebellion" broke out in the Kidal area.[52] As in the first rebellion

[50] Both Libya and Saudi Arabia grant generous scholarships for higher education in Arabic to Malian nationals. For some statistics on the former, see Lemarchand (1988).

[51] For changes in the Malian religious landscape, and the diversification of sources of Islamic knowledge, see Niezen (1990), Brenner (2000), Bouwman (2005), Soares (2005a, 2005b), and Schulz (2006, 2007).

[52] On the "democratic transition" of 1991 and 1992, see Bertrand (1992). A first rebellion had broken out in the north straight after independence (for detail, see Boilley 1999 and

of the 1960s, repression by the Malian army was brutal and led to reprisals on "blacks" by the rebels. Although a first agreement was quickly reached in 1991, granting substantial autonomy to the north, fighting continued, partly because the government was not seen to have kept its promise and partly because the rebel movement was splintering and had little control over its fighters (Klute 1995). The resulting insecurity provided ample opportunity for groups of armed bandits. It might have been the latter that triggered the establishment of "black defence groups," with assistance from the Malian army: *ganda koy*, or the "owners of the land," who claimed to represent "black interest" in the area and to defend their "sedentary way of life" against the "encroachment" of nomads.[53] They couched their policies in increasingly racist terms that for the first time publicly opposed the "blacks" and the "whites" in the area (Claudot-Hawad 1995), apparently in order to attract "black" Arabs and Tuareg to the movement – the *bellah* and *ḥarāṭīn*, descendants of former slaves. Some of these indeed redefined themselves as Songhay and joined the ranks of the *ganda koy*, others stayed neutral or benefitted quietly from their own relative immunity to redefine their former masters' property as their own, yet others protected and helped them (Giuffrida 2005b, Lecocq 2005).[54] Rhetoric tightened on both sides, and the threat and

Lecocq 2010). Grievances then expressed were hardly catered for in independent Mali, and many reoccurred in the 1990s. For a summary of these events, see Accord et al. (1995), Maiga (1997), and Ag Youssouf and Poulton (1998); for a more reflective collection of witnesses' accounts, see Grémont et al. (2004); for attempts at explanation, see Klute (1995, 2001) and Boilley (1996).

[53] The self-representation of the *ganda koy* as the "original inhabitants of the land," in an area where settlements had long been as mobile as nomads, points in itself towards a fundamental change in perspective (Hall 2011: 259). Struggles over access to land and grazing grounds had indeed been intense in the area, as more sedentary populations increasingly invested in livestock, and cultivated areas that in the past had been open for pasture (A. Marty 1993, Grémont 2005, Beeler 2006; for a parallel example from Mauritania, see Leservoisier 1994). Yet much of the rhetoric also seems to play to foreign observers and government policy, that, ever since colonial times, had more or less intentionally favoured settled agriculture. With the droughts of the 1970s and the 1980s, such problems had been exacerbated, especially as foreign aid in itself often clearly favoured the settlement of former nomads, as well as establishing clear and bounded ethnic labels (Giuffrida 2005a).

[54] Comparable logics of status and valorised foreign origin seem to have been at work in precolonial Zanzibar, leading to violent redefinitions in terms of race, class, and indegeneity that culminated in the 1964 revolution (Cooper 1980, Glassman 2000, Fair 2001), and that led again to tensions during general elections in 1995 and especially in 2001 (Cameron 2001). Yet the levels of violence that were reached there, backed up by state power and institutionalised economic inequality, remain incommensurable with events in northern Mali.

direct experience of violence made racial categories very real for a time, as all "whites" and "blacks" potentially were turned into enemies, leading to new patterns of segregation that are still noticeable in most northern Malian towns and smaller settlements (see Chapter 6).

Although these acts of violence furthered for a time a racial interpretation of difference, post facto, the "events" are often explained in terms of status. Hence, Lalla again: a "white" Arab of high status whose family was forced by the events to flee to Algeria, but who has now returned to Gao:

> People say we had problems with the *koro-boro* [Songhay, literally "town-dwellers"] but that is not true: we never had any quarrel with them. The government brought in the army and all the rabble that they could find in the gutter of Bamako, and they said to the *bellah* of the Tamasheq and of the Songhay and of the Arabs: look, you are black like us, we are all the same and we will take all the land. And if you had light skin or you just had a shop and were rich they came and killed you and burned all your stuff or took it away with them. As a result, there are hardly any Arabs left, and those who are left have stopped speaking Arabic and they have become black, just because they are fed up with killings and thievery.

Others accuse the army, generally seen to be composed of "lowly" people; in both explanations, disruption is thus blamed on low-status outsiders who are by definition unaware of local hierarchies and social subtleties and are therefore capable of all atrocities.[55] Their motivation is most commonly described either as inherent destructiveness and stereotypically "slave-like" lack of restraint, or as pure greed: most of the prominent "whites" killed had been influential traders, and people claim that their killers were mainly looking for money, or else were sent by people who wanted to rid themselves of commercial rivals. Racial explanations, even if they are put forward with as much violence as they were in northern Mali in the 1990s, thus only seem to have a temporary or at best partial hold on local imaginations – or rather, although they are locally frequently drawn on as cultural markers, they are always encompassed within notions of status based on genealogical patterns of identity; and indeed, the "events" were largely brought to an end by a local coalition of "notables" with no regard for ethnic boundaries (see Grémont et al. 2004). Yet until today, there is a widespread feeling among Tamasheq and

[55] The association between the army and low status or even slavery goes back nial times (see, e.g., R. L. Roberts 1987, Lovejoy 1983), and was strengthene colonial recruitment policies (Bouche 1968, S. Davis 1970, Echenberg 1991) ment to the Malian national army after independence, see Mann (2003).

Arabic speakers alike that they might quite simply "die out," less because of the number of people who were killed in the 1990s than because, confronted with the hazards of being "white," people might choose to drop out altogether: either by redefining themselves as "black," or by disappearing to the cities of the Maghreb.

One often-cited example here is Zayda's uncle, Mūlāy Sharīf. Of impeccable sharifian descent, but born to a Songhay mother, Mūlāy Sharīf ostensibly refuses to speak Arabic, claiming he is unable to do so; he publicly espouses a "black" lifestyle, is happily overweight, drinks, and receives Songhay girls in his house, where he lives on his own. He used to be married to a cousin of his, who divorced him because of his "loose" lifestyle; his brother was married to a girl from the Awlād Sīdi, Lalla's niece (see Chapter 3), who divorced him after he tried, according to her, to make her "dress like a *koro-boro*," that is to say, to go about with her hair and neck uncovered. Even worse, his sister is married to a wealthy Songhay businessman in Bamako, where she runs her household "just like a *sūdāniyya*," dressing her daughters in "mini-skirts." Arab women explain these many shortcomings by Mūlāy Sharīf's Songhay mother, although she herself was both noble and of notorious morality: "it's not her fault," they say, "it's in the blood: like witchcraft," while pointing to the veins in their forearms – using exactly the same phrases and gestures as Algerian women resigned to the moral shortcomings of their Malian stepchildren (see Chapter 2). Yet such logic is double-edged, as all families in the area necessarily have some kin connections with "blacks"; and, indeed, fears of children dropping out are widespread, and special care is taken, through food, clothing, and religious and linguistic training, to turn them into "real Arabs" (see Chapter 6). On closer acquaintance, however, one might wonder whether Mūlāy Sharīf really has lost any of his status, or even his truly sharifian capacity of encompassment. He spent much of his youth working with his "uncle" Sī Ḥammādi Zijlāwī (see Chapter 2) and was partly raised in Aoulef. He is as familiar with Algeria as with Mali and Niger – and Nigeria and Benin, where he spent years smuggling cars, petrol, and cigarettes for his Algerian in-laws. His house in Gao acts as a meeting point for notables and friends from all walks of life and all kinds of "ethnic groups" from the Bourem area, where Mūlāy Sharīf's father was mainly active. Mūlāy Sharīf makes and unmakes elections in the region, is on friendly terms with ministers in Bamako, and was instrumental in helping to defeat the second Tangara Arab candidate in the last elections, as he, despite his potentially Arab descent, put all his weight behind the leading Songhay candidate, a woman of good family, just like him. Despite or perhaps because of his drinking habit, Mūlāy Sharīf thus appears as the archetypal contemporary *sharīf* who can have "cousins everywhere" and "get along with anybody" while remaining an indispensable mediator in everybody's affairs – one of the "people who tie and untie," as even local Arabs grudgingly have to admit.

CONTEMPORARY GENEALOGICAL ENDEAVOURS

Mūlāy Sharīf's transnational success indirectly indicates that despite pressure put on older patterns of identity, genealogical logics have retained at least some of their importance. For one, interest in and controversies over genealogies and their universalising potential have not waned. Hence, in contemporary Kidal, Muḥammad al-Amīn Fāl, a Mauritanian scholar settled in the Malian Adagh, is busy working on a vast compilation of the genealogy of the Ifoghas, today the leading family in the Adagh, who claim sharifian descent. This undertaking is deeply controversial and has earned Muḥammad al-Amīn the title of "Ifoghas minister of propaganda" (Lecocq 2002: 25). Before the French colonial conquest, the Kel Adagh had no commonly recognised "noble" family (Clauzel 1962) but seemed to have muddled through at the margins of two centres of political influence: the Ahaggar to the north and the Iwellemeden in the south, paying tributes to either or neither if they could. To curtail Iwellemeden influence and to ascertain that the Adagh be included in French West Africa rather than Algeria, local French colonial administrators declared them independent and established the Ifoghas, nominal "nobles," at their head.[56] Claims to sharifian descent seem to date from this time; and the facility with which, throughout the colonial period and beyond, Algerian *shurafā'* established marital alliance with members of leading Ifoghas families (see Chapter 2) might have something to do with attempts to prove the veracity of such claims. Before then, the term "Ifoghas" seems to have referred to scholars rather than a particular tribe or family.[57] At independence, the Ifoghas continued to act as the "traditional chiefs" of the area and, as such, remained on the government payroll. Today, their

[56] For the rise of the Ifoghas, see Boilley (1999) and Lecocq (2002: 126). For the border dispute between French West Africa and Algeria, and the terms in which it was debated on either side, see the large number of documents and reports kept in CAOM 1H44.

[57] See, for example, Claudot-Hawad (1985), and the use of the term made by Shaykh Bāy, especially in CG, MS n° 92, when describing the "Idnān Kalāqa": "and most of them were Ifoghas and this is why they were better than the other Idnān in religion and practice." Grémont (2010: 106) found no mention of the term before the nineteenth century.

predominant position is resented by many, a resentment that was partly expressed in factional conflict with the last armed rebellion in the area in the mid-1990s (Klute 1995, Lecocq 2002) but that also, less dramatically, is aired in genealogical debates and private ridiculing of their genealogical pretensions.

Muḥammad al-Amīn's compilation of Ifoghas genealogy is an ongoing project and has been so for at least the last decade. So far, it spreads over forty-seven pages, in diagrams rather than as a running text (see Photo 4.1). All individual diagrams are numbered and feed back into a larger matrix that links them all to each other and to the family of the Prophet. They do not mention groups but deal exclusively with individuals, although to the initiated these, of course, stand for larger social formations – yet for everybody else, they remain forcibly obscure, especially as they go against most local received wisdom and legends of origin.[58] Hence, any reading of these diagrams presupposes prior local knowledge: in opposition to the texts discussed earlier, they cannot stand alone but rather provide props for more detailed expositions, or textual reminders of shared identity for internal consumption. Further, they are written in classical Arabic, a language with which only few people are sufficiently familiar locally to make sense of Muḥammad al-Amīn's scholarly scrawls. Yet everybody seems to agree that these genealogies are clearly publicity for the Ifoghas: ways to prove their sharifian descent and thus to justify their claims to local leadership. This apparent paradox – incomprehensible and inaccessible propaganda – can only be explained if we admit that much of the message of these diagrams lies in their form – and perhaps even in their incomprehensibility – rather than their content. Such a reading might go some way towards understanding the second paradox of Muḥammad al-Amīn's undertaking: only seven of his forty-seven genealogies refer to people known locally, six to various fractions of the Ifoghas, and one to a group of Imghad. The remaining forty are strikingly redundant, but they give a feeling of completeness and place local genealogies in an overall scheme that potentially covers everybody – or rather, everybody that matters. Again, hierarchies are established implicitly, through

[58] Local oral traditions refer to one common ancestor as central to Ifoghas identity: Muḥammad al-Mukhṭār Ayta, who is said to have arrived in the Adagh from Tabalbalt, a known sharifian centre (Boilley 1999). On arrival, his son married a local woman from the Taghat Mallat, although there is some debate over the exact status and position of this woman (see Badi 2001); in opposition to Muḥammad al-Amīn's neat genealogical model, by including women, such stories of local alliances allow for conflicting interpretation of lineage and hierarchy and localise stories of descent.

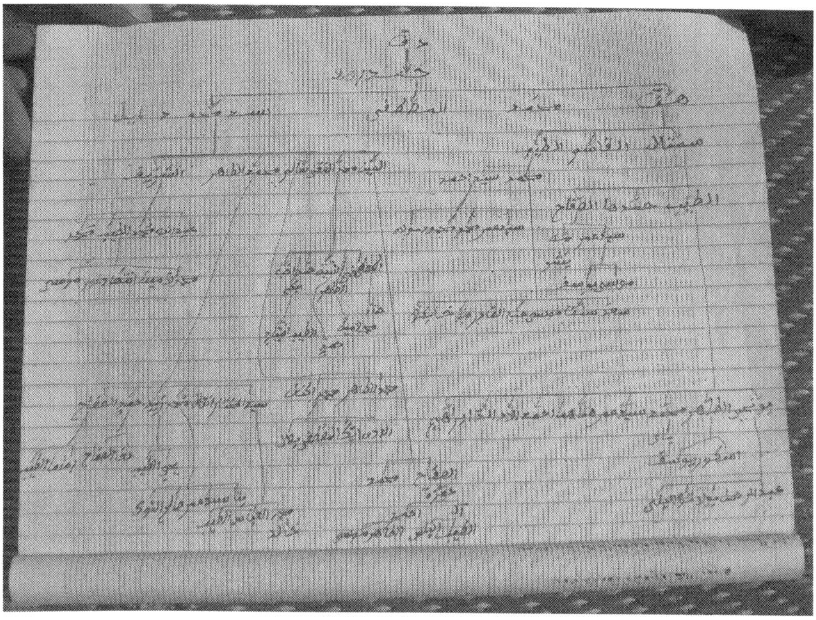

PHOTO 4.1. Genealogical diagram: Muḥammad al-Amīn Fāl.

omission; and, by their sheer size and "orthodox" appearance, these genealogies act as proofs of legitimacy, both for the Ifoghas as *shurafā'*, and for Muḥammad al-Amīn Fāl as a historian and religious scholar.

This penchant for genealogical models is in no way limited to people who are locally classified as "whites." In Gao, just down the road from Kidal, Younoussa Hamara Touré has put his training as a French-speaking sociologist at the service of a vast compilation of his own family's genealogies, as a preliminary framework for research into "local history." Younoussa defines himself as Arma, that is to say as belonging to Songhay speakers settled throughout the Niger bend who claim to descend from members of the Moroccan army that conquered Timbuktu in the sixteenth century and who have since then achieved considerable political clout in the area – one of their genealogies, used by Younoussa as a source text, was quoted at the beginning of this section.[59] For his compilation, he is drawing on Arabic and French colonial sources, but his main focus is on oral history, mostly as collected among his own family. He has filled several dozen Excel spreadsheets, one automatically linked to the

[59] CG, MS n° 87. For historical background on the Arma, see Abitbol (1979) and Saad (1983).

others, all carefully colour-coded according to the reliability of the information received, in an attempt to establish universal "generations" out of the various genealogical lore that he has recorded – an undertaking that is "extremely difficult," he says, as "local accounts hardly ever match at all." Younoussa's scheme links all major and minor Songhay settlements in the Niger bend to each other in a clear pattern of precedence, before in turn connecting them to Moroccan and eastern origins: in this way, these settlements and their inhabitants are first ranked and then inscribed into universal history. Notionally, at least, his genealogies are part of the same scheme as Muḥammad Maḥmūd and Muḥammad al-Amīn's, and all three could be connected, although this might mean having to trace genealogies back to their very origins, potentially leading to squabbles over precedence, encompassment, and the respective moral worth and authenticity of the connections claimed. Like Muḥammad Maḥmūd and Muḥammad al-Amīn, Younoussa is striving for completeness, to the point where the final point of his preliminary endeavour retreats with every step that he takes towards reaching it: by their universalising nature, genealogical schemes are always open-ended. Nonetheless, it is obvious that all three "histories" will only ever mention a very small fraction of society in northern Mali: like beads on a string, genealogical narratives only pick out those who were contained in the storyline before it even started to unfold. As a result, hierarchy and questions of status are, once more, implicit in the very structure of their undertaking.

Beyond Muḥammad al-Amīn's and Younoussa's scholarly endeavours, genealogical logics transpire in everyday interactions. At times, such genealogical patterns of ordering are even – unwittingly perhaps – endorsed by the Algerian nation-state, although here a strict moral ranking in terms of northern or southern descent is maintained throughout. Algerian nationality is currently given to most "white" Malians who demand it, by all accounts for political and strategic reasons; nonetheless, as a formality, Algerian descent – however many degrees removed – needs to be proven, either through written genealogies or the testimony of two Algerian witnesses.[60] In the past, people say, southern Algerian families with ties in

[60] "Everybody" can now get an Algerian passport, Arabs in northern Mali all agree, "ever since Ghaddafi said that all Saharans could be Libyans if they wanted to, and Algeria got jealous." The Libyan consulate that was opened for this purpose in Kidal had to be shut after a few weeks of functioning, allegedly due to interference and threats by the Algerian secret services. Nonetheless, Malians with Algerian papers know the fragility of their legal status, as they are clearly treated as second-class citizens in Algeria (*Algériens Taiwan*), and as, by all accounts, Algerian security forces have no qualms about ignoring or even ripping up their papers, if state policy changes or if they take a personal dislike to

Mali would never declare if any of their sons died, keeping their names and juridical identity for Malian relatives in need of a passport. Such logic is prominent throughout southern Algeria, where the presence of northern Malian "cousins" has grown steadily, with the droughts of the 1970s and 1980s and the general insecurity of the 1990s.[61] Although these northern Malian immigrants were publicly portrayed as "foreign refugees," and certainly looked the part in the national and international media – poor, disoriented, and starving – many among them, especially Arabic speakers, were in fact familiar with southern Algeria through longstanding exchange and trade relations, and considered themselves as cousins or at worst in-laws rather than foreigners, and they had no qualms about making their claims heard – and, more importantly, often succeeded in doing so. Thus, the Nūājī, an Arabic-speaking group from the Tilemsi in northern Mali, claim descent from a saint buried near Tamantit. On arrival in Algeria, rather than settling in one of the various Red Cross refugee camps near the border – camps readily described as "shameful" and reserved for the "rabble" – they chose to "remember," travelled straight to their ancestor's tomb, and settled there. More remarkably, their claims were heeded: they were allowed to stay, and, some years later, the local council decided to rebuild their shacks and to connect them to the local electricity and water network, thereby publicly legalising their settlement. Today, residents in Tamantit explain this with a resigned shrug: "After all," they say, "they had come to settle with their grandfather: they said that if we wouldn't let them stay, they would leave and take their grandfather with them – just imagine the fuss!" It is difficult to ascertain to what extent this was true, or rather, what other less publicly avowable factors might also have played a part in this decision. Nonetheless, this is how it is portrayed today, in a way that makes sense to all.

The Nūājī are by no means an exception: hardly any settlement in the Touat would be complete without a Sahelian quarter, inhabited by cousins, in-laws, or clients. *Zawāyā* played a particularly important role in this, and a large number of Sahelians, many of whom had for generations paid allegiance to them (see Chapter 1) are now settled on their

the holder. Despite the presence of the state, public identity thus still relies on connections and local recognition of status claims.

[61] On the droughts of the 1970s and 1980s and their impacts on local society, see Comité d'Information Sahel (1975), Ag Foni (1979), Ag Baye and Bellil (1986), Ag Ahar (1990), and Giuffrida (2005a, 2005b). Few scholars have studied the presence of Sahelian refugees and settlers in southern Algeria, but see Bellil and Badi (1993, 1996), Badi (2007, 2011), and Chapter 6.

land: this is the case, for instance, in Zaouiat Kounta, and in Aoulef Cheurfa and Akabli in the Tidikelt.[62] This does not mean, however, that the Nūājī or equivalent and their Algerian "cousins" have manifested much family feeling in other contexts. Throughout southern Algeria, Sahelians are generally described as "Tuareg," a term that bluntly denies any genealogical proximity and that has come to serve as pejorative shorthand for "white Malian settler, uncouth, immoral, uncivilised, dirty, involved in illegal transborder trade, and generally beyond the pale of good society." Consequently, Hassaniya, the Arabic dialect spoken throughout the Western Sahel, is described as the "Arabic of the Tuareg"; while the long veil, worn by most Sahelian women, has come to stand for their "Berber culture" – by which is meant lax religious precepts and general troublesomeness – hence Lalla's outrage at being mistaken for a "Tuareg," hence also the possibility of making this mistake in the first place. At the same time, however, Sahelian women remain a never-ending source of fascination, particularly for Algerian girls, as they are seen to represent a thoroughly despicable, but nonetheless alluring ideal of femininity, independence, and "freedom" – and as many of them are indeed cousins or in-laws. Moreover, most southerners remember their own mothers and grandmothers, clad in a long colourful veil, and perhaps even reciting poetry or genealogies in Hassaniya or Tamasheq (see also Chapter 6). Rather than foreign, these newly recovered "cousins" are thus all too close to the bone, bearing witness, not least through their shared genealogies, to the uncomfortable proximity of the *bilād al-sūdān*: not surprisingly, then, most local artisanal fairs displaying "Saharan traditions" are staffed by Sahelian refugees, admired by large groups of giggling local girls, in modern *ḥijāb* and baseball caps.

KUNTA NORTH AND KUNTA SOUTH

This uncomfortable but undeniable proximity is perhaps best illustrated by the example of the Kunta. As seen in Chapter 1 and earlier in this chapter, the Kunta have long been influential throughout the region, while controlling much trade with the Touat (Génevière 1950, McDougall 1986). Although in northern Mali, some of their political sway has been questioned recently (see Chapter 3), their scholarly credentials and

[62] In Akabli, Sahelian settlement dates to the nineteenth century (Chardenet, "Akabli," n.d. (early 1900s), CAOM 22H50). For a similar example of another set of Nūājī in Morocco, see di Tolla (1996).

spiritual prestige are still widely respected, as well as commanding many followers throughout West Africa. As 'Abd al-Ḥamīd, a Kunta *shaykh* from Timbuktu who trained in Libya to work as an Arabic teacher in the Gambia, recalls[63]:

Each year, they organise a great gathering, all our *talāmīdh* [students, or adepts of the Kunta branch of the Qādiriyya] who live in the Gambia.[64] They come together and do the *dhikr*, and then they give presents to the *shaykhs* who are present. I only turned up out of curiosity, and they just kept giving me presents, as soon as they found out that I was a real Kunta ... There was also an elderly *shaykh*, who had so far been the only Kunta they had met, but when he heard that I was there and wanted to meet him – he might have been a cousin, who knows – he ran away, maybe thinking that I had come to expose him, he must have been fake – as if I would have known just by looking at him![65]

'Abd al-Ḥamīd also houses a few *talāmīdh* from the Malian countryside – all non-Arabic speakers, and "blacks" – who have come to study the Qur'ān with his family, and in exchange perform menial duties around the house. Meanwhile, 'Abd al-Ḥamīd's uncle is one of the leading Kunta *shaykhs* in Bamako, where he commands many followers, who only approach him on their knees, and who retire crawling backwards. He also runs a successful business selling amulets and giving spiritual advice and has both the outer appearance and inner conviction of a powerful vehicle of God's knowledge and *baraka*; but even traditionally minded Malians sometimes think his activities are beyond the limits of the publicly acceptable.[66] Acceptable or not, they are certainly lucrative.

In Algeria, the Kunta are less prominent, but their central settlement, Zaouiat Kounta in the Algerian Touat, is similarly recognized as a place of *baraka* and scholarship. Its leading *shaykh* teaches a large number of students and followers, recruited from throughout Algeria. On his rare trips

[63] In addition to scholarships for Malian students, the Libyan government also funds Arabic-language schools throughout Mali, and independent teaching positions (for a description of these schools and some tentative figures, see Bouwman 2005). It further trains Arabic-language teachers of West African origin and sends them on teaching missions throughout the region, thereby providing one of the few career options for local scholars trained in classical Arabic, or wanting to be so.

[64] Paul Marty (1920: 155) describes the *talāmīdh* of the Kunta as their dependents, the religious equivalent of the *laḥma* of the Barābīsh. For a similar argument that links the Kunta's commercial success to their extensive control of labour, see McDougall (1986). On the Kunta branch of the Qādiriyya, see Batran (2001).

[65] Interviewed in Timbuktu in December 2007.

[66] For a description of similar practices in northwestern Mali and debates over their legitimacy, see Soares (2005b, 2007); for a case study from Niger, see Masquelier (2009).

to Adrar, he is greeted by crowds of people coming up to ask his advice or blessing, and sometimes stooping to kiss his hand. Nonetheless, the Algerian Kunta, like most religious figures in Algeria, propound notions of religious legitimacy that are in keeping with Algerian official Islam and indeed are keen to be recognized as "proper" religious dignitaries, in Algerian rather than Saharan terms. Of course, their standard recited genealogy still includes reference to southern connections; but whereas, in the older literature, Zaouiat Kounta was described as a subsidiary settlement established by Kunta from the Azawād in what is today northern Mali, contemporary versions stress direct descent from Middle Eastern and North African ancestors, with the subsequent establishment of missionary colonies further south.[67] Proud of their southern connections that indirectly prove their *baraka* and religious legitimacy, they are nonetheless careful to mark their distinctiveness from their Malian cousins. This has become a matter of some importance, as, with the general arrival of northern Malians in southern Algeria, a large number of Malian Kunta have settled throughout the Touat, some in Zaouiat Kounta, but many more in Bani w-Iskut, the Sahelian quarter of Adrar (see Chapter 6). These Malian Kunta have become famous for the kind of activities that 'Abd al-Ḥamīd's uncle indulges in: the writing of amulets, for instance, or the curing of mental illnesses and disquiet. Others, especially women, act as fortune-tellers, healers, and soothsayers, cure infertility, and provide means to attract husbands. 'Abd al-Ḥamīd's maternal uncle, also a Kunta and resident in Bani w-Iskut, is among the leading experts here, and people come from far and wide to draw on his services. If the legitimacy of these practices is open to some debate in Mali, in Algeria, there is no doubt whatsoever that they are beyond the pale.

Notionally, this would be no problem at all, if the Malian Kunta's clients only included Malians and if their activities hence safely remained within the cosmopolitan underbelly of Bani w-Iskut. But they do not, and his and his cousins' services are frequently drawn on by the Algerian middle classes, especially women of good families, who were always deeply embarrassed when I ran into them as they were skilfully picking their way through Bani w-Iskut's characteristic rubbish heaps and feral goats and children. Algerians are especially confident in the spiritual powers of the Malian Kunta as they have long been familiar with their Algerian cousins' religious reputation. Malian Kunta know this and

[67] Compare, for instance, the genealogies recorded by P. Marty (1920), with contemporary oral versions, and Hūtiya (2007).

proudly display the documents – mostly genealogical manuscripts – that prove these close connections and show that, indeed, the Algerian and Malian Kunta's *baraka* is but one. The mere existence of such "papers" is widely resented by Algerian Kunta and is the cause of some worry. As one of the Malian Kunta, resident in Adrar, recalls:

> When I first came here, I was curious about Zaouiat Kounta, I had heard so much about it, and especially I wanted to see their manuscripts, so I went out there and spoke to them. They were very cagey, very worried, especially when they saw that I was used to reading manuscripts and that I had some of my own ... and they never let me see theirs. It was later that I understood why: they were afraid I would find my own name in one of their papers, and that I had come to claim my inheritance![68]

By no stretch of the imagination could such claims be anything but symbolic, but then this is perhaps the crux of the matter: what is at stake here are not so much fears about property, but rather worries about the proper use of the genealogically transmitted *baraka* that is shared by all Kunta, and, even more importantly, about the written documents that "prove" these connections.[69] Yet to deny the value of these "papers" and the shared *baraka* altogether would deprive the Algerian Kunta of their own religious and scholarly legitimacy.

As long as the Malian Kunta stay in the spiritual and geographical underworld of Bani w-Iskut, even this remains tolerable; yet all attempts to go beyond this are deeply resented, especially if they amount to bids to be recognised by the state, and thereby take on an independent and possibly irrevocable position within the conceptual grid of officialdom. In late 2006, after much political wrangling, a national manuscript centre was opened in Adrar; in March 2007, local scholars were invited for a first meeting that indirectly would define who would, from then on, be classified as a "manuscript owner" (see also Scheele 2010a). Among the crowd dressed in carefully ironed white robes and modern suits, one group of *shaykhs* stood out by their colourful garb, unkempt beards, and wild hairstyles: the Malian Kunta, visibly shunned by all, but whose pockets were bulging with Islamic manuscripts. As soon as they spotted my presence, they beckoned me to come over, showing me various letters sent to them from Timbuktu. Within minutes, another *shaykh*, soberly dressed

[68] Interviewed in Tit in March 2008.

[69] As Ho (2006) points out in the very different context of the Indian Ocean, the problem here is not so much that the Malian Kunta further superstition, that is to say, practices that do not work, but rather, that their practices do work, but in illicit ways.

in white, pulled me away: "don't you waste your time with them," he whispered, "them and their scraps of paper – they have nothing to do with us, they are mere sorcerers." Yet there was no denying that these "sorcerers" were his own cousins, nourished by the same *baraka* as himself; that they owned as many and as valuable manuscripts as anybody else, if not more; and, worst of all, that most of the Algerian manuscripts contained as many embarrassing notions and "unorthodox" practices as theirs. In a sense, the Kunta found themselves in the same conundrum as Muḥammad Maḥmūd seventy years earlier when he attempted to establish an overarching scheme of genealogical ranking in northern Mali: the written word threatened to establish an equivalence that could not be doubted, but that could neither be allowed to stand publicly. Both groups were painfully aware that they were drawing on the same frame of reference, on which their identity as religious scholars depended, and which they could thus not reject out of hand; yet they could not endorse it either, as the connections it established were, due to the presence of the state, about to be officially recognised within a conceptual framework that by its nature claims to establish irrevocable boundaries.

CONCLUSION

Saharan hierarchies have long fascinated scholars and have been explained in different ways, with varying heuristic success. French colonial explanations especially, centred on questions of labour and plagued with the requirements of a nascent state bureaucracy, tended to focus on the local and reason in terms of ranks and bounded entities, thereby often setting the pattern for later scholarship. Here, we looked at a different set of terms with which social hierarchies can be discussed, and one that is much favoured by local scholars: genealogies, generally referred to as *tawārīkh*, or "histories," that constitute the most popular form of historical writing throughout the region. As genealogies, these texts at first appear to establish equivalence rather than distinction; yet when they are read with reference to the wider framework within which they situate themselves – that of Islamic history, refracted through local histories of conversion – they implicitly rank human difference and moral worth, through reference to more or less prestigious ancestors, different modes of descent and inheritance, an emphasis on the moral duty to remember, and, most importantly perhaps, through omission. As an inherently universalising view of the world, these genealogies bear within them a promise of knowledge of a preordained and universal world order, within which everybody can find his or her place: hierarchy and identity become a problems of textual criticism and range, rather than of philosophical debate. However, any attempt to fulfil this promise, to map everybody's *ta'rīkh* onto one unified canvas, is impossible and deeply resented, as it fixes once and for all relations that are by definition bound to perspective. Moreover, in the contemporary border region, genealogical logics have to compete with other, perhaps more recent ways of constructing identity and difference, in particular those put forward by regional nation-states that, by their nature, struggle to establish homogeneous bounded entities rather than gradations of boundless relations. Yet older logics persist, potentially leading to considerable embarrassment among reluctant cousins, but also to at times surprising local arrangements of tolerable coexistence.

What is at stake in many of the debates sketched out in this chapter – between "Kunta north" and "Kunta south," among different readings of genealogical lore, among conflicting moral interpretations, or even between racial and genealogical notions of identity – is perhaps best understood not in terms of conflict and opposition but rather as struggles over encompassment. The validity of genealogical schemes – of descent, identity, history, and religious legitimacy – is rarely questioned as such, not even by regional nation-states; rather, people attempt to contain the others' claims within their own genealogical past, as becomes especially obvious in Kunta debates over precedence and the direction of past migration. Such genealogical models and struggles over encompassment parallel our overall argument for the outside dependence and essential connectivity of Saharan place: following genealogical schemes of explanation, local identity is similarly a function of external ties, hence making it inherently fragile and vulnerable to outside interference; influence is not about territorial cover, but it is a result of extensive range. Genealogies structure reality in terms of individual names, rather than places and groups: although these names often stand for larger formations, the latter are never given, but remain negotiable and potentially unbounded, while boundaries might occur within as much as between different localities and places and are always the result of an additional effort. A similar pattern emerges in regional political and legal systems that remain strikingly delocalised, while deriving their legitimacy neither from local representation not from centralised rule but from reference to the universal framework of the *sharīʿa*.

5

Universal Law and Local Containment

Assemblies, Quḍāh, *and the Quest for Civilisation*

> In this society, social cohesion follows the many correlations that link the most self-contained particular to the general while constantly threatening to explode it: two rival principals fighting over the physical reality of the country. They can be detected in geography as well as in law. On the one hand, extravagant expanses of land where people persevere apathetically against precariousness and establish property as prestigious as vague. On the other, those places – I was going to say opportunities – where property becomes consolidated and precise. On one side the fluid and its possibilities. On the other, the contained and its laws. (Berque 1974: 103)

One of the key elements of outside images of the Sahara is the notion that it lacked political and legal control. In colonial descriptions, this "lawlessness," epitomised in the image of desert raiders, appears as both the result of ecological constraints and as their cause: had there only been more political order and reliable legal institutions, the argument runs, the desert would have blossomed.[1] "Anarchy" is thus seen to be reflected in the physical environment of the Sahara, Berque's "extravagant expanses of land" bereft of all visible markers of legal order or "civilisation." This

[1] See, for example, Montaudon (1883: 142): "Victims of exactions, of internal warfare, of warriors, the Arabs had to find a way of avoiding ruin, they had to mobilise their wealth, and instead of seeking their well-being and stability by tilling the soil, they became pastoralists, they took to living in tents, and acquired herds that were easier to keep away from the rapacity of their chiefs; they buried their money which thereby became unproductive." See also Pein, "Situation générale et projets d'occupation des oasis sahariennes," 28/12/1900, CAOM 22H33; and "Lettre du Colonel Cauchemez, commandant militaire des Oasis sahariennes au général commandant la subdivision de Laghouat," 24/11/1900, CAOM 22H33. For the most notorious exposition of the theory of an inevitable link between prosperity, climate, agriculture, and centralised rule, see Gautier (1927).

image is echoed in external Arabic sources, where the Sahara tends to be described as "lawless," as a place where legal contracts become void, and that is literally beyond civilisation.[2] Similar notions are reproduced on the ground, where, as we have seen throughout, notions of "civilisation" are opposed to that of "wilderness," all too easily associated with the *bādiya*, the uninhabited steppe bereft of legal boundaries. And indeed, as seen in Chapter 4, in the *bādiya*, notions of political influence, rights of access and predominance rarely took territorial forms. Rather, political power tended to be described in terms of overlapping influences radiating from a number of powerful centres, be their military, economic or religious.[3] "Community" was defined in social rather than territorial terms, and was inherently unbounded. Meanwhile, concepts of lawfulness, invariably tied up with Islam, were often developed in opposition to the powers that be.

At first sight, oasis towns, like those of the Algerian Touat that provide the material studied in this chapter, look rather different. Here, one is struck not only by the minute division of land, and the visible presence of nucleated settlement and neat and defined boundaries, but also by what looks like a surplus of law, or rather, by the vast quantities of legal documents, found in most households (see Photos 5.1 to 5.3). In the absence of a centralised state, these were produced by a variety of independent local institutions, mainly religious scholars and *quḍāh*, but also by local assemblies (*jamāʿāt*) of different sizes, scopes, and definitions, one of which will be described here in some detail. Most of these documents are concerned with private property, thereby creating, at least notionally, Berque's contained spaces where "property becomes consolidated and precise." Yet this visible containment is misleading: as Chapter 1 has shown, oases are necessarily part and parcel of larger networks that influence their internal

2 There has been some debate over the degree to which the Sahara was seen as beyond the reach of Islamic law, in particular among historians of trans-Saharan trade. Hence, Ralph Austen wrote in 1990, and then again in 2002, clearly after he had discussed the matter with Lydon, that "trans-Saharan trade was considered so risky as to be outside the jurisdiction of Islamic commercial law and even beyond the pale of general respectability" (1990: 340). Ghislaine Lydon, drawing on local archival documents of the kind used presented here, more convincingly argues that trans-Saharan trade could only function because of the possibilities offered by Islamic law (see especially 2008: 91). Both were probably right, depending on the range and social framework of transactions considered.

3 For further discussion of this point, see Bourgeot (1994), Claudot-Hawad (1998), Retaillé (1998), Lecocq (2003), Bonte (2008), and Grémont (2010). As the latter put it (2012): "From a Tuareg point of view ... to 'control space' seems to have had little meaning, and Tuareg of the eighteenth and nineteenth centuries rarely used this or similar concepts to express, construct, materialise, acknowledge or defend political pre-eminence."

PHOTO 5.1. Library in Talmin.

PHOTO 5.2. Legal documents.

constitution and rely on their relative legibility. Moreover, the law in question was the *sharī'a* and hence derives its validity and legitimacy from its correspondence to outside models, in other words, from its intellectual connectivity. Much as the genealogies discussed in Chapter 4 give universal names to local people, Islamic legal categories rephrase local transactions and thereby reconstitute them as part of a wider moral world. As a result, as it emerges from Touati sources, sedentary "community" appears as no more bounded or indeed "natural" than nomadic federations or trade networks of the kind discussed in Chapters 2 and 3. Little emphasis was placed on locality or even coresidence. Sources of legitimacy and even political power were rarely locally bounded, even though they acted to mark off a defined space of "civilisation" as against the encroaching *bādiya*. Nonetheless, torn between both universalising and localising tendencies, between porosity and containment, universalising legal aspirations – much like genealogical equivalences – often faltered on the ground, as local realities were recalcitrant to translation into the immutable categories of law, and necessarily remained socially determined. There is no doubt that *quḍāh* and notaries failed as often as saints, and that legal "papers," much as the "civilisation" they were describing,

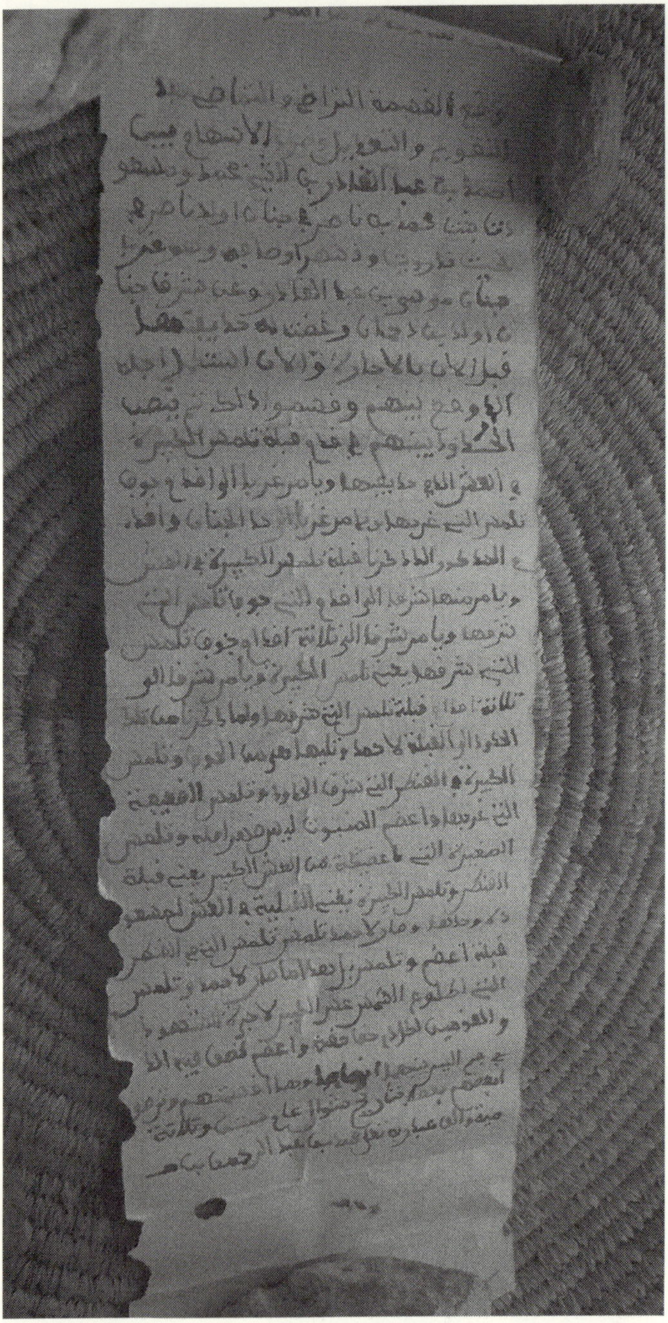

PHOTO 5.3. Contract.

were inherently fragile: but they nonetheless bore witness to the desire – or even the necessity – to be part of a wider world.

THE TOUAT: POLITICAL HISTORY AND COLONIAL INTERPRETATIONS

Until the French conquest at the turn of the twentieth century, state control in the Touat was at best rudimentary.[4] Nominally, the Touat came under the control of the Moroccan Sultan in 1526. But it regained independence in 1552, and Moroccan political influence remained patchy over the following centuries (Martin 1908). From 1795 until 1892, the region was "internally autonomous" (Grandguillaume 1973: 451) and paid no taxes. Precolonial local sources, such as the *Nawāzil al-ghuniya*, make no mention of Moroccan government representatives (*quyyād*, sing. *qā'id)* or even of the Moroccan sultan. Instead, they frequently deplore the absence of state authority. It is only with the last decade of the nineteenth century that Moroccan *quyyād* reappear in the Touat. Most of these seem to have been appointed to face the threat posed by the French army advancing south from Laghouat, either to strengthen Moroccan claims to the area, or in answer to local petitions.[5] These *quyyād* were nominally organised into a hierarchy centred on the newly appointed *āghā* of Timimoun, who attempted to levy taxes on the inhabitants of the Gourara proper, Touat and Tidikelt. His authority on the ground, as well as his own allegiance to the sultan, was however fragile. According to French colonial spies, "the *quyyād* transmit orders that they received from the *āghā* established in Timimoun: but these are rarely executed or even answered."[6]

[4] The question of the extent of Moroccan rule was then and remains until now highly politicised (Lecocq 2010: 61–8, see, e.g., Ma'zūzī 1978), and all information has to be treated with suspicion.

[5] "Lettre du capitaine Godron au colonel supérieur de Ghardaïa," 7/01/1894, CAOM 22H38. According to French colonial reports, these *quyyād* were either wealthy traders with extensive dealings with the west, that is to say with areas where Moroccan control was stronger, or religious dignitaries claiming, like the Moroccan sultan, descent from the Prophet, or the presidents of local assemblies (*jamā'āt*, sing. *jamā'a*), for whom this appointment by the sultan seem to have been merely an additional token of legitimacy. See "Notices sur les personnages influents Touat, Gourara, Tidikelt," 1893, CAOM 22H36.

[6] "Plan général d'occupation à adopter au Gourara et au Touat, après la prise de possession des oasis par nos colonnes, par le général commandant la division d'Alger," n.d., (early 1900s), CAOM 22H56. See also General de la Roque, "Lettre au Gouverneur Général de l'Algérie," 17/02/1896, CAOM 22H56; Simon, "Notices sur le Tidikelt," 20/06/1900,

On their arrival in the Touat in 1899–1901, the French adopted, more or less wholesale, the sultan's embryonic administrative structure.[7] And, presumably like him, they were dismayed by its inefficiency. In 1907, several years and a colonial conquest later, the annual report of the Touat notes with some misgiving the "habit of independence" displayed by local assemblies (*jamāʿāt*, sing. *jamāʿa*) that, "before 1901, were fully independent in their *qṣar* and had only vaguely submitted to the Moroccan sultan and his pashas."[8] The inhabitants of the Touat "hide with jealous care behind their ancient communal franchises"; their "judicial power" ought to be suppressed.[9] But what exactly were these "assemblies," "communal franchises," and "judicial power"? According to a late nineteenth-century report:

> In the districts of the Gourara and the Touat, every *qṣar* is administered by a *jamāʿa* ... The *jamāʿa* is the meeting of the notables of the *qṣar*. These notables or *kibār* are those who, by their age, their personal influence or their wealth, have influence over their fellow citizens. The number of *kibār* is not restricted. There is no special meeting place, the *kibār* meet at the house of one of them when this is necessary. The *jamāʿāt* suppress minor and criminal offences with disciplinary punishments, namely beating and fines. The fines are used to buy provisions for guests. As there is no public treasury, they are immediately converted into staples. These staples are kept in a communal house.[10]

These assemblies judged in all matters of public concern. Not surprisingly, traces of such judgements contained in the French colonial archives mainly relate to French spies: hence, in 1893, a trader from Metlili was brought before the assembly of Timimoun, where his letters to the French authorities were read out in public, as proof of his guilt; he was then condemned to a fine of five hundred francs and banned from Timimoun, but only after he had wound up his business transactions and recovered his

Swiney, "Lettre au Gouverneur Général de l'Algérie," 24/02/1894, both CAOM 22H36. In one case, if we believe the testimony of French spies to the area, as the *āghā*, accompanied by the local *qāʾid*, was attempting to intervene in a dispute over cultivated land, locals refused to listen, and the *āghā* had to "run away," as the opposing parties launched into a fight: Swiney, "Lettre au Gouverneur Général de l'Algérie," 25/05/1893, CAOM 22H36.

7 "Colonel Cauchemez, commandant militaire des oasis sahariennes, au général commandant la subdivision de Laghouat," 24/11/1900, CAOM 22H33.

8 "Rapport annuel, annexe du Touat," 1907, CAOM 23H91.

9 "Rapports annuels, poste du Touat," 1909 and 1910, CAOM 23H91.

10 "Plan général d'occupation." See also General de la Roque, "Lettre au Gouverneur Général de l'Algérie," 17/02/1896, CAOM 22H56; and the "Rapport annuel, poste du Touat," 1909, CAOM 23H91.

debts in the oasis.[11] Assemblies also represented their *qṣūr* to the outside and, before the French conquest of the Touat, sent several petitions to the French army command, asking them to "let everybody stay in their country: you where you are now, and we in ours."[12] Later, similar petitions asked for French protection.[13]

As time went by, however, French colonial reports on local municipal institutions became markedly less enthusiastic. In In Salah, the main oasis of the neighbouring Tidikelt, the French colonial officer Simon noted the relative absence of any political institutions beyond family councils. "In times of crisis, men of a certain age come together, and everybody can speak: but this is an assembly without a leader, and whose decisions are rarely put into practice." Similarly, in Foggarat ez-Zoua, there was no *qā'id*, no *shaykh*, no permanent assembly: "whosoever injures his neighbour, willingly or not, pays him a compensation that is equivalent to what he has lost. Mostly, such arrangements are concluded by private agreement. In disputed cases, the parties appeal to a few notables, whose wisdom is acknowledged by all."[14] General de la Roque described local political organisation in the Tidikelt in similar terms, noting the complexity of a political system "based on families and municipalities." Political life "blossoms within local assemblies" that are characterised by the "absence of all executive power" and hence difficult to coopt by the French state. Direct orders necessarily fail; what matters is general consensus.[15] Legislative power was even more elusive: although several reports list abstract references to past punishments, and even mention written law-codes established by assemblies, all of these "have been lost for at least two generations," or else might never have existed.[16] This, then, according to Simon again, was "a society free of conventions, but that nonetheless seems very happy."[17]

Although overall, French colonial officers found Saharan political institutions thus rather disappointing, they were impressed by the ability

[11] Swiney, "Lettre au Gouverneur Général de l'Algérie," 8/09/1893, CAOM 22H38.

[12] "Lettre des notables du Touat," n.d. (late 1890s), CAOM 22H26.

[13] "Lettre des Ouled bou Anane, Douï Menia, au commandant de la subdivision d'Aïn Séfra," 13/12/1318 AH (2/04/1901); and "Lettre de la djemaa des Assaça au chef du poste Djenan ed Dar," 1318 AH (1901), both CAOM 22H33.

[14] Simon, "Notices sur le Tidikelt," 20/06/1900, CAOM 22H50.

[15] de la Roque, "Lettre au Gouverneur Général de l'Algérie," 17/02/1896, CAOM 22H56; see also Chardenet, "Aoulef," n.d. (early 1900s), CAOM 22H50.

[16] Simon, "Notices"; and Didier, "Projet pour l'organisation du Gourara et du Touat," 5/05/1896, CAOM 22H56.

[17] Simon, "Notices sur le Tidikelt," 20/06/1900, CAOM 22H50.

and efficiency displayed by local assemblies with regards to hospitality and the management of communal stores and property:

> In the Touat, everybody who owns anything contributes to the food of guests passing through his *qṣar*. Specific days are ascribed to him over the course of the year in proportion to his wealth, generally assessed according to the share of water that he owns. The 365 days of the year are thus divided between all the inhabitants of the *qṣar* who can provide the *ḍiyāfa* [literally, hospitality, meal offered to guests]. This is written on a list that is used for several years. It is only changed in case of death or sale. The guests are fed by the inhabitant whose turn it is on the day when they arrive, on the condition however that their number does not exceed a certain limit, varying from one *qṣar* to the next.[18]

Or, in the neighbouring Wād Draʻa, near the contemporary Moroccan border:

> Strangers can travel in the entire Wād Draʻa without having to worry about food. They are lodged, for up to three days, in each *qṣar* where they arrive. In order to meet the expenses caused by this, the locals deduct a tenth of their date and grain harvest ... These staples are stored under the supervision of the *shaykh*, and the inhabitants take turns in being called on to prepare food for the guests.[19]

This hospitality was open to all: witness the experience of Karl Knelles, a German foreign legionnaire who had escaped from the French military and fled to Figuig in 1900, where he was put up in the town gatehouse alongside several other European deserters, fed, clothed, and eventually set to work with a local carpenter – only to find out that quite a number of other deserters had been incorporated into the *qṣar* before him, in much the same manner.[20] In an area plagued by a chronic shortage of labour, as well as by the necessity to tame potentially disruptive "guests" and attract regional trade, proactive hospitality clearly played a key role in local administration.

On a more practical level, hospitality necessarily relied on collective stores or levies, and hence a minimum of municipal organisation: and indeed, as indicated by local archival documents, such collective stores, as well as the administration of communal property and infrastructures, seem to have been at the heart of municipal institutions. In one case recorded in the French colonial archives, a local assembly was accused of

[18] "Annexe du Touat. Propositions du chef de l'annexe pour l'hébergement des hôtes arabes au chef-lieu," 9/04/1902, CAOM 22H48.

[19] Régnault, "Rapport sur le Oued Draa," 5/01/1904, CAOM 22H50.

[20] "Lettre du chef d'escadrons de Pimoden au commandant d'armes d'Ain Sefra," 26/10/1900, CAOM 22H33.

illegally selling water rights that were *muḥabbas*, indicating the role the assembly played in the administration of local infrastructure and communal property.[21] Assemblies routinely stepped in to claim estates left by owners who died heirless. They could further levy market taxes or individual contributions on all residents, in order to refill their stores earmarked for hospitality and to appoint officers in charge of managing them, alongside the irrigation system and the local mosque.[22] These officers could include the imam, the *waqqāf* (overseer) who was charged with the reception of strangers, the water measurer (*kayyāl al-mā'*), the *barrāḥ* in charge of public announcements, and the *wakīl*, who acted as steward to the mosque: mostly offices connected to the administration of communal property, in other words.[23] A similar image appears in the *Ghuniya*, where collective stores and hospitality seem to be among the defining features of local assemblies and where they are portrayed collectively offering "gifts" to nomads threatening to raid their town.[24] This emphasis on collectively managed property might go some way towards explaining the relative lack of political institutionalisation deplored by the French colonial officers: while they were looking for village assemblies on the European or perhaps the Kabyle model, Touati assemblies are perhaps better compared to Moroccan collective storehouses run by a council of co-owners (Montagne 1930b, Jacques-Meunié 1951), or to assemblies of shareholders in irrigation system in medieval southern Spain (Halpern 1934, Glick 1970).[25]

IRRIGATION RECORDS: PROPERTY AND POLITICS

Local irrigation records, the most common form of indigenous municipal documentation that survives in the Algerian Touat, confirm this emphasis on property and collective management of infrastructure. But they also undermine the French colonial assumption of locally bounded communities of coresidents as the primary focus of political action and legitimacy. The main purpose of these registers was to list, month after

[21] Swiney, "Lettre au Gouverneur Général de l'Algérie," 23/03/1894, CAOM 22H38.
[22] Didier, "Projet pour l'organisation du Gourara et du Touat," 5/05/1896, CAOM 22H56.
[23] Barthel, "In Salah et l'archipel touatien," 15/4/1902, CAOM 10H22.
[24] NG: 142.
[25] Notwithstanding French colonial models, this emphasis on property also runs through much European material on village assemblies: for a review, see Saboul (1956) and Blum (1971a, 1971b); for further European examples, see Reynolds (1984) and Davies (1988).

month, the ways in which the overall water produced by a given irrigation canal (*faggāra* or *sāqiya*) was divided among its owners. They are rather uniform, and the following extract from the register of the *faggāra* Adjellaoune in the Timmi drafted in the early 1950s can be taken as representative:

> Praise be upon the one God, and God's blessing upon our lord Muḥammad. 1370. [1950 AD. This is] the register of the division of the *sāqiya* Sīdi al-Kabīr. It concerns the repetition of its measure, on the day of the 18th of Ṣafar the blessed, in the year 1370. Altogether there are now 171 *mājil* and 5 of the *qīrāṭ* and 7 *qīrāṭ* and 19 *qīrāṭ* of the *qīrāṭ* with the addition of two *mājil* and 4 *qīrāṭ* and 15 of the *qīrāṭ* and a third from the large [*sāqiya*].[26] Of this, one *mājil* is for 'Abd al-Raḥmān b. al-Sāliḥ in care of (*'alā yad*) Mūlāy al-Sālim: 18 *qīrāṭ* from the *sāqiya* Tīlilān from the sons of Aḥmad b. Ajja 'Abd al- Raḥmān the second, and 6 *qīrāṭ* from the *sāqiya* al-Shaykh from 'Abd Allāh b. Aḥmad b. al-Walīd, and a *mājil* from the provisions (*'awl*) of the *faggāra* on lease (*bi-kirā'*) [the list continues for two pages] ... The servant of his Lord 'Abd al-Raḥmān b. Muḥammad al-Salām and the servant of his God Abī Anuwār b. Muḥammad al-Salām and the servant of his God the exalted 'Abd Allāh b. Aḥmad b. al-Walīd, may God protect him, *amīn*.[27]

Fagāgīr, as described in Chapter 1, are underground water canals that produce the majority of water that was consumed in the greater Touat before the French colonial administration started digging artesian wells; *sawāqin* (plural of *sāqiya*) are overground canals transporting parts of the overall quantity of water produced by a given *faggāra*. Due to their length and technical sophistication, *fagāgīr* needed heavy initial capital outlay and labour; and the water they produced was thus at a premium.[28] *Fagāgīr* were divided into original shares (*uṣūl*, sing. *aṣl*) that were owned individually. The distribution of shares followed the initial investment provided when the *faggāra* was first dug.[29] Over time, with the application

[26] A *mājil* is the largest quantity used in local irrigation records and corresponds to one large pool of water that notionally takes one day to fill up. A *qīrāṭ* is equivalent to one twenty-fourth of a *mājil*, a *qīrāṭ* of a *qīrāṭ* is a twenty-fourth of a *qīrāṭ*. Although these measurements clearly show their origins in water measurements based on time, that is to say, on proportion – as is still the case in both Ghadamès (Eldblom 1968) and southern Tunisia (Bédoucha 1987) – in the greater Touat, they have by all accounts long come to refer to absolute quantities (see also Grandguillaume 1975).

[27] ZF: 3 and 4.

[28] Although water as such cannot be owned according to Islamic law, once effort has been put into bringing it to the surface or transporting it, it can be bought and sold like cultivated land. For a brief outline of Islamic legal elaborations on water rights, see Vidal Castro (1995) on Islamic Andalusia and Powers (2002: 103–5) on Morocco.

[29] For a fuller description of ownership rights in Touati *fagāgīr*, see Grandguillaume (1973, 1975, 1978) and Marouf (1980).

of the Islamic laws of inheritance, the establishment of endowments and sales, patterns of ownership became exceedingly complex. Ownership more generally was conceived according to Islamic legal categories, and both the original shares and the water they produced could thus be sold, hired, leased, and mortgaged without much constraint, often, as seen in Chapter 1, to owners who were resident elsewhere.[30] Further, as the above extract shows, property rights in *fagāgīr* not necessarily indicated use rights in water, as usufruct was commonly held on lease (*bi-kirā'*), in the custody (*'alā yad*) or with the mediation (*bi-wasāṭa*) of a third person.[31] Ownership and possession hence did not necessarily overlap, and, as seen in Chapter 1, absentee owners were common. One, if not the main purpose of these irrigation registers was thus to note who, at a given point in time, had the right to use how much water and of which exact provenance.

Secondly, assemblies were in charge of the regular maintenance of *fagāgīr*. As indicated in Chapter 1, *fagāgīr* are necessarily dug in soft soil, and as soon as they are put to use, they start silting up. This means that they needed constant maintenance. As noted in Chapter 1, the registers repeatedly mention the subtraction of fixed amounts of water "for the emptying" (*li-kabūyihi*) or extension (*nafakh*, literally "swelling") of water canals, or for other urgent repairs decided collectively. As seen in the extract above, funds were also raised by leasing out water from the "provision" (*'awl*) of the *faggāra*, presumably a collectively held pool of water, against a fee paid "to the *faggāra*" itself. [32] This required a minimum of organisation. Today everybody simply states that both the keeping of records and the maintenance of a given *faggāra* were in the hands of the assembly, *al-jamā'a*. The irrigation registers themselves, however, phrased the matter rather differently, by focusing on ownership rather than local residence. Hence, the opening lines of the register of the *faggāra* Rawḍat al-Ḥājj:

And this [register] is written by he who was present for all of it and who verified it after the counting. And its exactitude was [verified by] the presence of several

[30] Grandguillaume (1973) claims that, in the Touat, the possibility of selling *uṣūl* was a recent innovation, but this seems difficult to prove. Throughout the *Ghuniya*, original water shares are explicitly described as analogous to land (also described as *aṣl*, a root that literally means "origin, root"), that is, they can be sold although they cannot, strictly speaking, be described as "moveable property," and although certain rights and obligations attach to them.

[31] See, for example, ZF: 8. Problems about leases of water are recurrent in the *Ghuniya*, see for instance NG: 138 and 140.

[32] ZF: 4.

of its owners (*arbāb*) [here follows a list of names]. Then the aforementioned *faggāra* was measured publicly in the middle of Ramadan in the aforementioned year by [more names]. And this was written by who was present and it was verified by the presence of several notables, owners of the *faggāra*.[33]

Other entries refer to the "associates" or "co-owners" (*shurakā'*) of a given *faggāra* or *sāqiya*; but there is no direct mention of the *jamā'a* independent of ownership.[34] Hence, what seems to matter, and indeed to confer the right of representation and decision making, is property rather than residence or any other kind of "citizenship" conceived according to territorial models or notions of descent. Keeping in mind the scattered nature of property described in Chapter 1, this meant that that political influence was not necessarily locally bounded, but followed the overlapping connections established by alienable property rights.

Starting, as the French colonial officers did, with an assumption of "traditional" bounded village communities, one might wonder at this absence of local protectionism, and perhaps blame it on the "alien" or even "alienating" influence of Islamic law. Islamic notions of property established few distinctions between potential buyers beyond the immediate family circle; Islamic law more generally finds it difficult to allow for municipal corporations of any kind, unless through legal ruse. Hence, Grandguillaume (1973, 1975, 1978) attempts to explain the permeability of local councils by arguing that Islamic law had gradually been imposed on a preexisting, autonomous, and bounded community governed according to "customary" law, and that this imposition, orchestrated by incoming *shurafā'* had indeed resulted in their current privileged position (see Chapter 4). Once applied, he states, Islamic law took its own inevitable course, leading to the growing "individualism" that he detects in the cases recorded in the *Ghuniya*. As shown in Chapter 1, however, the assumption of a prior autonomous community is problematic, and it is never quite clear who would have imposed the *sharī'a* on whom, and on what grounds other than religious and therefore legal prestige. Instead, all local sources indicate that local assemblies endorsed Islamic law quite willingly, eager to do the "right thing." Moreover, the notion of a direct correspondence between legal categories and local activities on the ground is hasty: the notion of property as an individual

33 *Zamām Rawḍat al-Ḥājj* (p. 1), courtesy of Shaykh b. al-Walīd.

34 For example, ZF: 1, 9, and 12. The term *sharika*, although a recognised type of legal association, seems to have been used rather loosely here: see below.

and alienable right, and the virtual absence of distinction between real estate and chattels put forward by Islamic law poses problems to all legally minded agricultural societies in the Islamic world. Where they thought it necessary, peasants have always found ways and means of circumventing such prescriptions in order to keep their landed property intact, without lessening their overall commitment to Islam (Wilkinson 1978: 58, Powers 1993, Mundy 1995). Other oasis societies in the Sahara, moreover, seem to have paid much less heed to Islamic requirements (Bédoucha 2001). In the Touati documents, by contrast, very little is made of legal loopholes that would make it possible to counteract these centrifugal tendencies. Islamic law proposes a large number of contracts that allow for collective ownership and management and that were clearly known throughout the area (see, e.g., Lydon 2008), none of which are drawn on locally: the chapter on "associations" (*sharika*) that occupies fifteen pages of the *Ghuniya* not once mentions municipal institutions or groups of owners beyond the family.[35] Similarly, the number of *aḥbās* established to protect family property from circulation is strikingly low.

The argument from legal determinism, then, seems faulty; neither does this look like a "community" struggling to protect itself against outside intruders imposing "law." Rather, as argued in Chapter 1, the opposition between the local and the external is misplaced here. Both are coterminous and bring each other into existence. Islamic law is at the heart of irrigation councils, much as oases rely on outside funds and investment to survive: cutting the local of from the wider connections that made it in the first place – in economic, social, and moral terms – was simply not an option. The establishment of family endowments (*aḥbās*), perhaps the best known means of circumventing the centrifugal tendency of the Islamic law of inheritance, can stand as an example here. *Aḥbās* are mentioned in almost a third of all documents in the *qāḍī*'s register mentioned in Chapter 1 (and discussed in more detail below). In almost half of these cases, however, this is not because new *aḥbās* are set up, or were transmitted intact, but rather because people petitioned to convert them back into private property, because, as they say, due to a lack of water and labour, the land has "died" or has been "invaded by sands."[36] In an area dependent on outside investment and exchange, "stopping" (the original

35 See NG: 288–303.

36 See, for instance, SQ: 19, quoted in full later.

sense of the Arabic root *ḥabasa*) property from normal circulation does not seem to have been a viable option in the long term.[37] In such circumstances, bounded communities were not necessarily the most salient local category of thought, aspiration and, indeed, political legitimacy.

APPEALS TO LEGAL SCHOLARS

Yet this picture needs to be nuanced further. The desire to apply Islamic law locally is one thing, while its practical execution is quite another. Assemblies necessarily relied on legal scholars as experts, but, in the absence of state enforcement or appointment, the relations between these scholars and local councils were complex, based on mutual dependence and numerous "arrangements." Colonial documents leave no doubt that the *jamāʿāt* were assisted in their "judgements" and in particular in their dealing with property by local Islamic scholars described variously as *ṭullāb* (schoolteachers, notaries), *fuqahāʾ* (jurisconsuls), *ʿulamāʾ* (scholars), or *quḍāh*. The annual report of 1908 explains that the *jamāʿāt* judged crimes and civil matters, but consulted *fuqahāʾ* of their choice in civil matters and those pertaining to personal status.[38] Other documents state that "conflicts between individuals are resolved by *ṭullāb*," or else that "a certain number of *ʿulamāʾ* settle local disputes."[39] In 1896, Didier noted, probably with some exaggeration, that there was "a *qāḍi* in every *qṣar*." He was mainly in charge of matters of personal status, property divisions, and inheritance:

> Inheritances are settled in the presence of members of the *jamāʿa*. An inventory of goods is drawn up by the *qāḍi* who then divides the inheritance among those who are entitled to it according to Muslim law ... If there are no heirs, all goods go to the *qṣar*; they are sold immediately, and exchanged for cereals and dates that are put into the communal storehouses.[40]

In 1929, after French colonial interference and in their characteristically muddled jargon, "Muslim justice" (meaning probably "indigenous

[37] This, however, is particular to the Touat: Eldblom (1968: 154, 196) notes that 80 per cent of land and water in Ghadamès and 50 per cent in Ghāt were held as family *aḥbās*, although this did not necessarily restrict actual sales. Yet we must keep in mind that Ghadamès was inhabited by successful Saharan merchants, who could channel their own investment into land and water back home.

[38] "Rapport annuel, annexe du Touat," 1908, CAOM 23H91.

[39] "Lettre du général Risbourg, commandant la division d'Oran, au Gouverneur Général de l'Algérie," 29/10/1900, CAOM 22H50; and Lt Ray Hardy. "Une terre qui meurt: le Touat," 30/04/1933, CAOM 10H86.

[40] Didier, "Projet d'organisation du Gourara et du Touat," 5/05/1896, CAOM 22H56.

justice") was rendered "according to ancient customs by the *jamā'āt* after consulting with *fuqahā'*, the three most influential of whom meet every three months in Adrar and know everything about personal status."[41]

In their daily practice, however, these scholars were quite as dependent on assemblies as the latter were on the knowledge they could offer. To cite, once more, French colonial sources:

> Judgements pronounced by the *quḍāh* of the Gourara are in fact considered in the courts of northern Algeria as having no legal value, because the Gourara *quḍāh* are not properly appointed, and because they have no assessors and no seals. The same applies to testimonies established by local *fuqahā'* that are not seen to be genuine because they are only signed [not sealed], and are thus not admitted as proofs by the magistrates of the Tell.[42]

Indeed, local documents and even oral history rarely refer to regular "appointments" of judges by a central authority that might grant them a seal. *Quḍāh* quite simply became *quḍāh* because they were recognised for their scholarship, or because they belonged to families long known to have provided *quḍāh*.[43] Examples of such families are the Bakrawiyyin in Tamantit and the Balbaliyyin in the Timmi (see also Grandguillaume 1975: 288), both recognised to be of sharifian descent and on whose family archives provide much of the documentation studied here.[44]

Although locally, this lack of official appointment does not seem to have posed a problem, strictly speaking and beyond the Touat, it clearly did, and local scholars were clearly aware of this. In Islamic law, there are three ways of establishing judicial evidence: self-accusation, testimony of reliable witnesses, or oath. A *qāḍi*'s judgement further counts as a proof that outweighs past testimony (Johansen 1990). As a result, much relies on the status of either "witness" or "*qāḍi*":

> The person who states the evidence has to be recognised as a witness or a judge. This recognition presupposes that he fulfils certain legal and social conditions,

41 "Poste du Touat, rapport annuel," 1929, CAOM 23H91. Although this *majlis* was endorsed by the French colonial authorities, it seems to have been an at least formal continuation of earlier practices: archival records mention precolonial judicial councils throughout, as does the *Ghuniya* (see NG: 222–31).

42 "Rapport annuel, poste du Gouara," 1908, CAOM 23H91.

43 Didier, "Projet"; and R. Hardy, "Une terre qui meurt." Simon, however, mentions that the *qāḍi* of Sahel claims to have been appointed by the Moroccan sultan: "Notices sur le Tidikelt," 20/06/1900, CAOM 22H50.

44 The hereditary nature of the judgeship is by no means exceptional: in Yemen, the title of *qāḍi* was long recognised to imply descent rather than calling (Dresch 1989, vom Bruck 1998).

> but requires especially that the representative of a public or legal authority recognise that the person in question can be admitted to exercise this power. (Johansen 1997: 336)

Hence, *quḍāh* ought to be appointed by a public authority, which in turn empowers them to ultimately decide on the reliability of witnesses. But, in the absence of a state, what does and what does not qualify as a "public or legal authority"?

This question is treated with some detail in the *Ghuniya*, indicating that it was locally considered to be important. Hence, the opening of the chapter on judges:

> About the general assembly (*al-jamāʿat al-ʿāmiya*) verily it appoints (*qaddamat*) who judges (*yaḥkum*) between them. Are they like a representative (*ka-muqaddam*) of the imam or an assembly of the just (*ʿadūl*) and the learned (*ʿulamā*ʾ) or are they like the governor (*al-ḥākim*)? ... And is [the decision] binding for those who do not attend, is it decided for them or does [the representative thus appointed] only rule in matters that are under the jurisdiction of *quḍāh*?
>
> And he answered as follows: as to the question of the appointment of the governor by the assembly (*naṣb al-jamāʿa li-l-ḥākim*) for what is arbitrated (*taḥkīm*) by judges. And the *shaykh* Sālim transmits that ... in the remotest parts of the country and when there is no sultan the most pious (*sāliḥūn*) in the country appoint the position of the imam. And al-Baghrawī said in his commentary on the *risāla*: and who appoints him, I mean the *qāḍi*, he is the most formidable imam or his representative if he is just. And if there is not one suitable in the assembly of the Muslims they are the ones who stand in his place inasmuch as the execution of authority (*iqāmat al-sulṭa*) is incumbent on them. And there are three conditions on those who among the people appoint the imam: integrity (*ʿadāla*), knowledge relating to whom deserves the position of imam, and opinion. And the court (*maḥkama*) of those who choose the imam: [they should be] the soundest and the most appropriate for the matter and those who know best.[45]

The *qāḍi*'s answer seems to be purposefully vague: it is not clear whether the "general assembly" refers to the inhabitants of a *qṣar*, or rather to a council of jurists, along the lines of the *majlis* of judges mentioned in the French colonial sources. In either case, it provides a rationale for the legitimacy of *quḍāh* who were appointed by their peers, and whose activities were endorsed by a local assembly of "notables," while further increasing their dependence on local backing.

As a result, relationships between the *qāḍi* and the assembly were close – all too close, perhaps, for legal scholars with exacting standards. An unnamed *qāḍi* cited in the *Ghuniya* notes ruefully that, in 1738, he

[45] NG: 616.

had endorsed a *ṣulḥ* that local "notables" (*a'yān*) had imposed on two quarrelling members against their will. Yet on further reflection, the *qāḍi* realises that such proceedings were "unlawful," "repents," and asks for "God's forgiveness" – the *ṣulḥ*, however, stands.[46] Later documents show that locally, *ṣulḥ* was often shorthand for a decision imposed by an assembly, at times against the claimants' wishes. There is much debate in Islamic legal scholarship as to under what conditions *ṣulḥ* could be imposed, and to what degree it could invalidate other Islamic prescriptions, but as a contract hinging on both parties' agreement, *ṣulḥ* concluded by force was clearly beyond the pale.[47] Yet the ten pages of the *Ghuniya* concerned with *ṣulḥ* primarily treat the conditions under which *ṣulḥ* could be imposed on reticent litigants. Quarrelling, one of these arguments goes, is reprehensible, and the *qāḍi*'s duty is to prohibit whatever is reprehensible; or else, fear of aggravation of conflict can justify *ṣulḥ* imposed by force.

Similarly, questions about witnesses mainly bear on their relationship with the assembly: whether witnesses were legitimised by the *qāḍi*'s approval, or by the assembly – or whether indeed the assembly as a whole was not the most suitable witness of them all. The relevant section of the *Ghuniya* opens with a question about the validity of the testimony of "the multitude" (*al-lafīf*), which, it is suggested, might be legitimised with reference to the local usage (*'amal*) of courts "in our country the Touat." This the *qāḍi* denies, somewhat vigorously.[48] Asked on a different occasion whether a "witness from the assembly" can be admitted, he answers that the validity of testimony depends uniquely on his integrity, not on membership in the assembly: "and the witness from the *jamā'a* if he is just (*'adlān*) then his testimony is licit and if not then not."[49] Yet a quick perusal of actual cases dealt with by the *qāḍi* shows that the assembly routinely acted as a collective witness: in one case, a substitution of goods is made in the absence of one of the owners but "in the presence of the assembly" and "they witnessed that it was sound" before it was signed by the *qāḍi*. Questioned later, a different *qāḍi* accepts the resulting document as valid.[50]

[46] NG: 222.

[47] For a discussion of *ṣulḥ*, its importance and its limits, see Schacht (1964), Othman (2007), and Hallaq (2009: 159–64).

[48] NG: 646. In Morocco in particular, judges were held to follow *'amal*, that is to say generally valid legal practices, although this is the only mention of the word that I have found in the Touat. On *'amal*, see Milliot (1952) and Toledano (1974).

[49] NG: 646.

[50] NG: 140.

A similarly close collaboration and interdependence between *quḍāh* and assemblies emerges, more than a century later, from the registers of the *qāḍi* of Timmi near contemporary Adrar, ʿAbd al-Karīm b. ʿAbd al-Ḥaqq al-Bakrī. These registers date from the 1930s and 1940s, when the *qāḍi*'s appointment had been endorsed by the French colonial authorities. The register was probably produced at their request, although it was kept in Arabic, and by the *qāḍi* and his family rather than the colonial administration or the court, and although French interference in the kind of matters treated by the *qāḍi* – mainly successions and legacies – was minimal at the time.[51] The register was written in a French account book, and contains 166 pages recording 272 transactions that took place between March 1944 and July 1946. The majority of these transactions concern divisions of inheritance, or the establishment or division of family *aḥbās*; others divide land between family members, exchange land for water, revoke earlier sales, or fix maintenance payment for divorced wives and children in contested cases: in other words, they are primarily concerned with property.[52] Even though the *qāḍi* was now backed up by the French colonial administration, roughly a quarter of all entries mention the assembly (*jamāʿa*) explicitly, mainly as acting to endorse the experts' evaluation of property or to "agree with" the *qāḍi*'s decision. Hence, a dispute over property held as a family endowment was concluded after "the evaluation and the adjustment took place among the people of the *ḥubus* with the attendance of the assembly of the Awlād Shaykh Sayyid Aḥmad ʿAbd Allāh b. ʿAmar and … who was present with

[51] Further, it bears no trace of official French endorsement, or reference to any kind of centralised government, as documents produced in *sharīʿa* courts in Italian-occupied Libya did (see Layish 1998, 2005). The dating system, however, is double, mentioning the CE date at the top, and the AH date at the end of each document.

[52] This emphasis on property is certainly in part due to the French colonial presence, as criminal matters were supposed to be brought before the French military administrator, not the *qāḍi*. But judging from the documents available, the proportion of property matters by no means increased with the French conquest. No traces of French-mediated litigation survive in the colonial archives, similar proportions are found in other local collections that pre-date French colonial involvement: 69 out of 106 documents kept in the Talmin archives are concerned with property, for instance. And for what it is worth, a similar emphasis emerges from the *Ghuniya*. More than half of its pages are devoted to matters of property, whereas only 24 out of 778 deal with punishable offences. Islamic law generally has little to say about secular crime, which is largely left to the discretion of the ruler or his agents (R. Peters 2005) – a problematic concept in the Touat, as seen previously. Nonetheless, this emphasis on property might give a hint as to what, from a local point of view, was taken to be a suitable field for legal intervention and documentation.

them of the good people (*min ahl al-khayr*)."[53] Elsewhere, the value of goods and their division were "firmly established after the calculation and adjustment and the adding of value of things in the presence of the aforementioned [claimants] and the assembly" or "with a just evaluation without fraud and without excess in the presence of the assembly."[54] In other cases, the assembly appointed a guardian for a minor (his maternal grandfather), acted as a guardian for an unmarried girl, or represented a female heir who could not attend the proceedings, without need for a formal appointment on her part.[55] Lastly, the assembly acted as the custodian for property bequeathed to the mosque, and, we might surmise, for property of people who died heirless, before French-appointed *quyyād* took over such claims.[56]

The assembly also played an important role in the validation of legal documents produced by the *qāḍi* or other local scholars, even in the absence of the original witnesses. This becomes clear in a somewhat lengthy inheritance suit, decided by a *majlis* of three judges in the *qṣar* of al-Mansūr on April 22, 1944. The claim was brought forward by Abū Flīja (whom we have already met in Chapter 1 owning water in numerous *qṣūr* scattered throughout the Touat and beyond). His half-brother Muḥammad 'Abd al-Raḥmān had passed away six months earlier, and his property had been taken over by Muḥammad 'Abd al-Raḥmān's full brother 'Abd Allāh, on behalf of the remaining members of the family, and without the *qāḍi*'s involvement. As a uterine half-brother, however, Abū Flīja had a right to one-sixth of the estate, which he had now come to claim: and in principle, there was no possible way in which 'Abd Allāh could invalidate his claim, enshrined in the *sharī'a*. His only hope was to prove that, at the time of his death, 'Abd al-Raḥmān's property had already passed out of his hands. This he attempts to do through the presentation of a series of documents: first a will (*rasm waṣiyya*) indicating that 'Abd al-Raḥmān had made his share of his father's estate over to 'Abd Allāh six months before his death. The *quḍāh* declare that this document was drafted according to legal norms, and duly witnessed, and they accept it as valid despite the absence of the two witnesses because

[53] SQ: 22.
[54] SQ: 18 and 28.
[55] SQ: 28 and 29. A similar case is reported in the *Ghuniya* (p. 140): here, however, the absent party is male but is, nonetheless, seen to be fully represented, without any formal appointment or transferral of agency, by the assembly and the *qāḍi*.
[56] SQ: 29–30.

they "knew them well." Beaten on this front, Abū Flīja then claims his share of the property left to Muḥammad 'Abd al-Raḥmān by his wife and paternal cousin: again, Muḥammad 'Abd Allāh is able to produce a document, established ten years earlier, in which she had renounced all her rights in return for compensation. Abū Flīja declares this document invalid, not on legal grounds, but rather because "everybody knows" that "she never received anything," appealing to the "crowd" (*malā'*): and indeed, on these grounds, the judges refuse to recognise the document as proof.[57] 'Abd Allāh reacts by playing his trump card: he produces a third document, undated, that testifies that the property in question was in fact a family endowment established by his grandfather, al-Ḥājj Bilqāsim al-Shabbāl, and that thus neither 'Abd al-Raḥmān's late wife, nor indeed Abū Flīja have the slightest claim on it – thereby making the entire foregoing debate redundant. The judges examine this document, noting that it was "sound and well constructed" and that its "meaning was very clear." They then read it out aloud "in the presence of the crowd (*malā'*)," and "the assembly (*jamā'a*) and the witnesses recognised their possessions before me." They then ask Abū Flīja whether he would like to oblige his half-brother to swear an oath, as he had originally declared he would, as a proof that the latter was not hiding parts of the estate that was lawfully due to him? Abū Flīja refrains. Then, in the name of peace and family harmony, the judges conclude a *ṣulḥ* between the two brothers, thereby foreclosing further dispute.[58]

TRANSLATING THE PARTICULAR

Ultimately, then, the value of legal documents depended on social backing, not by the original witnesses – as is standard practice in Islamic law – but rather by the local assembly. Yet the interdependence of assembly and *qāḍi* went deeper than political expedience. Islamic property rights, in particular in real estate, are always and necessarily the result of local negotiations, as they can only apportion shares but not fix value. In order to achieve the latter, the *qāḍi* had to rely on a group of local experts (*'urafā'*, sing. *'arīf*), invariably recruited from among the assembly, to establish a detailed description of the goods transacted and to fix their monetary value. This they did by "walking through" the property and

[57] A donation (*hiba*) indeed is only valid if the donee is publicly seen to have taken possession of them: see Powers (1993: 22).

[58] SQ: 21–2.

"taking stock of it."[59] The legacy of Abi Ibrīk b. Aī'īsh, divided on June 19, 1944, can stand as an example here: "And there came forward those who had knowledge of the value of the properties and the fixing of their prices. They [were] the aforementioned Ḥammād b. Abū Sālim and the aforementioned Abū Ḥasan b. Abū Aḥmad. And they walked round the estate and evaluated it."[60] Transactions were thus carried out, according to the documents themselves, "based on the Muslim *sunna*" but "their amount [was] decided by custom (*'urf*)."[61]

As Jacques Berque noted long ago, appeal to expert evidence in Moroccan *fiqh* "is so common that it has almost invaded all aspects of civil and commercial law.... Judgements almost always follow their conclusions ... this is in fact an indirect referral to arbitration" (Berque 1944: 25). Yet more was happening here than a simple framing of local decisions in legal terms. The recorded and duly witnessed description of land, water, and trees turned locally specific but legally amorphous and changeable matter into something saleable: something that was fixed, was evaluated in universal and everlasting terms, and could therefore be part of licit and permanent transactions. By doing so, these documents reconstituted the local as part of a wider moral universe, thereby, by reference to the outside, marking the boundary between what can and what cannot be legislated: between patches of legality and barbarity, between settled land and the *bādiya* or wilderness that surrounds them. This process, I think, was at the heart of the local appeal of the *sharī'a*: but it was never merely the *qāḍi*'s doing and relied on close collaboration between him and local assemblies. Moreover, due to the fragility and local particularism of agricultural resources, it was fraught with difficulties throughout.

This process of translation was particularly arduous with respect to water rights. Because *fagāgīr* silt up so easily, the overall amount of water they produce varies with time. As a result, owners do not possess absolute quantities, but a proportional share of the overall output, whatever that might be. Islamic law, however, requires that, at the time when a transaction is concluded, both parties know exactly what they are getting: hence, water leased or sold needs to be expressed in absolute or at least locally specific quantities that remain stable over time. The *Ghuniya* is explicit on this, thereby, incidentally, indicating that this was a longstanding problem: could water "measured according to the measure of the country" be

[59] SQ: 13.
[60] SG: 25–6.
[61] SQ: 19.

loaned or lent to somebody else? No, because local quantities are inherently variably, said the *qāḍi*, citing Ibn Rushd as his authority, and noting that it was common practice to defer the repayment of proportional water shares in order to hide interest payment, a practice that was utterly reprehensible.[62] When water is sold, who has to pay for the measuring, the seller or the buyer? And can the transaction be put off until the next day of measuring, if this date has not been fixed yet? No, said the *qāḍi*, as this again implies a degree of uncertainty that automatically invalidates all legal transactions.[63] In order to comply with Islamic legal standards, the output of a given *faggāra* hence needed to be measured on a regular basis, a costly undertaking that was usually entrusted to a specialist (*kayyāl al-mā'*), on the occasion of the "repetition of its measuring," as in the section of the irrigation register quoted earlier. In these registers, measures were repeated every other month, indicating the frequency of transactions, the limited life span of the results obtained, and the central part played by local customary experts in all legal transactions.[64]

More generally, the documents leave no doubt that, because of the inherent variability of local values and resources, the process of constant reevaluation was ongoing and generalised, whether transactions were concerned with land, water or chattels. In their final paragraph, all documents stake a claim to permanence and generality: transactions were, in a variety of set phrases, "total, general, irrevocable, final, definite, permanent," "with no conditions attached and with no right of withdrawal." Endowments in particular are set up "for generation after generation and womb after womb," to remain "a *ḥubus* forever and forever with no change, preserved forever."[65] Yet as a close look at the documents easily shows, this claim to immutability and permanence indicates an aspiration rather than a reality. Cultivated land easily reverted to fallow, and the *bādiya* always threatened to invade, through raiders as much as through sandstorms, or quite simply the passing of time. As seen earlier,

[62] NG: 206–9. See also 145–6.

[63] NG: 142.

[64] It seems that this strict observance of the Islamic requirement for exact quantities is particular to the Touat. In southern Tunisia, Bédoucha (2001) observes that although water could be sold independently from land, and although generally transactions of land implied the establishment of a legal record corresponding to the requirements of Islamic law, fixed quantities of water were never mentioned in writing but were left to be determined, orally, by local knowledge (*'urf*, again). In Morocco, proportional measurements were used throughout (see Chiche 1984, Hammoudi 1985, Bencherifa and Popp 1990, and Bellakhdar et al. 1992).

[65] SQ: 20–1.

endowments in particular often show all too clearly the fragility of human intentions:

Concerning the garden al-Nurmān and everything that the Shaykh Abū Qāsim b. Abi 'Alī has turned into a *ḥubus*. The wind and the sand have increased from the north so that it was kept from its turn [of water] and some palm-trees died and some remained without yield and without crop because of the lack of irrigation. And the wind and the sand got the upper hand and it became impossible to work it and it is now barren land filled with sand.[66]

This inherent fragility of value is further reflected in the imprecision and variability of measures used. Geographical descriptions often sprawl over several pages only in order to fix the situation of one palm-tree, with reference to the four cardinal points: it then becomes clear that the exact meaning of even these cardinal directions changes from one *qṣar* to the next. Measures of water varied widely from one *qṣar* or even from one *faggāra* to the next. Hence, Muḥammad, the adolescent son of Abi Ibrīk b. Aī'īsh (cited earlier) took his share of his father's legacy (among other things) in the form of:

9 *ḥabba* and 15 *qīrāṭ* from the spring worth 192 *dūru* and a half ... And 5 *ḥabba* and 13 *qīrāṭ* and 10 *qīrāṭ* of the whole *qīrāṭ* from the *faggāra* Talmatīn worth 976 *dūru* and 10 *salad*. And a third of ten *ḥabba* minus a sixth of a *ḥabba* from the *faggāra* Abnakūr worth 513 *dūru*. And two thirds of a *ḥabba* from the *faggāra* of the *qṣar* Batūlik worth 6 *dūru*. And in 3 big *ḥabba* from the *faggāra* Sayyid 'Alī in the hollow worth 9 *dūru*.[67]

Even in this short extract, a *ḥabba* of water could be worth anything between 2 and 40 *dūru*. Therefore, either the value of water varied considerably with its quality, source, and location, or else these measurements differed from one place to the next.

At a closer look, even the impression of fixity, immutability, and universality given by monetary values seems limited. Consider the following case, recorded in the register kept by the *qāḍi* of Tamantit: Abū Flīja (once again) had bought water rights, a storehouse, and a garden from his brother-in-law 'Abd al-Qādir in AH 1360, with a document established by the *qāḍi* himself. After the deaths of both 'Abd al-Qādir's and his father two years later, his brother Ḥammād successfully contests the earlier sale. Abū Flīja has to hand over the document of sale. The same witness then swears to the value of the property transacted at the time

66 SQ: 19.
67 SQ: 26.

of sale and now, claiming that it has increased from 77 to 163 *dūru* in three years. Abū Flīja hands over the missing sum, and remains owner of the garden.[68] There certainly was some inflation in land and water prices at the time, as traders and former French soldiers from other Saharan regions started to invest their profits and pensions in real estate (Capot-Rey and Damade 1962, J. Bisson 2003: 209, see also Chapter 2). However, an increase of more than 100 per cent seems excessive, and one is tempted to think that in this case, at least, monetary values were partly socially determined. After all, the revocation of the sale is part of a larger struggle between Abū Flīja and Ḥammād over the legacy left by the latter's father, fought through a series of acts and *qāḍī*'s judgements. Although elsewhere, price differentials are less blatant, it is important to keep in mind that the "evaluation" (*taqwīm*) and "fixing of prices" (*maqādir al-athmān*) were always left to local experts, and that the terms referring to the "amount" (*qadr*) of a property or the "right" (*ḥaqq*) of the owner were used interchangeably. The production and application of the "universal" categories of Islamic law was thus always necessarily the result of an ongoing process of translation, evaluation, and mediation between local particularisms and aspirations to universal validity.

THE NOTEBOOK OF THE ASSEMBLY OF TIT

Although local assemblies were crucial to this process of translation, apart from the irrigation registers discussed earlier they produced little lasting documentation that would provide their point of view, adding a different perspective and a summary of their activities as they themselves understood them. There is one exception, however: the notebook of the assembly of Tit, a small *qṣar* near Aoulef mentioned in Chapter 2 as home to Ḥammū Zafzaf and other trans-Saharan traders. The notebook is written in a school exercise book, with seventy-two carefully numbered pages, dealing with eighty-two separate transactions.[69] Even more so than the irrigation registers discussed earlier, this document by no means represents a pristine reality of life "before the state." First entries date from

[68] SQ: 16.

[69] The following is based on photographs of the original notebook (SJ) taken in Tit in March 2008, courtesy of 'Abd al-Raḥmān b. 'Abd al-Karīm. Page numbers used in the following paragraphs refer to those used in the manuscript itself: hence, earlier documents might be on later page numbers, while other page numbers are missing altogether. A few entries make reference to other documents or copies of documents, either held by the parties concerned, or by the regional administration. The notebook is discussed with further detail in Scheele (2010b).

autumn 1962, immediately after Algerian independence was achieved, and we can surmise that, although most activities recorded seem to follow more longstanding logics, this kind of record keeping was either encouraged by government officials or happened as a reaction to perceived state encroachment on their concerns. This close vicinity of the state makes it difficult to discern how the members of the assembly thought about themselves. Self-descriptions vary considerably throughout: from documents drawn up in the name of the owners (again, *arbāb*) of a given *faggāra*, via the "assembly of the residents of Tit" or the "national people (*al-sha'b al-waṭanī*, a decidedly nationalist term) in Tit," to "those who have signed below," or even, in 1972, to "the national assembly, those who were appointed in the booklet of ownership" – presumably a state survey. On the ground, however, entries seem to have been drafted by much the same people following a general logic of collective action, with the varying terminology indicating changing levels of relevance and sensitivity to context rather than different principles. Much like the *qāḍī*'s register and other legal documents, this notebook indicates an ongoing preoccupation with legality and the language and categories proposed by Islamic law, alongside a perhaps even more pronounced interest in local solidarity and the protection and management of communal property.

Although the notebook contains no lists of water shares comparable to those described previously (these might have been recorded in a separate document), the largest proportion of entries is concerned with the maintenance of irrigation works. Hence, one of the first entries, dated August 1963:

The registration of what was given to the group of workers on the *faggāra* al-Jadīda through the Sayyid Muḥammad b. Mūlāy 'Abd al-Raḥmān and al-Sāliḥ b. Būqādim and al-Ḥājj 'Abd al-Raḥmān

On August 3, 1962, they paid the workers 93,665 francs
On August 10 they paid 72,380 francs
On August 24 they paid 88,775 francs
On August 25 they paid 39,750 francs
On September 1 they paid 29,130 francs
On September 1 the Sayyid Muḥammad paid 4,200 francs
Altogether the workers on the *faggāra* al-Jadīda were paid 327,280 francs.[70]

Praise be upon the one God. December 2, 1962
The account of the money for the *faggāra* al-Jadīda that was in the hands of the assembly from the beginning of 1961 until September 1, 1962

[70] 7,500 € in today's money, for a population of perhaps 500 (133 of whom were represented in the assembly, see below).

Firstly 20,000 francs
Secondly 58,200 francs
Thirdly 120,000 francs
Fourthly the owners of the property (*arbāb milk*) of al-Jadīda collected 75,000 francs
Fifthly from those who divide [the water] among them 50,000 francs
Together 323,200 francs
Paid to all the workers 327,280 francs
The owners of the *faggāra* still owe 4,080 francs
December 4, 1962 ...
Witnessed by the servants of their Lord [followed by four names].[71]

Hence, the assembly decided when maintenance works were needed, employed workers on their account, advanced wages, carefully recorded them, and appointed delegates to pay them; the money advanced was then collected from communal – perhaps state – funds and from the owners and the users of the *faggāra*. At other times, money for immediate payment was borrowed from individual members of the assembly; also, the assembly could appoint an agent to take care of the recruitment of workers, their equipment, and their remuneration, against a set fee. Hence, on January 24, 1963, the assembly paid al-Ḥājj ʿAmar 228,295 F, 155,040 F for the "payment of the workers" and 73,255 F "for the ditch [irrigation canal]," noting that he had advanced corresponding sums to the workers.[72] Further maintenance works are recorded in great detail.[73] Overall, they amounted to the stately sum of 1,706,861 F, the most important part of the assembly's budget.

Although most of the money for maintenance was collected from owners of water shares, some of it at least came from communal landholdings: the maintenance works of summer 1974 were partly paid with money derived from the yields of a communal garden worked by a sharecropper, and partly with four gardens "from the share (*naṣīb*) of the assembly."[74] Although earlier entries do not mention such direct connections between land sales and irrigation works, in addition to sporadic government subsidies, revenues from land represented the assembly's main income.[75] A lengthy affair, recorded in December 1962 – and thus

[71] SJ: 5–6.
[72] SJ: 7 and 20.
[73] SJ: 7,10, 20, 39, 55, 114, and 116.
[74] SJ: 114 and 116.
[75] The budget, as represented in the notebook, is far from balanced, unless land sales are excluded as a source of revenue. Government subsidies were probably counterbalanced by taxation.

probably at least partly motivated by recent political changes – affords glimpses of the procedure used for such sales: land is first carefully measured by "experts," as already discussed, divided into lots, and sold off to individual villagers.[76] Later entries record similar land sales, sometimes referring to the prices fixed in December 1962; altogether, they amount to 1,279,350 F.[77] But what exactly was "communal land"? Some of it might have been heirless estates taken over by the assembly, but these were necessarily rare. Several entries concerned with land sales specify that the land sold was uncultivated (*arḍ bayḍā'*); others indicate that the assembly could grant usufruct of uncultivated land to sharecroppers.[78] In such cases, two thirds of the yield were paid to the assembly as long as the sharecropping agreement lasted; but sharecroppers could buy their halves and turn the land into private property. Hence, on May 28, 1966, Mūlāy Maḥammad bought a sixth of the garden of which he held a third in community with the assembly.[79] Here, the general rule is explicitly stated: "And the situation was that who wants to cultivate uncultivated land from the assembly, he gets a third of whatever the totality of the crops give him as long as he has not established the separation between him and the assembly." On May 15, 1970, Muḥammad b. 'Abd al-Raḥmān Maḥjūb asks the assembly to be granted "uncultivated land" in the "original land (*aṣl*) of Tasūt, the *aṣl* of al-Jadīda" – just next to Mūlāy Maḥammad's recently acquired sixth. He receives all cereals, fruit, vegetables, and grass grown on the land, and one-quarter of the dates; three-quarters of dates are paid to the assembly. The contract is limited to three years. After that, if the assembly so wishes, they can sell the land "in the general interest" (*fī 'l-maṣlaḥat il-'āma*), although Maḥjūb has first rights to buy it, if he is able to. If not, the entry continues, the land returns to the assembly and will be registered as "belonging to [the *faggāra*] al-Jadīda" in all land surveys. The assembly thus retained the right to sell virgin land in the *qṣar*: but judging by this later entry, such land had to be situated within the irrigated parameter of a particular *faggāra* to which it was seen to "belong," as, in this case, al-Jadīda, the main *faggāra* of Tit. Although strictly speaking, such sales were illegal, as the *sharī'a* does not recognise private property in uncultivated land, similar claims to property rights in fallow or virgin land

[76] SJ: 4, 8, and 11–13.

[77] SJ: 9, 21, 23, 32, 57, 61, and 69.

[78] SJ: 57 and 69. In the first case, the land is bought by a woman.

[79] SJ: 61.

that could potentially be irrigated are repeatedly refuted in the *Ghuniya*, indicating that they had long been common.[80]

Yet perhaps even more than the *fagāgīr*, the central institution mentioned in the notebook is the "moneybox of the assembly" (*ṣunduq mālī 'l-jamā'a*). Hardly an entry that does not mention it; meanwhile, several pages of the notebook are filled with what looks like straightforward accountancy, with great emphasis placed on the physical act of taking money out of the moneybox or putting it back in:

Praise to the one God. December 2, 1962.

The assembly put the preceding fines into the moneybox that is in the custody of 'Abd al- Raḥmān b. Biya: they amount to 33,765 francs.

Also the assembly enters into the moneybox that is with al-Ḥājj 'Abd al-Raḥmān 41,500 francs as remuneration for the land that the Ḥājj has granted to the *shurafā'*.

On the 5th of December 1962.

The assembly remembered that it had entrusted a loan to 'Abd al-Qādir b. 'Abd al-Raḥmān, which amounted to 17,000 F. And 'Abd al-Qādir b. 'Abd al-Raḥmān paid it to al-Ḥājj 'Abd al-Raḥmān b. Biya to put it into the moneybox, the goods of the people.[81]

The assembly routinely lent money to pay fines that they themselves imposed on their members, and that were then paid off in instalments, much as they advanced funds for maintenance works on the *fagāgīr* (see above).[82] Land sales rarely were paid off straight away, and most buyers continued to owe money to the assembly, and, as all entries specify, only received their documents of ownership once they had paid up.[83] In a way reminiscent of the *zawāyā* discussed in Chapter 1, but on a smaller scale, the assembly also loaned equipment and goods to its members: lengths or bales of cloth for trading purposes, but also "pipes" (*ja'aba*), water buckets, chains and scales, and other equipment relating to irrigation, as well as basic foodstuffs.[84] The assembly further gave land or granted a monthly salary (*shahriyya*) to village functionaries, such as the imam

[80] See, for example, NG: 138: "And he was also asked about the sale of a garden from somebody else ... and below it there was virgin land that had never been cultivated and that had never been planted. Does it enter into a sale or not?" It does not, says the *qāḍi*. In Tamantit, Capot-Rey and Damade noted in 1962 that land that is downstream from irrigated gardens and within the irrigated parameter, whether it lays fallow or not, can be owned, and is seen as the property of the owner of the irrigating water.

[81] SJ: 10.

[82] SJ: 29, 30, and 43.

[83] See, for example, SJ: 32 and 74.

[84] SJ: 3.

and two teachers in the local school, one of whom is described as the imam's son.[85] In some cases, the collective moneybox could be divided: in one instance, recorded in July 1963, the assembly collected money from among the "owners of the property (*arbāb al-milk*) of the *faggāra* al-Jadīda" and kept it "in the deposit (*amāna*) of the *faggāra*"; a month later, the measuring of the *faggāra* was paid for "from the box of the *faggāra*"; two months later, payment for maintenance works were noted with great care on the same page, thereby presumably referring to the same "deposit."[86] Individual residents of the *qṣar* kept their property in similar "boxes" (see later): individual and collective "households" thus tend to be pictured in similar terms, essentially as centred on common funds and expenses.[87]

At first sight, then, as suggested by the irrigation registers discussed earlier, we seem to be dealing here with straightforward accountancy, with the careful administration of communal funds that conceivably might constitute just one part of municipal administration, and perhaps the one that lent itself most easily to writing.[88] On several occasions, however, the assembly also acted as public prosecutor and judge. Hence, on December 22, 1962, Muḥammad b. Aḥmad Sīdi 'Alī was fined 3,000 F "for the transgression of the limits [of his property]" aggravated by insults to the "officer of the country" (*shurṭī 'l-bilād*).[89] Earlier that month, as seen previously, the notebook records the receipt of 33,765 F "from the precedent fines (*khaṭiyyāt*)," without any further explanations; in May 1963, the assembly threatens punishment (*'aqūba*) and imposes fines on those who refuse to participate in collective labour (see below). Mostly, however, the assembly adjudicates in conflicts between third parties, establishing *ṣulḥ* or "amicable agreements," more often than not "in the name of the *umma*" and painstakingly trying to follow Islamic law, if not by the letter, then at least in terms of procedure. Cases of *ṣulḥ* account

85 SJ: 4 and 17.

86 SJ: 55.

87 SJ: 100.

88 Accountancy was perhaps the most widespread use of basic literacy in the area. Shop registers (*kunnāsh*) or storehouse books (*dafātir makhzan*) are often mentioned both in the *qāḍi*'s register and in notarial documentation, not just for large trading families as has been recorded elsewhere (see for instance Pascon 1980, 1984), but also for small local shopkeepers: see for instance SQ: 21, and WK: 35.

89 SJ: 10. It is difficult to know who this "officer" or even "police officer," *al-shurṭī*, really was: it seems unlikely that he was just a state official, as people are repeatedly described as the sons or even grandsons of various *al-shurṭī*, who hence lived before the French colonial conquest. The term thus seems to refer to municipal officials acting on behalf of the assembly.

for roughly a sixth of all entries in the notebook. These mainly concern family conflicts, often quarrels that involve the "honour" of young girls and would suffer from too much publicity – "bring shame on Tit" (*ya'ud 'ayban li-Ṭīt*), as one of the entries puts it.[90] In one case, the father of a boy who had deflowered an eleven-year-old girl in the regional hospital was fined 30,000 francs, after the girl was duly examined by two female witnesses. The fine is paid straight away by the assembly to the offended party: the boy's father will have to reimburse as he is able to. Three months later, a similar case leads to the marriage between the boy and the girl, on the grounds that they were both from Tit and that they "have maternal kinship between them."[91] This amount was raised instantly "with the help of all his uncles." A marriage contract was drafted by the "Sayyids who were present (the members of the assembly)," and "the *umma* is led back to the straight path."[92] In the 1970s, a similar case involving maternal relations is also solved by marriage, with a dowry of 500,000 francs; whereas in August 1980, the "removal of virginity" of a fourteen-year-old girl by her male nurse – again, not from Tit, and external witnesses are present – leads to much debate, until the culprit and his family agree to the payment of 4,000 DA, or 400,000 francs.[93]

A case brought before the assembly in September 1963 shows a similar translation of individual rights that could potentially be backed up with reference to Islamic doctrine into logics of family or collective solidarity.[94] Aḥmad had taken advantage of the absence of his brother Muḥammad to sell their commonly held house, garden, and water to a *sharīf* from In Salah. On his return, Muḥammad refused to hand over his share of the property, arguing that Aḥmad had no right to sell it, and no documents to prove his ownership, and that the sale was thus null and void. The assembly looks into the case, finds that Muḥammad is in the right, and that Aḥmad had had no documents and hence no right to sell the property; nonetheless, they ask Muḥammad to give in, "for the general peace and because of their closeness, as they were from one seed and from one belly," and to give the deeds and a written commission to his brother,

[90] SJ: 105.

[91] Status distinctions might also have played a part here: the girl in the first case was a *sharīfa*, deflowered by a non-*sharīf*, whereas in the second case, the two were related, and hence, we can assume of comparable status, perhaps making the offence more easily redeemable. However, it is noteworthy that the amount of the fine is the same for both girls.

[92] SJ: 41.

[93] SJ: 105 and 115.

[94] SJ: 115.

in order to "legalise" the sale after the act. Further, he was required to hand over his share to the buyer without further ado – in exchange for a collective blessing.[95] Similarly, in February 1963, two brothers had been approached by third party to pay the hire for a car rented by their brother, who "was not to be found anywhere between Aoulef and In Ghar and In Salah." They had no intention to pay for their "rich brother," they said, and asked the assembly to authorise them to pay the missing amount from their brother's property, to which the assembly agreed, to the satisfaction of all.[96] Nine years later, their brother was "missing" again: he had been away for three months and 23 days, and his brothers and his wife asked the assembly to "open his moneybox" and to provide them with funds so that they could look after his family. The assembly complied, and found 446,340 francs in his moneybox, to which they added the value of his two houses, amounting to another 95,000 francs. Of this, 46,340 francs were handed over to his brother, but the assembly retained the rest, kept it in their stores, and took it upon themselves to pay the wife's monthly expenses, which they evaluated at 51,150 francs every six months.[97] Although the assembly commonly intervened to ensure that maintenance was paid to divorced or abandoned wives,[98] their direct intervention in a private moneybox is striking, after a mere three months' absence – no time at all, one should think, in a *qṣar* inhabited by trans-Saharan traders. Yet in this as in other cases recounted, the assembly clearly felt that they were acting in complete accordance with Islamic law, representing the *umma*, ultimate inheritor of all individual property.[99]

Relations with the increasingly powerful state and its regional representatives were less straightforward. On the one hand, the register shows a remarkable degree of linguistic eclecticism throughout. Standard Islamic greetings and references to the Prophet exist alongside or are even supplemented by "patriotic peace and revolutionary greetings" (*salām waṭanī wa-taḥiyya thawriyya*), while collective activities are justified both with reference to the "good of Islam" and to the "general interest"

[95] SJ: 51.

[96] SJ: 99.

[97] SJ: 100–2.

[98] Hence, in January 1967, Fāṭima bint Buqādir Muḥammad Sāliḥ comes before the assembly to claim maintenance for her daughter, who had been divorced the previous August, while pregnant. The assembly decides on the rate to be paid, taking into account that "the man is poor," and calls on his brother to make sure that the sum will be paid, retrospectively, counting from August 1966. SJ: 81.

[99] For explicit formulations of this, see SJ: 29, 41, and 115; see also al-'Uthmānī (2004) for similar municipal reasoning in Morocco.

(*al-maṣlaḥat al-'āma*) or the "interest of society" (*maṣlaḥat al-mujtama'*), echoing nationalist rhetoric.[100] Moreover, the assembly was clearly happy to act as a privileged interlocutor where state subsidies were concerned. Whereas in December 1962, major repairs on the main *fagāgīr* were paid for collectively, with a small amount of what might be state subsidies but are not clearly identified as such, works on the "ditch" in January 1963 were reimbursed by "members of the local council (*majlis al-waṭanī*) and members of the national political office (*al-maktab al-siyāsī 'l-waṭanī*)" to pay workers contracted from the outside and whose pay had been advanced from the moneybox.[101] In March 1963, the assembly received 124,462 francs "in Aoulef the house of the government," for work on specific *fagāgīr*, and again 559,140 francs in September of the same year.[102] Altogether, such transfers of funds amounted to 1,035,097 francs, covering just over half of the total cost of maintenance of irrigation works spent by the assembly throughout. None were recorded later on, and maintenance works undertaken in the 1970s were once more at the charge of the assembly.[103] Yet in other matters, state intervention failed, or was deeply resented: in May 1963, the assembly, presumably encouraged by overzealous officials attempting to impose the newly established Algerian egalitarianism by force, declared a *corvée* for all.[104] Judging by oral memories and the archival records, collective physical labour – rather than a levy on slaves or clients, or money paid to hire workers – was unthinkable in the *qṣūr*, if only because of the close connection between labour and low status (see Chapter 4). Several people, all of high status, refused to comply, and were fined. Yet these fines never seem to have reached the assembly's moneybox, and later maintenance works return

[100] Currencies and measurements used indicate a similar change: although in internal affairs, such as dowries and minor land sales, local measurements prevail until the 1970s, larger transactions refer to metres and francs, and then, gradually, also to Algerian Dinar. The Algerian Dinar is first mentioned in May 1966 (SJ: 45), two years after it became officially the national currency in Algeria.

[101] SJ: 20.

[102] SJ: 3 and 19.

[103] SJ: 106–12 are "statements about the budget of the commune Aoulef" for various tasks (the construction of a girls' school and showers, for instance, or a school in Tamgat), drafted in the second half of 1962; it is impossible to tell whether they were subsidies, taxation, or merely intended as models for village accountancy. They never mention the assembly, or indeed any common witnesses; and the sums dealt with are considerable, in any case, and totally out of proportion with other items of accountancy mentioned throughout the notebook: altogether, they amount to 17,334,345 F.

[104] SJ: 33. Such attempts were common throughout the Algerian south, see, for example, Keenan (1977) for examples from the Ahaggar.

to the more common pattern of collective levies to hire workers – thereby clearly revealing tensions between state and local conceptions of collective duties, the practical limits of state intervention, and the assembly's longstanding ability to effectively deal with outside intervention without rejecting it altogether.

Other conflicts with state officials were even more explicit. On May 12, 1970, the assembly "who have signed below" sent a series of petitions to the prefect, complaining about "the matter of Aḥmad Abū 'Abd Allāh," a regional tax collector who had been "in charge of the assembly" (*fī ḥaqq il-jamā'a*). He had abused his power in order to "take an indulgence (*al-'āfiya*)," "from property that does not concern him," and without "consulting with the assembly," although the latter had been "indulging him for many of his personal inclinations."[105] Three and a half years later, a long note proudly proclaims the conclusion of the affair: the assembly "took back" the garden "that they had originally (*fī 'l-aṣl*) owned," but "that had been usurped" by the "thief" Aḥmad Abū 'Abd Allāh, "with the help of some of the powerful who are biased." It now rented it out to a sharecropper, receiving three-quarters of his date harvest. The sharecropper, however, continued to pay nine measures of wheat to Abū 'Abd Allāh.[106] This, perhaps, best illustrates the role of the assembly in local administration: sometimes acting as the agent of the state, accepting its subsidies, and having a hand in tax collection, they were never simply coopted by it, and, where they felt threatened in their own prerogatives, could act to protect their interests, with the necessary concessions made to changing political circumstance – to the detriment of poorer *qṣar* dwellers, such as the sharecropper who now finds himself burdened with an additional level of taxation. And indeed, although transactions recorded became less frequent by the early 1980s, and eventually ceased altogether, everybody locally agrees that this was not the result of state pressure, but rather due to the decline of agriculture, "family strife," and the gradual reorientation of livelihoods and careers.

CONCLUSION

Oases, then, are perhaps best imagined as nodes of legal density and containment, patches of "civilisation" established by local inhabitants – municipal assemblies, scholars, *shaykh*s, and *quḍāh* – not merely for the

105 SJ: 90, 95, and 103.
106 SJ: 104.

better ordering of the social, but also because the establishment and maintenance of proper place has spiritual value. This "civilisation" is partly represented by the fragmented, orderly, and thriving gardens of oases: and it is thus not surprising that throughout the archival record, property rather than crime and punishment emerges as the key legal category, as well as the basis of political representation. Nonetheless, although it established boundaries, the law was also a sign of fundamental permeability of the local, on the most intimate level: by putting Islamic notions of ownership at the heart of local councils, assemblies made their very existence dependent on legal categories that were beyond their control. This means, first of all, that we need to question the common sense assumption of the equivalence of law and power, or of the necessary imposition of law from above: it seems that Touati oases imported the *sharīʿa* quite voluntarily. We further need to refine implicit notions of local assemblies that all too often draw on images of "primitive democracy," in favour of a model more closely akin to a collective management of shared property based on individual ownership, in itself a legal category governed by external standards. Lastly, we need to move away from legal functionalism. Although the importance accorded locally to property rights might go some way towards explaining the local preoccupation with Islamic law, it cannot fully account for it: as shown throughout, adherence to Islamic legal categories and procedures created quite as many problems as it solved. Moreover, the local application of the *sharīʿa* only rarely fulfilled its inherent promise of permanence and universal validity. On that ground, religious scholars, representatives of eternal law, had to rely on local experts to determine value and on local councils for their backing and support; what seems to have mattered were less the practical results than the process of translation that underpinned them. In such a context, concepts of law and legality only take their full meaning if we understand them as ways in which Saharan localities, swamped in a sea of "wilderness," could imagine themselves as part of a wider world of universal truth and regulations – economically, socially, and morally. Like the founding saint discussed in Chapter 2, a *qāḍi* and his law-books were thus first and foremost a living sign of the village's membership in the larger Islamic community, a central element in the establishment of just society, and hence in the making of civilisation and place – as important, perhaps, as the careful maintenance of property rights, safe storage, and irrigation systems.

6

Settlement, Mobility, and the Daily Pitfalls of Saharan Cosmopolitanism

> Settlements in the Mediterranean, many of them extremely small, have slipped in and out of whatever category established to contain them ... We should imagine them as being in flux from year to year, even from day to day – just like other microregions made by mobile Mediterranean people. They may evolve at a very great pace, exhibiting frequent changes of population density and disposition, social institution or economic function – all perhaps beneath a relatively immutable architectural carapace ... The unifying feature is not the accident of a nucleated pattern, whether or not this qualifies as urban; it is the intricate and often far-flung engagement with a wider, kaleidoscopic, world. (Horden and Purcell 2000: 94, 122)

This final chapter is intended to sum up the overall argument of this book and to draw together the ethnographic and historical evidence presented, in a conceptual framework that echoes and confirms the reflections put forward in Chapter 1. Here, they are applied to what might at first look like a radically different setting: three contemporary Saharan cities, Adrar and Tamanrasset in southern Algeria and Gao in northern Mali, that so far have mainly figured as a backdrop and anchorage to regional mobilities and connections. Over the last three decades, Saharan cities and towns, in particular those situated in the oil-rich states of the Maghrib, have experienced exponential demographic growth and have been the subject of various monographs, in particular by Fran
geographers.[1] Most of these works address Sahar
terms of state investment and control, and portray

[1] See, for instance, URBAMA (1989), Pliez (2003), Côte (2005),
(2007), and Choplin (2009).

and cities as artificial creations, independent of or even hostile to their environment (see, e.g., J. Bisson 2003, Côte 2005); and indeed, electric water pumps and seemingly inexhaustible oil revenues seem to have done away with the intrinsic problems of oasis agriculture and management, the subject of the preceding chapter. However, as I have attempted to show throughout, outside funds and investment have always been key to the establishment of most kinds of Saharan settlement; and although the new financial and technical possibilities developed by rich and powerful regional states dwarf any other income and resource, they exist alongside and at times within older networks. As a result, certain underlying logics of outside dependency and regional connectivity remain relevant, although they might be expressed in different ways and subject to new sets of constraints (see also Pliez 2003: 17). In other words, we still need to understand Saharan cities, much like older and perhaps more dispersed settlements, as "loci of contact and overlap between different ecologies" or "nodes of intensity in an overlapping matrix of connectivity," to echo once more Horden and Purcell's (2000: 100, 393) expressions, and this despite state pressure towards containment and homogeneity – or rather, towards a different and more centralised form of dependency.

Al-Khalīl, where this book began, is a striking example of such modern outside dependency, and of the resulting fragility of Saharan settlement: it houses an essentially mobile population relying on resources created by trade, and that might conceivably just vanish over night. Every single building in al-Khalīl refers to other places, other buildings, and other people, at times hundreds of kilometres away. Adrar, Tamanrasset, and Gao house most of these "other people," the great majority of them women who, although culturally associated with fixity and "civilisation," are in actual fact no less mobile than their brothers and husbands. More generally, migration and mobility are and remain integral features of settled life. As shown in Chapters 1 and 4, immigration is essential not merely for the foundation of Saharan settlement and its maintenance, but also for the ways local identities and hierarchies are construed: the population of all kinds of Saharan settlement was never homogeneous in any sense.[2]

[2] This heterogeneity is attested through the (rather patchy) historical record. The inhabitants of tenth-century Sijilmāsa were primarily "merchants from Iraq" (Ibn Hawqal, in Levtzion and Hopkins 1981: 45), or "many foreigners from every country" (al-Maqqadasī, ibid. 53). Eleventh-century Awdaghust was inhabited by "natives of Ifrīqiya [eastern Algeria and Tunisia]" but also by "a few people from other countries" (al-Bakrī, ibid. 68). Fourteenth-century Ghadamès was "very populous and extensively urbanized because it has become the staging post for companies of pilgrims from the Sūdān and caravans of merchants going to Cairo and Alexandria" (Ibn Khaldūn, ibid. 340).

At the same time, as seen in Chapter 5, political representation and legal frameworks were delocalised. This social, cultural, and political heterogeneity is reflected in the spatial outlay of most Saharan settlements with their neat division into quarters, explained with reference to a history of migration and to status, but also as a reflection of the mutual independence and supposedly inherent moral incommensurability that opposes the different groups and networks that meet on city grounds.[3] This is reminiscent of the kind of social coexistence described by scholars of the Indian Ocean, where settlements, similarly dependent on movement and outside influence and populations, also strike by their segregation (Simpson and Kresse 2007). In such an historical setting of exchange, "integration" would be the obvious assumption, yet people persist in claiming to be different, and put much effort and social labour into maintaining this difference, thereby giving a new meaning to notions of "cosmopolitism," based on detachment rather than integration (see also Tarrius 2000, Anderson 2001). Similarly, in the Sahara, as shown throughout, connectivity is the norm, but people strive to maintain distinction, to keep their relations manageable and morally contained. Cross-cutting ties of course exist, and they are indeed indispensable to urban life; but the more intimate such relations are, and the more fragile boundaries between groups are conceived to be, the more emphasis is placed on them, as inherent or even "natural" markers of moral value. Saharan cities, then, are best understood in the constant tensions between the cultivation of the right kind of connections, and the containment of those, more recalcitrant to moral evaluations, that are potentially corrupting.

GHETTOES AND QṢŪR

Let us start with that part of the population of contemporary Saharan cities whose mobility seems to be beyond doubt, although they might in fact, due to the myriad restrictions imposed on them, be the least mobile

[3] Again, this segregation has a long history. Hence, a late nineteenth-century colonial description of Akabli in the Tidikelt: "Akabli is composed of small villages, constructed at different times by natives from the most diverse backgrounds, settled there by the hazards of Saharan life. This is why next to the Foulanes from Sudan we find some Oulad Zenani; next to the Kunta from the Azawād some Oulad Sidi Mohammed who say they are descendants of the Ansar [companions of the Prophet] of Medina. All these families live next to each other without mixing too much and keeping their traditions and religious attachments. They all have their own little *qṣar*" (Chardenet, "Akabli," n.d. (early 1900s), CAOM 22H50). A similar description is given by Miner (1950: 43) of Timbuktu in the 1940s.

of all Saharans: the so-called "trans-Saharan migrants," whose projects and fate have come to dominate academic writing on the contemporary Sahara.[4] Most of these nationals of sub-Saharan countries, hoping to reach Europe overland, get stuck in the Sahara due to EU pressure on North African states to tighten their migration policies. Here, they join more longstanding seasonal migrants from the Sahel as well as "white refugees" from the Malian and Nigerien Sahara (see Chapters 3 and 4).[5] While some writers have hailed this forced coexistence as the beginnings of a "new cosmopolitanism" of cultural interaction and transformation (Boesen and Marfaing 2007),[6] and others have looked for traces of emerging "urbanity" in cultural exchange and the establishment of "new centralities" (Pliez 2003), migrants themselves tend to talk about their experiences in terms of segregation, exclusion, ongoing but often frustrated projects of mobility, and social and cultural autonomy: elements that are most frequently summed up by the local term and institution of the "ghetto." These ghettoes are simple houses or courtyards, rented by more established foreign residents of the city, who in turn sublet rooms to newly arrived migrants, mostly to nationals of their home country. Yet the term itself is somewhat ambiguous: in the immediate vicinity of the Algero-Malian border, it also refers to ad hoc camps set up for protection against hostile people and climate; in Tamanrasset, it can indicate a shared house as well as a makeshift shelter established in the rocks in the vicinity of the town proper. Lastly, it has come to stand for translocal communal associations, divided along lines of nationality or, at times, language, that organise life abroad and act as mediators with the host society and state institutions.[7] In all three cases, the image of the ghetto acts as an ongoing sign of and symbol for the migrants' fundamental aspiration to mobility, whether this translates into actual movement or not.

On arrival in any major town on the road north, migrants either look for or are pointed to their respective ghetto. Every newcomer pays a set sum, between 50 and 100 euros, into the communal moneybox. This

[4] For references on trans-Saharan migration, see the introduction.

[5] See Brachet (2009) and the overlap between seasonal and transit migration between northern Niger and Libya and Algeria; see Choplin (2009) and Marfaing (2010) for a similar scenario in Mauritania. For archival references to seasonal migration from northern Mali to southern Algeria, see Chapter 2.

[6] The idea of a "new cosmopolitanism" has attracted some reflection in both French- and English-speaking academia; see especially Werbner (1999, 2006, 2008).

[7] For descriptions of ghettoes throughout the contemporary Sahara, see Ba and Choplin (2005) and Brachet (2009). Similar institutions have long existed in the region, initially to facilitate overland travel to Mecca: see Birks (1978).

moneybox is kept by the national "president," chosen from among those who have lived in the city longest. Its contents are used for emergencies: illness, for instance, or problems with the authorities. Funds might also be advanced to newcomers who lost all their money on the way, to be reimbursed once they find a job or have money sent to them from home by Western Union. Although everybody I spoke to thought that such communal funds were necessary, doubts were frequently expressed about the way the moneybox was run, and the lack of accountability. This is of some importance, as membership in these ghettoes is never quite voluntary:

> You come to this place and you think: nobody knows me here, but then somebody will come up to you and tap you on the shoulder, saying: you are from Ghana or you are from Cameroon and so on, everybody knows even before you arrive, the drivers tell them and it is written all over your face. They will point you to your ghetto. Usually, people are happy to find that they are not on their own; but some don't want to pay, and if that happens, if you decide to just go and sleep rough, they will come and beat you up at night, until you understand that you cannot live on your own. Or people from a different country might come and beat you up because they know that the ghetto won't protect you, or the police will – they all know.[8]

Ghettos act as travel agencies and organise transport. The president of the ghetto gathers a sufficient number of people to fill a four-by-four, and then gets in touch with a transport agent against a commission: in Gao for instance, the standard commission is the price of one passage to Algeria, for every fourteen "adventurers." Presidents are also in touch with the few nongovernmental organisations in the area, channel funds from the Red Cross if they are forthcoming, talk to journalists and researchers, and help obtain certificates as "refugees" from the United Nations Commissioner for Refugees (UNHCR): they act as privileged intermediaries between migrants and the host society.[9]

Much more than just initial lodgings, the ghettoes hence provide networks of solidarity and sites of collective and transnational representation

[8] This section is based on interviews with sub-Saharan migrants in Tamanrasset, Kidal and Gao, conducted in winter and spring 2007–8.

[9] These certificates are routinely handed out by the Algiers representation of the UNHCR. They are of little use in Algeria itself, and stories abound of Algerian security forces quite simply destroying them when they are presented with one. Nonetheless, they imply that sub-Saharan migrants will not be able to demand asylum once they reach Europe, as they have already transitted via a country considered to be safe. On the role increasingly played by the UNHCR in policing international migration, see Agier (2006).

for an essentially mobile population. They organise and symbolise a certain mode of interaction with the host society that excludes all notions of permanence or "integration," through coopted intermediaries who have special knowledge of both societies.[10] They also stand for translocal communal accountability, justice, and autonomy, beyond state borders and institutions:

> In Algeria for instance, you cannot go to the police, they are the greatest thieves of all. So if somebody steals your mobile phone, say, and you know who it was, you can go to your president and you complain, and they will catch him and he will be judged by everybody – he has to pay a fine and return what he has stolen, and sometimes he will get lashes, we all come together and decide. Or if somebody doesn't pay his debts before leaving, or he has stolen somebody else's phone, or has caused trouble with other people, and people have seen him travel north, the spokesman in Gao will ring his colleagues in Algeria and say "if so-and-so arrives, you must stop him, he still owes money," and there is no way he could ever escape that, because there are only so many places that he can go to on the way. So as soon as he gets off the truck and to the city, somebody will talk to him and take him away, and the assembly will already be waiting for him. Or else if he had trouble with other people from a different country, their president and our president will have been informed, and they will try to arrange things between them.

This transnational efficacy at times becomes a cause of pride, and is often compared favourably to the many shortcomings of regional states: "the Nigerians, for instance," people whisper in awe, "they can take you all the way from the coast through to the Tell, and nobody will ever know; if they don't like their president – you know they all deal in drugs and are dangerous – they complain to Lagos, and somebody will come up here and take him out, without anybody seeing anything, especially not the police." Yet stories of punishment also serve as tropes in moral evaluation and differentiation, indicating a fundamental ambivalence: "the Nigerians, if they catch a thief, they cut his hand off – you know the barber down the road with one arm? He says it was an accident ... We, no, we are not like that, we are more humane, this is why we cannot live with them."[11]

How much of this is true or mere rumour is of course difficult to ascertain; but all these stories speak of a feeling of segregation and social, cultural, moral, and judicial autonomy, with a mix of resignation

[10] The position of a *jatigi* or "landlord," a local intermediary who acts as a privileged intermediary between foreign settlers or traders has a long history in West Africa: see for instance Hill (1966) and Brooks (1993). See Bredeloup (2007) on the use of the term *jatigi* to refer to lodgers for migrants in contemporary Mauritania.

[11] Nigerians are widely assumed to be involved in the international drug-trade, independently of the "mafia" based in al-Khalīl, see Bayart, Ellis, and Hibou (1999).

and pride. And there is no doubt that on one level, these communal associations are a dire necessity. In spring 2008, trouble broke out in Bordj Badji Mokhtar. Apparently, a sub-Saharan migrant on his way north had refused to pay his debts to an Arab trader, the ghetto did not intervene, and in retaliation, sub-Saharan migrants were randomly chased from town with sticks and machetes. They had to "run" all the way to Gao, where they finally reached safety: in a context where everybody is only as powerful and protected as their connections, migrants quite simply have to play the same game.[12] Nonetheless, everybody knows that in most cases, personal obligations rather than communal organisations offer most protection, and, generally speaking, those migrants who have established individual ties with their host society, mostly through work, and who rent private accommodation, are the ones who do best.[13] And there is no doubt that from a local point of view, people are worried about migrants not because they fail to integrate, but rather because they might integrate too much, and thereby erode existing boundaries and question local hierarchies. Hence, all migrants agree that in their experience, the most "racist" of Algerians are "the local blacks" (the *ḥarāṭīn*, defined as descendants of former slaves), "who are worried that we (and others) might take them for our cousins."[14] Hence perhaps the public and somewhat reassuring emphasis on the ghetto, as a sign and symbol of social, moral, and cultural autonomy, of vulnerability and of an ongoing project of mobility; a public emphasis that is readily understood by all, and that makes sense within the broader social organisation and spatial conception of Saharan settlements more generally. And indeed, accounts of city life in the Sahara invariably dwell on social differentiation and spatial segregation into autonomous districts, whether they are described as ghettoes or not.

[12] Otherwise, when trouble breaks out in al-Khalīl or related areas, negotiations are undertaken by the relevant "tribal elders" in accordance with "tradition," thereby integrating it once more into regional social norms, if only retrospectively. How much the actual composition of such councils corresponds to historical precedence is, of course, a different question: but there is no doubt that sub-Saharan migrants are outside the system. For more detail on Khalīlī conflict resolution, see Scheele (2009b).

[13] Conversely, migrants who do well prefer to hire private accommodation. This is true of Algeria (Badi 2007) much as of Mauritania (Choplin 2008, Marfaing 2010).

[14] This fragility of boundaries between Algerian *ḥarāṭīn* and *suwādīn* is echoed in a large number of jokes, told in private, and that are funny only by the taboo broken: "A *sūdānī* and a *ḥarṭānī* were working together in this man's garden. One day, the *ḥarṭānī* was in the car, driving out, and shouted at the *sūdānī*: hey, *sūdānī*, open the gate will you? The *sūdānī* got angry and shouted back: I might be a new *sūdānī*, but you are an old *sūdānī* (*anā sūdānī jdīd, wa inta sūdānī qdīm*)!"

ADRAR: THE EMBATTLED OUTPOST OF ALGERIAN MIDDLE-CLASS MORALITY

The most striking example here is perhaps Adrar and its Sahelian twin, Bani w-Iskut. The first time I visited Bani w-Iskut was with my friend Jamāl. Jamāl is from a well-respected maraboutic family from a *qṣar* near Zaouiat Kunta, seventy kilometres south of Adrar; a devout Muslim, teacher at a local high school, he had put me in touch with several *shaykh*s and *'ulamā'* in the area. One of these had been the current leading religious *shaykh* of the Kunta (see Chapter 4), Sīdi Muḥammad, who had spent many a summer in Jamāl's second house in Oran. Asked for information about Mali, Sīdi Muḥammad had professed his own ignorance, and sent us to Bani w-Iskut in order to look up Sīdi N'Goma, a "very knowledgeable cousin" of his. Jamāl was at first reluctant, as he feared for his car, he said; but one day during Ramadan we finally went. We started asking for directions as soon as we turned off the broad paved road behind the *sūq* Būdā and were sent down various wrong turns by veiled men squatting in the dusty streets, in the shade of trans-Saharan trucks, looking at us with suspicious curiosity. Goats were feeding on large rubbish heaps in the streets and were periodically tortured by half-naked and incredibly dirty children. "*Shūfi 'l-safāj*" ("Look at these savages"), Jamāl said sadly, before he was mesmerised by large plates of steaming lentils carried past: in the middle of Ramadan! When we finally found the house, we were ushered into a large mud-brick building, past three well-nourished ladies whose colourful *malāḥif* (full-body veil, sing. *milḥafa*) left much of their charms uncovered ("See! And I can barely afford one," Jamāl whispered), and then across a courtyard full of chickens and goats, to a small square room with little furnishing, lit by a tiny window just below the low ceiling. Sīdi N'Goma was squatting on a cheap carpet, clutching his prayer beads; he mumbled in hardly audible Hassaniya that he knew nothing of Mali, had indeed hardly ever been there, but that he might be able to afford me "protection" if I really wanted to go there, but then of course I would have to pay … Jamāl quickly pulled me away, past the giggling ladies, into his car, and back to "civilisation." "These people sleep on pots of gold," he mumbled all the way back, and days later still, "and they live in holes like animals."

The second time I went to Bani w-Iskut was almost a year later, after having been to Mali and back. I had come on my own this time, to visit Minatou, the elder sister of my northern Malian host Lalla. The veiled men still seemed to be squatting where I had left them, but this time

I recognised them straight away: I had met most of them either in Gao or al-Khalīl, and they were little surprised that I had made good my promise to visit. Sīdi N'Goma was Minatou's next-door neighbour, and his three daughters (not wives) insisted I stay for dinner, gave me one of their *malāḥif* as a present, and introduced me to their father, who spoke Algerian Arabic fluently, and was now rather chatty. In Timbuktu, I had spent much time with one of their cousins and fiancé, and the girls were eager to hear family gossip. They did not recognise me, of course: last year's foreign visitor introduced by an "Adrari" had long slipped their minds. On acquaintance, what had seemed like the heartland of debauchery turned out to be an ordinary Timbuktu household, were it not for the slight markers of distinction that the girls had borrowed from Algerian mainstream culture: fizzy drinks, for instance, and elaborate sweets and dry biscuits rather than meat to greet the visitors. Bani w-Iskut as perceived by Jamāl – and as I had seen it the first time, watching as I was through his eyes – thus disappeared at first touch; indeed, all the traits that Jamāl had expected to see on his visit, and found – irreligion, debauchery, illicit wealth, lack of "civilisation" – were perceived by Sīdi N'Goma's daughters in much the same negative way, as characterising black migrants and more recent arrivals from the *bilād al-sūdān*. But without a prior visit to Timbuktu, this "normality" was simply not visible: much like al-Khalīl, Bani w-Iskut could only make sense if it was understood in a broader context of connectivity, as referring to other places beyond the limits of Adrar, and mostly beyond the national borders of Algeria.

Bani w-Iskut, "build and keep quiet about it," is the largest "informal" quarter of Adrar. According to most descriptions, its first houses were built, overnight and in a clandestine way, in the 1970s, following the arrival of Malian refugees (see also J. Bisson 2003: 129–32).[15] Bani w-Iskut further grew during the 1980s and 1990s, as more and more Sahelian Tuareg and Arabs settled in town, either directly from their home countries, or after having been expelled from Bordj Badji Mokhtar; it continues to expand, spilling over into the empty lands around the city. By now, other Sahelian quarters have sprung up throughout town, but Adrari imagination continues to see Bani w-Iskut as representing "the *bilād al-sūdān*," its moral shortcomings and its gradual "encroachment" on Algeria: it is a world on its own, where "normal" social and cultural

[15] Dates are subject to some debate: Adraris tend to insist on the newness of Bani w-Iskut, whereas its inhabitants stress just how long they have been living there, pointing to family history and the "traditional" architecture of their houses.

norms do not apply, where people dress "foreign," divorce easily, and everybody is a smuggler. From an Adrari point of view, it is a place of dangerous porosity and instability, with uncountable people moving in and out, but never truly resident; a site that by its proximity and excessive outside connections leaves Adrar vulnerable to all kinds of contamination: disease, drugs, prostitution, witchcraft, HIV. With its anarchic layout and architecture where Adraris infallibly get lost, with its dirty mud-roads, rubbish heaps, and spontaneously constructed houses made out of all kinds of possible and impossible materials, and with its goats, chicken, and intense street life, Bani w-Iskut stands in stark opposition to the clear and well-built town centre of Adrar, whose broad paved road, right angles, and large administrative buildings, all uniformly painted in terracotta, breathe at the rhythm of the Algerian nation-state. "Why do you want to go to Bani w-Iskut," as an Algerian friend of mine put it, very seriously, "when you have already been to Gao? They are the same." Bani w-Iskut's "crookedness" and permeability is also reflected in its economy, whose mainstay, at least according to Adrari perceptions, remains illegal transborder trade: rather than an integrated part of the city's economy, Bani w-Iskut is thus portrayed as external to the city's life, as a parasite that feeds on Algerian wealth and hands it over to outsiders, without submitting to its social and economic norms – Jamāl's "pots of gold" that ought to be invested locally, or at least deposited in a bank, rather than left to rot or be used to feed dubious transborder networks and other unmentionable ties.

My host Minatou, Lalla's (see Chapters 3 and 4) older sister, arrived in Adrar in the 1970s with her husband, having spent several years in Mecca. Her house is situated in the oldest part of Bani w-Iskut, near the mosque. On my first visit, it was still partly built in mud bricks, although Minatou was gradually replacing them with concrete. A shaggy door made out of corrugated iron opened into a large courtyard, where a satellite dish was suspended from crumbling walls, occasionally head-butted by goats feeding on plastic bags, and where the little black maid was busy preparing large dishes of rice on an open fire, seasoned with rancid sheep's butter imported from Mali. There was no running water, and the little available electricity was mainly used to power the television and to charge the ubiquitous mobile phones. The courtyard led into a reception room, sparsely furnished and with its cheap blue paint peeling off the walls, but that was always replete with family members and visitors, squatting on the floor and drinking endless rounds of strong sweet tea. Bani w-Iskut primarily acts as a way station and relay for traders travelling through the border region, and as such Minatou's house is perhaps best thought about as the "civilised" – read: feminised – equivalent of a Khalīlī *garāj*. Lakhḍar, al-Shaykh, and everybody else whom I had met in al-Khalīl sporadically made their appearance, continuing conversations began in Gao; Lalla turned up one day, wanting to visit another of her sisters who had come up to Adrar to go to hospital. Conversations turned on family members spread out between Gao, Bordj Badji Mokhtar, and Adrar, on the ups and downs of trade and security in northern Mali, and on Arab soap operas followed either side of the border on satellite TV.

On a permanent basis, however, Minatou's house is almost exclusively inhabited by women: Minatou herself, her daughter Faṭūma, a young niece sent to Adrar to go to school, her daughter-in-law, a young girl from their home area in northern Mali, and her little granddaughter. Minatou's son Rashīd, the petrol smuggler encountered in Chapter 3, is mostly absent, while her husband, of a venerable age, generally keeps to his bed; Faṭūma's former husband lives in Bamako. This predominance of women is typical of households in Bani w-Iskut: Minatou's neighbour Hanna, a Tamasheq speaker from Kidal, lives with her two sisters and their three small daughters. Her only brother, a former transborder trader, has set up house in Kidal, where I first met him; her husband, a smuggler, has "disappeared" into the world of al-Khalīl, without giving any sign of life for more than a year; her brother-in-law, also a trader, works in a Khalīlī *garāj*, and will be "back shortly." Next door, Sīdi N'Goma's three daughters look after their ageing father, with no husband in sight; meanwhile, 'Abd al-Ḥamīd, the Timbuktu Kunta scholar met in Chapter 4, the fiancé of the eldest, is sorting out family affairs at his main residence in Timbuktu. Like most of her neighbours, Minatou runs a business of her own, dealing in veils and other female paraphernalia.[16] Some of these are sent to her by her eldest sister from Mauritania, who herself spends much time travelling between Nouakchott, Gao, and Adrar; other goods are brought to her by exclusively female traders from northern Mali and Niger, and in particular from Western Saharan refugee camps near Tindouf. This predominance of women reinforces Adrari perceptions of the immorality of Bani w-Iskut; further, it seems to confirm Jamāl's notion that Bani w-Iskut is little better than a ghetto, home to a mobile population whose primary social ties, husbands, and cultural references

[16] Trading is a common and utterly respectable occupation for Hassaniya as much as for Songhay and most West African women: for case studies of successful traders, see Lesourd (2006) on Mauritania, Lambert (1993) on Mali, Cordonnier (1982) and Weigel (1987) on Togo; see Humarau (1997) for an overview.

are situated elsewhere: not really part of Adrar, and even less so of contemporary Algeria. Yet, here as for sub-Saharan migrants, at a closer look these distinctions become fragile, and reveal myriad cross-cutting ties and fundamental parallels that are underplayed in everyday conversation, but that remain nonetheless crucial to city life.

This is most obvious from an economic point of view. Inhabitants of Bani w-Iskut run stalls and shops in the market, where they sell goods of more or less dubious provenance that, by their low prices, often bring relief to strained middle-class household budgets. Bani w-Iskut's female population have specialised in certain services that have by now become indispensable to Adrari cultural life: they braid hair, for instance – a recent fashion among the Adrar wealthy – or supply amulets, foretell the future, cure depression or sterility, or remedy the absence of suitable husbands, alongside other services that "orthodox" Algerian morality condemns as un-Islamic (see also Chapter 4). Other women in Bani w-Iskut go out to work in subaltern positions – cleaners, for example – in Adrar. Meanwhile, transborder trade is never just in the hands of Sahelians, but relies on the collaboration or at least the tacit endorsement of a whole cross section of the Algerian population (see Chapter 3); and many "real Adraris" are more familiar with Bani w-Iskut's tangled streets than they would like to admit. Former Algerian trading families, such as those described in Chapter 2, still have family connections in Bani w-Iskut and cultivate them, although they might be loath to mention them in public. Hence Zayda, daughter of one of the Zijlāwī, whose maternal grandfather had been Minatou's father's best friend and patron, and who the Awlād Sīdi draw on in times of crisis.[17] Zayda deals in veils and other "women's stuff" (incense, perfumes, jewellery, shoes), and often collaborates with Minatou, but she tends to cater for a "better sort" of clients, who regularly visit her large house in the recent Mille-quatre-cents housing development where Zayda's nieces – dressed in jeans and brought up in Niamey – dish out generous helpings of rice and couscous (see Chapter 2). Although, to the unpractised Algerian eye, Zayda's visitors are dressed in much the same way as their "maternal cousins" in Bani w-Iskut, their *malāḥif* speak of wealth, elegance, and access to the latest fashion through connections with Mauritania, Mali and Niger. Zayda reigns supreme over a group of women like her: daughters of Algerian trans-Saharan traders and Malian or Nigerien mothers, who act as living

[17] Such as the imprisonment of their younger brother, Muḥammad, recounted in Chapter 3.

connections between the Adrari bourgeoisie and Bani w-Iskut, and whose frequent social gatherings she organises and directs. Her clients include girls from "real" Algerian families, some of local origin, but mostly daughters of civil servants from the north, eager to buy the latest Sahelian fashion and especially curious about the unknown world of the *bilād al-sūdān* that here comes adorned with sufficient helpings of respectability and wealth.

From an administrative point of view, Bani w-Iskut's position is similarly ambiguous: even though the construction of Bani w-Iskut was indeed originally unauthorised by state officials, it was nonetheless conducted with the tacit consent of the town's people and administration (J. Bisson 2003: 129). It has now been connected to the municipal water and electricity networks, roads have been paved, children go to school, and the local town hall is gradually replacing old mud-brick houses with new concrete buildings. Hence, on my last visit, I found that Minatou's house had fallen down; neighbours pointed me to the neighbouring quarter, where I found the family sheltering in their second house, bought by Minatou's father for his second wife in the early 2000s. Minatou had just returned from the local town hall, and enthusiastically asked me to help her spell out the official document she had brought back: the "government" (*al-dawla*) was to reconstruct her old house, properly, in concrete, and with running water. Meanwhile, her daughter Faṭūma was busy in the kitchen, sweating from work she was not quite used to: the black servant had decided that she wanted to go to school, and indeed turned up later, proudly wearing the regulation Algerian school pinafore, in bright pink. They had all become Algerian, sighed Minatou, yet she was unable to suppress her smile at the thought of the future life of luxury in her new house – perhaps with air-conditioning … Like Minatou, many women in Bani w-Iskut dream of a state-constructed house in one of the new quarters, complete with satellite television, an inside kitchen, air-conditioning, a paved courtyard and no livestock, allowing for stylish female reclusion: if such outward signs of Algerian social mobility remain mostly unaffordable to them, a painful awareness of Algerian middle-class values and ambitions is shared by all. In the meantime, they attempt to react to Algerian prejudice that stamps them as "barely better than prostitutes" by less costly attempts to surpass them in "morality": leaving their house only with their face covered, for instance, and emphasising their own religious status and superiority; or sending their daughters and younger siblings to quranic school, while jealously restricting their movements. Conversely, "real Algerian" girls are fascinated by the fashion, beauty, allure, and especially the freedom of movement that they associate with the women of Bani w-Iskut, their erstwhile "cousins" (see Chapter 4). They never tired of stories I told them about female traders, and jealously watched me go off to visit Bani w-Iskut, while secretly trying on the *malāḥif* I had brought back from Mali while I was away. Of course, such intimacy makes relations more strained rather than less, and leads to an even more pronounced emphasis on radical, that is to say moral, distinction. But it also shows their underlying fragility, and it is clearly no coincidence that those Algerian women who publicly dare showing themselves in West African clothing tend to be northerners, or educated girls who are most unquestionably removed from their own past.

Yet parallels between Bani w-Iskut and Adrar go much deeper than mere cross-cutting economic and social ties and mutual awareness of embarrassing intimacy. Few parts of Adrar are older than Bani w-Iskut, and the town as a whole is made of socioculturally distinctive districts that exist only because of a more or less recent history of migration. When the French established a military post here in 1901, they chose to set up their camp just outside the seat of the former regional *qāḍi* in Timmi (whose registers were discussed in Chapter 5). They opened a market nearby that in 1906 counted seventeen shops, all held by "foreign" traders.[18] The first houses were rented out to indigenous soldiers in the French army, most of whom came from El Goléa and Metlili; several coffee shops mainly served soldiers; so did the market, although it also attracted a growing number of Touata customers, who were chronically short of cash.[19] As they did not own livestock, the Touata remained totally dependent on foreign transporters and traders to supply the town, until trucks were introduced; by then, however, trade had been monopolised by Sha'anba former French military, such as the Akacem family, whose history was traced in Chapter 2.[20] At independence, Algerian civil servants, mainly recruited in the north, replaced the French army. In 1974, as migrants from northern Mali and Niger started to settle in Bani w-Iskut, Adrar was made capital of the *wilāya* (department) of the same name. This led to ambitious building projects and to the creation of hundreds of

[18] They were: four Jews, one Mzabi, three Sha'anba from El Oued, two Arabs from Laghouat, three from Ouargla, one from Metlili, one from Khenafsa, two from the Jabal Nafūz in Tunisia, and one from El Goléa. See "Rapport annuel, annexe du Touat," 1906, CAOM 23H91, and the various documents on the "Création de l'annexe du Touat" kept in CAOM 22H48.

[19] "Rapport annuel, annexe du Touat," 1906, CAOM 23H91.

[20] "Rapport annual, annexe du Touat," 1910, CAOM 23H91.

administrative jobs, mainly taken up by "northerners," who settled in government housing projects near their places of work. Northerners, especially from Algiers and Kabylia, staffed schools and hospitals; others followed, attracted by the oil-rich south that seemed to offer possibilities of social mobility that by now had become illusory on the Mediterranean coast. In the 1990s, civil war in both northern Mali and northern Algeria sent waves of refugees to the Algerian south, considered relatively safe; they settled on the outskirts of town, generally following regional and linguistic boundaries, and invested in the service sector and retail trade throughout the town. The northwest, long linked to the Touat through trade and seasonal migration (see Chapters 1 and 2), provided wholesale traders and building contractors to cater for these new arrivals. Meanwhile, inhabitants of the nearby *qṣūr* who chose to move to Adrar mainly settled near the historic Timmi, on the road to Tamantit; the only people who might plausibly claim some degree of "indegeneity" – and generally refrain from doing so – are hence clearly marginal to city life, both geographically and socially.

These histories of migration still determine contemporary hierarchies and sociabilities. Marital alliances, social ties, and mostly also capital investment tend to be directed outwards, towards a more or less distant place of origin and the "cousins" who still live there; few are the residents of Adrar, wealthy or not, who do not have some kind of home elsewhere. The great Sha'anba families, literally at the heart of the Adrari bourgeoisie, tend to marry among themselves, and women and girls follow a never-ending circle of engagements, weddings, and funerals with people "just like them" but resident in Tamanrasset, El Goléa, or Algiers. Once a year, the Adrar residents of the Kalloum family invite everybody else to their large compound in the centre of Adrar (see Chapter 2); but all year round, their social life is turned towards their cousins in Timimoun, Abiodh Sidi Cheikh, and Oran, while relations of distant politeness prevail with their neighbours. Weddings organised by Becharis unite Becharis; and every Adrari who can afford to do so spends the hot summer months in the northwest or, more frequently, on the Mediterranean coast, in Oran or Mostaghanem. Northern civil servants mostly keep their families back home, and dream of retirement in the north; indeed, many younger men quite simply come to the south to earn enough money to get married and set up a family elsewhere; and their mobility, actual and conceptual, stands comparison with any sub-Saharan resident of the local ghetto or former or current trans-Saharan trader. Even where such mobility is interrupted, for reasons of family strife, lack of means, or insecurity, regional ties and origins translate into the general pattern of everyday social life. Dahman and his family, for instance, are unmistakeably Kabyle. Dahman has spent most of his life in the south and prides himself in his ability to "bear it": he used to run a restaurant-cum-truck stop in the Tanezruft, all on his own. He is now Adrar's most sought-after mechanic, and he brought his wife here after life in northern Algeria became too dangerous.[21] The only time they went back, he says, they were caught in a fake roadblock, and everybody else was killed: never again. Nonetheless, his wife mainly speaks Kabyle and about Kabylia; at home they eat Kabyle food and keep Kabyle hours, and she stays aloof from anybody but their nearest relatives – which means that she leads a very restricted social life indeed.

Similar patterns of social interaction apply even to those residents who might be most plausibly classified as "locals." Hence, the Cherfaoui, a family of sharifian descent originally from Mtarfa in the nearby Gourara. They moved to Adrar, to one of the new quarters built near the road to Tamantit, in the hope of finding employment, and the head of the family now works as a taxi driver. This is one of the more "mixed" residential quarters of town, and they cultivate some ties with their neighbours, especially through their children; yet publicly, their social life is centred on family connections, with Mtarfa itself, but also with sharifian families in neighbouring *qṣūr*, especially Tamantit, Tsabit, and Fenoughil. This is where suitable spouses are recruited, and where the family spend all religious holidays. They tend to stay aloof from Adrari Sha'anba, northern civil servants and Sahelian immigrants alike, not on grounds of indigeneity – after all, as *shurafā'*, they originally came from Morocco – but rather because they see them as arrogant and morally tainted, irreligious, materialist (with a slight hint of envy here), racist, and superficial. Hence, the rhetoric of moral incommensurability cuts in all directions; the rejection of Bani w-Iskut is only one among many, although, in many respects, it remains the most public and overdetermined one. On the ground, moreover, Bani w-Iskut encompasses quite as many hierarchical distinctions as Adrar, based on date of arrival, status, language, wealth, and nationality. Hence, Bani w-Iskut and Adrar mirror each other in a constant game of distinction and differentiation; they are both made of overlapping social networks, maintained by ongoing projects of mobility and the active remembrance of outside origins; and their main point of reference remains elsewhere.

[21] Certain parts of Kabylia were particularly hard hit by the violence of the 1990s: see Martinez (1998) and H. Roberts (2003).

TAMANRASSET: AFRICA ALREADY

If Adrar admits only unwillingly to its cosmopolitanism and strives hard to give itself a public image of homogeneity, thereby forcefully excluding the "messiness" of Bani w-Iskut, Tamanrasset publicises it proudly and self-consciously: it is "not really Algerian," its inhabitants say, "Bani w-Iskut writ large," "free," "easy," "anarchic," "mobile," and "open," like the *bilād al-sūdān*.[22] This difference is surprising, as the two cities share a similar history: like Adrar, Tamanrasset started as a French army post and was made the capital of a *wilāya* in 1974; its exponential growth has been and still is due to state investment, army personnel, and trade. Indeed, the influential commercial families who built the contemporary city centre are the same as those who remain at the heart of Adrar; and Tamanrasset's growth is also mainly due to immigration from northern Algeria and the Sahel.[23] Yet where in Adrar people attempt to establish a firm boundary between Bani w-Iskut and the "town," no such binary distinction exists in Tamanrasset. There is not one, but several Sahelian quarters defined by language, place of origin, date of arrival, wealth, and degree of involvement with the Algerian state. Sahelian industries flourish throughout the city (Badi 2012), and sub-Saharan migrants are much more visible: whereas they have failed to establish their own quarter in Adrar, in Tamanrasset, black Sahelian restaurants have sprung up all over the town, to be seen by all, even if they mainly cater for their own countrymen (Badi 2007). Tamanrasset's main market has developed around what used to be the "trans-Saharan fair" (the Assihar) and is known for its broad array of Sahelian goods and vendors. Distinctions between the various quarters of town are nonetheless pronounced and phrased in terms of moral incommensurability; but this is a subtle game of local hierarchies, and if there is a clear binary opposition at all, it is the one that opposes an undifferentiated group of "northerners" – locally referred to as *shināwa*, Chinese, that is to say the most foreign of all – to the people from the Sahara.

[22] On the "cosmopolitanism" of Tamanrasset, see also Spiga (2002), Badi (2007, 2011), and Nadi (2007).

[23] Beyond the overall demographic growth of Tamanrasset, from 30,000 in 1974 to an estimated 76,000 today, it is difficult to come by reliable figures on the provenance of new residents; and even overall figures exclude the many inhabitants of the city who are not officially registered, live in makeshift dwellings, or are inherently mobile. Estimates tend to be impressionistic and are generally politically motivated: some claim that two-thirds of the population of Tamanrasset are "foreign" or "migrants" (see, e.g., Spiga 2002), without stating any sources or proposing valid definitions for these categories.

Like Adrar, Tamanrasset consists of a number of distinctive districts, and this spatial segregation reflects both a history of migration and the town's complex contemporary social life. The centre, near the few remaining French administrative buildings, is inhabited by the descendants of large trading families, mainly Sha'anba, who came with the French army in the early twentieth century. They constitute a close-knit community, with strong ties to their cousins in Adrar, not least through repeated marital alliances, and much like their Adrari cousins, their social life closely links Sha'anba from throughout the Sahara, in an endless round of exclusive women's tea parties and wedding preparations marked by their strong reference to northern Algerian models. Further towards the Oued, in the historic commercial centre, live Tamanrasset's oldest inhabitants: families from In Salah some of whom arrived before the Sha'anba and the French, invited by leading nomadic Ahaggar families to set up agricultural colonies and centres of scholarship.[24] Whereas Sha'anba houses tend to be large, square, well-aired, and modern, and speak of their owners' wealth and endorsement of the state, the quarter occupied by people from In Salah near the market seems to reproduce a Tidikelt *qṣar*, both in its overall layout and in its architectural style: open doors lead through winding passages into small courtyards and rooms with floors covered in sand; parts of the quarter are reserved for "whites," whereas others are for *ḥarāṭīn* former agricultural labourers. While Sha'anba women dress in *jallāba* and *ḥijāb* and speak with a standard Touati accent with northern inflections, women from In Salah sport colourful *malāḥif*, leaving the *jallāba* to unmarried girls, and their dialect contains words from eastern Algeria and Hassaniya by turns. This is due to a longstanding close interaction between the Tidikelt and the Ahaggar, and a long history of settlement and intermarriage (see Chapter 1). Nonetheless, they remain consciously set apart from the "locals," through their language, social networks, privileged involvement in the state administration in minor positions, and often also their religious descent.

Across the Oued are various Sahelian quarters, most notoriously Guett el-Oued, where the Assihar is located, and which is today the busiest part of the city. This is where the first generation of "white" Sahelian migrants settled, and owning a house in Guett el-Oued has in itself become a sign of relative seniority and status; yet the quarter is far from homogeneous and continues to attract relative newcomers who rent rooms or rely on the support of more established residents of the same origin and linguistic

[24] As discussed in more detail in Chapter 1; for references, see Chapter 1.

group. Many of the most longstanding residents of Guett el-Oued are Arab wives of Algerian traders (see Chapter 2) who started to settle in Tamanrasset in large numbers in the 1970s and 1980s. They still constitute the "aristocracy" of the Malian Arab community, which, here as in Bani w-Iskut, is largely run by women with a flair for commerce and an outstanding degree of mobility and concomitant social ties. My first visit to Guett el-Oued took place on the occasion of a naming ceremony.[25] All the women attending were Malian Arabs from Timbuktu, many of whom had been married to Algerian traders, who still travelled to Mali on a regular basis, where they often owned secondary residences.[26] The house was large and constructed in concrete, but most social life took place in the large courtyard and the open-air kitchen, while the Algerian-style lounge had been stripped of its furniture. All the women were dressed in colourful *malāḥif* and plentiful gold-plated jewellery from Mauritania, exuding Chadian incense. They spoke the Arabic-inflected Songhay of Timbuktu; there were no biscuits and cakes, but rather generous helpings of *to*, the Malian national dish. Within five minutes of squatting in the kitchen near the steaming pot of millet, bags that still bore visible traces of trans-Saharan crossings were pulled out from underneath *malāḥif* or dragged across the kitchen floor. Rings, necklaces, wristbands, and ear rings in bright yellow, transparent veils in pink, purple, and orange, perfumes, sandals and incense: the latest fashion from Mauritania, brought back from last week's trip or else sent by the sister or cousin resident in

[25] Naming ceremonies take place seven days after a child is born, on the day when the child's name is chosen, often in the presence of the imam, and publicly announced. They are especially popular among women, to whom a lavish meal is offered, and who leave presents of money with the child. Although these ceremonies are common throughout the northern Sahel (where, confusingly, they are called "*baptêmes*" in French), they are unknown in Algeria, and only celebrated by migrants from the south. In Tamanrasset, however, they are gradually starting to become popular among the commercial middle classes, who tend to translate them into tea-drinking and biscuit-eating events.

[26] Strictly speaking, they are thus in-laws rather than refugees. This made their arrival in Tamanrasset easier from an administrative point of view; however, it also, according to their own recollection, added to the hostility they experienced at the hand of "real Algerians," especially women: "They are jealous of us, all of them, because they know that when their husbands come to Mali, they see all these beautiful women there, especially in Timbuktu, and they simply cannot resist. And once they get used to us, they can never go back. It's because Timbuktu women are beautiful, they are white, as you can see, much whiter than their own *ḥarṭāniyyāt* [here used as a derogative term to refer to high-status southern Algerian women, who tend to be of darker skin than many of their northern Malian "cousins"]. Also, they are real women, they know how to be beautiful, and they know how to live and how to please men." Again, differences between the "host" society and "migrants" are thus couched in moral terms, although here, moral judgement is reversed, and stereotypes of sexual allure are turned into assertions of pride.

Timbuktu, Nouakchott, or Bamako and on offer for a "special price," just for the occasion. Every self-respecting Sahelian Arab in Tamanrasset is to some extent a trader and exploits her transnational connections to the full.

Most *shināwa*, or northerners, live in peripheral districts, constructed by the state if they are civil servants, or increasingly also by private companies, if they have come on their own account to try their luck in the south. Like their "cousins" in Adrar, their social horizons and aspirations are mainly turned towards the Tell.[27] Formerly nomadic Ahaggar who have settled in town tend to live towards their former pastures, where they can claim land, and try to run camp sites and thereby capture their share of the tourism industry – attempting to feed on another type of transnational mobility;[28] generally, much like the *qṣūr*-dwellers in Adrar, they remain marginal to the city itself. Less well-connected Sahelians settle in Tahaggant, the new quarter near the recently constructed university. Here, everything speaks of recent arrival, instability, misery, and improvisation. Houses are constructed with modern materials, as soon as these can be procured, and are held together by faith rather than mortar. Most residents I met on my visits were Tuareg from the area of Kidal, who stay aloof both from Malian Arabs and from their Ahaggar "cousins" who view them with much suspicion (see Bellil and Badi 1993, 1996); they have picked up Algerian Arabic, but speak Tamasheq at home, and only sporadically send their children to school. Tahaggant is the centre of illegal transborder ventures, and no house would be complete without a shabby four-by-four in front of its door, or traces of recent truck repairs: mobility is not an option, but the mainstay of the local economy, and the quarter breathes at the rhythm of trans-Saharan arrivals and departures. At first sight, much like Bani w-Iskut, Tahaggant thus appears like a world on its own, turned towards Kidal, and instinctively avoided by all

[27] An exception here are Kabyles, often teachers, who came to Tamanrasset attracted by the "shared Berber culture" they were hoping to find. Mostly, they are disappointed: Tamanrasset is clearly a town of Arabic speakers, and local Tuareg are often rather suspicious of Kabyles, whom they see not as "Berber cousins" but rather as a particularly irreligious kind of *shināwa*.

[28] Until very recently, Tamanrasset and its surroundings were the only area in Algeria that remained open to tourism. It was accessible by direct flights from Paris and known for guided tours and "safaris," by car or camel, through the Ahaggar national park. Alongside state employment, largely taken by people from In Salah or by northerners, it was the most important official source of income in town; and people joked that "every Tuareg with a mobile phone owned a travel agency." With recent threats of "terrorism," tourism has plummeted, to the great despair of locals, especially Algerian Tamasheq speakers; see Keenan (2003).

"respectable" citizens and their daughters; but here as in Adrar, individual cross-cutting ties are manifold and link places like Tahaggant to the bourgeois heart of Tamanrasset society. Hence Bohanna, mentioned in Chapter 2, who, originally from Kidal and closely connected to Ḥammū Zafzaf, joined the ALN during the war, stayed with them after independence, lived in Tit for a while, and has now moved to Tahaggant. Or else Ighles, the truck driver who took me to Gao, as described in Chapter 3: originally from Timiaouine on the Algero-Malian border, he shares a large house with his brothers in Tahaggant, while his elder brother lives in Bani w-Iskut, his sister is married in a small *qṣar* near In Salah, and his mother remains in the Tilemsi: he works for a Sha'anbī *patron*. Or Tadman, of outstanding beauty, who owns a large house and even larger *garāj* of much higher standing, with shiny new tiles and Moroccan cushions in the living room, with a second, even more luxurious house in Kidal, and who turned out to be quite familiar with various "real Algerians" of my acquaintance – although there is no doubt that they would never publicly admit to such a relation.

Such cross-cutting ties in no way erode existing boundaries; rather, they confirm them and lend considerable prestige to those who can transgress them routinely, and thereby draw on various regional networks and histories of mobility. Māma is outstanding here. She is from a family of Tajakanat, was born in Timbuktu, and was married to an Algerian trader as a second wife when she was fourteen.[29] Her husband had grown rich trading on the black market during the Second World War and in the 1950s (see Chapter 2); with national independence and state-sponsored socialism, the family moved to Niger to establish a sweet and ice cream factory in Maradi. They "returned" to Tamanrasset in the late 1980s. The family now lives in a quietly sophisticated part of town, just behind the buzz of Guett el-Oued. Māma is a conspicuous figure in all Malian Arab gatherings and family events; she knows everything and everybody, and her opinion is much valued. She owes this respected position not merely to her early arrival, but also to her excellent connections to "real Algerians": she is intimately acquainted with all parts of Tamanrasset

[29] Māma considers herself to be Algerian as much as she is proud of her connection to Timbuktu. As seen in Chapter 4, this is not at all contradictory: throughout the region, the Tajakanat, a federation known for their trading abilities and religious descent, are primarily associated with the market of Tindouf, which is situated within the borders of contemporary Algeria. Taking a slight historic shortcut, Tindouf is indeed indicated as Māma's place of birth in her (Algerian) passport, conferring her Algerian nationality beyond doubt.

society, except the *shināwa*. Māma runs a sewing workshop, where she produces clothes of all possible styles, for resident white Sahelians, but increasingly also for the Algerian middle classes. Due to the large presence of sub-Saharan migrants, labour is cheap in Tamanrasset, and because of her own experience in Timbuktu and Maradi, Māma is in an excellent position to appreciate the various skills that sub-Saharan and especially black Sahelian workers might have. Her linguistic ability – she speaks Songhay and Arabic fluently, of course, but also some Bambara, Hawsa, and French – helps her here, even if many of her workers are from Ghana ("that's where the really good tailors come from"): they are nonetheless impressed by her "local" knowledge of "African ways", and trust her as one whose moral standards are intelligible to them.

Māma employs four to six tailors at any one time, in a workshop inside her large compound. She is well aware that most of her employees are here to travel on, ideally to Europe, but that they need to earn some money first – "adventurers", as she calls them, with a resigned shrug. Most stay for six months to a year, but many come back after they have once again been picked up by the police, and relieved of all their earthly possessions. They are of course aware that Māma's wealth is based on their labour, and that she takes advantage of their difficult situation; but they know that she can protect them, and that, in Tamanrasset, such protection comes at a price:

> It's good to work for her, we sleep in the workshop, and the police cannot get us here. I used to work in the market: every morning when I started, a policeman came and watched me, and every time I earned some money, I could see him counting. When I had just enough to leave, he knew as well as I did, and the day before, he came and arrested me – I had to give him everything I had to get out of prison again. And I am sure he was waiting for me the next day, to start counting again. If you work for Māma, even if they pick you up in the streets, she will try to get you out, if only because she wants you to finish the work you have started.[30]

Māma rarely travels to Mali herself, and if she does, it is for family reasons rather than business. Her success is thus based less on her own

[30] Interview in Tamanrasset, November 2007. Accounts of the various systems and institutions through which local security forces routinely exploit sub-Saharan "adventurers" are legion: the man who owns the trucks that dump illegal migrants on the Algerian border also sells them passages back and has them working on his own building sites in the border area, for instance. In addition to their own structural mobility, large parts of the local security forces hence feed on that of others. For comparable systems in Niger and Mauritania, see Brachet (2005) and Choplin (2009), respectively.

mobility than on her ability to draw on that of others, and to accommodate conflicting notions of morality and propriety: as a wife to a known Algerian, and of an impeccable social, religious and moral reputation, she can cater for all, has friends in all places, always knows what is appropriate, and never causes any embarrassment to her clients: she knows how to keep apart what, according to local standards, ought to be separate. When coming to her house, her Algerian middle class clients are always certain that they will not run into an "adventurer," a notorious transborder trader – or indeed, any man at all.

Māma is not alone in her success: like Zayda and Minatou, she is supplied by a number of Sahelian Arab women who deal in West African cloth. The perhaps most famous and widely respected of these is Deija. As soon as a wedding comes up, women of all kinds and origins start trekking to her large, new, and comfortable house, near Māma's, to order suitable outfits; news of her imminent departure to Mali results in a similar throng of women at her door, trying to get their orders in. Deija travels to Bamako on a regular basis, to carefully choose her goods and to supervise their initial treatment.[31] She has her own car and driver; in addition to the house in Tamanrasset and her old home in Gao, she has bought a large villa in Bamako, where her husband spends most of his time, managing her other investment: a tea company, importing tea directly from China, and packaging and selling it throughout Mali. She has also opened a shop in Tamanrasset, near her house, which is run by a nephew of hers, "for the children." Deija owes her success to her professionalism and commercial ability, but also to her close connection to a formerly very successful Sha'anbī trading family with whom her husband collaborated closely when they were still living in Timbuktu. Yet there is nothing "natural" about it: as she says laughingly, she herself had to learn how to speak Bambara, and how to tell good *bazin* from bad, before she could even start; as an Arab from Timbuktu, when she started trading out of economic necessity, she had never been to the Malian capital or indeed worn anything but a *milḥafa*; but she knew "how to travel," as she puts it herself. Like Māma, Deija is utterly respectable, and this is what allows her to succeed in her balancing act between two different

[31] Although Chinese products are now flooding the market, *bazin* of the highest quality is uniquely produced in Germany. It is then shipped to West Africa, where it is beaten to give it its characteristic shine, and then dyed. Conscientious traders supervise all stages of this process, and Deija only deals with her own trusted collaborators in these matters. In Algeria, a full high-quality *bazin* costume for a wedding can cost several million centimes (up to 30,000 DA, or 300 euros, two to three times the average monthly salary).

and mutually exclusive "worlds": she invariably sells her goods from her own living room, from which men are strictly excluded; she keeps her daughters and nieces carefully in seclusion, marries them off as early as possible, and minimises their school attendance: in a sense, the restriction of movement she imposes on her dependents excuses her own wide-ranging mobility. As a result, in the privacy of their own bedrooms, many "real Algerian" women who, publicly, are quick in their condemnation of "Sudanese ways" but who are chronically short of cash, see her as a potential example of how to be rich and independent while remaining unquestionably respectable.[32]

GAO: PAST VIOLENCE AND FRAGILE BOUNDARIES

At first, it might seem absurd to compare Gao to Adrar and Tamanrasset, both recent and artificial creations by an alien colonial state. Gao, on the other hand, is situated in the Sahel, near agricultural lands and a permanent water source; it is one of the oldest cities in West Africa, with a long imperial past, as all Malian school children learn from an early age.[33] Yet pre-colonial accounts and colonial reports give a very different image of Gao: they rather seem to echo the inherent fragility and the waxing and waning of Saharan settlement or, in this case, of settlement that largely depended on Saharo-Sahelian exchange and state investment and revenue. Hence, in the early 1850s, Heinrich Barth (1857–8, vol. 3: 480–1) described Gao, formerly the "most splendid city of Negroland" as a "desolate abode of a small and miserable population," a "hamlet, which altogether consists of about three hundred huts, grouped in separate clusters, and surrounded by heaps of rubbish, which seemed to indicate the site of some larger buildings of the former city." All that remained of Gao's glorious past were the ruins of the great mosque and the tomb of Askia Mohammed, where people still pray, but "lack the energy" for necessary repairs.[34]

[32] When it became known that I was about to go to Mali, I was approached by a number of women of my acquaintance who wanted me to send them clothes, or ideally, establish contact with Malian traders, to have a direct line to the much coveted *bazin*.

[33] Founded in the seventh century, Gao was the capital of the Songhay Empire. It then became part of the Empire of Mali and regained independence in the fifteenth century, until it declined with the Moroccan conquest of Timbuktu in 1591. It is one of the few cities in the area were archaeological excavations have taken place; see Insoll (1997, 2000). On the Songhay Empire more generally, see Hama (1968), Cissoko (1975), and Hunwick (2003).

[34] Askia Mohammed was the first Songhay emperor to have converted to Islam and is still seen as emblematic of past regional grandeur, justice, and splendor.

There is no market, and Barth comments repeatedly on the difficulties of procuring food, if only to feed his horses (ibid. 482). Fifty years later, this is echoed in French colonial reports. Administrators struggled to find supplies in the absence of a market; trade was in the hands of a few "*dioula*," mostly former French soldiers classified as Bambara and Moroccan Arabs from Timbuktu who came to buy grain. The main stimulus for trade and settlement was the presence of the French army, and here as in Adrar and In Salah, soldiers often doubled as traders.[35] Yet by 1923, cattle trade with Kano in northern Nigeria had developed, and traders from Niger "have settled in Gao in a quarter that is considered to be the wealthiest, and that plainly looks the most appealing."[36] In 1930, Gao was inhabited by "some Peulh" who spoke Songhay, a few Arma who had their own separate quarter, and by the "most cosmopolitan *dioula*": "traders, Arabs, Syrians, Bambara, Wolof, and so on."[37] The town was organised in independent "villages" organised according to language and origin, and whose taxes were, as in colonial Kidal described in Chapter 2, collected by individual headmen; the largest was "Gao-Dioula," founded in the 1900s, and inhabited by former French soldiers and traders.[38]

Contemporary Gao still shows traces of the "many villages" of French colonial times. It is divided into eight distinct districts all identified with specific populations, variously defined in terms of language, "culture," "race," social standing, and wealth: Arabs and Tuareg from the Tilemsi, Arabs from Timbuktu, Algerian traders and their descendants, Arma and Songhay of good families, Bozo fishermen, *bellah* and *ḥarāṭīn*, civil servants from southern Mali, army personnel, Dogon traders and domestic servants, traders from Niger and Nigeria, European aid workers, U.S. peace corps and army. All have their own separate districts with their own characteristic architecture, and contact between them remains, on a public level at least, sporadic and strongly hierarchical. The *quatrième quartier*, settled by Tilemsi Arabs and Tuareg, can stand as an example here. Situated at a certain distance from the town centre, straddling the road north, it is separated from the rest of the town by a large open space used as a football pitch; on turning the corner, stray visitors are watched suspiciously, and the main language in the street changes from Songhay to

35 "Monographie du cercle de Gao," 1905, ANM (fonds anciens) 1D39.

36 "Monographie du cercle de Gao," 1923, ANM (fonds anciens) 1D39.

37 "Monographie du cercle de Gao," 1930, ANM (fonds anciens) 1D39. See also "Rapports commerciaux confidentiels, Gao," 1933, ANM (fonds récents) 1Q285, and "Rapports commerciaux, cercle de Gao," 1922–44, ANM (fonds récents) 1Q338.

38 "Droit coutumier à Gao," 1932, ANM (fonds anciens) 1D39.

Arabic and perhaps Tamasheq. In terms of architecture, the boundary is similarly marked: whereas in the neighbouring *cinquième quartier*, inhabited by Arab traders from Timbuktu and their few remaining Algerian colleagues, houses are closely huddled together and constructed according to northern Saharan models, with inner courtyards covered in sand and winding passage ways leading to small secretive rooms protected by thick mud-brick walls from both the heat and curious onlookers, here, houses are large enclosures, marked by bare concrete walls, that shelter some livestock, cars, and trucks as well as a large family tent, in a fashion more reminiscent of a Khalīlī *garāj* than of the venerable urban tradition of Timbuktu. Two or three rooms, constructed hastily in a corner, serve as storage rather than living space; indeed, Lalla's mother, a longstanding resident of the *quatrième*, declared that it would be sheer madness to attempt to sleep in them, as they might "fall down on your head" at night – and she was probably quite right.[39]

Like al-Khalīl and Bani w-Iskut, the *quatrième* thus stands as a marker of ongoing mobility. It is mostly of recent construction, and houses a flexible population of former nomads and current transborder smugglers. This is where trans-Saharan journeys of all kind are organised; trucks unload parts of their cargo in their respective *gawārij* in the *quatrième* before driving round to the customs office on the other side of town. The conspicuous villas of "Tangara Arabs" who have come to wealth and fame (see Chapter 3) are situated here, as is the mansion of the "prince of the Tilemsi," a descendant of the formerly ruling Kunta family (see Chapter 4); this is where Algerian preachers on their way south stop over, resting from the fatigue of their trans-Saharan journey, and trying their rhetorical skills on a willing audience of elderly Arab ladies. Social life in the *quatrième* is largely autonomous, or rather tributary to trans-Saharan rather than urban networks: visiting takes place within its boundaries, and life-cycle rituals – such as, here too, naming ceremonies – assemble women from throughout the quarter, and only rarely beyond, although they frequently include sisters and cousins from Bani w-Iskut, Tahaggant,

[39] Some of the mobile aspects of the *quatrième* can be explained with reference to the formerly nomadic lifestyle of many of its inhabitants. Yet nomads can settle in radically different way; "sedentarisation" might proceed in stages, while the term only badly explains the various strategies of mobility put forward (see also Giuffrida 2005a), in the same way in which "nomadic" can cover a whole array of different lifestyles; and not all residents of the *quatrième* were ever nomadic at all. Ongoing rather than past outside connections – often of a radically different kind – thus often seem to be of more importance. On sedentarisation in the Sahel and the Maghreb more generally, see J. Bisson (1986), Lefébure (1986), Rasmussen (2002), and Choplin (2006).

or Nouakchott. More prosperous families own shops in the central market that act as outlets for the supplies arriving in the *quatrième* (and many of which they have taken over from Algerian trading families with profits made in the Lahda and cigarette trade, as described in Chapter 3); nonetheless, business largely functions within networks based on fellow inhabitants of the *quatrième*, or else on contacts in al-Khalīl, Bani w-Iskut, and beyond. Hence, like al-Khalīl, Bani w-Iskut, and Tahaggant, the *quatrième* is a half-world, where people often feel more closely connected to their brothers, sisters, and cousins living across the border than to their next-door neighbours; and indeed, here as in Bani w-Iskut, daily conversations turn on family gossip with an utter disregard for national borders or geographical distance.

Yet whereas in Adrar and Tamanrasset, spatial and cultural segregation is uniquely explained in terms of outside connections, migration, and morality, in Gao, it is also seen to be the result of civil strife and violence. Most inhabitants of the *quatrième* settled here in the 1990s or 2000s, when their formerly nomadic or seminomadic way of life had become unsafe, due to army reprisals after the 1990s rebellion, or because of the "war of the Kunta" (see Chapters 3 and 4), and this history of violence is still echoed in contemporary accounts of settlement. "We have to live here, ever since they tried to kill us all," as Khadīja, Lalla's next-door neighbour, insists, "it is much safer: there are no *koroboro* [Songhay, literally town-dwellers] between us and Algeria here."[40] As seen in Chapter 5, Songhay and Arab, "black" and "white" agree that ever since the "events" of the 1990s, morally speaking at least, Gao has been declining; it has become "rotten," life has ceased to prosper, and people live in fear. In my Gao hostess Awa's words:

> Money does not prosper anymore, food does not nourish you, and the fields are barren. Life has lost its sweetness: you just run and run and run and you will never get anywhere, you just work and work and work and nothing will come from it. Your children are not like your own anymore, they do not recognise you: they are like animals.

Since then, too many people from the south have moved in, and those from the north have been cut off from their past networks and livelihoods.

[40] Khadīja's husband, an influential Arab trader from the Tilemsi with a somewhat tarnished reputation, was killed at the same time, hence perhaps her rhetorical excess. The *quatrième* is literally situated behind the Algerian consulate, where, in the 1990s, Arabs and Tuareg found shelter; and although Malian Arabs are well aware of the duplicity of the Algerian state, they invariably describe the presence of the consulate as "reassuring."

In addition to the strongly felt presence of the Malian army, deeply mistrusted since the 1990s (and probably also before), this also reflects more banal changes in the commercial and transport infrastructure. With the recent construction of a bridge over the Niger and of a paved road that links Gao directly to the Nigerien capital Niamey, the city has turned into a trading hub, and one that largely escapes the control of older trading families. Hence, while all inhabitants of Gao are still defined by their ongoing mobility, for most Arabic and Tamasheq speakers, their actual ability to move has been severely curtailed by the "events," and reoriented towards the border area and illegal trade. From an Arab point of view, this is disastrous: from being "Arabs," that is to say, people who are by definition in control of their and other people's movements (see Chapter 4), they have forcibly been turned into *koro-boro*, city-dwellers, while remaining marginal to the city itself; the mobility of transborder traders, meanwhile, is increasingly at the command of others. Hence, perhaps, the emphasis on spatial segregation and mutual incompatibility; and hence also the effort put into maintaining sociocultural and linguistic distinctions in everyday life, in an area where, racial political rhetoric notwithstanding, most linguistic groups have long intermarried and roughly look the same, and where people might quite conceivably drop out of whatever category is assigned to them at birth – as was indeed the case with Mūlāy Sharīf, Zayda's uncle, described in Chapter 4.

As a result perhaps, Arabs in Gao explain much of what they do with reference to what other people do not do; the aspects most stressed are those of their own superior restraint, refinement, literacy, knowledge of religion, and awareness of the historical significance of things (see also Chapter 4); these express themselves on a daily basis through food, clothing, and language. Although most people in Gao eat roughly the same thing – rice or millet every day, with a bit of meat and some vegetables if they are available – a great issue is made of culinary differences. "Whites" eat meat, on such a reading, and "blacks" eat spicy rice and vegetables. An elderly Arab who had been told by his (Bambara) doctor to eat fish asked me in a rather perplexed way whether he could be sure that it would do him no harm, him, a "pure" Arab with not a drop of "black blood" in him. Children are brought up to follow such preferences, and Arabs teach even very young toddlers to appreciate small bits of cooked meat and liver in much the same way as European children are given sweets. Special attention is paid to Arab children of black mothers, and there is much suspicion by Arab husbands of black wives that the latter might secretly put too much chilli in their children's food, in order to "turn them black." Dress is equally, if not more important. Arab women wear the *milḥafa*, a five metre long veil that covers the whole body, as do high-status Tuareg; Songhay ladies of a certain age and standing wear ample *boubous*, and a turban; girls wear a sarong and T-shirt, or might even dress like Europeans; low-status and poor people are easily recognisable by their rags.[41] In fact, of course, women might change their clothes, and the *milḥafa* especially can be adjusted according to circumstance, thus in turn defining the situation at hand. Nonetheless, choices of clothing are construed to be irreversible and intimately related to morality and identity. Hence, as seen in Chapter 4, Lalla's niece Faṭūma divorced her husband, Mūlāy Sharīf's brother, because he insisted on her "dressing like a *sūdāniyya*," a shorthand here for a whole series of transgressions; conversely, wearing a *milḥafa* influences the way women move and is an indispensable prop for a whole series of highly stylised gestures that are seen as constitutive of "true Arab women," whose "modesty" speaks both of their superior knowledge of Islam and of their power of seduction.[42]

Language is the third most commonly cited marker of distinction.[43] As much as a matter of descent, "Arabness" and status are understood as a function of the capacity to master the grammatical and poetic subtleties of Arabic; similarly, religious understanding and morality are seen as intertwined with linguistic skill. This is especially true as Arabic is the language of the Qur'ān, and the two are seen to be necessarily bound up with each other: it is impossible, people insist, to say impious things in "pure" Arabic; and a simple *bismillāh* before starting a meal will earn more compliments on one's knowledge of Arabic than even the most complex and sustained conversation. Language learning is thus essential for the moral shaping of personhood.[44] As such, it is all-encompassing and

[41] There is clearly also an economic rationale here: cloth used to be among the one most expensive item traded in the area, and was often used as currency (Hunwick 1999b, Webb 1999) or as a way of keeping savings (Spittler 1993). Nowadays, both *malāḥif* and *boubous* made out of *bazin* vary considerably in price, and can be extremely expensive in local terms. To the initiated, they immediately reveal the economic status of their wearer.

[42] See also Lesourd (2006). These gestures include tucking the *milḥafa* around one's toes when sitting down with legs stretched out, adjusting it so that it reveals the appropriate the amount of hair, tugging it in behind the ears, using it as a cover when lying down, or hiding the face in it when laughing.

[43] What follows is mostly based on an Arab point of view. For an excellent discussion of the close link between language, status, and personhood among Tamasheq speakers, see Casajus (1990).

[44] In different settings and from distinct perspectives, both Abu Lughod (1986) and Caton (1990) describe a similarly close connection between the true mastery of language and

ongoing: Arab women exchange poetry, and explain it to each other, by way of mutual improvement. Young children are taught quranic expressions before anything else, and their relative quickness to babble Arabic sounds or else their stubborn insistence on speaking, say, Songhay, is seen as a sign of their moral worth or lack thereof. Conversely, if somebody "turns evil," women assured me repeatedly, he or she will become incapably of remembering or even pronouncing quranic Arabic, although they might "repent" and "remember." Mothers who fail to teach Arabic to their children are publicly upbraided because they have neglected a moral rather than a purely technical duty. Yet a mastery of Arabic is not merely a living sign of moral distinction but also a rare good. In a general environment marked by multilingualism, Arabs proudly maintain that whereas they can learn all other languages – and indeed often speak them to some degree – nobody else can truly learn Arabic, the mother of languages that encompasses and contains them all, much like sharifian genealogies are seen to encompass everybody else's.[45] Today, however, this intimate link between language, status, and "Arabness" renders the latter even more fragile than before. Many children of Arab descent speak little or no Arabic, especially if they were brought up in Timbuktu or Bamako. Meanwhile, about half of all Malian schoolchildren go to Arabic-language schools, sponsored by Libya and mostly staffed by "blacks" with a degree from a Libyan or Egyptian university (Bouwman 2005: 2, 4); Arabic is omnipresent on television, on radio, and in local missionary endeavours.[46] As a result, the Hassaniya spoken by Malian Arabs is compared to "real Arabic," and is generally found wanting, and claims to linguistic superiority and the concomitant privileged access to God's words, central to Arab identity in northern Mali, vanish at one stroke, to be even more hotly defended that before (see also Chapter 4).

Despite such discourses and practices of radical difference, people interact daily, of course, and all function, with more or less success, in

fully achieved moral personhood, in Yemen and Egypt, respectively. On the personal transformation linked to the memorisation and recitation of the Qur'ān, see Colonna (1995); on Mauritanian poetry, see Ould Bah (1971), which contains a full bibliography.

45 Similarly, *koro-boro* cannot learn Tamasheq. Such assumptions about languages are both mirrored and practically perpetuated by marriage strategies: while Arabs often have Tuareg or Songhay mothers, the reverse is hardly ever true, due to the principle of Arab female hypogamy.

46 On Arabic-language schooling in Mali, see also Brenner (2000). On Islamic missionary endeavours in northern Mali, see Niezen (1990), Gutelius (2007), and Lecocq and Schrijver (2007).

a multilingual environment. Perhaps the closest of these interactions is marriage. Following the principle of *kafā'a*, status equivalence between marriage partners, Arab women are barred from marrying either Tuareg or *koro-boro* unless these latter are of very high status; and this prohibition is often seen as the last bulwark against "the total disappearance" of Malian Arabs. Arab men, however, can marry whom they please and have long done so. After the fact, such unions might be portrayed as invariably harmonious, and there has indeed been, some time ago, a certain *engouement* in anthropology for "hybridity."[47] Yet as Ho (2001) observes, and as already touched on in Chapter 2, what matters is not marriage in itself, but the circumstances under which it is concluded, the ways in which children of such unions are defined, the relative status of the spouses, and the degree to which they are consciously chosen because of rather than despite their own background and family: once more, it is a question of the "right" or the "wrong" kinds of connections. These circumstances are never merely given or mechanically reproduced; rather, they are redefined at each marriage and according to its social context, in a process that can be very painful and fraught with daily difficulties. Thus, my friend Awa: although her mother was Tuareg, and, as she herself maintained, "white," her father was Peulh, and in Gao, Awa is generally classified as "black."[48] She was sixteen when she got married to 'Abd al-Karīm, a "Tangara Arab." 'Abd al-Karīm is resolutely Malian and aspires to a career as a civil servant rather than a transborder trader: he presented himself as a candidate to the local elections and is now busy pulling strings in order to obtain a government job in Bamako. His choice of a non-Arab wife can hardly be seen as an attempt to establish connections with powerful in-laws, as he was loath to acknowledge them; rather, much as 'Abd al-Salām, the Algerian trader discussed in Chapter 2 did with his many Malian wives, he treats her as if she had no family at all. And this, apart from her beauty, is perhaps what made her so attractive to him, as it allowed him to reduce undesirable connections, including

[47] See, for example, Young (1995) and Papastergiadis (1995) for the sudden popularity of the term in the 1990s. More recently, hybridity has been claimed not as a political aspiration, but rather as the natural order of things (Latour 1991, 2005), with social scientists – and the people they study – striving to maintain distinction and to cross-cut inevitable connectedness in order to stabilise relations, persons, and things (Strathern 1996). This is certainly a more useful approach for the material discussed here.

[48] Her mother, Awa says, turned "black" with grief and shame, after her husband's death, her resulting poverty, and due to the general "rottenness" of contemporary Gao. Judging from family photographs, this is true.

the influence his own family might have over her and his household: he can be confident that Awa will always be impervious to counsel given her by his older sister, and that there is no danger of the two of them uniting behind his back.

Yet in reality, such links are of course there and cannot be denied. Although ʿAbd al-Karīm is trying very hard to turn his house into a truly Arab home, "civilised" according to North African or at least Mauritanian standards, all his attempts fail, never opposed, but just quietly ignored. Awa prefers the vast open courtyard of their modern house and its string of male and female visitors to the seclusion of her living room; the door is always left wide open, to ʿAbd al-Karīm's exasperation. Curtains put up in doorways get pulled down within the hour, the costly Moroccan-style living room has been stripped of its coverings, while Bambara neighbours lounge on it watching Mexican soap operas, having tampered with the satellite dish that was intended to broadcast only Arab channels. The house rings with the voices of children of Awa's family whom she "fosters," especially teenage girls who seem all too fond of tight T-shirts and miniskirts. Awa herself wears the veil inside the house, mostly, but refuses to wear it outside: she would fall over it straight away, and what would people think?

> I also keep making holes in them, at the bottom, you see, because of my high heels, so I wear them once and then I have to throw them away … Once, I went outside wearing the veil, and I got so flustered – with my bag you know, and the shopping, and the veil kept falling down, and I tried to hold it, and I got all hot – a shop-keeper laughed and said I should come inside, sort it all out, and I did. You cannot believe how angry ʿAbd al-Karīm was when he found out.

Moreover, according to ʿAbd al-Karīm, Awa's food is too African, despite occasional attempts to make it "Arab" – mainly by adding a lot of meat and butter – and she always adds too much chilli, or else cannot control her servant as she should.

Meanwhile, Awa similarly feels that she has to defend her house against onslaughts of "savages," threatening the kind of sedentary "civilisation" – that of the *koro-boro*, the longstanding town dwellers – that she was brought up with. ʿAbd al-Karīm's family was furious when they got married, and his sister came to live with them straight away, to keep watch over him. "They destroyed the whole house," as Awa says, "they are not used to this kind of thing – houses, I mean, and electricity and so on. Where they come from they do not know such things, they break everything and pee on the carpet." Now, if Arab guests turn up, they are lodged in the courtyard. She sees her in-laws' resulting hostility less as a personal offence than as a structural given:

> Arab women do not like it when their men marry blacks, because then they never come back and their daughters can't find a husband unless they take a black man and they'd rather die first. But Arabs love black women so much: it's because Arab women are dirty, and don't wash, always wearing those dirty old veils, and they are lazy and never work, and they cannot cook. All they ever do is talk about other people behind their backs, and all they care about is money: I know so many Arab girls who have eaten their husbands, they want gold and cars, and more gold and more cars – that's why all these poor Arabs have to go smuggling and live in the desert in the cold and risk their lives.[49]

Such mutual contempt and divergence of opinion about the nature of "civilisation," of course in no ways preclude a lasting and harmonious marriage. More worrying, however, is the education of their only son, Sīdi. 'Abd al-Karīm wants him to be Arab, and Arab only, despite his dark hue that his female relatives never tire of remarking upon. However, an Arab child should be educated by his mother mainly, which means that he spends most time with people who cannot speak Arabic, and, worse, who have a "loose" way of life: namely, Awa's cousins, despite all attempts made by 'Abd al-Karīm's female relatives to "lighten him up" – at least morally, or so they say. Sīdi is doing quite well with all this, his pockets full of treats, and speaking Arabic, Songhay, and French fluently. One day, however, he will have to "choose sides," at least publicly.

CONCLUSION

Not all marriages lead to quite so much conflict, of course, and even where they do, such squabbles do not matter in the overall scheme of things: but they remind us of the fragility of boundaries and the daily effort necessary to maintain them. Here, as in Tamanrasset and Adrar, clear spatial segregation and the public emphasis on moral and cultural incommensurability thus seem to result less from an inability to "integrate" but rather from conscious attempts to maintain distinctions, in a context of longstanding exchange, ongoing mobility, and vital connectivity that constantly threaten to blur boundaries. This is perhaps most visible in Gao, where a violent homogenisation of lifestyles resulting in a clear reduction of mobility and control has led to an overemphasis on "culture"; yet

[49] This echoes description of Algerian women given by northern Malian Arab women married to Algerian husbands: see above.

boundaries are similarly fragile and thus overdetermined in Adrar, where Bani w-Iskut resembles local *qṣūr* and houses distant cousins, and in Tamanrasset, where sub-Saharan migrants complain about the "racism" of local *ḥarāṭīn*, while the commercial success of women with multiple identities is envied by all. This emphasis on boundaries, put forward in public, but often contraverted by everyday practice, runs through all accounts of Saharan settlement, large or small, historic or modern, blurring the boundaries between *qṣūr* and contemporary towns, and it is perhaps here that we have to look for a particularly Saharan cosmopolitanism, based less on integration than on the ability to maintain distinctions despite longstanding and often all too intimate interaction. Hence, the image of the ghetto is pertinent not merely when talking about regional migrants but also when analysing Saharan settlement more generally; moreover, like the ghetto, its underlying logic of boundaries, communal autonomy and segregation needs to be understood in terms of ongoing real or putative mobility: all Saharan settlements are made by migrants, and, more importantly, by migrants who continue to remember their outside origin. Large parts of contemporary Saharan towns, if not all of them, refer by their architectural layout, their self-definition, their social practices, their economy, and, most importantly, the daily whereabouts and demeanour of their inhabitants, to places that lie beyond the limits of the town itself, thereby creating different and sometimes mutually exclusive regions that in turn are central to identity locally. The image developed in Chapter 1, of oases acting as "truck stops" or as nodes of overlap among various socioeconomic regions of interdependence, therefore still holds, although the regions created today and the means by which they are maintained may differ profoundly from their historical predecessors – if only because of state involvement. Notwithstanding, Saharan settlement, of whatever kind, appears as tributary to prior movement, both imagined and real, and to an ongoing engagement with a truly kaleidoscopic world – hence its fragility and its fragmentation but also its openness, changeability, and vitality.

Conclusion

Saharan Connectivity and the "Swamp of Terror"

This book began in al-Khalīl, among veiled men huddling around trucks and four-by-fours, drinking tea, boasting of their exploits, and, from time to time, concluding more or less dirty deals. In this book, issues that are of daily concern in al-Khalīl – regional supplies, the maintenance of social networks, the fragility of settlement, the inherent problems of outside dependence, aspirations to moral autonomy and containment, and the shifting boundaries between wilderness and civilisation – served as a starting point to develop an approach to Saharan settlement more generally, portraying regional connectivity as the key to local ecologies, and avoiding common sense assumptions of a necessary radical break in Saharan history and society. However, relying on al-Khalīl in this way has its own dangers, worse perhaps than a mere conceptual lack of imagination. "Trouble comes from ungoverned places" in the words of a leading U.S. general[1]; and al-Khalīl all too easily seems to confirm images of the Sahara as a "swamp of terror" (Powell 2004) and anarchy put forward in international security reports and media coverage. Seen from Washington, Brussels, Paris, or London, places like al-Khalīl, as international smuggling outposts, are first and foremost abodes of disorder that foster and finance "Islamism," house trans-Saharan migrants and are pivotal to the organisation of the international cocaine trade. And indeed, in publications on the contemporary Sahara, whatever the subject matter, eager readers and seminar audiences inevitably pick out the familiar, or the "facts" that, from the point of view of political science or journalism,

[1] Lt. Gen. Wallace C. Gregson Jr., commander of the Marine Corps forces in the Pacific, cited in Powell (2004: 54).

appear the most relevant. Surely, it matters little what Saharan smugglers think and whether they pray (and whether they invest in cows or irrigation), as long as we know where the cocaine is going and how many guns they have got? As a result, the few scholarly works that are based on an actual knowledge of the areas concerned are increasingly swallowed up by the budding literature on security concerns in the Sahara that, through its initial postulate of "great danger" and "radical changes" precludes in-depth local case studies or historical approaches.[2] Here, the leap from local driver to "international drug trafficker" is easily made; much as concerns about the AQIM (al-Qā'ida in the Islamic Maghrib) and a chronic underestimation of the vastness and complexity of the Sahara readily sweep all religiously minded locals into the vast bucket of "Islamism" or even "terrorism."[3]

"Across the broad Sahara," as *Air Force Magazine* notes, in a much quoted article published in November 2004, "a desolate expanse of sand and rock covering 3.3 million square miles – al-Qaeda and its terrorist affiliates are setting up shop, taking advantage of the lawless and trackless badlands stretching from the Atlantic to the Indian Ocean. Unless checked, the terrorist infestation could turn parts of Africa into launchpads for tomorrow's murderous outrages" (Powell 2004: 51). More recent reports establish a direct link between "Islamic terrorism" and the international drug trade – or indeed all kinds of illegal trade – on the tenuous grounds of common sense. Hence, Alain Rodier, member of the

[2] See for instance a recent report by the Thomas More institute: "Towards a sustainable security in the Maghreb: an opportunity for the region, a commitment for the European Union," that elaborates the threat posed by migration, smuggling, and "terrorism" in the Sahel, citing mainly newspaper reports and statements made by various army officials. It makes no reference to any scholarship on the area, and claims to be based on one [sic] "study trip to the Maghreb." Newspaper reports cited bear such alluring titles as Joseph Braude's "Gang Rape and al-Qaeda Infiltration: A No Man's Land in North Africa Grows Dangerous" (*The New Yorker*, 25/02/2010, according to the report, but the reference is untraceable). For more detail on U.S. security policy in the area, see McGovern (2005, 2010), Keenan (2005, 2007a), Jourde (2007), Gutelius (2007) and Lecocq and Schrijver (2007) for a fuller list of references; and Keenan (2006a, 2006b, 2007b, 2009) for an ongoing, albeit rather controversial and idiosyncratic commentary on current events.

[3] In 2007, the GSPC (Groupe salafiste pour la prédication et le combat), a splinter group that had emerged in the civil war that threatened northern Algeria in the 1990s, changed its name to the AQIM, thereby becoming the only group based on the African continent that made open reference to al-Qā'ida. This change of name, however, implies a much tighter institutional connection than can be shown on the ground, and it seems to have been largely "rhetorical" (McGovern 2005: 7). Nonetheless, it forcefully speaks to the Western mind.

Centre Français de Renseignement, in a presentation given to the French military research centre on strategy, in May 2010[4]:

> If, up to now, no formal proof has confirmed the involvement of the AQIM in drug trafficking, it seems that at least the Sahelian part of the movement is linked to it, if only to provide "protection" to this illegal trade. In fact, this provides a new source of funding to the AQIM that very conveniently supplements their income derived from kidnappings that are now very common in the Sahel. Moreover, it has been proven that drug trafficking is always connected to arms trading, which is of course of great interest to the AQIM.

In the "swamp" of the Sahara (a particularly ill-chosen metaphor if ever there was one), then, conjecture easily takes the place of knowledge or research, as long as it conforms to overarching stereotypes of fear. The Sahara, although now literally open to the gaze of U.S. military intelligence (Lecocq and Schrijver 2007), continues to attract Western fantasies whose "truth-value" remains largely independent of factual analysis.

Partly, this easy neglect of complexities on the ground stems from the conceptual and visual habits discussed in the introduction to this book: in Power Point presentations, the Sahara, portrayed as a homogeneous space marked by boundless and arbitrary movement, is easily shaded in as "dangerous," and, on the large-scale maps generally used, symbols of threat and random photographs downloaded from the Internet seem to fill it rather nicely. Partly, it is linguistic: submitting a paper (Scheele 2009b), in French, to a highly respected French anthropological journal, I received it back, with few comments or highlighted changes, only to find that those whom I had called, following local usage, "smugglers" (*fraudeurs*), now appeared as "drug traffickers" (*narco-traffiquants*), ironing out any attempt at comprehension and all moral ambiguity; meanwhile, presidents of local ghettoes, whose main preoccupation is with the running of hostels and the provision of food, are increasingly referred to, throughout the literature, as "people smugglers" (Collyer 2006: 18–20) or, again, "traffickers," giving an impression of large-scale organisation and outside agency that has little or no grounding in reality. It seems that nobody really wants to know that most Saharans are not rabid fundamentalists, or apprentice criminals, but that they are just trying to get by, mostly relying on older networks and occupations, as much as international security concerns still allow them to do so; neither is it acceptable

4 The presentation was given during a meeting of the Groupe d'études et de recherches sur l'Afrique stratégique (GERAS) at the Institut de recherche stratégique de l'Ecole Militaire (IRSEM) in Paris, on 21/05/2010.

news that there are no "waves" of trans-Saharan migrants "flooding" Europe, and victimised by international criminal networks of "people smugglers."[5] Careful scholarly analyses that do not correspond to the current Euro-American worldview are quite simply misunderstood, and generously misquoted, often not even out of malice or manipulation, but because, as with the legendary wealth of Timbuktu and trans-Saharan trade, prior assumptions prove to be stronger than factual proof. And once more, such prior assumptions are directly linked to political interests: even the most innocuous paper given on the Sahara, in the United Kingdom, the United States, or France, is inevitably followed up by compliments transmitted by slick young men in designer suits, distributing business cards that cite organisations such as the Brussels Council against the Threat, whereas questions invariably turn on the exact routes of the cocaine trade – to little avail, of course.[6]

This kind of interest is echoed locally, where there is a growing awareness of the strategic importance of the area – indeed, it would be difficult for locals to overlook the pink, sweaty and well-nourished U.S. army officers in Gao attempting to train the Malian army in "surveillance techniques," the large transport planes familiar from footage from the Iraq war flying overhead that wake you in the early hours of the morning in Kidal, or the Algerian Sonatrach and Canadian oil companies prospecting north of Timbuktu, with Chinese assistance.[7] Before embarking on research in the Algerian Sahara, I spent years working in the north of the country, in Kabylia, an area that had long been in outright rebellion against the central government, without experiencing more than the

[5] On this point, see, for example, Streiff-Fénart and Poutignat (2008) and San Marco (2009).

[6] This is not to say that all criminal activities in the Sahara are simply "made up" by exaggerated security concerns or national secret services (as argued most forcefully by Keenan 2009). The recent (November 2011) kidnapping of three European tourists in Timbuktu, and the fact that hostages taken earlier in Niger are still held in northern Mali, clearly shows the presence of radical armed groups in Mali. Nonetheless, this is not all that can be said about the area, and one needs to be cautious not to overestimate the local influence of these groups, or indeed to explain all local social changes by their presence. In other words, whatever is going on is clearly misrepresented through the categories of international demagogy.

[7] For a review of the various U.S. military initiatives and programmes in the Sahel countries, and the funding accorded to each, see McGovern (2005: 27–31). On the search for oil in northern Mali, see S. Y. Dembélé, "Pétrole malien: mythe ou réalité?," *Les Echos*, 5/06/2006; A. Niangaly, "Ressources minérale au Mali: le pétrole en 2009," *Le Quotidien de Bamako*, 29/10/2008; Chahana Takiou, "Le Mali fait appel à l'Algérie pour trouver du pétrole," *Forum Algérie*, 24/11/2008; and J.-P. James, "Pétrole au Mali: du rêve au cauchemar," *Le Quotidien de Bamako*, 31/03/2010.

usual bother from national security forces; yet what seemed to me like the much more innocent pursuit of local legal traditions in the Sahara sparked extraordinary interest by men in dark suits, who proceeded to visit anybody who had ever hosted me throughout the country. In northern Mali, on the other hand, Timbuktu Arabs were delighted by my presence, and especially by my interest in manuscripts. They claimed that "vast quantities of oil" were about to be discovered near Tawdanni, the regional salt mine, eight hundred kilometres to the north of Timbuktu, "ways of tapping the Algerian oil-fields," of "making them run dry," as people whispered, stunned by (certainly illusory) images of their own future prosperity. And who would be their rightful owners, if not the Arabs of Timbuktu, who had long controlled the salt mines of Tawdanni, and who certainly had some "papers" to prove it – if only I could oblige them with a quick rummage through various sand-filled chests of manuscripts, rescued from ruins in Arawān, their home town. There is no doubt then that the Sahara is "exciting," all too exciting perhaps, and that the various issues faced by Saharan populations are politically overdetermined, in a whole new pattern of connectivity of international security concerns and struggles over primary resources, to the point where it seems at times impossible to address them in terms that, both from a local and a scholarly point of view, make sense. "The threat" thereby risks becoming a self-fulfilling prophecy: if even established academics feel the need to tailor their research programmes towards "resource management" of the worse kind, and if more vulnerable junior researchers are paid to find "Islamic terrorists," they will of course do so, with no conscious falsification on their part – and who will then come and ask whether the terms used in the initial questions were ever appropriate?

There are many reasons, then, to refrain from the slippery slope of potentially "useful" information gathering and to stick to water management and oasis agriculture – with perhaps a nod to legal truck-trade. But, as I have tried to show throughout, such a limited approach would make no sense, and would indeed reinforce existing conceptual divisions, between north and south, the past and the present, that to my mind have strongly contributed to much of the current misunderstanding of contemporary Saharan realities. Al-Khalīl is too much an integral part of the everyday experience of life in the Central Sahara to be artificially excised; further, as argued throughout, it can provide a unique glimpse into the underlying logics of Saharan connectivity, and therefore help us ask useful questions both of contemporary and historical Saharan material. Chapter 1 took the questions posed by al-Khalīl as a guiding threat to establish a framework to understand Saharan patterns of exchange, drawing on the literature discussed in the introduction, and on local archival material. It showed that oases could only be established with the help of outside investment and ongoing maintenance. As a result, their very existence depended on networks of exchange, most of which were Saharan rather than trans-Saharan. These networks created regional complementarities that remained flexible in their configuration, but without which neither sedentary agriculturalist nor pastoral nomads could survive. Meanwhile, trans-Saharan trade is best understood as one possible manifestation of this overarching regional connectivity. Chapter 2 illustrated this argument with reference to accounts of early twentieth-century trade given today by traders from the Algerian south. It showed the importance of longstanding regional ties, as well as the dominance of "civilisational" models in personal and family memories. Traders could only succeed if they established intimate ties with their host society, mostly through marriage; yet this necessary intimacy invariably led to worries about moral containment that continue to shape the lives and social positions of their descendants even today. Chapter 3 returned to al-Khalīl in order to further develop this close connection between trade, settlement and morality, with an analysis of contemporary transborder trade and of the social and moral quandaries it causes. Most Saharan trade is now in the hands of nationals of Sahelian countries, although past networks and alliances continue to be important. However, control over the more lucrative aspects of this trade, drugs and arms, is gradually transferred to places beyond the Sahara, and the resulting loss of agency is resented by most, and felt to be morally corrosive.

Chapter 4 looked at notions of local identity and social hierarchies. It argues that, much like Saharan ecology and economy, these cannot be grasped from a purely local point of view, but need to be understood in relation to the ability to move, to gain access to a wide range of resources, and credibly to claim far-reaching connections – as is done, in particular, by genealogies, the most common form of historical writing in the Sahara. Nationalism and the ethnic categories that accompany it have since put forward another very powerful way of thinking about identity; genealogical models persist nonetheless, and, as migrants from northern Mali and Niger have moved in large numbers to southern Algeria, can lead to great embarrassment among their Algerian "cousins." Chapter 5 looked at ways in which, in the absence of the state, patches of legality were construed locally. It argued that property was central to notions of social and political representation, hence creating a boundless and inherently delocalised system of overlapping administrative spheres and jurisdictions.

Quḍāh and local assemblies worked in close collaboration, not merely to maintain order, but rather to create pockets of civilisation, validated and made permanent through reference to the universal categories of Islamic law. Chapter 6 concluded the book with ethnographic glimpses of life in three Saharan cities, showing the historical depth and particular nature of the "Saharan cosmopolitanism" that has recently attracted much attention, and of which al-Khalīl, with its visible and often violent segregation, appears as an extreme version. As argued throughout, Saharan cities have long owed their existence to movement and overlapping outside connections, and their spatial outlay and contemporary patterns of sociability bear witness to this. People are proud to live apart, they conceive of urban society as inherently hierarchical, and they seldom talk about the city as a concrete social unit, but continue to derive their identity and standing from external links, despite the real but downplayed importance of cross-cutting social ties.

Al-Khalīl, then, prompts us to ask new questions of Saharan material, leading at times to unexpected answers. Yet at the same time, it might also stand for the demise of the regional patterns described throughout: Saharan smuggling, or the most illegal and most valuable part of it, is increasingly controlled by "mafias," centralising agencies that function "just like a state" and that are locally much resented. This resentment is partly due to a longstanding resistance against changes in local hierarchies, especially by those who envy the rise of the *nouveaux riches* and fear for their own position, but some of it also stems from a real concern about the loss of moral autonomy and independence and the resulting increasing vulnerability felt by all local inhabitants. For everybody who has followed the recent history of the Algerian Sahara, gleeful accounts of future oil wealth pronounced by formerly nomadic Arabs from northern Timbuktu who now return from their "exile" in Mauritania to get "their share" are chilling rather than cheerful: their fate will depend on decisions made beyond their grasp and reach. Similarly, if increased military intervention in the area becomes more than the underfinanced media stunt that it has proven to be so far (McGovern 2005: 25, Keenan 2007b), up to now regionally containable balances of power will quite literally blow up; and the track record of U.S. military intervention and intelligence is so poor as to make one fear the worst.[8] Perhaps, then, we are finally entering

[8] This was written before the "Arab spring" in North Africa. The effects of these events, and foreign military intervention relating to them, in particular in Libya, will be momentous throughout the Central Sahara, although it is impossible to predict in what way.

a stage where the historical emphasis on forced Saharan passivity, or at least on trans-Saharan trade and intervention, will become justified; military intervention and exaggerated political strategising might indeed turn the Sahara into the unified and homogenous space of nineteenth-century fantasies; and one might wonder just how resilient the regional patterns of connectivity, described throughout the preceding chapters, will prove when faced with international surveillance and centralised funding. In al-Khalīl, however, this growing feeling of loss of autonomy is mostly met with ever more outrageous and self-glorifying boasts: nobody, people say, will ever be able to rule the "democratic and popular Republic of al-Khalīl" – "Colombians" and "Islamic terrorists" will have to marry local Tuareg wives, and then they will soon learn how to keep quiet – and at the very worst, Khalīlīs will pick up their goods, water tanks and satellite phones, and simply move somewhere else.

Glossary

(all words are in Arabic, unless indicated otherwise)

ʿarīf, ʿurafāʾ	customary expert
aṣl, uṣūl	literally "root," family land or water share
badawī, badū	nomad, inhabitant of the *bādiya*
bādiya	the steppe or "wilderness"
baraka	blessing
bazin (French)	shiny and vivdly coloured material, used in West African clothing
bellah (Tamasheq)	descendant of a former slave
bilād al-sūdān	literally "country of the blacks": sub-Saharan West Africa as seen from the Sahara or the Mediterranean
dioula (Bamanan)	Muslim trader
dhikr	literally "remembering," Sufi recitation
faggāra, fagāgīr	underground water canal
frūd	smuggling, from French *fraude*
garāj, gawārij	trading entrepôt, from French *garage*
ghazū	raid
ḥabba, ḥubūb	water measurement
ḥarṭānī, ḥarṭāniyya, ḥarāṭīn	here: descendents of former slaves
ḥubus, aḥbās	pious endowment
iqāla	sale with right of restitution
jamāʿa, jamāʿāt	assembly
khammās	sharecropper

koro-boro (Songhay)	literally "town dweller": sedentary Songhay-speaker
milḥafa, malāḥif	full-body veil
mithqāl	weight of gold : 4.25 g or thereabouts
nāzila, nawāzil	legal case cited as precedent
qāḍi, quḍāh	Islamic judge
qā'id, quyyād	literally "leader," here : representative of the Moroccan sultan
qariya	village
qaṣba	forteresse
qaṣīda, qaṣā'id	poem
qīrāṭ, qarārīṭ	water measurement
qṣar, qṣūr	fortified village, oasis town
rahn, ruhūn	mortgage
sāqiya, sawāqin	subsidiary water canal
sharī'a	Islamic law
shināwī, shināwa	literally "Chinese," in southern Algeria: people from the north of the country
sūdānī, sūdāniyya, suwādīn (classical Arabic *sūdān*)	literally "black": non-Arabic speaker from the Sahel or sub-Saharan Africa
sunna	recognized Islamic practice as based on the deeds and sayings of the Prophet
sūra, suwar	quranic verse
ta'rīkh, tawārīkh	literally "history," here mostly genealogy
umma	the community of all Muslims
wathīqa, wathā'iq	written document
wilāya	administrative district in Algeria
zakāt	religious tax
zāwiya, zawāyā	literally "corner," here : religious stronghold

References

Archives Consulted

ACK – Archives du cercle de Kidal, Kidal, Mali
ALN – Archives nationales du Mali, Bamako, Mali
CAOM – Centre d'archives d'outre-mer, Aix-en-Provence, France
CEDRAB – Centre de documentation et de recherches Ahmed Baba, Timbuktu, Mali
SHAT – Service historique de l'armée de terre, Vincennes, France

Principal Manuscript Sources

NG – *Nawāzil al-ghuniya,* late eighteenth/early nineteenth century, courtesy of Shaykh Bilkabīr in Mtarfa
KT – *Kitāb al-turjamān*, 1930s, accessible at the CEDRAB
SJ – *Sijill al-jamā'a*, SJ, 1962 to 1977, courtesy of 'Abd Allāh b. 'Abd al-Karīm in Tit
SQ – *Sijill al-qāḍi*, SQ, 1930s to 1950s, courtesy of Mohamed Bakraoui in Tamantit
WK – *Wathā'iq Kūsān*, WK, 1820s to 1950s, courtesy of shaykh Ṭayyib al-Balbālī in Kusan
WT – *Wathā'iq Talmīn*, WT, 1830s to 1950s, courtesy of 'Abd al-Qādir Ma'zūz in Talmin
ZF – *Zamām al-faggāra*, ZF, 1940s to 1950s, courtesy of Shaykh Belaïd in Adrar

Bibliography

Abdelhamid, A. 2006. *Manuscrits et bibliothèques musulmans en Algérie.* Méolans-Revel: Atelier Perrousseaux.
Abitbol, M. 1979. *Tombouctou et les Arma.* Paris: Maisonneuve et Larose.

Abu Lughod, L. 1986. *Veiled sentiments: honor and poetry in a Bedouin society*. Berkeley: University of California Press.

Abun-Nasr, J. 1965. *The Tijaniyya*. Oxford: Oxford University Press.

Accord, Novib, Oxfam (eds.). 1995. *Nord du Mali: de la tragédie à l'espoir*. Bamako: AMAP.

Ag Ahar, E. 1990. L'initiation d'un *ashamur*. *REMMM* 57, 141–52.

Ag Baye, Ch., and R. Bellil. 1986. Une société touarègue en crise: les Kel Adrar du Mali. *Awal* 2, 49–84.

Ag Foni, E. 1979. *L'impact socio-économique de la sécheresse dans le cercle de Kidal*. Bremen: BORDA.

Ag Youssouf, I., and R. E. Poulton. 1998. *A peace of Timbuktu. Democratic governance, development and African peacemaking*. New York: United Nations.

Agier, M. 2006. Protéger les sans-États ou contrôler les indésirables: où en est le HCR? *Politique africaine* 103, 101–5.

Alaoui, M. I., and P. Carrière (eds.). 1991. *Aspects de l'agriculture irriguée au Maroc*. Montpellier: Laboratoire de géographie rurale de l'Université Paul-Valéry.

Amat, C. 1888. *Le M'zab et les M'zabites*. Paris: Challamel.

Amselle, J.-L., and E. Grégoire (eds.). 1988. *État et réseaux marchands transnationaux en Afrique de l'Ouest*. Paris: Club du Sahel.

Anderson, A. 2001. *The powers of distance: cosmopolitanism and the cultivation of detachment*. Princeton: Princeton University Press.

Appadurai, A. 1996. *Modernity at large: cultural dimensions of globalization*. Minneapolis: University of Minnesota Press.

Ardener, E. 1970. Witchcraft, economics and the continuity of beliefs. In *Witchcraft: confessions and accusations* (ed.) M. Douglas, 141–60. London: Tavistock.

Arnaud. 1861. Siège d'Ain Madhi par El-Hadj Abdelkader. *Revue Africaine* 16, 354–7 and 453.

Attia, H. 1965. Modernisation agricole et structures sociales. Exemple des oasis du Djerid. *Revue tunisienne des sciences sociales* 2, 59–79.

Austen, R. A. 1990. Marginalization, stagnation and growth: trans-Saharan caravan trade, 1500–1900. In *The rise of merchant empires: long-distance trade in the early modern world* (ed.) J. Tracy, 311–50. Cambridge: Cambridge University Press.

2010. *Trans-Saharan Africa in world history*. Oxford: Oxford University Press.

Ba, C.O., and A. Choplin. 2005. 'Tenter l'aventure' par la Mauritanie: migrations transsahariennes et recompositions urbaines. *Autrepart* 36, 21–42.

Badi, D. 2001. Ifoghas. *Encyclopédie Berbère* 24, 3649–54.

2002. L'archéologie du peuplement de Tadmekka d'après les traditions orales Kel Essuk. http:://www.kidal.info.

2007. Le rôle des communautés sahéliennes dans l'économie locale d'une ville saharienne: Tamanrasset (Sahara algérien). In *Les nouveaux urbains dans l'espace Sahara-Sahel: un cosmopolitisme par le bas* (eds.) E. Boesen and L. Marfaing, 259–78. Paris: Karthala.

2012. Cultural interaction and the artisanal economy in Tamanrasset. In *Saharan frontiers: space and mobility in northwest Africa* (eds.) J. McDougall and J. Scheele, 200–11. Bloomington: Indiana University Press.

Baduel, A.-F., and P. Baduel. 1980. Le pouvoir de l'eau dans le Sud tunisien. *ROMM* 30, 101–31.

Bahous, M. 2001. *L'insurrection des Ouled Sidi Cheikh*. Oran: Dar el-Gharb.

Baier, S. 1977. Trans-Saharan trade and the Sahel: Damergu, 1870–1930. *Journal of African History* 18/1, 37–60.

1980. *An economic history of central Niger*. Oxford: Clarendon Press.

Baier, S., and A. Lovejoy. 1975. The desert-side economy of the Central Sudan. *International Journal of African Historical Studies* 8/4, 551–81.

1977. The Tuareg of the Central Sudan: gradations in servility at the desert's edge (Niger and Nigeria). In *Slavery in Africa: historical and anthropological perspectives* (eds.) I. Kopytoff and S. Miers, 291–311. Madison: University of Wisconsin Press.

Barbour, B., and M. Jacobs. 1985. The Mi'raj: a legal treatise on slavery. In *Slaves and slavery in Muslim Africa* (ed.) J. R. Willis, 125–59. London: Frank Cass.

Barkey, K. 1994. *Bandits and bureaucrats: the Ottoman route to state centralization*. Ithaca: Cornell University Press.

Barth, H. 1857–8. *Travels and discoveries in North and Central Africa*. London: Frank Cass.

Batran, A. 2001. *The Qadiriyya brotherhood in West Africa and the Western Sahara: the life and times of Shaykh Mukhtar al-Kunti, 1729–1811*. Rabat: Institut des études africaines.

Baude, J.-J. 1841. *L'Algérie*. Paris: Arthur Bertrand.

Bāy Bil'ālim, M. 2004. *Qabīla fulān fī 'l-māḍī wa-l-ḥādir wa mā lahā min al-'ulūm w-al-ma'rifa wa-l-ma'āthir*. Algiers: Dār Hūmaha.

2005. *Al-riḥla al-'aliyya ilā minṭaqa Tuwāt*. Algiers: Dār Hūmaha.

Bayart, J.-F. 2004. Le crime transnational et la formation de l'État. *Politique Africaine* 93, 93–104.

Bayart, J.-F., S. Ellis, and B. Hibou. 1999. *The criminalization of the state in Africa*. Oxford: James Currey.

Beaussier, M. D. 1958. *Dictionnaire pratique arabe français*. Algiers: Bencheneb.

Beaumont, P., M. Bonine, and K. McLachlan (eds.). 1989. *Qanat, kariz and khattara: traditional water systems in the Middle East and North Africa*. Wisbech: Galipoli House.

Bédoucha, G. 1987. *L'eau, l'amie du puissant. Une communauté oasienne du sud tunisien*. Paris: Éditions des archives contemporaines.

2001. Libertés coutumières et pouvoir central. L'enjeu du droit de l'eau dans les oasis du Maghreb. *Études rurales* 155–6, 117–41.

Beeler, S. 2006. *Conflicts between herders and farmers in north-western Mali*. London: International Institute for Environment and Development.

Bellakhdar, J., A. Benabid, J. Maréchal, and J. Vittoz. 1992. *Tissint, une oasis du Maroc présaharien. Monographie d'une palmeraie du Moyen Dra*. Rabat: Al Biruniya.

Bellil, R. 1999–2000. *Les oasis du Gourara, Sahara algérien*. Louvain: Peeters.

Bellil, R., and D. Badi. 1993. Évolution de la relation entre Kel Ahaggar et Kel Adagh. In *La politique dans l'histoire touarègue* (ed.) H. Claudot-Hawad, 95–110. Aix-en-Provence: IREMAM.

1996. Les migrations actuelles des Touaregs du Mali vers le Sud de l'Algérie. *Études et documents berbères* 13, 79–98.

Ben Hounet, Y. 2009. *L'Algérie des tribus: le fait tribal dans le Haut Sud-Ouest contemporain*. Paris: L'Harmattan.

Bencherifa, A., and H. Popp. 1990. *L'oasis de Figuig. Persistance et changement*. Passau: Passauer Mittelmeerstudien.

Bendjelid, A. et al. 1999. Mutations sociales et adaptation d'une paysannerie ksourienne du Touât: Ouled Hadj Mamoun (wilaya d'Adrar, Algérie). *Insaniyat* 7, 39–52.

Benissad, H. 1994. *Algérie: restructurations et réformes économiques*. Algiers: OPU.

Benjaminsen, T. A., and G. Berge. 2004. *Une histoire de Tombouctou*. Paris: Actes Sud.

Benkheira, H. 1990. Un désir absolu: les émeutes d'octobre 1988 en Algérie. *Peuples méditerranéens* 52–3, 7–18.

Bensaâd, A. 2002. La grande migration africaine à travers le Sahara. *Méditerranée* 99/3–4, 41–50.

2005a. Eau, urbanisation et mutations sociales dans le Bas-Sahara. In *La ville et le désert, le Bas-Sahara algérien* (ed.) M. Côte, 95–122. Paris: Karthala.

2005b. Les migrations transsahariennes, une mondialisation par la marge. *Maghreb – Machrek* 185, 13–36.

(ed.). 2009. *Le Maghreb à l'épreuve des migrations subsahariennes*. Paris: Karthala.

Bernard, A., and N. Lacroix. 1906. *L'évolution du nomadisme en Algérie*. Algiers: Jourdan.

Bernus, E. 1981. *Touaregs nigériens. Unité culturelle et diversité régionale d'un peuple pasteur*. Paris: ORSTOM.

1990. Histoires parallèles et croisées: nobles et religieux chez les Touaregs Kel Denneg. *L'Homme* 115, 31–47.

1999. Exodes tous azimuts en zone sahélo-saharienne. In *Déplacés et réfugiés. La mobilité sous contrainte* (eds.) V. Lassailly-Jacob, J.-Y. Marchal, and A. Quesnel, 195–208. Paris: IRD.

Bernus, S. 1981. Relations entre nomades et sédentaires des confins sahariens méridionaux: essai d'interprétation dynamique. *ROMM* 32, 23–35.

Berque, J. 1944. *Essai sur la méthode juridique maghrébine*. Rabat: Leforestier.

1953. Problèmes initiaux de la sociologie juridique en Afrique du nord. *Studia Islamica* 1, 137–62.

1974. *Maghreb: histoire et société*. Algiers: SNED.

Bertrand, M. 1992. Un an de transition politique: de la révolte à la troisième République. *Politique Africaine* 47, 9–22.

Bibed, F. 1997. Les Kunta à travers quelques extraits de l'ouvrage Al-Tarâ'if wa al-talâ'id de 1756 à 1826. PhD dissertation, University Aix-Marseille 1.

Birks, J. S. 1978. *Across the savannas to Mecca: the overland pilgrimage route to West Africa*. London: Hurst.

Bisson, J. 1986. De la zaouïa à la ville: El Abiodh Sidi Cheikh, ou la naissance d'une ville nomade. In *Petites villes et villes moyennes dans le monde arabe* (Vol. 1), 139–52. Tours: Urbama.

2003. *Mythes et réalités d'un désert convoité: le Sahara*. Paris: L'Harmattan.

Bisson, V. 2005. Défi à Kébili. Enjeux fonciers et appropriation urbaine au Sahara tunisien. *Annales de géographie* **644**, 399–421.

Blok, A. 1974. *The Mafia of a Sicilian village, 1860–1960: a study of violent peasant entrepreneurs*. Oxford: Blackwell.

Blum, J. 1971a. The European village community: origins and functions. *Agricultural History* **45**, 157–78.

1971b. The internal structure and polity of the European village community from the fifteenth to the nineteenth century. *Journal of Modern History* **43**, 541–76.

Bodichon, E. 1847. *Études sur l'Algérie et l'Afrique*. Paris: E. Bodichon.

Boesen, E., and L. Marfaing (eds.). 2007. *Les nouveaux urbains dans l'espace Sahara-Sahel: un cosmopolitisme par le bas*. Paris: Karthala.

Boilley, P. 1993. L'organisation commune des régions sahariennes (OCRS): une tentative avortée. In *Nomades et commandants: administration et sociétés nomades dans l'ancienne A.O.F.* (eds.) E. Bernus et al., 215–40. Paris: Karthala.

1996. Aux origines des conflits dans les zones touarègues et maures. *Relations internationales et stratégiques* **23**, 100–7.

1999. *Les Touaregs Kel Adagh. Dépendances et révoltes: du Soudan français au Mali contemporain*. Paris: Karthala.

Bonète, Y. 1962. Contribution à l'étude des pasteurs nomades Arbâʿa. Doctorat de 3e cycle, Paris.

Bonte, P. 1981. Ecological and economic factors in the determination of pastoral specialization. *Journal of Asian and African Studies* **16/1–2**, 33–49.

1987. Donneurs des femmes ou preneurs d'hommes? Les Awlād Qaylān, tribu de l'Adrar mauritanien. *L'Homme* **102**, 54–79.

1989. L'ordre de la tradition. Evolution des hiérarchies dans la société maure contemporaine. *REMMM* **54**, 118–28.

1994. Les risques de l'alliance. Solidarités masculines et valeurs féminines dans la société maure. In *Les complexités de l'alliance, vol. 4: économie, politique et fondements symboliques* (eds.) F. Héritier and E. Coupet-Rougier, 107–42. Paris: Editions des archives contemporaines.

1998a. Fortunes commerciales à Shingīti (Adrar mauritanien) au XIXe siècle. *Journal of African History* **39**, 1–13.

1998b. Esclaves ou cousins. Évolution du statut servile dans la société mauritanienne. In *Terrains et engagements de Claude Meillassoux* (ed.) B. Schlemmer, 157–82. Paris: Karthala.

2000. Faire fortune au Sahara: permanences et ruptures. *Autrepart* **16**, 49–65.

2001. Droit musulman et pratiques foncières dans l'Adrâr mauritanien. *Études rurales* **155–6**, 93–106.

2008. *L'émirat de l'Adrar mauritanien: harîm, compétition et protection dans une société tribale saharienne*. Paris: Karthala.

Bordes, P., and A. Labrousse. 2004. Économie de la drogue et réseaux de corruption au Maroc. *Politique Africaine* **93**, 63–82.

Botte, R. 1999. Économies trafiquantes et mondialisation. *Politique Africaine* 88, 139–50.

Boubakeur, H. 1999. *Un soufi algérien, Sidi Cheikh*. Paris: Maisonneuve et Larose.

Boubekri, H. 2000. Échanges transfrontaliers et commerce parallèle aux frontiers tuniso-libyennes. *Maghreb – Machrek* 120, 39–51.

Bouche, D. 1968. *Les villages de liberté en Afrique noire française*. Paris: Mouton.

Boukhobza, M. 1982. *L'agro-pastoralisme traditionnel en Algérie: de l'ordre tribal au désordre colonial*. Algiers: OPU.

Bourdieu, P. 1965. The sentiment of honour in Kabyle society. In *Honour and shame: the values of Mediterranean society* (ed.) J. G. Peristiany, 191–241. London: Weidenfeld and Nicolson.

Bourgeot, A. 1994. Une rupture du couple écologie-économie. La crise du pastoralisme touareg. In *A la croisée des parcours. Pasteurs, éleveurs, cultivateurs* (eds.) C. Blanc-Pamard and J. Boutrais, 63–78. Paris: Orstom.

1995. *Les sociétés touarègues. Nomadisme, identité, resistances*. Paris: Karthala.

Bouterfa, S. 2005. *Les manuscrits du Touat: le Sud algérien*. Algiers: Editions Barzakh.

Bouwman, D. 2005. Throwing stones at the moon: the role of Arabic in contemporary Mali. PhD thesis, University of Leiden.

Bovill, E. W. 1968. *The Golden Trade of the Moors*. Oxford: Oxford University Press.

Bowen, J. 1992. On scriptural essentialism and ritual variation: Muslim sacrifice in Sumatra and Morocco. *American Ethnologist* 19/4, 656–71.

Brachet, J. 2005. Migrants, transporteurs et agents d'état: rencontre sur l'axe Agadez-Sebha. *Autrepart* 36, 43–62.

2009. *Migrations transsahariennes: vers un désert cosmopolite et morcelé (Niger)*. Bellecombe-en-Bauges: Éditions du Croquant.

2011. The blind spot of repression: migration policies and human survival in the Sahara. In *The migration-development-security nexus* (eds.) T.-D. Truong and D. Gasper, 57–66. London: Springer.

Braudel, F. 1966 [1949]. *La Méditerranée et le monde méditerranéen à l'époque de Philippe II*. Paris: Armand Colin.

1967–79. *Civilisation matérielle et capitalisme (XVe–XVIIIe siècle)*. Paris: Armand Colin.

Bredeloup, S. 2007. *La diams'pora du fleuve Sénégal. Sociologie des migrations africaines*. Toulouse: Presses universitaires du Mirail, IRD Éditions.

Bredeloup, S., and O. Pliez (eds.). 2005. Migrations entre les deux rives du Sahara. *Autrepart* 36 (special issue).

Brenner, L. 2000. *Controlling knowledge*. London: Hurst and Company.

Brooks, George E. 1993. *Landlords and strangers. Ecology, society and trade in Western Africa 1000–1630*. Boulder: Westview Press.

Brower, B. C. 2009. *A desert named peace: the violence of France's empire in the Algerian Sahara, 1844–1902*. New York: Columbia University Press.

2010. Rethinking abolition in Algeria. Slavery and the "indigenous question." *Cahiers d'études africaines* 195/3, 805–28.

Bryceson, D. F. 2000. Of criminals and clients. African culture and afro-pessimism in a globalised world. *Canadian Journal of African Studies* 34/2, 417–42.

Bugéja, M. 1930. L'estivage des Larbaâ dans le Tell. *Bulletin de la Société de Géographie d'Alger et de l'Afrique du Nord* 35, 1–19.

Caillié, R. 1830. *Journal d'un voyage à Tembouctou et à Jenné, dans l'Afrique centrale.* Paris: Imprimerie royale.

Cameron, G. 2001. The Tanzanian general elections on Zanzibar. *Review of African Political Economy* 28, 282–6.

Capot-Rey, R. 1942. Le nomadisme pastoral dans le Sahara français. *Travaux de l'institut de recherches sahariennes* 1, 63–86.

1953. *Le Sahara français.* Paris: PUF.

1956. Greniers domestiques et greniers fortifiés au Sahara. Le cas du Gourara. *Travaux de l'institut de recherches sahariennes* 14, 139–59.

Capot-Rey, R., and W. Damade. 1962. Irrigation et structure agraire à Tamentit. *Travaux de l'institut de recherches sahariennes* 21, 99–119.

Caratini, S. 1989. *Les Rgaybat (1610–1934).* Paris: L'Harmattan.

Carette, E. 1844. *Étude sur les routes suivies par les Arabes dans la partie méridionale de l'Algérie et de la Régence de Tunis pour servir à l'établissement du réseau géographique de ces contrées.* Paris: Imprimerie Royale.

1848. *Études sur la Kabilie proprement dite.* Paris: Imprimerie nationale.

Carette, E., and A. Warner. 1846. Carte de l'Algérie divisée par tribus. In *Les tableaux des établissements français en Algérie.* Paris: Imprimerie Royale.

Casajus, D. 1987. *La tente dans la solitude: la société des morts chez les Touaregs Kel Ferwan.* Paris: MSH.

1990. Islam et noblesse chez les Touaregs. *L'Homme* 115, 7–30.

Caton, S. 1990. *'Peaks of Yemen I summon': poetry as cultural practice in a North Yemeni tribe.* Berkeley: University of California Press.

Cauneille, A. 1968. *Les Chaanba.* Paris: Éditions du CNRS.

Chaintron, J.-F. 1957. Aoulef. Problèmes économiques d'une oasis à foggaras. *Travaux de l'institut de recherches sahariennes* 16, 101–30.

Chaker, S. 1999. *Berbères aujourd'hui, Berbères dans le Maghreb contemporain.* Paris: L'Harmattan.

Chancel, A. de. 1858. *D'une immigration des Noirs libres en Algérie.* Algiers: Bastide.

1859. *Cham et Japhet ou de l'émigration des nègres chez les blancs considérée comme moyen providentiel de régénérer la race nègre et de civiliser l'Afrique intérieure.* Paris: Hennuyer.

Chapman, M. 1978. *The Gaelic vision in Scottish culture.* London: Croom Helm.

Châu, L. 1992. Politiques économiques et crises pendant les 30 années d'indépendance. *Politique Africaine* 47, 31–42.

Chaudhuri, K. N. 1985. *Trade and civilisation in the Indian Ocean: an economic history from the rise of Islam to 1750.* Cambridge: Cambridge University Press.

1990. *Asia before Europe: economy and civilisation in the Indian Ocean from the rise of Islam to 1750.* Cambridge: Cambridge University Press.

Chentouf, T. 1984. Les monnaies dans le Gourara, le Touat et le Tidikelt dans la seconde moitié du 19e siècle. In *Enjeux sahariens* (ed.) P.-R. Baduel, 79–94. Paris: Éditions du CNRS.

Chiche, J. 1984. Description de l'hydraulique traditionnelle. In *La question hydraulique*, 119–319. Rabat: Institut agronomique et vétérinaire Hassan II.

Choplin, A. 2006. Le foncier urbain en Afrique: entre informel et rationnel, l'exemple de Nouakchott (Mauritanie). *Annales de Géographie* 647, 69–91.

2008. L'immigré, le migrant et l'allochtone: circulations migratoires et figures de l'étranger en Mauritanie. *Politique Africaine* 109, 73–90.

2009. *Nouakchott: au carrefour de la Mauritanie et du monde*. Paris: Karthala.

Cissoko, S. M. 1975. *Tombouctou et l'Empire songhay*. Dakar: NEA.

Claudot-Hawad, H. 1985. Adrar des Ifoghas. *Encyclopédie Berbère* 2, 556–8.

1990. Honneur et politique. Les choix stratégiques des Touaregs pendant la colonisation française. *REMMM* 57, 11–47.

1995. 'Négrafricanisme' et racisme. *Le Monde diplomatique*, April 1995, 30.

1996. Identité et alterité d'un point de vue touareg. Éléments pour un débat. *Cahiers de l'IREMAM* 7–8, 132–40.

1998. La hiérarchie des savoirs et des pouvoirs dans la société touarègue précoloniale et la récomposition des roles socio-politiques pendant la guerre anticoloniale et après la défaite. *Nomadic Peoples* 2/1–2, 17–38.

2000. Captif sauvage, enfant esclave, affranchi cousin. La mobilité statutaire chez les Touareg. In *Groupes serviles au Sahara* (ed.) M. Villasante-de Beauvais, 237–68. Paris: Éditions du CNRS.

Clauzel, J. 1960. Transports, automobiles, et caravanes dans le Sahara soudanais. *Travaux de l'institut de recherches sahariennes* 19, 161–8.

1962. Les hiérarchies sociales en pays touareg. *Travaux de l'institut de recherches sahariennes* 31, 120–75.

Cleaveland, T. 1998. Islam and the construction of social identity in the nineteenth-century Sahara. *Journal of African History* 39, 365–88.

2002. *Becoming Walata: a history of Saharan social formation and transformation*. Portsmouth: Heinemann.

Cohen, W. 1980. *The French encounter with Africans. White responses to blacks, 1530–1880*. Bloomington: Indiana University Press.

Collyer, M. 2006. States of insecurity: consequences of Saharan transit migration. Working paper 06–31, COMPAS, University of Oxford.

Colonna, F. 1995. *Les versets de l'invincibilité. Permanence et changements religieux dans l'Algérie contemporaine*. Paris: Presses des Sciences Po.

Comité d'Information Sahel. 1975. *Qui se nourrit de la famine en Afrique?* Paris: Maspéro.

Conklin, A. 1997. *A mission to civilize: the republican idea of empire in France and West Africa, 1895–1930*. Stanford: Stanford University Press.

Conrad, D. C., and B. Frank (eds.). 1995. *Status and identity in West Africa: Nyamakalaw of Mande*. Bloomington: Indiana University Press.

Constable, R. O. 2003. *Housing the stranger in the Mediterranean world: lodging, trade, and travel in late antiquity and the Middle Ages*. Cambridge: Cambridge University Press.

Conte, B. 1994. L'après-dévaluation: hypotheses et hypothèques. *Politique Africaine* 54, 32–46.

Cooper, F. 1980. *From slaves to squatters: plantation agriculture in Zanzibar and coastal Kenya*. New Haven: Yale University Press.
Cordell, D. 1977. Eastern Libya, Wadai, and the Sanusiya: a tariqa and a trade route. *Journal of African History* 18/1, 21–36.
1999. No liberty, not much equality, and very little fraternity: the mirage of manumission in the Algerian Sahara in the second half of the nineteenth century. In *Slavery and colonial rule in Africa* (eds.) S. Miers and M. A. Klein, 38–56. London: Frank Cass.
Cordell, D., J. W. Gregory, and V. Piché. 1996. *Hoe and wage. A social history of a circular migration system in West Africa*. Boulder: Westview Press.
Cordonnier, R. 1982. *Les revendeuses de tissues de la ville de Lomé*. Paris: Orstom.
Cornet, A. 1952. Essai sur l'hydrologie du Grand Erg Occidental et des régions limitrophes. Les Foggaras. *Travaux de l'institut de recherches sahariennes* 8, 71–122.
Côte, M. (ed.). 2005. *La ville et le désert, le Bas-Sahara algérien*. Paris: Karthala.
Cressier, P. 1988. *Programme Azawagh. Première propspection comparative des sites médiévaux et modernes de l'Adrar des Iforas (rapport préliminaire)*. Paris: ORSTOM/CNRS.
Daumas, E. 1864. *Mœurs et coutumes de l'Algérie: Tell, Kabylie, Sahara*. Paris: Hachette.
Davis, M. 2001. *Late Victorian holocausts: El Niño famines and the making of the Third World*. London: Verso.
Davis, S. 1970. *Reservoirs of Men: a history of the black troops of French West Africa*. Westport: Negro University Press.
Davies, W. 1988. *Small worlds. The village community in early mediaeval Brittany*. London: Duckworth.
Direche-Slimani, K. 1997. *Histoire de l'émigration kabyle en France au XXe siècle*. Paris: L'Harmattan.
Dresch, P. 1989. *Tribes, government and history in Yemen*. Oxford: Oxford University Press.
2000. Wilderness of mirrors: truth and vulnerability in Middle Eastern fieldwork. In *Anthropologists in a wider world: essays on field research* (eds.) P. Dresch, W. James and D. Parkin, 109–28. Oxford: Berghahn.
2006. *The rules of Barat. Texts and translations from tribal documents in Yemen*. San'â: CEFAS.
2009. Les mots et les choses: l'identité tribale en Arabie. *Etudes rurales* 184, 185–202.
Dunn, R. E. 1971. The trade of Tafilalt: commercial change in southeast Morocco on the eve of the Protectorate. *African Historical Studies* 4/2, 271–304.
Dupraz, P. 1994. Paroles de 'dévalués'. *Politique Africaine* 54, 117–26.
Echard, N., and P. Bonte. 1976. Histoire et histoires. Conception du passé chez les Hawsa et les Touareg Kel Gress de l'Ader (République du Niger). *Cahiers d'études africaines* 61–2, 237–96.
Echenberg, M. J. 1991. *Colonial conscripts: the* Tirailleurs Sénégalais *in French West Africa, 1857–1960*. Oxford: James Currey.

El Hamel, C. 2002a. *La vie intellectuelle islamique dans le Sahel ouest-africain*. Paris: L'Harmattan.

2002b. 'Race', slavery and Islam in Maghribi Mediterranean thought. *Journal of North African Studies* 7/3, 29–52.

Elboudrari, H. 1985. Quand les saints font les villes: lecture anthropologique de la pratique sociale d'un saint marocain du XVIIe siècle. *Annales E. S. C.* 40/3, 489–508.

Eldblom, L. 1968. *Structure foncière, organisation et structure sociale. Une étude sur la vie socio-économique dans les trois oasis libyennes de Ghat, Mourzouk et particulièrement Ghadamès*. Lund: Uniskol.

Emerit, M. 1954. Les liaisons terrestres entre le Soudan et l'Afrique du Nord au XVIIIe siècle et au début du XIXe siècle. *Travaux de l'institut de recherches sahariennes* 11, 29–47.

Ennaji, M. 1994. *Soldats, domestiques et concubines. L'esclavage au Maroc au XIXe siècle*. Tunis: Cérès Editions.

Evans-Pritchard, E. E. 1940. *The Nuer*. Oxford: Clarendon Press.

Fair, L. 2001. *Pastimes and politics: culture, community and identity in post-abolition Zanzibar, 1890–1945*. Athens: Ohio University Press.

Fall, Y. 1982. *L'Afrique à la naissance de la cartographie moderne*. Paris: Karthala.

Fardon, R. (ed.). 1995. *Counterworks: managing the diversity of knowledge*. London: Routledge.

Farias Moraes, P. F. 2003. *Arabic medieval inscriptions from the Republic of Mali*. Oxford: Oxford University Press.

Fay, C. 1995a. La démocratie au Mali, ou le pouvoir en pâture. *Cahiers d'études africaines* 35/1, 19–53.

1995b. Car nous ne faisons qu'un: identités, equivalences et homologie au Maasina (Mali). *Cahiers des sciences humaines* 31/2, 427–56.

Ferme, M. C. 2001. *The underneath of things: violence, history and the everyday in Sierra Leone*. Berkeley: University of California Press.

Freitag, U., and W. G. Clarence-Smith (eds.). 1997. *Hadrami scholars, traders, and statesmen in the Indian Ocean, 1750s–1960s*. Leiden: Brill.

Gambetta, D. 1993. *The Sicilian mafia: the business of private protection*. Cambridge: Harvard University Press.

Garrard, T. 1982. Myths and metrology: the early trans-Saharan gold trade. *Journal of African History* 23/4, 443–61.

Gast, M. 1968. *Alimentation des populations de l'Ahaggar, étude ethnographique*. Paris: Arts et métiers graphiques.

1989. Échanges transsahariens et survie des populations locales. *Bulletin d'écologie humaine* 7/2, 3–24.

Gautier, E. F. 1927. *L'islamisation de l'Afrique du Nord: les siècles obscurs du Maghreb*. Paris: Payot.

Gellner, E. 1969. *Saints of the Atlas*. London: Weidenfeld and Nicolson.

Génevière, J. 1950. Les Kountas et leurs activités commerciales. *Bulletin de l'IFAN* **B.12**, 1111–27.

Geoffroy, A. 1887. Arabes Pasteurs Nomades de la tribu des Larbas. *Les Ouvriers des deux mondes* 1/8, 409–64.

Geschiere, P. 1997. *The modernity of witchcraft*. Charlottesville: University of Virginia Press.

Gilsenan, M. 1976. Lying, honor and contradiction. In *Transaction and meaning: directions in the anthropology of exchange and symbolic behavior* (ed.) B. Kapferer, 191–219. Philadelphia: Institute for the Study of Human Issues.

Gironcourt, G. de. 1920. *Missions de Gironcourt en Afrique occidentale 1908–1909 et 1911–1912. Documents scientifiques*. Paris: Société de Géographie.

Giuffrida, A. 2005a. Clerics, rebels and refugees: mobility strategies and networks among the Kel Antessar. *Journal of North African Studies* 10/3–4, 529–43.

2005b. Métamorphose des relations de dépendance chez les Kel Antessar au cercle de Goundam. *Cahiers d'études africaines* 179–80, 805–29.

Glassman, J. 2000. Sorting out the tribes: the creation of racial identities in colonial Zanzibar's newspaper wars. *Journal of African History* 41/3, 395–428.

Glick, T. 1970. *Irrigation and society in mediaeval Valencia*. Cambridge: Harvard University Press.

Granier, J.-C. 1980. Rente foncière et régulation économique dans le Gourara algérien. *Revue Tiers-Monde* 83, 649–64.

Grandguillaume, G. 1973. Régime économique et structure du Pouvoir. Le système des foggara du Touat. *Revue de l'Occident musulman et de la Méditerranée* 13–14, 437–57.

1975. Le droit de l'eau dans les foggara du Touat au XVIIIe siècle. *Revue des études islamiques* 43/2, 287–322.

1978. De la coutume à la loi: droit de l'eau et statut des communautés locales dans le Touat précolonial. *Peuples méditerranéens* 2, 119–33.

Grégoire, E. 1986. *Les Alhazai du Maradi (Niger): histoire d'un groupe de riches marchands sahéliens*. Paris: ORSTOM.

1998. Sahara nigérien: terre d'échanges. *Autrepart* 6, 91–104.

1999. *Touaregs du Niger, le destin d'un mythe*. Paris: Karthala.

2000. Les communautés marchandes d'Agadès (Niger). Accumulation et exclusion, 1945–1998. In *Politiques et dynamiques territoriales dans les pays du Sud* (ed.) J.-L. Chaléard and R. Pourtier, 231–46. Paris: Sorbonne.

Grémont, C. 2005. Comment les Touaregs ont perdu le fleuve. Eclairage sur les pratiques et les représentations foncières dans le cercle de Gao (Mali), XIXe–XXe siècles. In *Patrimoines naturels au Sud. Territoires, identités et stratégies locales* (eds.) M. C. Cormier-Salem et al. 237–90. Paris: IRD.

2010. *Les Touaregs Iwellemmedan (1647–1896). Un ensemble politique de la boucle du Niger*. Paris: Karthala.

2012. Villages and crossroads: changing territorialities among the Tuareg of Northern Mali in the twentieth century. In *Saharan frontiers: space and mobility in Northwest Africa* (eds.) J. McDougall and J. Scheele, 131–45. Bloomington: Indiana University Press.

Grémont, C., A. Marty, R. ag Moussa, and Y. Hamara Touré. 2004. *Les liens sociaux au Nord-Mali. Entre fleuve et dunes*. Paris: Karthala.

Grévoz, D. 1994. *Les méharistes français à la conquête du Sahara: 1900–1930*. Paris: L'Harmattan.

Guillermou, Y. 1993. Survie et ordre social au Sahara. Les oasis du Touat-Gourara-Tidikelt en Algérie. *Cahiers des sciences humaines* **29**/1, 121–38.

Guitart, F. 1989. Le rôle des frontières coloniales sur le commerce transsaharien central (région d'Agadez 1900–1970). *Cahiers géographiques de Rouen* **32**, 155–62.

Gutelius, D. 2002. 'The path is easy and the benefits large': the Nasiriyya, social networks and economic change in Morocco, 1640–1830. *Journal of African History* **43**, 27–49.

2007. Islam in northern Mali and the war on terror. *Journal of Contemporary African Studies* **25**/1, 59–76.

Guyer, J. I. 1993. Wealth in people and self-realisation in equatorial Africa. *Man* (n.s.) **28**/2, 243–65.

Haarmann, U. 1998. The dead ostrich: life and trade in Ghadamès (Libya) in the nineteenth century. *Die Welt des Islams* **38**/1, 9–94.

Haas, H. d. 2007. The myth of invasion. Irregular migration from West Africa to the Maghreb and the European Union. Research Report, International Migration Institute, Oxford.

Hall, B. 2005. The question of 'race' in the pre-colonial southern Sahara. *Journal of North African Studies* 10/3–4, 339–68.

2011. *A history of race in Muslim West Africa, 1600–1960*. Cambridge: Cambridge University Press.

Hallaq, W. B. 2009. *Sharī'a: theory, practice, transformations*. Cambridge: Cambridge University Press.

Halpern, E. 1934. La huerta de Valence. *Annales de Géographie* **242**, 146–62.

Hama, B. 1968. *Histoire des Songhay*. Niamey: Publications de la République du Niger.

Hammoudi, A. 1974. Segmentarité, stratification sociale, pouvoir politique et sainteté. *Hespéris – Tamuda* **16**, 147–80.

1980. Sainteté, pouvoir et société: Tamgrout aux XVIIe et XVIIIe siècles. *Annales E. S. C.* 35/3–4, 615–41.

1985. Substance and relation: water rights and water distribution in the Drâ valley. In *Property, social structure and law in the modern Middle East* (ed.) A. Mayer, 27–57. Albany: State University of New York Press.

Hampshire, K., and S. Randall. 1999. Seasonal labour migration strategies in the Sahel: coping with poverty or optimising security? *International Journal of Population Geography* 5, 367–85.

Hanoteau, A., and A. Letourneux. 1872. *La Kabylie et les coutumes kabyles. Tome 1*. Paris: Challamel.

Harbi, M., and B. Stora (eds.). 2004. *La guerre d'Algérie: 1954–2004. La fin de l'amnésie*. Paris: Robert Laffont.

Harris, W. V. (ed.). 2005. *Rethinking the Mediterranean*. Oxford: Oxford University Press.

Heffernan, M. 2001. 'A dream as frail as those of ancient time': the incredible geography of Timbuctoo. *Environment and Planning D: Society and Space* 19/2, 203–25.

Henkel, H. 2005. 'Between belief and unbelief lies the performance of *salat*': meaning and efficacy of a Muslim ritual. *Journal of the Royal Anthropological Institute* 11/3, 487–507.

Herzfeld, M. 1980. Honour and shame. Some problems in the comparative analysis of moral systems. *Man* (n.s.) 15, 339–51.

1987. *Anthropology through the looking glass: critical ethnography in the margins of Europe*. Cambridge: Cambridge University Press.

Hibou, B. (ed.). 1999. *La Privatisation des États*. Paris: Karthala.

Hill, P. 1966. Landlords and brokers: a West African trading system. *Cahiers d'études africaines* 6/23, 349–66.

Ho, E. 2001. Le don précieux de la généalogie. In *Emirs et présidents. Figures de la parenté et du politique dans le monde arabe* (eds.) P. Bonte, E. Conte, and P. Dresch, 79–102. Paris: Editions du CNRS.

2004. Empire through diasporic eyes: a view from the other boat. *Comparative Studies in Society and History* 46/2, 210–46.

2006. *The graves of Tarim. Genealogy and mobility across the Indian Ocean*. Berkeley: University of California Press.

Hodges, T. 1983. *Western Sahara: the roots of a desert war*. Beckenham: Croom Helm.

Holsinger, D. 1979. Migration, commerce and community. The Mzabites in nineteenth-century Algeria. PhD Dissertation, Northerwestern University.

1980. Migration, commerce and community: the Mizabis in eighteenth- and nineteenth-century Algeria. *Journal of African History* 21/1, 61–71.

Hopkins, A. G. 1973. *An economic history of West Africa*. London: Longman.

Horden, P., and N. Purcell. 2000. *The corrupting sea*. Oxford: Blackwell.

Humarau, B. 1997. Grand commerce féminin, hiérarchies et solidarités en Afrique de l'Ouest. *Politique Africaine* 67, 89–102.

Hunwick, J. 1985. *Sharīʿa in Songhay: the replies of al-Maghīlī to the questions of Askia al-Hājj Muhammad*. Oxford: Oxford University Press.

1999a. Islamic law and polemics over race and slavery in North and West Africa (16th–19th century). In *Slavery in the Islamic Middle East* (ed.) Shaun E. Marmon, 52–9. Princeton: Markus Wiener.

1999b. Islamic financial institutions: theoretical structures and aspects of their application in sub-Saharan Africa. In *Credit, currencies and culture: African financial institutions in historical perspective* (eds.) E. Stiansen and J. Guyer, 72–99. Uppsala: Nordiska Afrikainstitutet.

2003. *Timbuctu and the Songhai Empire*. Leiden: Brill.

Hutchinson, S. 1996. *Nuer dilemmas: coping with money, war and the state*. Berkeley: University of California Press.

Hūtiya, M. S. 2007. *Tuwāt w-Azawād*. Algiers: Dār al-kitāb al-ʿarabī.

Insoll, T. 1997. *Islam, archaeology and history: Gao region*. Oxford: Tempus reparatum.

2000. *Urbanism, archeology and trade: further observations on the Gao region (Mali): the 1996 fieldseason results*. Oxford: British Archeaological Reports.

Jacques-Meunié, D. 1951. *Greniers-citadelles au Maroc*. Paris: Arts et métiers graphiques.

Janson, M. 2005. Roaming about for God's sake: the upsurge of the Tabligh Jamaʿat in the Gambia. *Journal of Religion in Africa* 35/4, 450–81.

Johansen, B. 1990. Le jugement comme preuve. Preuve juridique et vérité religieuse dans le droit islamique hanéfite. *Studia Islamica* 72, 5–17.

1997. Formes de langages et fonctions publiques: stereotypes, témoins et offices dans la preuve par l'écrit en droit musulman. *Arabica* 44, 333–76.

Johnson, M. 1968. The nineteenth-century gold 'mithqal' in West and North Africa. *Journal of African History* 9, 547–69.

1976. Calico Caravan: the Tripoli-Kano trade after 1880. *Journal of African History* 45/4, 95–118.

Jourde, C. 2007. Constructing representations of the 'global war on terror' in the Islamic Republic of Mauritania. *Journal of Contemporary African Studies* 25/1, 77–100.

Kea, R. A. 2004. Expansions and contractions: world-historical change and the Western Sudan world-system. *Journal of World-Systems Research* 10, 723–816.

Keenan, J. 1977. *The Tuareg, people of Ahaggar*. London: Allen Lane.

2003. Contested terrain: tourism, environment and security in Algeria's extreme south. *Journal of North African Studies* 8/3–4, 226–65.

2005. Waging war on terror: the implications of America's 'new imperialism' for Saharan peoples. *Journal of North African Studies* 10/3–4, 619–47.

2006a. Military bases, construction contracts and hydrocarbons in North Africa. *Revue of African Political Economy* 33/109, 601–8.

2006b. Turning the Sahel on its head: the 'truth' behind the headlines. *Revue of African Political Economy* 33/110, 761–9.

2007a. The banana theory of terrorism: alternative truths and the collapse of the 'second' (Saharan) front in the war on terror. *Journal of Contemporary African Studies* 25/1, 31–58.

2007b. US silence as military base gathers dust. *Revue of African Political Economy* 34/113, 588–90.

2009. *The dark Sahara: America's war on terror in Africa*. London: Pluto Press.

Khadraoui, A. 2007. *La foggara dans les oasis du Touat – Gourara et du Tidikelt. Définition – propositions de réhabilitation et de sauvegarde*. Algiers: Ministère des ressources en eau.

Klein, B., and G. Mackenthun (eds.). 2004. *Sea changes: historicising the ocean*. London: Routledge.

Klute, G. 1995. Hostilités et alliances. Archéologie de la dissidence des Touaregs au Mali. *Cahiers d'études africaines* 137, 55–71.

2001. Die Rebellionen der Tuareg in Mali und Niger. Habilitationsschrift, Universität zu Siegen.

Lambek, M. 1990. Certain knowledge, contestable authority: power and practice on the Islamic periphery. *American Ethnologist* 17/1, 23–40.

Lambert, A. 1993. Les commerçantes maliennes du chemin de fer Dakar – Bamako. In *Grands commerçants d'Afrique de l'Ouest* (eds.) P. Labazée and E. Grégoire, 37–70. Paris: Karthala.

Latour, B. 1991. *Nous n'avons jamais été modernes*. Paris: La Découverte.

2005. *Reassembling the social: an introduction to actor-network-theory*. Oxford: University Press.

Lawless, R., and L. Monahan (eds.). 1997. *War and refugees: the Western Sahara conflict*. London: Pinter.

Layish, A. 1998. *Legal documents on Libyan tribal society in the process of sedentarisation*. Wiesbaden: Harrassowitz.

2005. *Sharīʿa and custom in Libyan tribal society. An annotated translation of decisions from the sharīʿa courts of Ajdābiya and Kufra*. Leiden: Brill.

Leclerc, L. 1858. *Les oasis de la province d'Oran, ou les Oulad Sidi Cheikh*. Algiers: Tissier.

Lecocq, B. 2002. 'That desert is our country'. Tuareg Rebellions and competing nationalisms in contemporary Mali (1946–1996). PhD Thesis, University of Amsterdam.

2003. This country is your country: territory, borders, and decentralisation in Tuareg politics. *Itinerario* 27/1, 58–78.

2005. 'The Bellah Question': slave emancipation, race and social categories in late twentieth-century northern Mali. *Canadian Journal of African Studies* 39/1, 42–68.

2010. *Disputed desert: decolonisation, competing nationalisms and Tuareg rebellions in Mali*. Leiden: Brill.

Lecocq, B., and P. Schrijver. 2007. The war on terror in a haze of dust: potholes and pitfalls on the Saharan front. *Journal of Contemporary African Studies* 25/1, 141–66.

Lefébure, C. 1986. Ayt Khebbach, impasse sud-est. L'involution d'une tribu exlue du Sahara. *Revue de l'Occident musulman et de la Méditerranée* 41, 136–57.

Lemarchand, R. (ed.). 1988. *The green and the black: Qadhafi's policies in Africa*. Bloomington: Indiana University Press.

Lenz, O. 1884. *Reise durch Marokko, die Sahara und den Sudan, ausgeführt im Auftrage der Afrikanischen Gesellschaft in Deutschland in den Jahren 1879 und 1880*. Leipzig: Brockhaus.

Leriche, A. 1946. Contribution à l'étude de l'histoire maure. Les guerres des Kountas (traduit du wasit). *Notes africaines* 30, 4.

1953. De l'origine du thé au Maroc et au Sahara. *Bulletin de l'IFAN* 15, 731–6.

Leservoisier, O. 1994. *La question foncière en Mauritanie. Terres et pouvoirs dans la région du Gorgol*. Paris: L'Harmattan.

Lesourd, C. 2006. 'Au bonheur des dames'. Femmes d'affaires mauritaniennes de nos jours. PhD dissertation, Social Anthropology, EHESS, Paris.

Levtzion, N., and J. F. P. Hopkins (eds.). 1981. *Corpus of early Arabic sources for West African history*. Cambridge: Cambridge University Press.

Linebaugh, P., and M. Rediker. 2000. *The many-headed Hydra: sailors, slaves, commoners and the hidden revolutionary history of the Atlantic*. London: Verso.

Lo, A. 1953–4. Les foggaras du Tidikelt. *Travaux de l'institut de recherches sahariennes* 10, 139–79 and 11, 49–77.

Loimeier, R. 1997. *Islamic reform and political change in northern Nigeria*. Evanston: Northwestern University Press.

Lorcin, P. 1995. *Imperial identities: stereotyping, prejudice and race in colonial Algeria*. London: I. B. Tauris.

Lovejoy, P. E. 1978. The role of the Wangara in the economic transformation of the central Sudan in the 15th and 16th centuries. *Journal of African History* 19, 173–93.

1983. *Transformations in slavery*. Cambridge: Cambridge University Press.
1984. Commercial sectors in the economy of the nineteenth-century central Sudan: the trans-Saharan trade and the desert-side salt trade. *African Economic History* 13, 85–116.
Lucas, P., and J.-C. Vatin. 1975. *L'Algérie des anthropologues*. Paris: Maspero.
Lydon, G. 2005. Slavery, exchange and Islamic law: a glimpse from the archives of Mali and Mauritania. *African Economic History* 33, 117–48.
2008. Contracting Caravans: Partnership and Profit in Nineteenth-Century Trans-Saharan Trade. *Journal of Global History* 3/1, 89–113.
2009a. *On trans-Saharan trails. Islamic law, trade networks, and cross-cultural exchange in nineteenth-century Western Africa*. Cambridge: Cambridge University Press.
2009b. A paper economy of faith without faith in paper: a reflection on Islamic institutional history. *Journal of Economic Behavior and Organization* 71, 647–59.
McDougall, E. A. 1980. The Ijil salt industry: its role in the pre-colonial economy of the Western Sudan. PhD thesis, University of Birmingham.
1985. Camel caravans of the Saharan salt trade: traders and transporters in the nineteenth century. In *The workers of African trade* (eds.) P. E. Lovejoy and C. Coquery-Vidrovitch, 99–122. London: Sage.
1986. The economies of Islam in the Southern Sahara: the rise of the Kunta clan. *Asian and African Studies* 20, 45–60.
1990. Salts of the Western Sahara: myths, mysteries and historical significance. *International Journal of African Historical Studies* 23/2, 231–57.
2002. Perfecting the 'fertile seed': the *Compagnie du Sel Aggloméré* and colonial capitalism, c.1890–1905. *African Economic History* 30, 53–80.
2005. Conceptualising the Sahara: the world of nineteenth-century Beyrouk commerce. *Journal of North African Studies* 10/3–4, 369–86.
MacGaffey, J. 1991. *The real economy of Zaire. The contribution of smuggling and other unofficial activities to national wealth*. Philadelphia: University of Pennsylvania Press.
McGovern, M. 2005. Islamist terror in the Sahel: fact or fiction? International Crisis Group Africa Report n° 92.
2010. Chasing shadows in the dunes: Islamist practice and counterterrorist policy in West Africa's Sahara-Sahel zone. In *Securing Africa. Post-9/11 discourses on terrorism* (ed.) M. Smith, 79–97. Farnham: Ashgate.
Maiga, M. 1997. *Le Mali: de la sécheresse à la rébellion nomade*. Paris: L'Harmattan.
Malkin, I., C. Constantakopoulou, and K. Panagopoulou (eds.). 2009. *Greek and Roman networks in the Mediterranean*. London: Routledge.
Mann, G. 2003. Violence, dignity and Mali's new model army, 1960–1968. *Mande Studies* 5, 65–82.
Marchal, R. (ed.). 2001. *Dubaï. Cité globale*. Paris: Éditions du CNRS.
Marcus, G. 1995. Ethnography in/of the world system: the emergence of multi-sited ethnography. *Annual Review of Anthropology* 24, 95–117.
Marfaing, L. 2010. De la migration comme potentiel de développement local: étrangers et migrants en Mauritanie. *Migrations Société* 22/127, 9–25.

Marfaing, L., and S. Wippel (eds.). 2004. *Les relations transsahariennes à l'époque contemporaine*. Paris: Karthala.
Markovits, C. 2000. *The global world of Indian merchants, 1750–1947*. Cambridge: Cambridge University Press.
Marouf, N. 1980. *Lecture de l'espace oasien*. Paris: Sindbad.
2005. *Les fondements anthropologiques de la norme maghrébine: hommage à Jacques Berque*. Paris: L'Harmattan.
Martin, A.-G.-P. 1908. *À la frontière du Maroc: les oasis sahariennes (Gourara, Touat, Tidikelt)*. Algiers: Imprimerie algérienne.
Martinez, L. 1998. *La guerre civile en Algérie*. Paris: Karthala.
Marty, A. 1993. La gestion de terroirs et les éleveurs: un outil d'exclusion ou de négociation. *Tiers-Monde* 34/134, 327–44.
Marty, G. 1948a. À Tunis: éléments allogènes et activités professionnelles, djerbiens, gabésiens, gens du Sud, et autres tunisiens. *IBLA* 11/42, 159–87.
1948b. Les algériens à Tunis. *IBLA* 11/43–4, 301–34.
Marty, P. 1920. *Études sur l'islam et les tribus du Soudan. Tome 1: Les Kounta de l'Est. Les Berabich. Les Iguellad*. Paris: E. Leroux.
Marx, E. 2006. The political economy of Middle Eastern and North African pastoral nomads. In *Nomadic societies in the Middle East and North Africa: entering the 21st century* (ed.) D. Chatty, 78–97. Leiden: Brill.
Masquelier, A. 2009. *Women and Islamic revival in a West African town*. Bloomington: Indiana University Press.
Masud, M. K. (ed.). 2000. *Travellers in faith: studies of the Tablîghî Jamâ'at as a transnational Islamic movement for faith renewal*. Leiden: Brill.
Mattingly, D. (ed.). 2003. *The archaeology of Fezzan. Volume 1: Synthesis*. London: Society for Libyan Studies.
Mauny, R. 1961. *Tableau géographique de l'ouest africain au Moyen Âge*. Dakar: IFAN.
Ma'zūzī, M. 1978. *La Marocanité du Sahara central: Tidikelt, Touat, Gourara, Saoura*. Rabat: Éd. Mithaq Almaghrib.
Mbok, E. 1994. Un ajustement improbable… *Politique Africaine* 54, 104–10.
Meillassoux, C. 1986. *Anthropologie de l'esclavage: le ventre de fer et d'argent*. Paris: PUF.
Mezzine, L. 1987. *Le Tafilalt: contribution à l'histoire du Maroc aux XVIIe et XVIIIe siècles*. Rabat: Publications de la Faculté des Lettres et des Sciences Humaines.
Miège, J.-L. 1981. Le commerce trans-saharien au 19e siècle. Essai de quantification. *Revue de l'Occident musulman et de la Mediterranée* 32, 93–120.
Milliot, L. 1952. *Recueil de jurisprudence chérifienne*. Paris: E. Leroux.
Miner, H. 1953. *The primitive city of Timbuctoo*. Princeton: American Philosophical Society.
Mollat de Jourdin, M. 1984. *Les explorateurs du XIIIe au XVIe siècle. Premiers regards sur des mondes nouveaux*. Paris: J. L. Lattès.
Montagne, R. 1930a. *Les Berbères et le Makhzen dans le Sud du Maroc*. Paris: Alcan.
1930b. *Un magasin collectif de l'Anti-Atlas, l'agadir des Ikounka*. Paris: Larose.
Montaudon. 1883. La colonisation en Algérie. *La Réforme Sociale* 6, 71–99 and 138–48.

Morvan, T. 1993. Nouïel, oasis du Nefzaoua (Tunisie): de la source aux forages illicites. *Cahiers d'Urbama* 8, 29–49.

Moussaoui, A. 2002. *Espace et sacré au Sahara. Ksour et oasis du sud-ouest algérien*. Paris: Éditions du CNRS.

Mundy, M. 1995. *Domestic government: kinship, community and polity in north Yemen*. London: Tauris.

Nadi, D. 2007. Installation dans une ville de transit migratoire. Le cas de la ville de Tamanrasset en Algérie. In *Les nouveaux urbains dans l'espace Sahara-Sahel: un cosmopolitisme par le bas* (eds.) E. Boesen and L. Marfaing, 279–94. Paris: Karthala.

Naylor, R. T. 2002. *Wages of crime: black markets, illegal finance, and the underworld economy*. Ithaca: Cornell University Press.

Newbury, C. W. 1966. North African and Western Sudan trade in the nineteenth century. A reevaluation. *Journal of African History* 7/2, 233–46.

Nicolaisen, J., and I. Nicolaisen. 1997 [1963]. *The pastoral Tuareg: ecology, culture and society*. New York: Thames and Hudson.

Niezen, R. W. 1990. The 'community of the helpers of the sunna': Islamic reform among the Songhay of Gao (Mali). *Africa* 60/3, 399–423.

Nijenhuis, K. 2003. Does decentralization serve everyone? The struggle for power in a Malian village. *European Journal of Development Research* 15/2, 67–92.

Nixon, S. 2009. Excavating Essouk-Tadmekka (Mali): new archaeological investigation of early Islamic trans-Saharan trade. *Azania* 44/2, 217–55.

Nordstrom, C. 2007. *Global outlaws: crime, money, and power in the contemporary world*. Berkeley: University of California Press.

Norris, H. T. 1975. *The Tuaregs: their Islamic legacy and its diffusion in the Sahel*. Warminster: Aris and Phillips.

1986. *The Arab conquest of the Western Sahara. Studies of the historical events, religious beliefs and social customs which made the remotest Sahara a part of the Arab world*. London: Longman.

1990. *Ṣūfī mystics of the Niger desert*. Oxford: Clarendon Press.

Nouhi, M. L. 2009. Religion and society in a Saharan tribal setting: authority and power in the Zwaya religious culture. PhD dissertation, University of Alberta.

Olivier de Sardan, J.-P. 1984. *Les sociétés Songhay-Zarma*. Paris: Karthala.

Osswald, R. 1986. *Die Handelsstädte der Westsahara. Die Entwicklung der arabisch-maurischen Kultur von Sinqīt, Wādān, Tīsīt und Walāta*. Berlin: Reimer.

1993. *Schichtengesellschaft und islamisches Recht: die Zawāyā und Krieger der Westsahara im Spiegel von Rechtsgutachten des 16.–19. Jahrhunderts*. Wiesbaden: Harassowitz.

Othman, A. 2007. And amicable settlement is the best: *sulh* and dispute resolution in Islamic Law. *Arab Law Quarterly* 21, 63–90.

Ould Bah, M. 1971. Introduction à la poésie mauritanienne (1650–1900). *Arabica* 18/1, 1–48.

Ould Cheikh, A. W. 1985. Nomadisme, Islam et pouvoir politique dans la société maure précoloniale (XIe–XIXe). Essai sur quelques aspects du tribalisme. PhD dissertation, Paris V.

Parkin, D., and R. Barnes (eds.). 2002. *Ships and the development of maritime technology in the Indian Ocean*. London: Routledge.
Pascon, P. 1980. Le commerce de la maison d'Ilîgh d'après le register comptable de Husayn b. Hachem. *Annales E. S. C.* 35, 700–29.
1984. *La Maison d'Iligh*. Rabat: P. Pascon.
Papastergiadis, N. 1995. Restless hybrids. *Third Text* 9/32, 9–18.
Pearson, M. N. 2003. *The Indian Ocean*. London: Routledge.
Pellicani, M., and S. Spiga. 2007. Analyse comparée des espaces charnières de la mobilité migratoire entre 'Nord' et 'Sud': le cas de Pouilles (Italie) et du Touat (Algérie). In *Les migrations internationales. Observation, analyse et perspectives*, 277–96. Paris: PUF/ AIDELF.
Peters, E. 1976. From particularism to universalism in the religion of the Cyrenaica Bedouin. *British Journal of Middle Eastern Studies* 3/1, 5–14.
Peters, R. 2005. *Crime and punishment in Islamic law: theory and practice from the sixteenth to the twenty-first century*. Cambridge: Cambridge University Press.
Phelinas, P. 1991. La commercialisation des céréales au Mali: comportement des agents économiques privés et régulation du marché. *Chroniques du Sud* 6, 225–32.
1992. La stratégie alimentaire entre la famine et l'autosuffisance. *Politique Africaine* 47, 43–50.
Pliez, O. 2003. *Villes du Sahara, urbanisation et urbanité dans le Fezzan libyen*. Paris: Éditions du CNRS.
2004. De l'immigration au transit? La Libye dans l'espace migratoire euro-africain. In *La nouvelle Libye. Sociétés, espaces et géopolitique au lendemain de l'embargo* (ed.) O. Pliez, 139–57. Paris: Karthala.
2006. Nomades d'hier, nomades d'aujourd'hui. Les migrants africains réactivent-ils les territoires nomades au Sahara? *Annales de Géographie* 652, 688–707.
Pouillon, F. 1993. Simplification ethnique en Afrique du Nord: Maures, Arabes et Berbères (18ᵉ–20ᵉ siècles). *Cahiers d'études africaines* 33/1, 37–49.
Powell, S. M. 2004. Swamp of terror in the Sahara. *Air Force Magazine*, November 2004, 50–4.
Powers, D. 1993. The Islamic inheritance system: a socio-historical approach. *Arab Law Quarterly* 8, 13–29.
2002. *Law, society and culture in the Maghrib, 1300–1500*. Cambridge: Cambridge University Press.
Purcell, N. 2003. The boundless sea of unlikeness? On defining the Mediterranean. *Mediterranean Historical Review* 18, 9–29.
Rabinow, P., and G. Marcus. 2008. *Designs for an anthropology of the contemporary*. Durham: Duke University Press.
Rain, D. 1999. *Eaters of the dry season: circular labor migration in the West African Sahel*. Boulder: Westview Press.
Rasmussen, S.-J. 1992. Disputed boundaries: Tuareg discourse on class and ethnicity. *Ethnology* 31/4, 351–65.
2002. Tuareg labor migration, gendered spaces, and the predicament of women. *City and Society* 14/2, 281–311.
Renan, E. 1873. La société berbère. *Revue des deux mondes* 107, 138–57.

1882. *Qu'est-ce qu'une nation? Conférence faite en Sorbonne, le 11 mars 1882*. Paris: Calman Lévy.

Retaillé, D. 1986. Les oasis dans une géographie méridienne Sahara-Sahel. *Cahiers géographiques de Rouen* **26**, 3–16.

1998. L'espace nomade. *Revue de géographie de Lyon* 73/1, 71–81.

Reynolds, S. 1984. *Kingdoms and community in Western Europe, 900–1300*. Oxford: Clarendon Press.

Richer, A. 1924. *Les Touaregs du Niger (région de Tombouctou-Gao): les Oulliminden*. Paris: Larose.

Roberts, H. 2003. *The battlefield: Algeria. Studies in a broken polity*. London: Verso.

Roberts, R. L. 1987. *Warriors, merchants and slaves: the state and the economy in the middle Niger Valley, 1700–1914*. Stanford: University Press.

Roitman, J. 1998. The garrison-entrepôt. *Cahiers d'études africaines* 38/150–2, 297–329.

2005. *Fiscal disobedience: an anthropology of economic regulation in Central Africa*. Princeton: Princeton University Press.

Romey, A. 1983. *Les Sa'īd 'Aṭbā de N'Goussa: Histoire et état actuel de leur nomadisme*. Paris: L'Harmattan.

Rossi, B. 2009. Slavery and migration: social and physical mobility in Ader (Niger). In *Reconfiguring Slavery* (ed.) B. Rossi, 182–206. Liverpool: Liverpool University Press.

Saad, E. 1983. *Social history of Timbuktu: the role of Muslim scholars and notables 1400–1900*. Cambridge: Cambridge University Press.

Saboul, A. 1956. The French rural community in the eighteenth and nineteenth centuries. *Past and Present* 10, 78–95.

Sahlins, M. D. 1983. Other times, other customs – the anthropology of history. *American Anthropologist* 85/3, 517–44.

San Marco, P. 2009. Migrations transsahariennes et ensemble eurafricain. In *Le Maghreb à l'épreuve des migrations subsahariennes* (ed.) A. Bensaâd, 411–25. Paris: Karthala.

Schacht, J. 1964. *An introduction to Islamic law*. Oxford: Clarendon Press.

Scheele, J. 2007. Recycling *baraka*: knowledge, politics and religion in contemporary Algeria. *Comparative Studies in Society and History* 49/2, 304–28.

2009a. *Village matters: knowledge, politics and community in Kabylia (Algeria)*. Oxford: James Currey.

2009b. Tribus, États et fraude: la region frontalière algéro-malienne. *Études rurales* 184, 79–94.

2010a. Coming to terms with tradition: manuscript conservation in contemporary Algeria. In *The Trans-Saharan Book Trade: Arabic Literacy, Manuscript Culture, and Intellectual History in Islamic Africa* (eds.) G. Krätli and G. Lydon, 291–318. Leiden: Brill.

2010b. Councils without customs, qadis without states: property and community in the Algerian Touat. *Islamic Law and Society* 17/3, 350–74.

Schendel, W. van, and I. Abraham. 2005. *Illicit flows and criminal things: the other side of globalization*. Bloomington: Indiana University Press.

Schroeter, D. 1988. *Merchants of Essaouira: urban society and imperialism in southwestern Morocco, 1844–1886*. Cambridge: Cambridge University Press.

Schulz, D. 2006. Promises of (im)mediate salvation: Islam, broadcast media, and the remaking of religious experience in Mali. *American Ethnologist* 33/2, 210–29.

2007. Evoking moral community, fragmenting Muslim discourse. Sermon audiorecordings and the reconfiguration of public debate in Mali. *Journal of Islamic Studies* 26, 39–71.

Scott, J. C. 2009. *The art of not being governed: an anarchist history of upland Southeast Asia*. New Haven: Yale University Press.

Shryock, A. 1997. *Nationalism and the genealogical imagination: oral history and textual authority in tribal Jordan*. Berkeley: University of California Press.

Simpson, E., and K. Kresse (eds.). 2007. *Struggling with history: Islam and cosmopolitanism in the Western Indian Ocean*. London: Hurst.

Soares, B. F. 2005a. *Islam and the prayer economy: history and authority in a Muslim town*. Edinburgh: Edinburgh University Press.

2005b. Islam in Mali in the neoliberal era. *African Affairs* 105/418, 77–95.

2007. Les sciences ésotériques musulmanes et le commerce d'amulettes au Mali. In *Magie et écriture islamique dans les mondes africains et européens* (ed.) C. Hamès, 209–18. Paris: Karthala.

Spiga, S. 2002. Tamanrasset, capitale du Hoggar: mythes et réalités. *Méditerranée* 99, 83–90.

Spittler, G. 1993. *Les Touareg face aux sécheresses et aux famines: les Kel Ewey de l'Aïr*. Paris: Karthala.

Stewart, C. 1973. *Islam and social order in Mauritania*. Oxford: Clarendon Press.

Stora, B. 1993. *Histoire de la guerre d'Algérie, 1954–1962*. Paris: La Découverte.

1994. *L'histoire de l'Algérie depuis l'indépendance*. Paris: La Découverte.

Strathern, M. 1996. Cutting the network. *Journal of the Royal Anthropological Institute* 2/3, 517–35.

Streiff-Fénart, J. and Ph. Poutignat. 2006. De l'aventurier au commerçant transnational, trajectoires croisées et lieux intermédiaires à Nouadhibou (Mauritanie). *Cahiers de la Méditerranée* 73, 129–49.

2008. Nouadhibou, 'ville de transit'? *Revue européenne des migrations internationales* 24/2, 193–217.

Tag, S. 1994. *Paysans, état et démocratisation au Mali: Enquête en milieu rural*. Hamburg: Institut für Afrika-Kunde.

Tagliacozzo, E. 2005. *Secret trades, porous borders: smuggling and states along a Southeast Asian frontier, 1865–1915*. New Haven: Yale University Press.

Tarrius, A. 2000. *Les nouveaux cosmopolites*. La Tour d'Aigues: Éditions de l'Aube.

Taussig, M. 1977. The genesis of capitalism amongst a South American peasantry: devil's labor and the baptism of money. *Comparative Studies in Society and History* 19/1, 130–55.

Tennyson, A. 1829. *Timbuctoo. A poem, which obtained the chancellor's medal at the Cambridge commencement, M.DCCC.XXIX*. Cambridge: Cambridge University Press.

Thom, M. 1990. Tribes within nations: the ancient Germans and the history of France. In *Nation and narration* (ed.) H. K. Bhabha, 23–43. London: Routledge.

Thomson, A. 1993. La classification raciale de l'Afrique du Nord au début du 19e siècle. *Cahiers d'études africaines* 33/1, 19–36.

Tilly, C. 1985. War making and state making as organized crime. In *Bringing the state back in* (eds.) P. B. Evans, D. Rueschemeyer, and T. Skocpol, 169–87. Cambridge: Cambridge University Press.

Toledano, H. 1974. Sijilmasi's manual of maghribi 'amal, *Al-'amal al-mutlaq:* a preliminary examination. *International Journal of Middle East Studies* 5/4, 484–96.

Tolla, A. M. di. 1996. Les Nouaji, 'Touaregs' du Tafilalet. *Cahiers de l'IREMAM* 7/8, 215–22.

Touati, H. 1992. Prestige ancestral et système symbolique sharifien dans le Maghreb central du 17e siècle. *Arabica* **39**, 1–24.

Trautmann, T. R. 1997. *Aryans and British India.* New Delhi: Vistaar.

Triaud, J.-L. 1983. Hommes de religion et confréries islamiques dans une société en crise, l'Aïr aux 19e et 20e siècles. *Cahiers d'études africaines* **91**, 239–80.

Triaud, J.-L., and D. Robinson (eds.). 2000. *La Tijaniyya: Une confrérie musulmane à la conquête de l'Afrique.* Paris: Karthala.

URBAMA. 1989. *Le nomade, l'oasis et la ville.* Tours: Laboratoire URBAMA.

Urvoy, Y. 1936. *Histoire des populations du Soudan central (colonie du Niger).* Paris: Larose.

al-'Uthmānī, M. 2004. *Alwāḥ jazūla w'al-tashrī' al-islāmī.* Rabat: Wazāra al-awqāf w'al-shū'ūn al-islāmiyya.

Vallet, J. 1973. Une oasis à foggara, Tamentit. In *Oasis du Sahara algérien* (eds.) C. Nesson, M. Rouvillois-Brigol, and J. Vallet. Paris: Institut Géographique National.

Varese, F. 2001. *The Russian Mafia: private protection in a new market economy.* Oxford: Oxford University Press.

Vaughan, M. 2005. *Creating the creole island: slavery in eighteenth-century Mauritius.* Durham: Duke University Press.

Venkatesh, S. A., and S. D. Levitt. 2000. 'Are we a family or a business?' History and disjuncture in the urban American street gang. *Theory and Society* **29**, 427–62.

Vidal Castro, F. 1995. El agua en el derecho islámico: introducción a sus origines, propriedad y uso. In *El agua en la agricultura de al-Andalus* (ed.) T. Quesada Quesada, 99–117. Granada: El Legado Andalusí.

Villasante-de Beauvais, M. 1991. Hiérarchies statutaires et conflits fonciers dans l'Assaba contemporain, Mauritanie. *Revue du monde musulman et de la Méditerranée* **59–60**, 181–210.

1997. Genèse de la hiérarchie sociale et du pouvoir politique bidân. *Cahiers d'études africaines* **147**, 587–633.

(ed.). 2000. *Groupes serviles au Sahara.* Paris: IREMAM-CNRS.

Vom Bruck, G. 1998. Disputing descent-based authority in the idiom of religion: the case of the Republic of Yemen. *Die Welt des Islams* 38/2, 149–91.

Wallerstein, I. 1974–1989. *The modern world-system*. New York: Academic Press.

Webb, J. L. A. 1982. Towards the comparative study of money: a reconsideration of West African currencies and neoclassical monetary concepts. *International Journal of Historical Studies* 15/3, 455–66.

1995a. The evolution of the Idaw al-Hajj commercial diaspora. *Cahiers d'études africaines* 35, 455–75.

1995b. *Desert frontier: ecological and economic change along the Western Sahel, 1600–1850*. Madison: University of Wisconsin Press.

1999. On currency and credit in the Western Sahel, 1700–1850. In *Credit, currencies and culture. African financial institutions in historical perspective* (eds.) E. Stiansen and J. I. Guyer, 38–55. Uppsala: Nordiska Afrikainstitutet.

Weigel, J. Y. 1987. Nana et pécheurs du port de Lomé: une exploitation de l'homme par la femme? *Politique Africaine* 27, 37–46.

Werbner, P. 1999. Global Pathways. Working Class Cosmopolitans and the Creation of transethnic worlds. *Social Anthropology* 7, 17–53.

2006. Vernacular cosmopolitanism. *Culture & Society* 23/2–3, 496–98.

(ed.). 2008. *Anthropology and the new cosmopolitanism*. Oxford: Berg.

Whitcomb, T. 1975. New evidence on the origin of the Kunta. *Bulletin SOAS* 38, 103–23, 403–17.

Wilkinson, J. C. 1977. *Water and tribal settlement in south-east Arabia: a study of the Aflāj of Oman*. Oxford: Clarendon Press.

1978. Islamic water law with special reference to oasis settlement. *Journal of Arid Environments* 1/1, 87–96.

Wilson, A. 2006. The spread of foggara-based irrigation in the ancient Sahara. In *The Libyan desert: natural resources and cultural heritage* (eds.) D. Mattingly, S. McLaren, E. Savage, Y. al-Fasatwi, and K. Gadgood, 205–16. London: Society for Libyan Studies.

Wing, S. D. 2008. *Constructing democracy in transitioning societies of Africa: constitutionalism and deliberation in Mali*. Basingstoke: Palgrave Macmillan.

Young, R. 1995. *Colonial desire: hybridity in theory, culture and race*. London: Routledge.

Zunes, S., and J. Mundy. 2010. *Western Sahara: war, nationalism and conflict irresolution*. Syracuse: Syracuse University Press.

Index

Books in This Series

1 *City Politics: A Study of Léopoldville, 1962–63*, J. S. LaFontaine
2 *Studies in Rural Capitalism in West Africa*, Polly Hill
3 *Land Policy in Buganda*, Henry W. West
4 *The Nigerian Military: A Sociological Analysis of Authority and Revolt, 1960–67*, Robin Luckham
5 *The Ghanaian Factory Worker: Industrial Man in Africa*, Margaret Peil
6 *Labour in the South African Gold Mines*, Francis Wilson
7 *The Price of Liberty: Personality and Politics in Colonial Nigeria*, Kenneth W. J. Post and George D. Jenkins
8 *Subsistence to Commercial Farming in Present Day Buganda: An Economic and Anthropological Survey*, Audrey I. Richards, Fort Sturrock and Jean M. Fortt (eds.)
9 *Dependence and Opportunity: Political Change in Ahafo*, John Dunn and A. F. Robertson
10 *African Railwaymen: Solidarity and Opposition in an East African Labour Force*, R. D. Grillo
11 *Islam and Tribal Art in West Africa*, René A. Bravmann
12 *Modern and Traditional Elites in the Politics of Lagos*, P. D. Cole
13 *Asante in the Nineteenth Century: The Structure and Evolution of a Political Order*, Ivor Wilks
14 *Culture, Tradition and Society in the West African Novel*, Emmanuel Obiechina
15 *Saints and Politicians*, Donald B. Cruise O'Brien
16 *The Lions of Dagbon: Political Change in Northern Ghana*, Martin Staniland
17 *Politics of Decolonization: Kenya Europeans and the Land Issue, 1960–1965*, Gary B. Wasserman
18 *Muslim Brotherhoods in Nineteenth Century Africa*, B. G. Martin
19 *Warfare in the Sokoto Caliphate: Historical and Sociological Perspectives*, Joseph P. Smaldone
20 *Liberia and Sierra Leone: An Essay in Comparative Politics*, Christopher Clapham
21 *Adam Kok's Griquas: A Study in the Development of Stratification in South Africa*, Robert Ross
22 *Class, Power and Ideology in Ghana: The Railwaymen of Sekondi*, Richard Jeffries
23 *West African States: Failure and Promise*, John Dunn (ed.)
24 *Afrikaners of the Kalahari: White Minority in a Black State*, Margo Russell and Martin Russell
25 *A Modern History of Tanganyika*, John Iliffe
26 *A History of African Christianity, 1950–1975*, Adrian Hastings
27 *Slave, Peasants and Capitalists in Southern Angola, 1840–1926*, W. G. Clarence-Smith
28 *The Hidden Hippopotamus: Reappraised in African History: The Early Colonial Experience in Western Zambia*, Gwyn Prins
29 *Families Divided: The Impact of Migrant Labour in Lesotho*, Colin Murray
30 *Slavery, Colonialism and Economic Growth in Dahomey, 1640–1960*, Patrick Manning
31 *Kings, Commoners and Concessionaires: The Evolution and Dissolution of the Nineteenth-Century Swazi State*, Philip Bonner
32 *Oral Poetry and Somali Nationalism: The Case of Sayid Mahammad 'Abdille Hasan*, Said S. Samatar

33 *The Political Economy of Pondoland, 1860–1930*, William Beinart
34 *Volkskapitalisme: Class, Capital and Ideology in the Development of Afrikaner Nationalism, 1934–1948*, Dan O'Meara
35 *The Settler Economies: Studies in the Economic History of Kenya and Rhodesia, 1900–1963*, Paul Mosley
36 *Transformations in Slavery: A History of Slavery in Africa*, Paul E. Lovejoy
37 *Amilcar Cabral: Revolutionary Leadership and People's War*, Patrick Chabal
38 *Essays on the Political Economy of Rural Africa*, Robert H. Bates
39 *Ijeshas and Nigerians: The Incorporation of a Yoruba Kingdom, 1890s–1970s*, J. D. Y. Peel
40 *Black People and the South African War, 1899–1902*, Peter Warwick
41 *A History of Niger, 1850–1960*, Finn Fuglestad
42 *Industrialisation and Trade Union Organization in South Africa, 1924–1955*, Stephen Ellis
43 *The Rising of the Red Shawls: A Revolt in Madagascar, 1895–1899*, Stephen Ellis
44 *Slavery in Dutch South Africa*, Nigel Worden
45 *Law, Custom and Social Order: The Colonial Experience in Malawi and Zambia*, Martin Chanock
46 *Salt of the Desert Sun: A History of Salt Production and Trade in the Central Sudan*, Paul E. Lovejoy
47 *Marrying Well: Marriage, Status and Social Change among the Educated Elite in Colonial Lagos*, Kristin Mann
48 *Language and Colonial Power: The Appropriation of Swahili in the Former Belgian Congo, 1880–1938*, Johannes Fabian
49 *The Shell Money of the Slave Trade*, Jan Hogendorn and Marion Johnson
50 *Political Domination in Africa*, Patrick Chabal
51 *The Southern Marches of Imperial Ethiopia: Essays in History and Social Anthropology*, Donald Donham and Wendy James
52 *Islam and Urban Labor in Northern Nigeria: The Making of a Muslim Working Class*, Paul M. Lubeck
53 *Horn and Crescent: Cultural Change and Traditional Islam on the East African Coast, 1800–1900*, Randall L. Pouwels
54 *Capital and Labour on the Kimberley Diamond Fields, 1871–1890*, Robert Vicat Turrell
55 *National and Class Conflict in the Horn of Africa*, John Markakis
56 *Democracy and Prebendal Politics in Nigeria: The Rise and Fall of the Second Republic*, Richard A. Joseph
57 *Entrepreneurs and Parasites: The Struggle for Indigenous Capitalism in Zaïre*, Janet MacGaffey
58 *The African Poor: A History*, John Iliffe
59 *Palm Oil and Protest: An Economic History of the Ngwa Region, South-Eastern Nigeria, 1800–1980*, Susan M. Martin
60 *France and Islam in West Africa, 1860–1960*, Christopher Harrison
61 *Transformation and Continuity in Revolutionary Ethiopia*, Christopher Clapham
62 *Prelude to the Mahdiyya: Peasants and Traders in the Shendi Region, 1821–1885*, Anders Bjørkelo
63 *Wa and the Wala: Islam and Polity in Northwestern Ghana*, Ivor Wilks
64 *H. C. Bankole-Bright and Politics in Colonial Sierra Leone, 1919–1958*, Akintola Wyse

65 *Contemporary West African States,* Donald Cruise O'Brien, John Dunn, and Richard Rathbone (eds.)
66 *The Oromo of Ethiopia: A History, 1570–1860,* Mohammed Hassen
67 *Slavery and African Life: Occidental, Oriental, and African Slave Trades,* Patrick Manning
68 *Abraham Esau's War: A Black South African War in the Cape, 1899–1902,* Bill Nasson
69 *The Politics of Harmony: Land Dispute Strategies in Swaziland,* Laurel L. Rose
70 *Zimbabwe's Guerrilla War: Peasant Voices,* Norma J. Kriger
71 *Ethiopia: Power and Protest: Peasant Revolts in the Twentieth Century,* Gebru Tareke
72 *White Supremacy and Black Resistance in Pre-industrial South Africa: The Making of the Colonial Order in the Eastern Cape, 1770–1865,* Clifton C. Crais
73 *The Elusive Granary: Herder, Farmer, and State in Northern Kenya,* Peter D. Little
74 *The Kanyok of Zaire: An Institutional and Ideological History to 1895,* John C. Yoder
75 *Pragmatism in the Age of Jihad: The Precolonial State of Bundu,* Michael A. Gomez
76 *Slow Death for Slavery: The Course of Abolition in Northern Nigeria, 1897–1936,* Paul E. Lovejoy and Jan S. Hogendorn
77 *West African Slavery and Atlantic Commerce: The Senegal River Valley, 1700–1860,* James F. Searing
78 *A South African Kingdom: The Pursuit of Security in Nineteenth-Century Lesotho,* Elizabeth A. Eldredge
79 *State and Society in Pre-colonial Asante,* T. C. McCaskie
80 *Islamic Society and State Power in Senegal: Disciples and Citizens in Fatick,* Leonardo A. Villalón
81 *Ethnic Pride and Racial Prejudice in Victorian Cape Town: Group Identity and Social Practice,* Vivian Bickford-Smith
82 *The Eritrean Struggle for Independence: Domination, Resistance and Nationalism, 1941–1993,* Ruth Iyob
83 *Corruption and State Politics in Sierra Leone,* William Reno
84 *The Culture of Politics in Modern Kenya,* Angelique Haugerud
85 *Africans: The History of a Continent,* John Iliffe
86 *From Slave Trade to 'Legitimate' Commerce: The Commercial Transition in Nineteenth-Century West Africa,* Robin Law (ed.)
87 *Leisure and Society in Colonial Brazzaville,* Phyllis Martin
88 *Kingship and State: The Buganda Dynasty,* Christopher Wrigley
89 *Decolonization and African Life: The Labour Question in French and British Africa,* Frederick Cooper
90 *Misreading the African Landscape: Society and Ecology in an African Forest Savannah Mosaic,* James Fairhead and Melissa Leach
91 *Peasant Revolution in Ethiopia: The Tigray People's Liberation Front, 1975–1991,* John Young
92 *Senegambia and the Atlantic Slave Trade,* Boubacar Barry
93 *Commerce and Economic Change in West Africa: The Oil Trade in the Nineteenth Century,* Martin Lynn
94 *Slavery and French Colonial Rule in West Africa: Senegal, Guinea and Mali,* Martin A. Klein

95 *East African Doctors: A History of the Modern Profession*, John Iliffe
96 *Middlemen of the Cameroons Rivers: The Duala and Their Hinterland, c.1600–c.1960*, Ralph Derrick, Ralph A. Austen, and Jonathan Derrick
97 *Masters and Servants on the Cape Eastern Frontier, 1760–1803*, Susan Newton-King
98 *Status and Respectability in the Cape Colony, 1750–1870: A Tragedy of Manners*, Robert Ross
99 *Slaves, Freedmen and Indentured Laborers in Colonial Mauritius*, Richard B. Allen
100 *Transformations in Slavery: A History of Slavery in Africa, 2nd Edition*, Paul E. Lovejoy
101 *The Peasant Cotton Revolution in West Africa: Côte d'Ivoire, 1880–1995*, Thomas J. Bassett
102 *Re-imagining Rwanda: Conflict, Survival and Disinformation in the Late Twentieth Century*, Johan Pottier
103 *The Politics of Evil: Magic, State Power and the Political Imagination in South Africa*, Clifton Crais
104 *Transforming Mozambique: The Politics of Privatization, 1975–2000*, M. Anne Pitcher
105 *Guerrilla Veterans in Post-war Zimbabwe: Symbolic and Violent Politics, 1980–1987*, Norma J. Kriger
106 *An Economic History of Imperial Madagascar, 1750–1895: The Rise and Fall of an Island Empire*. Gwyn Campbell
107 *Honour in African History*, John Iliffe
108 *Africans: History of a Continent, 2nd Edition*, John Iliffe
109 *Guns, Race, and Power in Colonial South Africa*, William Kelleher Storey
110 *Islam and Social Change in French West Africa: History of an Emancipatory Community*, Sean Hanretta
111 *Defeating Mau Mau, Creating Kenya: Counterinsurgency, Civil War, and Decolonization*, Daniel Branch
112 *Christianity and Genocide in Rwanda*, Timothy Longman
113 *From Africa to Brazil: Culture, Identity and an Atlantic Slave Trade, 1600–1830*, Walter Hawthorne
114 *Africa in the Time of Cholera: A History of Pandemics from 1817 to the Present*, Myron Echenberg
115 *A History of Race in Muslim West Africa, 1600–1960*, Bruce S. Hall
116 *Witchcraft and Colonial Rule in Kenya, 1900–1955*, Katherine Luongo
117 *Transformations in Slavery: A History of Slavery in Africa, 3rd Edition*, Paul E. Lovejoy
118 *The Rise of the Trans-Atlantic Slave Trade in Western Africa, 1300–1589*, Toby Green
119 *Party Politics and Economic Reform in Africa's Democracies*, M. Anne Pitcher
120 *Smugglers and Saints of the Sahara: Regional Connectivity in the Twentieth Century*, Judith Scheele

Made in the USA
Las Vegas, NV
15 March 2022

45678573R00169